D1001314

Social Security Policy in a Changing Environment

**A National Bureau
of Economic Research
Conference Report**

MGEN
MR914

Social Security Policy in a Changing Environment

Edited by **Jeffrey R. Brown, Jeffrey Liebman, and David A. Wise**

The University of Chicago Press

Chicago and London

b32152346

JEFFREY R. BROWN is the William G. Karnes Professor of Finance at the University of Illinois at Urbana-Champaign, and a research associate of the National Bureau of Economic Research. JEFFREY LIEBMAN is the Malcolm Wiener Professor of Public Policy at the John F. Kennedy School of Government, Harvard University, and a research associate of the National Bureau of Economic Research. DAVID A. WISE is the John F. Stambaugh Professor of Political Economy at the John F. Kennedy School of Government, Harvard University, and director of the program on the economics of aging at the National Bureau of Economic Research.

The University of Chicago Press, Chicago 60637
The University of Chicago Press, Ltd., London
© 2009 by the National Bureau of Economic Research
All rights reserved. Published 2009
Printed in the United States of America

18 17 16 15 14 13 12 11 10 09   1 2 3 4 5
ISBN-13: 978-0-226-07648-5 (cloth)
ISBN-10: 0-226-07648-2 (cloth)

Library of Congress Cataloging-in-Publication Data

Social security policy in a changing environment / edited by Jeffrey R.
    Brown, Jeffrey Liebman, and David A. Wise.
        p. cm. — (A National Bureau of Economic Research conference report)
        "This volume consists of papers presented at a conference held in Woodstock, Vermont in October 2006"—Acknowledgments.
        Includes bibliographical references and index.
        ISBN-13: 978-0-226-07648-5 (cloth : alk. paper)
        ISBN-10: 0-226-07648-2 (cloth : alk. paper) 1. Social security—Government policy—United States I. Brown, Jeffrey R. II. Liebman, Jeffrey B. III. Wise, David A.
        HD7125.S599286 2008
        368.4'300973—dc22
                                                                2008031051

HD
7125
.S599286
2009

♾ The paper used in this publication meets the minimum requirements of the American National Standard for Information Sciences— Permanence of Paper for Printed Library Materials, ANSI Z39.48-1992.

National Bureau of Economic Research

Officers

John S. Clarkeson, *chairman*
Kathleen B. Cooper, *vice-chairman*
James M. Poterba, *president and chief executive officer*
Robert Mednick, *treasurer*

Kelly Horak, *controller and assistant corporate secretary*
Alterra Milone, *corporate secretary*
Gerardine Johnson, *assistant corporate secretary*

Directors at Large

Peter C. Aldrich
Elizabeth E. Bailey
Richard B. Berner
John H. Biggs
John S. Clarkeson
Don R. Conlan
Kathleen B. Cooper
Charles H. Dallara
George C. Eads

Jessica P. Einhorn
Mohamed El-Erian
Jacob A. Frenkel
Judith M. Gueron
Robert S. Hamada
Karen N. Horn
John Lipsky
Laurence H. Meyer
Michael H. Moskow

Alicia H. Munnell
Rudolph A. Oswald
Robert T. Parry
James M. Poterba
John S. Reed
Marina v. N. Whitman
Martin B. Zimmerman

Directors by University Appointment

George Akerlof, *California, Berkeley*
Jagdish Bhagwati, *Columbia*
Glen G. Cain, *Wisconsin*
Ray C. Fair, *Yale*
Franklin Fisher, *Massachusetts Institute of Technology*
Mark Grinblatt, *California, Los Angeles*
Saul H. Hymans, *Michigan*
Marjorie B. McElroy, *Duke*

Joel Mokyr, *Northwestern*
Andrew Postlewaite, *Pennsylvania*
Uwe E. Reinhardt, *Princeton*
Nathan Rosenberg, *Stanford*
Craig Swan, *Minnesota*
David B. Yoffie, *Harvard*
Arnold Zellner (Director Emeritus), *Chicago*

Directors by Appointment of Other Organizations

Jean-Paul Chavas, *American Agricultural Economics Association*
Gail D. Fosler, *The Conference Board*
Martin Gruber, *American Finance Association*
Timothy W. Guinnane, *Economic History Association*
Arthur B. Kennickell, *American Statistical Association*
Thea Lee, *American Federation of Labor and Congress of Industrial Organizations*

William W. Lewis, *Committee for Economic Development*
Robert Mednick, *American Institute of Certified Public Accountants*
Angelo Melino, *Canadian Economics Association*
Harvey Rosenblum, *National Association for Business Economics*
John J. Siegfried, *American Economic Association*

Directors Emeriti

Andrew Brimmer
Carl F. Christ
George Hatsopoulos
Lawrence R. Klein

Franklin A. Lindsay
Paul W. McCracken
Peter G. Peterson
Richard N. Rosett

Eli Shapiro
Arnold Zellner

Relation of the Directors to the
Work and Publications of the
National Bureau of Economic Research

1. The object of the NBER is to ascertain and present to the economics profession, and to the public more generally, important economic facts and their interpretation in a scientific manner without policy recommendations. The Board of Directors is charged with the responsibility of ensuring that the work of the NBER is carried on in strict conformity with this object.

2. The President shall establish an internal review process to ensure that book manuscripts proposed for publication DO NOT contain policy recommendations. This shall apply both to the proceedings of conferences and to manuscripts by a single author or by one or more coauthors but shall not apply to authors of comments at NBER conferences who are not NBER affiliates.

3. No book manuscript reporting research shall be published by the NBER until the President has sent to each member of the Board a notice that a manuscript is recommended for publication and that in the President's opinion it is suitable for publication in accordance with the above principles of the NBER. Such notification will include a table of contents and an abstract or summary of the manuscript's content, a list of contributors if applicable, and a response form for use by Directors who desire a copy of the manuscript for review. Each manuscript shall contain a summary drawing attention to the nature and treatment of the problem studied and the main conclusions reached.

4. No volume shall be published until forty-five days have elapsed from the above notification of intention to publish it. During this period a copy shall be sent to any Director requesting it, and if any Director objects to publication on the grounds that the manuscript contains policy recommendations, the objection will be presented to the author(s) or editor(s). In case of dispute, all members of the Board shall be notified, and the President shall appoint an ad hoc committee of the Board to decide the matter; thirty days additional shall be granted for this purpose.

5. The President shall present annually to the Board a report describing the internal manuscript review process, any objections made by Directors before publication or by anyone after publication, any disputes about such matters, and how they were handled.

6. Publications of the NBER issued for informational purposes concerning the work of the Bureau, or issued to inform the public of the activities at the Bureau, including but not limited to the NBER Digest and Reporter, shall be consistent with the object stated in paragraph 1. They shall contain a specific disclaimer noting that they have not passed through the review procedures required in this resolution. The Executive Committee of the Board is charged with the review of all such publications from time to time.

7. NBER working papers and manuscripts distributed on the Bureau's web site are not deemed to be publications for the purpose of this resolution, but they shall be consistent with the object stated in paragraph 1. Working papers shall contain a specific disclaimer noting that they have not passed through the review procedures required in this resolution. The NBER's web site shall contain a similar disclaimer. The President shall establish an internal review process to ensure that the working papers and the web site do not contain policy recommendations, and shall report annually to the Board on this process and any concerns raised in connection with it.

8. Unless otherwise determined by the Board or exempted by the terms of paragraphs 6 and 7, a copy of this resolution shall be printed in each NBER publication as described in paragraph 2 above.

Contents

Acknowledgments

This volume consists of papers presented at a conference held in Woodstock, VT in October 2006. Most of the research was conducted as part of the NBER Retirement Research Center with financial support from the U.S. Social Security Administration (SSA) through grant #10-P-98363-1 to the National Bureau of Economic Research as part of the SSA Retirement Research Consortium. Additional funding sources are noted in individual papers.

The findings and conclusions expressed in this volume are those of the respective authors and do not represent the views of SSA, any agency of the federal government, or the National Bureau of Economic Research.

Introduction

Jeffrey R. Brown, Jeffrey Liebman, and David A. Wise

This volume compiles selected studies conducted through the National Bureau of Economic Research (NBER) Center for Retirement Research. The center was created in 2003 with funding from the U.S. Social Security Administration and is structured to provide analysis that can inform Social Security policy. In setting our research agenda, we have been guided by three principles. First, reform must recognize the changing and uncertain environment in which the Social Security system will operate. Second, several alternative routes to sustainable solvency should be explored. Third, the potential routes to solvency should be evaluated for "resiliency" to future uncertain demographic, economic, and social trends.

While some of the center's research focuses directly on Social Security reform, other research aims to inform Social Security policy by analyzing the changing economic environment in which future Social Security beneficiaries will live. For example, several of our center's projects have studied trends in private-sector retirement saving—particularly the shift from defined benefit (DB) to defined contribution (DC) pension plans—because the "optimal" Social Security replacement rate may evolve as the structure of private retirement savings changes over time. We have also studied trends in health care costs because decisions about Social Security benefits, and indeed how much of society's resources to devote to So-

Jeffrey R. Brown is the William G. Karnes Professor of Finance at the University of Illinois at Urbana-Champaign, and a research associate of the National Bureau of Economic Research. Jeffrey Liebman is the Malcolm Wiener Professor of Public Policy at the John F. Kennedy School of Government, Harvard University, and a research associate of the National Bureau of Economic Research. David A. Wise is the John F. Stambaugh Professor of Political Economy at the John F. Kennedy School of Government, Harvard University, and director of the program on the economics of aging at the National Bureau of Economic Research.

cial Security, may depend in part on health care costs. And we have studied the uncertain nature of future demographic, economic, and social trends—such as the age structure of the population, marriage and divorce rates, women's labor force participation, productivity, market rates of return, and the like.

The volume is organized into five parts. Part I introduces several innovative approaches to Social Security reform. Part II examines individual behavior in making retirement saving decisions, such as how much to save or how to allocate savings among alternative investment options. Part III analyzes different approaches to reducing the financial market risk faced by individuals who invest in personal retirement accounts. Part IV looks at aggregate trends in retirement asset flows and their effect on macroeconomic markets. Part V considers health trends and their projected effects on future mortality. This introduction summarizes each of the chapters, drawing heavily on the authors' own summaries.

Innovative Approaches to Social Security Reform

In recent years, the debate about Social Security reform in the United States has focused on a limited range of proposals, a fact which may have contributed to the partisan nature of reform discussions. An important aim of our center is to expand the range of approaches considered and to assess the resiliency of alternative proposals to uncertain future demographic, financial, and other trends. The first three chapters in this volume analyze new ideas for Social Security reform. The first considers reforms that would remove the disincentive in Social Security for long careers. The second analyzes notional defined contribution social security systems and evaluates their ability to self-adjust to uncertain future circumstances, and thus to retain their financial stability over the long term. The third develops a reform proposal based on progressive personal accounts, which blend characteristics of funded personal accounts with some of the core objectives of traditional social security policy.

In chapter 1, "Removing the Disincentives in Social Security for Long Careers," Gopi Shah Goda, John B. Shoven, and Sita Nataraj Slavov explore the relationship between Social Security policy and labor market behavior at older ages. Since Social Security was instituted in 1935, life expectancy at age twenty has increased from sixty-six to seventy-six for men and from sixty-nine to eighty for women. Health at older ages has also improved. Such dramatic advances in health and longevity mean that people have the physical and mental capability to work until older ages. Yet people are retiring younger, even as they live longer and healthier lives. Indeed, the duration of retirement has grown by even more than the increase in life expectancy at retirement.

Godi, Shoven, and Slavov consider the role of Social Security policy in influencing—or, more precisely, distorting—the work and retirement decisions of older workers. They highlight the features of Social Security that discourage long careers, discourage work at older ages, and increase the number of years in retirement. The main finding of the chapter is that Social Security imposes high implicit tax rates on workers late in their careers. As a result of this distortion, the duration of retirement is suboptimally long, compounding the financial stress on public and private retirement support systems.

One example of the distortion in Social Security is how benefits are calculated based on the highest thirty-five years of earnings. This means that the thirty-third, thirty-fourth, and thirty-fifth years of work noticeably improve retirement benefits by replacing a "zero" in the benefit calculation formula. The thirty-sixth year of work, on the other hand, may or may not count, and if it does, it will replace a lower year of earnings and not a zero in the calculation. Thus, the benefit formula discourages careers of more than thirty-five years. Another aspect of the benefit formula offers disproportionately higher benefits to workers with short careers, treating them with the same redistributive advantages as if they were lower earners. Both characteristics of the benefit formula lead to high implicit tax rates at older ages and for longer careers.

The authors suggest three reforms that would reduce the distortionary impact of Social Security at older ages. First, they propose using forty years, rather than thirty-five, in benefit computation. Second, they propose disentangling career length and progressivity in the benefit formula. And third, they propose to establish a "paid-up" category of workers who have more than forty years of contributions, who would no longer be subject to the payroll tax. The study finds that these proposed changes would eliminate most of the large positive tax rates for older workers. They would also reduce the association between age and tax rate and move tax rates closer to zero for most workers in most years of their lives. With these changes, the implicit tax rates associated with Social Security remain roughly constant over a worker's life, resulting in less distortion of career length choices. The authors find, in addition, that the proposed reforms need not affect the overall progressivity of the Social Security system. However, by reallocating benefits from those with shorter careers to those with longer careers, the reforms would result in less insurance against adverse shocks that cause people to work for fewer years.

The study concludes that by eliminating the disincentives against working longer careers, we can capitalize on the good fortunes of increasing life expectancy and favorable health status by paving the way for those in good health to stay in the labor force longer.

In chapter 2, "Notional Defined Contribution Pension Systems in a Stochastic Context: Design and Stability," Alan J. Auerbach and Ronald Lee explore a new approach to Social Security reform that is known as "Notional Defined Contribution" or "Nonfinancial Defined Contribution" (NDC). Sweden was the first country to introduce an NDC system. A number of other countries have introduced NDC plans, including Italy, Poland, Latvia, Mongolia, and the Kyrgyz Republic, and proposed plans for France and Germany have NDC aspects.

The NDC programs differ in detail, but the basic principle is that they mimic defined contribution plans without actually setting aside financial assets. Thus, some of the benefits of fully funded defined contribution plans can be achieved—particularly the improved labor supply incentives from a more transparent link between current taxes and future retirement benefits—while avoiding the transitional difficulties of converting from an unfunded pay-as-you-go (PAYGO) system. Under an NDC program, a "notional" capital account is maintained for each participant. Balances in this account earn a rate of return that is declared by the pension plan each year, and notional payments into this account are made over the entire life history to mirror actual taxes or contributions by plan participants. After a designated age such as sixty-two, a participant can begin to draw benefits, which is done by using the account to purchase an annuity from the pension plan. The terms of the annuity will depend on mortality risk at that time and on a rate of return stipulated by the pension plan.

While NDC plans are seen as having various potential advantages over traditional PAYGO systems, the focus of this chapter is on their financial stability over the long term. The stability results from three factors. First, the rate of return in the notional accounts reflects the underlying PAYGO nature of the program and is based on what is expected to be affordable over time. Second, the annuity structure should buffer the system from the uncertain costs of rising longevity. And third, in the event that the program's finances move toward imbalance, a braking mechanism can be incorporated that automatically modifies the rate of return to help restore the plan to financial health. Given the political difficulties of making frequent changes in PAYGO pension programs, the attractiveness of an inherently stable and self-adjusting system is clear.

In this chapter, Auerbach and Lee use a stochastic macroeconomic model for forecasting and simulating the long-term finances of NDC-type public pension programs in the context of demographic and economic trends in the United States. Because future patterns of demographic and economic change are uncertain, the model generates a probability distribution of outcomes (benefit flows and rates of return) for generations of plan participants for the NDC program, as well as for the overall financial stability of the NDC system.

The study finds that an NDC system similar to that currently in use in Sweden, which bases rates of return on the growth rate of average wages and utilizes a brake to adjust the rate of return during periods of financial stress, effectively eliminates the accumulation of debt in the Social Security system, even under the most adverse demographic and economic circumstances. Thus, the system is effective in preventing inadequate funding of Social Security obligations over the long term.

What this version of an NDC system does not do is adjust automatically to situations when there is excess money accumulating in the system. Put differently, the braking mechanism is asymmetric, automatically making corrections when the financial balances of the system move toward increased debt, but without correction when the financial balances move toward asset accumulation. Only a symmetric brake, which raises rates of return during periods of financial strength, avoids large accumulations of financial assets.

Other findings from the simulations are first, that the brake can be more gradual than under the Swedish system and still provide a stable distribution of outcomes; second, that an NDC system in which rates of return are based on total rather than per capita economic growth is inherently more stable; and third, that a considerable share of the volatility in the financial performance of NDC systems is attributable to economic uncertainty, rather than demographic uncertainty.

In chapter 3, "Reforming Social Security with Progressive Personal Accounts," John Geanakoplos and Stephen P. Zeldes develop yet another approach to Social Security reform. Their reform plan is designed to preserve the core objectives of the current Social Security system and, at the same time, gain the benefits of personal accounts.

Advocates for retaining the current system argue that Social Security should redistribute wealth from those who have earned more over their whole working lives to those who have earned less. They also suggest that different generations should share in the risks and benefits of macroeconomic growth. So if real wages go up over time, retirees should get some benefit from those macroeconomic gains, even though they are no longer working. Advocates for personal accounts, on the other hand, support ownership by individuals of tangible assets that cannot be revoked by a future government. They also like the idea that people know the current market valuation of their retirement resources, as they are accrued over time, so that rational planning for retirement can take place outside of Social Security.

Geanakoplos and Zeldes seek to find a common ground between these two approaches and to develop a plan that preserves the core goals of each one. They demonstrate that it is possible to convert Social Security into a system of personal accounts with irrevocable ownership of market priced assets, while at the same time redistributing benefits based on lifetime income and sharing macroeconomic gains across generations. They refer to the plan as *progressive personal accounts.*

The proposed system uses the payroll tax to buy assets in a personal retirement account for each Social Security recipient. Income-based redistribution is accomplished through a variable government match (or tax) on these Social Security contributions. High lifetime earners receive lower matches (or a tax) on contributions to their personal account, while low lifetime earners receive a higher government match. Risk sharing across generations is accomplished through the creation of a new kind of derivative security whose payoffs depend on the average earnings of those working at a specific point in time. So if younger workers are doing well and receiving high wages, the old will get higher payoffs from their investment in the derivative security. Every year a worker would pay the Old-Age and Survivors Insurance (OASI) payroll tax and receive a certain number of these securities in the worker's account.

According to the authors, it is possible to create a system of progressive personal accounts that exactly mimics the promised taxes and payouts of the current Social Security system. The resulting system would preserve some of the core goals of Social Security, as it is structured today, but would also improve upon it due to the increased transparency, enhanced property rights, and lower political risk (of legislation removing benefits) that naturally come with individual accounts. Chapter 3 lays out the mechanics of such a system in detail.

Retirement Plan Choice

With the growth of 401(k)-type plans, retirement saving is becoming an increasingly important complement to Social Security as a component of financial support in retirement. In addition, some Social Security reform proposals would supplement the defined benefits provided by the current U.S. Social Security system with either voluntary or mandatory personal retirement accounts (PRAs). The increasing importance of individually-owned retirement savings accounts, whether integrated within the Social Security system or outside the system, will make decision making by individuals a more important aspect of retirement planning in the future. The next two chapters in the volume look at how people make decisions about retirement plans when individual decisions need to be made.

In chapter 4, "Who Chooses Defined Contribution Plans?," Jeffrey R. Brown and Scott J. Weisbenner analyze the decisions made by a group of 50,000 workers who currently have a choice between a defined benefit (DB) and a defined contribution (DC) pension system. Their study is based on the experience of employees in the State Universities Retirement System (SURS) of Illinois, where workers make a one-time, lifetime, irrevocable choice among three retirement plans: (1) a traditional formula-based DB plan; (2) a "portable DB plan," which is slightly less generous than the traditional DB program if one retires from the system, but more generous if the worker takes an early lump-sum distribution; and (3) a completely self-managed DC plan. Individuals who fail to make an active choice within the first six months of employment are automatically defaulted into the traditional DB plan.

Other aspects of the SURS experience are also relevant to the study. First, the wages of individuals earned from SURS-covered employment are not also covered by Social Security. So for most, the decision made is a decision about people's primary source of income in retirement. Second, the combined employer/employee retirement contributions to the SURS system are at least 14.6 percent of annual salary, which is larger than the payroll tax paid by those in the Social Security system. Therefore, the SURS system looms large as part of a participant's lifetime financial plan. And third, the choice of retirement programs is available to employees with diverse job characteristics and earnings, including campus administrators, faculty members, clerical staff, university police and fire protection workers, and others.

There are two major findings from the study. First, despite initial projections that a majority of new employees would actively select the self-managed DC plan or portable DB plan, the evidence is that a majority of new employees never makes an active pension choice and, thus, are defaulted into the traditional DB plan. The proportion of new employees not making a choice among plans, and hence defaulting into the traditional DB plan, has been roughly three-fifths over the period 2001 to 2004.

Second, approximately 15 percent of new employees choose the self-managed DC plan, despite the fact that the DC plan is likely inferior to the portable DB plan, given the financial features of the various plans and reasonable assumptions about future financial market returns. Interestingly, individuals are more likely than average to choose the self-managed DC plan if they are more highly educated, have higher earnings, are married, and work in a location where a higher fraction of other employees also chose the self-managed plan. The findings suggest that these "educated, high earning, young professionals" have a strong preference for DC plans, even when the financial terms are unfavorable. For example, among the 650 individuals in the sample who are full-time, aged thirty to thirty-nine, academics at a university, married, have earnings in excess of $50,000, and are still active employees as of spring 2006, 52 percent of them chose the self-managed DC plan, compared with 15 percent in the sample as a whole.

The analysis raises the question of why some individuals appear to make suboptimal choices. The authors speculate that there are at least five reasons why they may do so. First, participants may simply have difficulty processing the complex information that they are provided when making this choice, due either to time constraints or some form of bounded rationality. Second, the information provided by SURS may not be optimally designed to facilitate meaningful comparisons between the self-managed DC plan and the portable benefits package. Third, individuals may understand the rules, but may overestimate their investment abilities, or the expected market return of the DC plan. Fourth, individuals may believe there is political risk in the traditional or portable benefit plans, arising from the chronic underfunding of the SURS system. Fifth, individuals may place a high value on choice for its own sake. In continuing research, the authors are exploring these alternative hypotheses using a survey of current SURS participants.

In chapter 5, "The Importance of Default Options for Retirement Saving Outcomes: Evidence from the United States," John Beshears, James J. Choi, David Laibson, and Brigitte C. Madrian look at a very similar issue in the context of 401(k) plans. In this case, the worker's decision is about whether to enroll in the 401(k) plan, what portion of their income to allocate to the plan, and how to invest it among the various investment options offered in the plan. Much like the previous chapter, a core finding is that defaults matter a lot. Many people avoid making an active decision about their retirement saving, and so the default provisions of their 401(k) plan are what people end up doing "by default."

The chapter summarizes a breadth of empirical evidence on how the default provisions of retirement saving plans impact savings behavior along multiple dimensions, such as savings plan participation, savings rates, asset allocation, and postretirement savings distributions. The findings are that defaults impact savings outcomes at every step along the way. For example, some 401(k) plans have automatic enrollment, requiring employees to explicitly "opt-out" of the plan. Others require eligible employees to actively enroll in the plan, or "opt-in." Automatic enrollment is found to dramatically raise participation rates.

When the 401(k) plan has a default savings rate and a default investment allocation, employees are much more likely to choose those defaults, rather than to specify an alternative. As a result, the higher the default contribution rate, the higher the savings rate among those participating. Defaults even matter when employees leave their jobs, and their 401(k) balances may be left in the account, or they may be distributed to employees with the option to roll over the funds to another retirement plan. When the funds are distributed (which happens automatically in most smaller accounts), they are much more likely to be removed permanently from retirement saving, while undistributed funds tend to be left in the plans.

The findings of this study are relevant not only to the design of a company's 401(k) plan, but also to how one would structure a personal account system within Social Security. For example, a voluntary PRA system within Social Security would lead to higher participation and higher saving if it has automatic enrollment (rather than requiring active enrollment) and if the default savings rate is higher. The findings on asset allocation are also relevant and suggest careful attention to the investment options made available to participants as well as to the default allocations among them. A clear conclusion of this research is that defaults are not neutral—they can either facilitate or hinder better savings outcomes. The authors emphasize that current public policies toward saving include examples of both.

Reducing Financial Market Risk in Personal Retirement Accounts

The next section of the volume also relates to the increasing importance of individual retirement saving and, particularly, to the potential implications of a PRA component in Social Security. A significant concern, particularly if PRAs were to become part of Social Security, is with the imposition of investment risk on plan participants. The concern is that the economic well-being of some retirees could be undermined by poor investment returns. There is, therefore, great interest in strategies that could reduce the riskiness of PRAs while preserving the other features of PRAs. While the chapters in this section are focused on reducing the risk of PRAs, the results are also relevant to retirement saving taking place in 401(k) plans and other financial accounts that are separate from Social Security.

The first chapter in this section considers financial market products that cap downside market risk. The second analyzes an approach in which the government would guarantee a minimum investment return. The third studies the extent to which life-cycle investment strategies could reduce the variance in retirement income levels. The fourth investigates the extent to which increased progressivity in the traditional Social Security system could be used to buffer lower-income retirees against PRA market risk.

In chapter 6, "Reducing the Risk of Investment-Based Social Security Reform," Martin Feldstein presents a market-based approach to reducing the risk of investment-based Social Security that could be tailored to individual risk preferences. With this new form of risk reduction, substituting an investment-based PRA for the traditional pure PAYGO plan could achieve both a significantly higher expected retirement income and a very high probability that the investment-based annuity would be at least as large as the PAYGO benefit. A key feature of the approach developed in the chapter is guarantee that the individual would not lose any of the real value of each year's PRA savings and might be guaranteed to earn at least some minimum real rate of return.

In one example of such a plan, the current 12.4 percent PAYGO tax is compared with a mixed plan that has a 6.2 percent PAYGO tax and 6.2 percent annual PRA savings. This new mixed plan, when fully phased in, would have the following desirable characteristics: (1) The median value of the combined retirement income (i.e., the sum of the PAYGO benefit and the PRA annuity) would be 147 percent of the traditional PAYGO benefit. (2) There would be a 95 percent probability that the combined retirement income (the PAYGO benefit and the PRA annuity) exceeds the traditional PAYGO benefit. (3) There would be less than one chance in 100 that the combined retirement income would be less than 96 percent of the traditional PAYGO benefit. (4) Each year's PRA saving would be guaranteed to earn at least a 1 percent real rate of return between the time that it is saved and its value at age sixty-six. It is, therefore, referred to in the chapter as a "No Lose" plan. (5) The variable annuity purchased at age sixty-six would have a similar "No Lose" feature, that is, a guaranteed real rate of return of at least 1 percent.

The "No Lose" concepts developed in the chapter rely on financial instruments already available in the marketplace. The idea is that the amount saved in a PRA each year would be guaranteed to retain at least its real value by age sixty-six. The simplest way to achieve such a No Lose PRA account would be to combine Treasury Inflation-Protected Securities (TIPS, which have a guaranteed real return) with equities. The fraction of the annual PRA saving that would have to be invested in TIPS to guarantee that the annual PRA saving would retain its real value by age sixty-six depends on the age of the saver and the rate of return on the TIPS of the relevant maturity. For example, if the saver is twenty-one years old and the real return on TIPS is 2 percent, a $1,000 PRA saving would be divided between $410 in TIPS and the remaining $590 in equities. The 2 percent real return and the forty-five-year investment period imply that the $410 would accumulate to $1,000 at the initial price level by age sixty-six. Even if the equity portion became completely worthless, the PRA account would be worth the initial $1,000 real dollars.

At older working ages, there are fewer years for the TIPS to accumulate and, therefore, a larger fraction of the initial saving must be invested in TIPS. For example, a forty-year-old would have to invest $598 out of each $1,000 of new saving in TIPS to guarantee the $1,000 value of the account at age sixty-six with the remaining $402 invested in equities. In practice, of course, the value at age sixty-six of the annual PRA saving would be worth substantially more than the guaranteed amount because the equity portion of the account would add additional value. Indeed, the likelihood (based on past market returns) is that the equity portion would add very substantial additional value.

The chapter considers a range of "No Lose" options with varying trade-offs between the guaranteed minimum return and the distribution of possible higher returns. For example, the approach can be easily modified to increase the guarantee from a zero real return (No Lose) to a 1 percent real rate of return. Indeed, different trade-offs might be more or less desirable to different individuals, based on their particular risk preferences. These options are then evaluated relative to the baseline values that would be provided through a traditional PAYGO Social Security system. Simulations are used to derive the probability distributions of retirement incomes relative to the "benchmark" benefits specified in current law. Calculations of expected utility show that the risk reduction techniques developed in the chapter can raise expected utility relative to investment-based plans with no guarantees. Finally, the chapter shows how these approaches might be applied to deal with the aging of the population without the large rise in the payroll tax that would otherwise be required.

In closely related work reported in chapter 7, "Pricing Personal Account Benefit Guarantees: A Simplified Approach," Andrew Biggs, Clark Burdick, and Kent Smetters develop a methodology for estimating the market cost of return guarantees. Given the size of Social Security benefit entitlements and the market risks inherent in personal account investing, guarantees constitute a significant contingent liability to the guarantee provider.

Most of the existing research on guarantees has estimated their cost, based on a probability distribution of possible investment outcomes, and then used the distribution to calculate an "expected" cost of the minimum guarantee. According to the authors, however, this approach does not reflect fully how guarantees would be priced in the financial marketplace. In particular, it ignores the greater valuation placed by the market on losses relative to the expected value of the losses. Indeed, the total "market cost" of a benefit guarantee, including the associated cost of market risk, could be several times larger than its "expected cost." This chapter demonstrates how a model for calculating the expected cost of a benefit guarantee can be modified to present the market price of personal account guarantees as a supplement to expected cost valuations. The simplified method for estimating the market price of a guarantee is shown to produce results equivalent to the Black-Scholes model.

The approach is illustrated using a Social Security reform proposal from Senator John Sununu (R-NH) and Representative Paul Ryan (R-WI). This proposal would introduce personal accounts investing from 5 to 10 percent of wages, depending upon the worker's earnings level. At retirement, individuals would receive either the proceeds of their personal account or their currently scheduled benefit, whichever is greater. Thus, this plan effectively guarantees that accounts would produce benefits no lower than those scheduled for the current program. In the illustrative policy, the "expected cost" valuation of the proposed guarantee is calculated to be 11.3 percent of total benefits to new retirees in 2050, while the "market value" cost is calculated to be 28.2 percent of benefits.

In chapter 8, "Reducing Social Security PRA Risk at the Individual Level: Life-Cycle Funds and No-Loss Strategies," James M. Poterba, Joshua Rauh, Steven F. Venti, and David A. Wise explore the implications for asset accumulation of different investment strategies. In a Social Security system with a personal retirement account (PRA) component, retirement savers would have to decide how to allocate their PRA portfolios across a broad range of asset classes and financial products. Asset allocation decisions have important consequences for retirement wealth accumulation because they affect the expenses of investing as well as the risk of low returns. The goal of this study is to assess the relative risk associated with alternative asset allocation strategies in PRAs, though it also offers insight on the consequences of different asset allocation rules in 401(k)-type plans.

The approach used in the study is to simulate the distribution of balances in PRA retirement saving accounts under various assumptions about the asset allocation strategies that investors may choose. In addition to a range of age-invariant strategies, such as an all-bond and an all-stock strategy, the chapter considers several different "life-cycle funds" that automatically alter the investor's mix of assets as he or she ages. These funds allocate a higher fraction of an investor's portfolio to stocks at the beginning of a working career and then gradually decrease the equity fraction as the worker approaches retirement. The authors also consider a "no lose" allocation strategy for retirement saving, in which households purchase enough riskless bonds at each age to ensure that they will have no less than their nominal contribution when they reach retirement age and then invest the balance in corporate stock. This strategy combines a riskless floor for retirement income with some upside investment potential, along the lines of what is described in chapter 6.

The best asset allocation strategy—the one with the highest expected utility to the investor—is found to depend on the relative importance of four issues: the expected return on stocks, the risk aversion of the investing household, the amount of financial wealth held outside the PRA, and the expenses associated with different investment options. At modest levels of risk aversion, or when the household has access to substantial non-PRA wealth at retirement, the historical pattern of stock and bond returns implies that an all-stock investment strategy brings higher expected utility than any of the more conservative strategies. When the expected return on stocks is reduced, however, other strategies may dominate the all-equity allocation for investors with high levels of relative risk aversion. In these circumstances, the value of a mix of stocks and inflation-indexed bonds (TIPS) or an inexpensive life-cycle product may be higher than an all-stocks strategy.

The findings also underscore the importance of avoiding high expense ratios. Many of the available life-cycle products have higher expense ratios than could be achieved by the household simply holding a stock index fund and some TIPS (or bonds) and either holding them in fixed proportions throughout their lifetime or rebalancing toward TIPS (or bonds) as they get older. Households who are unable to do this on their own will not do terribly in life-cycle funds, but they will lose money relative to what they could get if they executed very simple investing strategies on their own.

A very different approach to reducing PRA risk is explored in chapter 9, "Changing Progressivity as a Means of Risk Protection in Investment-

Based Social Security," by Andrew A. Samwick. This chapter analyzes changes in the progressivity of the Social Security benefit formula as an alternative means of lessening the overall risk for lower-income Social Security beneficiaries. Because Social Security benefits provide a larger share of retirement income for lower-income households, Samwick argues, the most direct way to make sure that they do not fall into poverty in old age is to increase the progressivity of the benefit formula. Doing so would lessen the need to provide insurance against the possibility of low returns in the PRAs because low-income retirees would depend less on their PRAs to stay out of poverty.

In the illustrative reform plans studied by Samwick, individual PRA accounts are created with contributions of 2 percent of covered earnings per year. At the same time, traditional Social Security benefits are reduced by 40 percent. Samwick evalues four different approaches to the 40 percent aggregate benefit cut, each with a different degree of progressivity in the benefit formula. The least progressive version would maintain the progressivity of Social Security benefits at its current level, but reduced all benefits by 40 percent. The most progressive version would provide an equal retirement benefit to everyone, regardless of past earnings. The other two scenarios are in between, offering moderate increases in benefit progressivity.

A series of simulations are conducted to analyze the implications of these policy alternatives on the economic well-being of lower income households, as well as to evaluate the optimal allocation of PRA assets among different asset classes. The key finding is that under baseline parameters, a flat Social Security benefit independent of earnings (the most progressive option) allows the bottom 30 percent of the earnings distribution to achieve a higher expected utility than under the proportional reductions to the current benefit formula even with no investments in equity. An additional 30 percent of earners can lessen their equity investments without loss of welfare relative to those available under the scaled-back current formula. Under more realistic and less extreme changes to the traditional benefit, about half of the equity risk can be eliminated for the lowest earnings decile, and some equity risk can be eliminated for the bottom six deciles.

The optimal allocation to equities in the PRA is not particularly sensitive to the progressivity of the reductions in the traditional benefits—in most simulations, the optimal share in equities increases slightly for low earners and decreases slightly for higher earners with more progressive reductions in the traditional benefits.

Demographics, Asset Flows, and Macroeconomic Markets

Many analysts have suggested that population aging will adversely affect the assets of baby boomers when they retire. These analysts argue that when a large population cohort is working and accumulating resources for retirement, their demand for investments is high, thereby increasing asset prices. Conversely, when a large cohort retires, they are more likely to sell their assets to finance consumption and thereby drive down asset prices. This argument suggests that the rapidly increasing population of older people in the United States and around the world might lead to lower returns in financial markets in the decades ahead.

The extent to which these predictions will be realized is difficult to predict. It is particularly difficult in an international context, where macroeconomic markets are interrelated, and where financial capital flows freely across countries. The next two chapters in the volume consider the effects of population aging on asset markets, one focused on retirement saving in the United States and one on global financial markets.

Chapter 10 is part of a series of investigations by James M. Poterba, Steven F. Venti, and David A. Wise aimed at forecasting the flow of funds into and out of retirement-related asset holdings in the United States. In "The Decline of Defined Benefit Retirement Plans and Asset Flows," these investigators focus on the flow of funds into and out of "traditional" defined benefit (DB) pension plans. A companion study, also referenced in the chapter, focuses on the flow of funds into and out of 401(k)-type savings plans. Together, these studies project the direction and magnitude of asset flows for a very significant portion of retirement-related investments.

These analyses provide quantitative documentation, as well as future forecasting, of a fundamental transition in saving for retirement in the United States. What we have experienced over the last twenty-five years is a massive shift from saving through employer-managed defined benefit (DB) pensions to saving in individually managed defined contribution (DC) retirement plans, particularly 401(k) plans. Thus, to understand the effect of demographic trends on the demand for retirement assets in the coming decades, it is important to evaluate the likely flows into and out of both 401(k)-type plans and DB plans.

The projections in the chapter suggest that the average (over all people) of the present value of real DB benefits at age sixty-five attained an historical maximum in 2003, when the value was about $73,000. The present value declines after 2003, as the proportion of new retirees covered by DB plans declines. The projections also suggest that the average value of 401(k) assets at age sixty-five surpasses the average present value of DB benefits at age sixty-five in about 2010. Thereafter, the value of 401(k) assets grows rapidly, attaining levels much greater than the maximum present value of DB benefits. If equity returns between 2006 and 2040 are comparable to those observed historically, by 2040 average projected 401(k) assets will be over six times larger than the historical maximum level of DB benefits at age sixty-five, attained in 2003. Even if equity returns average 300 basis points below their historical value, the authors project that average 401(k) assets in 2040 would be 3.7 times as large as the value of DB benefits in 2003.

The offsetting and dominating influence of 401(k)-type saving, compared with flows in DB assets, is the central conclusion of the analysis. Focusing on DB assets alone suggests that an aging population, in conjunction with a shift away from DB plans, will lead to a decline in the real value of pension assets averaged across all retirees in future cohorts. When combining projected 401(k) assets with projected DB assets, however, the study finds that real pension assets not only increase, but increase substantially, in future decades.

These results underscore the need for further analysis of the factors that determine the diffusion of 401(k) plans across corporations, especially small companies with low-wage workers, as well as the contribution behavior and withdrawal behavior of 401(k) participants. The growing role of 401(k)-type plans in the retirement landscape suggests that understanding asset accumulation and drawdown in these plans is a critical component of any analysis of the effect of demographic change on financial markets.

Chapter 11 extends the analysis of demographic change and asset markets from the United States to international financial markets. In "Demographic Change, Relative Factor Prices, International Capital Flows, and Their Differential Effects on the Welfare of Generations," Alexander Ludwig, Dirk Krüger, and Axel Börsch-Supan develop a simulation model to analyze the impact of demographic change on macroeconomic markets around the world.

While the size, rate of growth, and age distribution of the population is changing worldwide, the magnitude of demographic changes and the timing and character of those changes differ significantly across countries and across regions of the world. There is variation in aggregate population growth rates and trends, variation in the ratio of the working-age population to the total adult population, and variation in the portion of the population at older ages. These demographic variations, and the varying paths of demographic change over time, affect international flows of capital and other resources. And these flows, in conjunction with the demographic changes themselves, affect the macroeconomic characteristics of different countries and the welfare of different generations within them.

The authors present the following intuitive explanation, which plays out in their more rigorous macroeconomic modeling. First, changes in the population structure will alter aggregate labor supply and aggregate savings that, in turn, alter the prices for labor and capital. As the working age population declines, for example, labor will become scarcer, relative to capital; real wages will increase; and real rates of return to capital will decrease. Second, as countries reform their PAYGO pension systems to partially funded systems, the additional supply of capital from those reforms reinforces the downward pressure on the rate of return to capital. The welfare implications of changing factor prices differ across generations, as younger generations gain from wage increases and older generations lose from lower capital returns.

The goal of this study is to quantify these effects in an international context, accounting for international flows of resources across countries. Much of the work leading up to this study has been in developing an economic model to make these calculations.

The study finds that the rate of return to capital decreases by roughly 80 to 90 basis points if capital is allowed to flow freely across regions. The simulations indicate that capital flows from rapidly aging regions to the rest of the world will initially be substantial, but that trends are reversed subsequently. However, because long-term demographic trends are highly correlated across Organization for Economic Cooperation and Development (OECD) countries, the capital flows across countries do not affect much the long-run decrease in the rate of return on capital. In other words, the impact of open markets in moderating the macroeconomic impact of demographic change within countries is less important because of the similarities in demographic change across countries in the long term.

In terms of the generational welfare effects, the simulations suggest that for younger households with few capital assets, increases in wages will dominate the decline in rates of return on capital. For example, abstracting from Social Security and its reform, the cohort born in 2005 will gain about 0.6 to 0.9 percent in terms of lifetime consumption. Older, asset-rich individuals, on the other hand, tend to lose because of the decline in interest rates on capital. However, if demographic changes necessitate reforms in Social Security, then reduced benefits or increased taxes will moderate the welfare gains to the younger generation.

Mortality Projections

The financial footing of the Social Security system depends importantly on the longevity of program participants. In the past several decades, longevity in the United States has increased substantially, adding to the financial burden on the Social Security program. What the future holds is less clear and requires the consideration of multiple factors. In chapter 12, "Is the U.S. Population Behaving Healthier?," David M. Cutler, Edward L. Glaeser, and Allison B. Rosen compare the risk factor profile of the population in the early 1970s with that of the population in the early 2000s and consider the implications of recent trends for future reductions in mortality.

The first part of the chapter estimates the impact of demographics, smoking, drinking, obesity, blood pressure, and cholesterol on ten-year mortality rates, comparing the predicted ten-year mortality in the two time periods. For the population aged twenty- to seventy-four, the ten-year probability of death fell from 9.8 percent in 1971 to 1975 to 8.4 percent in 1999 to 2002. For the population aged fifty-five to seventy-four, the ten-year risk of death falls from 25.7 percent to 21.7 percent. The largest contributors to these changes are reductions in smoking and better control of blood pressure.

While overall health has improved, not all risk factor trends have been in a positive direction. Smoking rates have fallen by more than a third since 1960, and alcohol consumption has declined by 20 percent since 1980, both leading to better health. Demographically, the population is better educated, and better-educated people live longer than less-educated people. On the other hand, obesity rates have doubled in the past two decades, and diabetes has increased as a result.

The second part of the analysis considers the impact on mortality if current trends continue. The mortality forecast integrates together several of the most important risk factors associated with mortality. Smoking and obesity are found to be the most important and offsetting components of the forecast. Based on reduced smoking, the mortality risk for the entire population aged twenty-five and older would be expected to decline by 8 percent. Increasing obesity, however, with current treatment rates—leads to increased hypertension and high cholesterol—and a 13 percent increase in mortality risk.

While suggestive, the authors emphasize that there is considerable uncertainty in making health projections for the future. For example, two-thirds of the U.S. population is overweight or obese. As a result, continued increases in weight from current levels have a bigger impact on health than did increases in weight from lower levels of body mass index (BMI). At the same time, however, the detrimental impact of BMI on health can be moderated dramatically by controlling hypertension and high cholesterol. So the question is not just whether weight will continue to increase. Also critical is the extent to which those who are overweight or obese take medications to control the health risks associated with high BMI. That, too, is highly uncertain. Understanding how to improve utilization of and adherence to recommended medications are key issues.

I

Innovative Approaches to Social Security Reform

1

Removing the Disincentives in Social Security for Long Careers

Gopi Shah Goda, John B. Shoven, and
Sita Nataraj Slavov

1.1 Introduction

When Social Security was instituted in 1935, the period life expectancy at age twenty for males was sixty-six and for females sixty-nine. Today, twenty-year-old males have a period life expectancy of seventy-six and females eighty. This increase in life expectancy has been accompanied by a corresponding improvement in health at all ages. Cutler, Liebman, and Smyth (2007) find that, in terms of mortality, men at age sixty-eight in 2000 have roughly the same mortality risk as men at age sixty-two in 1960. Thus, at a same age, men in the year 2000 are roughly six years younger. In terms of self-assessed health status, they find that the difference is even larger, approximately ten years. Their bottom line is, "Our best guess is that people aged 62 in the 1960s are in equivalent health to people aged 70 or more today" (p. 14). In related work, Shoven (2004) suggests that the age of elderly people is more appropriately measured by remaining life expectancy than by years since birth.

These improvements in life expectancy and health status enable individuals to prolong their careers and delay retirement. However, the length of retirement has actually grown by more than the increase in life expectancy

Gopi Shah Goda is a Robert Wood Johnson Scholar in Health Policy Research at Harvard University. John B. Shoven is the Charles R. Schwab Professor of Economics at Stanford University, and a research associate of the National Bureau of Economic Research. Sita Nataraj Slavov is an assistant professor of economics at Occidental College.

This research was supported by the U.S. Social Security Administration (SSA) through grant #10-P-98363-1-01 to the National Bureau of Economic Research (NBER) as part of the SSA Retirement Research Consortium. The opinions and conclusions expressed are solely those of the authors and do not represent the opinions or policy of SSA or any agency of the Federal Government.

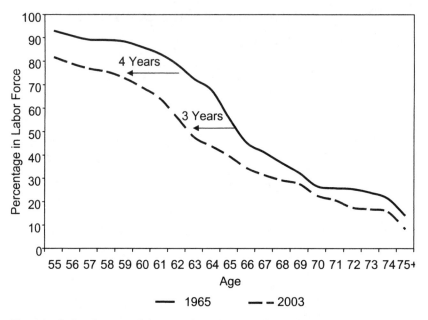

Fig. 1.1   Labor force participation of men by age, 1965 and 2003

at retirement. Figure 1.1 shows labor force participation rates by age in 1965 and 2003. Both early retirees and median retirees are retiring earlier in 2003 than they were in 1965. Figure 1.2 displays labor force participation rates by remaining life expectancy rather than age and shows that the average length of retirement for men has increased almost 50 percent since 1965. In 1965, the average length of retirement for the median male retiree was thirteen years. By 2003, it was nineteen years. Roughly half of the additional years were due to improvements in life expectancy, and half were due to earlier retirement.

Individuals may choose to use increases in their life expectancy for additional leisure or additional consumption, and it is possible that the shift toward longer retirements is optimal. However, there are a number of features of Social Security that distort incentives toward increased retirement length by imposing high implicit tax rates on longer careers and working at older ages. For example, Social Security benefits are computed based on the average of an individual's highest thirty-five years of earnings. An individual with fewer than thirty-five years of earnings has a relatively strong incentive to work for an additional year as the additional earnings clearly raise the average upon which the benefit is based. On the other hand, an individual who has already worked for thirty-five years has a diminished incentive to work an additional year—the earnings from that year will, at best, replace one of the previous highest thirty-five in the benefit computa-

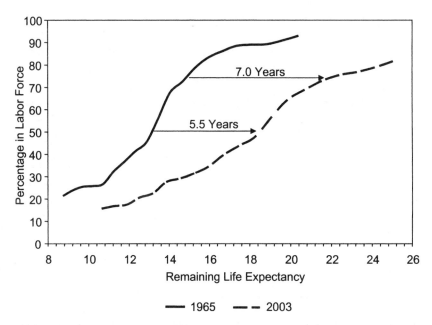

Fig. 1.2 Labor force participation of men by remaining life expectancy, 1965 and 2003

tion. Thus, the benefit formula encourages careers of thirty-five years or less. Several other features of the benefit computation—which we will discuss in detail in the following—contribute to the disincentives for long careers.

In this chapter, we examine the disincentives for long careers created by Social Security. Our main finding is that the structure of these programs imposes high implicit tax rates on workers late in their careers. As a result of this distortion, we believe retirements are suboptimally long. The consequences of this distortion are significant: a lot of the stress on public and private pension systems is caused by the increased length of retirement. We also outline ways to reduce or eliminate the implicit taxes on long careers and working at older ages. The potential benefits of a larger work force for Social Security and Medicare (and gross domestic product [GDP]) are large.

1.2   Work Incentives in U.S. Social Security

In this section, we investigate the impact of Old Age and Survivors Insurance (OASI) on the career-length incentives of both stylized and actual workers. In each year of their working life, we compute the workers' present value of Social Security taxes minus benefits under the assumption that they stop working after the current year (i.e., they accumulate no further earnings). The *implicit Social Security tax rate* is defined as the increase in the net tax burden from working an additional year as a percentage of the current year's earnings. In other words, this is the additional net tax the worker incurs by prolonging his or her career by one year. This variable captures the worker's incentive to continue working for an additional year as opposed to retiring. Throughout our analysis, OASI benefits are computed under 2005 law. That is, we sum each worker's highest thirty-five years of wage-indexed earnings that fall below the earnings cap and divide this amount by 420 months to get the worker's average indexed monthly earnings (AIME). We then compute the worker's primary insurance amount (PIA): the PIA is equal to 90 percent of the first x of AIME, plus 32 percent of the amount between x and y, plus 15 percent of the remainder of AIME, where x and y are the constructed bend points for the appropriate retirement year.[1] The worker receives the PIA—indexed for inflation—every month from retirement until death. A minimum of ten years of work is required to qualify for any benefits. In computing taxes and benefits, we assume an aggregate wage growth rate of 3.5 percent, an inflation rate of 2.5 percent, and a discount rate of 4.5 percent. The OASI tax rate is assumed to be 10.6 percent applied to capped earnings using the historical earnings caps. Benefit streams are discounted for mortality using the Social Security Administration's intermediate scenario mortality rates.

Our analysis is similar to that of Feldstein and Samwick (1992). Feldstein and Samwick compute marginal net tax rates for stylized workers who vary by gender, income, and marital status. They show that the additional tax paid on an additional dollar of income varies significantly across workers and over a worker's lifetime—in particular, marginal tax rates are significantly higher for single workers and for younger workers. Their finding that marginal tax rates decline with age comes from the fact that as a worker approaches retirement, the present value of the additional benefit received increases. However, they only compute marginal tax rates for workers between ages twenty-five and sixty, and each year of earnings over this thirty-five-year period is assumed to count in the benefit computation. This assumption overlooks a major disincentive for long careers: after a worker has accumulated thirty-five years of earnings, additional years are likely to have little, if any, impact on benefits. As we will show in the following, taking account of this fact implies that older workers face significantly higher implicit tax rates than younger workers.

1.2.1   A Stylized Computation

To illustrate our argument, we compute implicit tax rates for a set of four male stylized workers under current law. Three of our stylized workers re-

---

1. The 2005 bendpoints ($627 and $3,779) were multiplied by the appropriate wage adjustment factor to be in line with the year in which the worker retires.

ceive simulated earnings profiles equal to either the average, 10th percentile, or 90th percentile earnings for their age group. In order to simulate wage histories, we use Outgoing Rotation Groups from the 2001 and 2002 Current Population Survey to compute the wage for each of the three earnings levels within each age group. We then divide this by the aggregate average wage across all age groups. This ratio is multiplied by the historical average wage in each year of the worker's life to arrive at a wage for the worker. For example, consider an average male thirty-year-old worker in 1950. The national average annual wage in 1950 was $2,763. According to our computations, a thirty-year-old male earns 1.13 times the national average; therefore, his simulated wage would be $2,763 × 1.13 = $3,122. A fourth stylized worker earns the historical earnings cap in each year.

We assume that all stylized workers start work at age twenty and retire at the normal retirement age. The implicit Social Security tax rate for a given career length is calculated as described previously. The results of this exercise are shown in figure 1.3. Note that for less than ten years of work, the worker is not yet vested in the system and, therefore, faces an implicit tax rate of the full 10.6 percent. (These years are not shown in figure 1.3.)

Two points should be clear from the graph. First, all workers experience a sharp increase in their implicit tax rate at thirty-five years of work. The reason for this increase is that Social Security benefits are calculated based

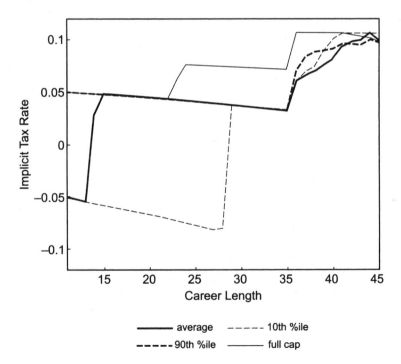

Fig. 1.3   Implicit tax rates by career length

on the highest thirty-five years of indexed annual earnings. This means that the thirty-third, thirty-fourth, and thirty-fifth year of work noticeably improve retirement benefits because the earnings of that year replace a zero in the calculation of average indexed monthly earnings (AIME). On the other hand, the thirty-sixth year of work may or may not enter the calculation, and if it does, it will replace a lower year of earnings and not a zero in the calculation. The marginal incentive to work for the thirty-sixth year and beyond is much lower than for the first thirty-five years. Part-time work after a career of thirty-five years or more will, in particular, usually have no impact on subsequent benefits, and, therefore, the 10.6 percent OASI payroll tax is simply a tax and has no component of deferred benefits. For people who enter the workforce immediately after high school and who do not leave the labor force for an extended period, thirty-five years of earnings will be accumulated by the age of fifty-three.

Second, the median and low earners each experience a sharp increase in their implicit tax rate earlier in their careers—for the middle-income earner, after twelve years of work, and for the low-income earner, after twenty-two years of work. This increase results from the fact that the PIA formula is sharply progressive, combined with the fact that the AIME calculation does not distinguish between workers with lower earnings and those with higher earnings but shorter covered careers. At the beginning of their careers, workers tend to have a low AIME because they have significantly fewer than thirty-five years of positive earnings. The benefit computation replaces the missing years of earnings with zeros, and these workers appear to be in a lower income group than their true lifetime earnings would imply. The progressivity of the PIA formula translates this low AIME into a disproportionately high monthly benefit. As workers accumulate positive earnings years, the benefit computation begins to treat them as if they have higher lifetime incomes. A sharp increase in the implicit tax rate occurs when a worker accumulates enough positive earnings years to cross a PIA bend point. Thus, the current formula favors workers with short careers by treating them as if they were low earners. In some cases, for instance, where the short career was necessitated by poor health, that may be appropriate. In most cases, however, the current treatment seems inappropriate and blunts the incentive to work long careers. This effect is most pronounced for low-income workers, who face the sharpest increase in their implicit tax rate.

These distortions lead us to evaluate the following three reforms:

1. *Use forty years, rather than thirty-five, in the AIME computation.*

If forty years were used instead of thirty-five, this would remove some of the discouragement currently built into the system for staying in the workforce. An extra five years of work would count toward the calculation of retirement benefits.

2. *Disentangle career length and progressivity.*

Average indexed monthly earnings could be calculated only for the months with covered earnings (eliminating the zeros from the computation and dividing by the number of months of nonzero earnings rather than 420). The PIA would be calculated using this modified AIME formula. However, a single person would only get the full PIA at the Normal Retirement Age (NRA) if they worked a full career (currently thirty-five years, proposed to be forty years under the first reform). If they worked fewer years, their benefits would be reduced proportionately. For example, consider how we currently treat someone with a ten-year high-income career. Their benefits are determined as if they were a relative low earner with the twenty-five years of zeros in the earnings calculation. The alternative would be to give them 10/35ths of the PIA of a high earner. This would result in a reduction of benefits for short career workers. This reform is illustrated in figure 1.4.

3. *Establish a "paid-up" category of workers who have more than forty years of contributions.*

Under the first proposed reform, the number of years in the benefit calculation is forty. A complementary policy is to only collect forty years of payroll taxes from workers. After forty years of covered employment, the worker would be declared "paid-up" for Social Security. This should be relatively easy to administer—conceivably an indicator would be added to the individual's Social Security number reflecting the fact that paid-up

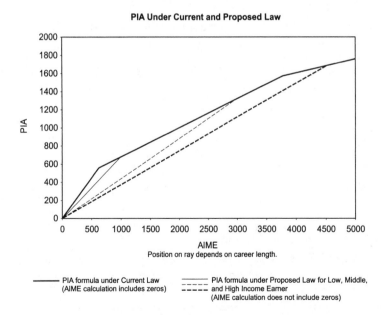

Fig. 1.4   **PIA under current and proposed law**

status had been achieved. A related idea was mentioned in Burtless and Quinn (2002), namely allowing workers who reach the NRA to opt out of additional Social Security contributions.

There is a theoretical justification for these policies. The intuition of optimal tax theory would be to place heavier taxes on more inelastic supply (and demand) and lighter taxes or no taxes on highly elastic behavior. Our hypothesis is that the forty-first and forty-second years of work, for instance, are far more sensitive to incentives than the twenty-first and twenty-second years of work. The practical significance of these three reforms is to make employment of veteran workers more attractive for both the employee and the employer.

Taken together, these three proposals result in a benefit cut. In order to compensate for this and keep the reforms benefit-neutral in aggregate, we increase retirement benefits proportionately in order to keep aggregate benefits constant before and after the reforms.[2] Assuming no behavioral changes, the adjustment needed is a 19.4 percent increase in benefits. The proposals also result in redistribution from those with shorter careers to those with longer ones. Figure 1.5 illustrates this by depicting our stylized average earner's PIA, as a function of career length, under both the current and the proposed law. Under the proposed law, a worker's PIA would rise more sharply as he or she accumulated years of work—that is, benefits are more responsive to a decision to delay retirement. Workers with fewer than thirty-one years of covered earnings would receive a smaller PIA than under the current system; however, as their career length extends beyond thirty-one years, their PIA rises above the current level. A similar result holds for the low and high earners.

On the revenue side, introducing the "paid-up" category of workers who have worked forty years constitutes a reduction in the amount of tax revenues the system receives. We estimate that at most 4.35 percent of OASI revenue comes from income that was earned after an individual worked forty years.[3] Thus, instituting the "paid-up" reform would require a payroll tax increase of 0.5 percent, changing the current OASI tax from 10.6 percent to 11.1 percent. All future calculations of the impact of the three proposed reforms account for the tax and benefit adjustments to ensure benefit- and revenue-neutrality.

---

2. The revenue effects are estimated using the Social Security Benefits and Earnings Public-Use File described in the following section.

3. The estimate of the fraction of OASI revenue earned in years 41+ comes from the Social Security Benefits and Earnings Public-Use File, 2004, described in more detail in the following section. The beneficiaries' earnings were indexed to 2003 using the historical Social Security average wage index. This estimate is biased upward because the data set only includes earnings below the taxable maximum, which has increased significantly over the period 1951 to 2003. This implies the program has expanded over this time period, and earnings in the earlier part of this period are underrepresented.

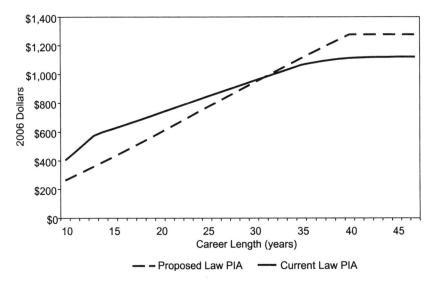

Fig. 1.5   Monthly primary insurance amount under current and proposed law: Average income earner

We repeat our implicit tax rate computations for the four stylized workers under the proposed reforms. The results are shown in figure 1.6 and labeled "Proposed Law." Current Law results are also shown for comparison purposes. Note that implicit tax rates remain roughly constant over each worker's life, resulting in less distortion of career length choices. Moreover, implicit tax rates for all income groups are closer to zero. The decreasing trend arises from the present value of future benefits increasing as a worker gets closer to the NRA. At forty years of work, all workers enter the "paid-up" category and no longer participate in the system.

The proposed reforms do not affect the overall progressivity of the Social Security system as is shown in table 1.1. At the thirty-five-year career length, the average income earner's internal rates of return (IRRs) are constant before and after the reforms at 1.17 percent. The three policies do not change the relative position of the low- and high-income earners. After an individual has worked thirty-five years, he or she is always better off under the proposed reforms.

1.2.2   Data and Results

The drawback of using stylized workers is, of course, that they do not reflect the diversity of actual workers' labor market experiences. In particular, the stylized workers' ages and career lengths are perfectly correlated. This makes it difficult to capture the experience of, for example, a woman who takes time out of the labor force to raise children. Thus, we repeat our computations using the Social Security Benefits and Earnings Public-Use

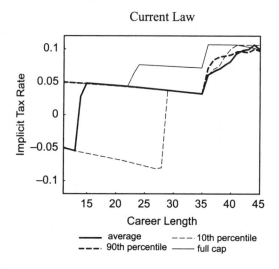

Current Law

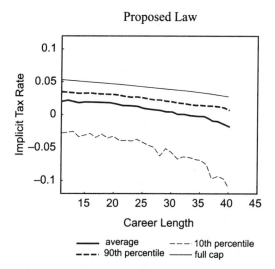

Proposed Law

Fig. 1.6   Implicit tax rates by career length under current and proposed laws

Table 1.1	Internal rates of return for workers with 35-year career (%)	
	Current law	Proposed law
Low-income earner	2.47	2.46
Average-income earner	1.17	1.17
High-income earner	0.66	0.66

File, 2004, which contains benefit and earnings data on a 1 percent random, representative sample entitled to receive a Social Security benefit in December 2004. The full sample contains data on 473,366 beneficiaries. Unfortunately, this data set provides no way to link couples; therefore, we include only workers who are receiving benefits based on their own earnings records. We limit our attention to beneficiaries receiving retirement benefits who started working in 1951 or later, which leaves 123,552 individuals born between 1910 and 1942.[4] We continue to use Social Security intermediate scenario assumptions for mortality.

For the actual worker computations under the proposed law, we introduce an earnings threshold: years in which earnings are less than 5 percent of the earnings cap are not counted toward the years of work calculation, but are subject to payroll taxes.[5] The rationale for the earnings threshold is that many individuals—particularly as they get older—have years in which they work a small number of hours. Without an earnings threshold, these individuals' benefits would increase disproportionately (given the modified AIME computation and the progressivity of the PIA formula), and they would accumulate years of credit toward the paid-up status. The result is that many older individuals in the sample would face large negative implicit tax rates. The earnings threshold reduces this distortion. Of course, this means that years where earnings were under the threshold face the full tax, unless the individual had attained paid-up status by working more than forty years. On balance, however, we find that distortions are significantly less with the earnings threshold. (This issue did not arise with the stylized workers as our simulated earnings profiles never fell below the 5 percent threshold.)

In order to illustrate the complexity of patterns that actual individuals face, we plot histograms of the ages at which individuals attain ten years of covered earnings (vesting age at which individuals become eligible for benefits), thirty-five years of covered earnings (the current number used in the benefit computation), and forty years of covered earnings (the proposed number to be used in the benefit computation). The results are broken down by gender and appear as figures 1.7 to 1.9.

While workers tend to reach ten years of work at age thirty, thirty-five years at age fifty-five, and forty years at age sixty (like our stylized workers), there is considerable individual variation, particularly for females. A sizeable number of females reach these experience levels considerably later than assumed in our stylized example. These figures illustrate the impor-

---

4. Only aggregate earnings are recorded for years 1937 to 1950.

5. This is not unlike the earnings needed to obtain a quarter of coverage in the current system, $920 in 2005. To receive four quarters of coverage, an individual would need $3,680 in earnings, approximately 4 percent of the 2005 earnings cap of $90,000. Earnings below this level are subject to the payroll tax even though benefits are not increased.

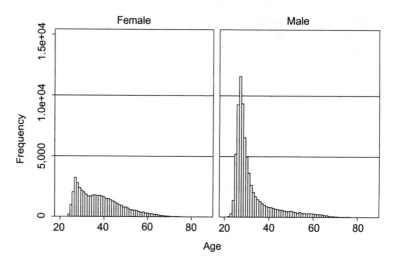

Fig. 1.7   Distribution of vesting age: Graphs by gender

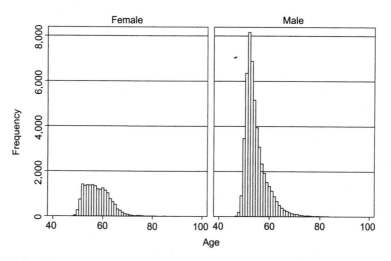

Fig. 1.8   Distribution of thirty-five-year career age: Graphs by gender

tance of using actual workers to study the career length incentives created by the system, particularly if we are interested in the impact on women.

Figures 1.10 and 1.11 show our calculations of the average implicit tax rate broken down by career length (figure 1.10), age (figure 1.11), and gender. The current law computations exhibit the same features as did those for stylized workers. Workers face increases in their implicit tax rates under current law as they age and increase their career length. This is a result of moving from one PIA bend point to the next and from accumulating thirty-five years of earnings. This result occurs for both male and female

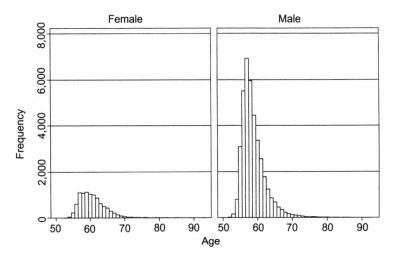

Fig. 1.9   **Distribution of forty-year career age: Graphs by gender**

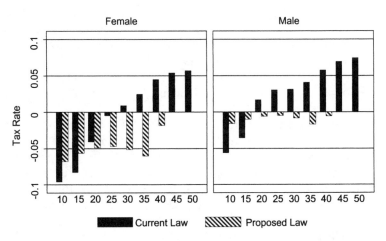

Fig. 1.10   **Average implicit Social Security tax rates, by career length: Graphs by gender**

workers, and it is present whether we look at means or medians (not shown).

Under the proposed law, male workers' implicit tax rates move closer to zero for all age and experience groups. There is also a much smaller association between implicit tax rate and age. Most of the large, positive implicit tax rates—which occur late in their careers—are eliminated. Those that remain are faced by individuals who earn less than the earnings threshold and, therefore, are being subject to the full OASI tax rate of 10.6 percent. Individuals with earnings below the threshold drive up the aver-

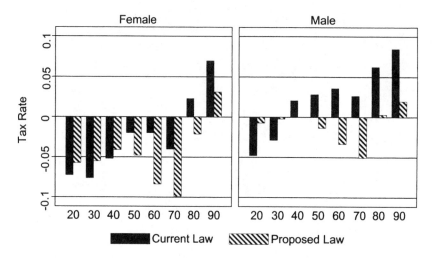

Fig. 1.11   Average implicit Social Security tax rates, by age: Graphs by gender

age implicit tax rates faced under the proposed reforms at older ages; however, the average annual income earned by people who face the full OASI tax rate is only $1,115. One of the main differences between the treatment under the current law and the proposed law is the sharp decrease in the number of people *and* the amount of income facing the full tax rate under the three reforms.

The changes redistribute from short-careered workers to long-careered workers as shown in figure 1.12. Individuals who work more than forty years and are thus subject to the paid-up policy reform no longer see earlier earnings years being replaced by later, potentially higher earning years. While this could lead to a decrease in their calculated PIA, the IRR would be higher under the proposed reforms because the added benefit from replacing a year of earnings in the current calculation is small relative to the amount of taxes paid.

Females tend to experience a larger subsidy under both current law and the proposed policies due to the fact that the system is progressive and females in the sample have lower earnings, and also because their mortality probabilities are more favorable, making the expected future additional benefits larger. We define the Gender Gap to be the difference between average male and female implicit Social Security tax rates. Table 1.2 summarizes calculations of the Gender Gap under different mortality assumptions and shows that approximately 40 percent of the difference between male and female implicit tax rates is due to more favorable female mortality; the remaining is attributed to differences in underlying earnings levels.

The reforms may disproportionately penalize women, who are more likely to take time out of the labor force for child or elderly care and expe-

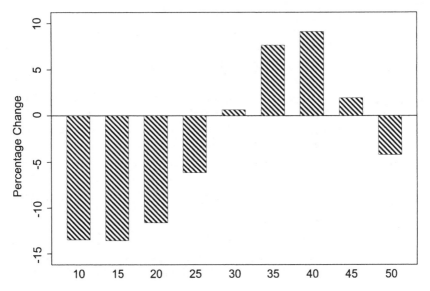

Fig. 1.12   **Percentage change in PIA by career length**

Table 1.2   Average implicit Social Security tax (ISST) rates under different
                       mortality assumptions (%)

	Average ISST	Gender gap
Current law		
Males	0.90	
Females using female mortality	−3.99	4.89
Females using male mortality	−2.18	3.08
Portion of gender gap explained		
by mortality differences		37
Proposed law		
Males	−0.93	
Females using female mortality	−5.33	4.40
Females using male mortality	−3.34	2.41
Portion of gender gap explained		
by mortality differences		45

rience shorter careers. Benefit levels are 0.89 percent higher for males but 1.45 percent lower for females under the three reforms. One possible policy to alleviate this effect would be to give women an across-the-board credit for working of one, two, or three years. This policy is similar to the treatment of individuals who take time out of the labor force to raise children in countries such as Germany. In the German system, a child-raising parent is treated as though he or she earned the average wage until the child's third birthday. The differences between the PIA in the current system and the PIA under the proposed reforms along with a credit for women are given in table 1.3. Note that offering a credit to women of even one year has a substantial effect on the level of benefits.

Our calculations of mean implicit tax rates mask a considerable amount of variation across workers. To illustrate this variation, we plot individual implicit tax rates as a function of age for a small subsample of individuals under both current law and the proposed reforms. These are shown in figures 1.13 (current law) and 1.14 (proposed law). Most individuals experience features similar to the stylized workers: under current law, there are sharp increases in implicit tax rate as they cross PIA bend points and another sharp increase when they accumulate thirty-five years of work. There is considerable variation across workers in the timing of these increases. The proposed law eliminates most of the large positive tax rates for older workers. It also reduces the association between age and tax rate and moves tax rates closer to zero for most workers in most years of their lives. However, many of the workers experience single years with large negative implicit tax rates. These are years in which earnings are low—these years

Table 1.3   Percentage change in primary insurance amount by gender and years of credit given for women (%)

	No credit	1-year credit	2-year credit	3-year credit
Male benefits	0.89	0.89	0.89	0.89
Female benefits	−1.45	1.69	4.73	7.67
Total	−0.02	1.20	2.39	3.53

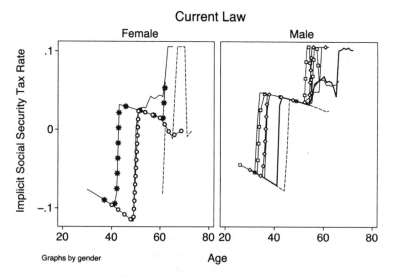

Fig. 1.13   Current law: Graphs by gender

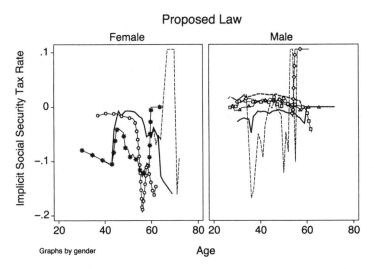

Fig. 1.14   Proposed law: Graphs by gender

disproportionately increase PIA (due to the progressivity of the formula) and contribute toward paid up status.

1.3   Conclusion

The U.S. labor market has proved to be very flexible in absorbing new workers as evidenced by its ability to accommodate large numbers of workers as women entered the labor force in the past several decades, and the economy has benefited greatly as a result of the larger workforce. By eliminating the disincentives against working longer careers, we can capitalize on the good fortunes of increasing life expectancy and favorable health status by paving the way for more capable individuals to stay in the labor force.

References

Burtless, Gary, and Joseph Quinn. 2002. Is working longer the answer for an aging workforce? Center for Retirement Research. Issue in Brief no. 11. Center for Retirement Research at Boston College.

Butrica, Barbara A., Richard W. Johnson, Karen E. Smith, and Eugene Steuerle. 2006. The implicit tax on work at older ages. *National Tax Journal* 59:211–34.

Cutler, David M., Jeffrey B. Liebman, and Seamus Smyth. 2007. How fast should the Social Security eligibility age rise? NBER Retirement Research Center Working Paper no. NB04-05. Cambridge, MA: National Bureau of Economic Research.

Feldstein, Martin, and Andrew Samwick. 1992. Social Security rules and marginal tax rates. *National Tax Journal* 45 (1): 1–22.

Fenge, Robert, Silke Uebelmesser, and Martin Werding. 2002. Second-best properties of implicit Social Security taxes: Theory and evidence. CESifo Working Paper no. 743.

Gruber, Jonathan, and David A. Wise. 1997. Social Security and retirement around the world. NBER Working Paper no. 6134. Cambridge, MA: National Bureau of Economic Research, August.

Shoven, John B. 2004. The impact of major improvement in life expectancy on the financing of Social Security, Medicare, and Medicaid. In *Coping with Methuselah: The impact of molecular biology on medicine and society,* ed. Henry J. Aaron and William B. Schwartz, 166–97. Washington DC: Brookings Institution.

Comment   Erzo F. P. Luttmer

This chapter tackles the important question of how the Social Security benefit formula can be adjusted so that it generates fewer incentives for individuals to retire early. Social Security provides retirement incentives when the additional Social Security taxes paid by postponing retirement for a year exceed the increase in the present value of future Social Security benefits from working this additional year. Goda, Shoven, and Slavov refer to this difference, when expressed as a fraction of earnings, as the implicit Social Security tax. Two features in the current Social Security law cause this implicit Social Security tax to be high for individuals with long careers. First, the current Social Security law bases benefits on the average of the thirty-five highest years of indexed earnings. Thus, current earnings will increase this average less for individuals who already have worked for thirty-five years than for individuals who have not yet worked thirty-five years because for the former group the current year's earnings crowd out a prior year's earnings in the benefit formula. Second, the progressivity of Social Security benefits depends on the average indexed earnings of the highest thirty-five years of earnings (including years with zero earnings) rather than basing this average only on those years with positive earnings. As a result, Social Security redistributes from workers with long careers to those with short careers even if these two groups have the same earnings per year worked. This redistribution further raises the implicit Social Security tax on those with longer careers.

Goda, Shoven, and Slavov analyze a reform proposal that would reduce the implicit early retirement incentives in the Social Security benefit rules. This reform would base benefits on the average of the forty highest years of

Erzo F. P. Luttmer is an associate professor at the John F. Kennedy School of Government, Harvard University, and a faculty research fellow of the National Bureau of Economic Research.

positive indexed earnings (i.e., excluding years with zero earnings) and reduce benefits pro rata based on the number of years with positive earnings for people who have fewer than forty years of positive earnings. For example, a person with twenty years of positive earnings would receive half the benefits of someone who has the same average earnings based on forty years of positive earnings. Finally, after forty years of positive earnings, one would become "paid-up," that is, exempt from paying any further Social Security taxes. Under this proposal, Social Security benefits and the Social Security tax rate are adjusted such that average benefits and average Social Security tax revenue are the same as under the current law.

Using data on a 1 percent random sample of Social Security beneficiaries in 2004 who started working after or during 1951 and claim benefits based on their own earnings record, Goda, Shoven, and Slavov carefully evaluate the reform proposal's impact on the Social Security incentive to retire as well as its distributional impact. They find that this reform would lead to a sharp reduction in retirement incentives: the implicit Social Security tax rate would fall substantially, typically by 4 to 7 percentage points, for men and women between the ages of fifty and seventy. As a result, Social Security would no longer provide this group of workers with an incentive to retire early. By design, this proposal would increase benefits for those with longer careers at the expense of those with shorter careers. However, the reform does not substantially affect the overall progressivity of the Social Security system. The proposed reform would reduce the average benefits of women relative to those of men, but this can be fixed with a minor adjustment.

Goda, Shoven, and Slavov analyze one of three implicit marginal Social Security taxes, namely the implicit Social Security tax "on postponing retirement by one year." In other words, it is the implicit tax on working this year when the counterfactual is retiring in the following year. This is probably the most plausible counterfactual for older workers. The second implicit Social Security tax is the tax on the extensive margin of working this year holding labor supply constant in the future years. In other words, it is the incentive to take one year off from working, for example, for child care or schooling reasons. This margin is probably the more relevant one for younger workers. Finally, there is the implicit Social Security tax on the intensive margin: the effect of earning one extra dollar on expected Social Security benefits net of taxes holding earnings in all other years constant.

Feldstein and Samwick (1992) also calculate implicit Social Security taxes and find, in apparent contradiction to Goda, Shoven, and Slavov's findings, that these tax rates fall with age. Goda, Shoven, and Slavov attribute this difference to the fact that Feldstein and Samwick only calculate implicit marginal Social Security tax rates for workers with at most thirty-five years of earnings. This, however, is not the reason why Feldstein and Samwick obtain different results. The difference in findings arises because

Feldstein and Samwick examine the implicit Social Security tax *on the intensive margin,* while Goda, Shoven, and Slavov examine the implicit Social Security tax on *postponing retirement.* The implicit Social Security tax on the intensive margin is lowest in those years included in the thirty-five highest years, whether or not they crowd out other years, and, therefore, this tax will remain relatively low for workers with a long work history as long as current earnings end up belonging to the thirty-five years of highest earnings. The Social Security system distorts labor supply decisions on both the intensive and extensive margins and may cause significant deadweight loss on each of these margins because of preexisting distortions. It would, therefore, be worthwhile to also examine how the proposed reform would affect these other two implicit marginal Social Security tax rates.

While Goda, Shoven, and Slavov present a compelling case that the reform proposal would improve incentives without having a major redistributive impact, it is less clear that the reform proposal is optimal. For example, the rules on the treatment of spouses imply high implicit Social Security taxes for individuals who will claim benefits based on their spouse's earnings. Perhaps the political viability of altering these rules is low, but it would be interesting to explore whether these rules can be adjusted to reduce implicit marginal Social Security tax rates with a distributional impact that is roughly neutral. More narrowly, the proposal currently analyzed by Goda, Shoven, and Slavov contains two parameters: the number of years of earnings that are included in the Social Security benefit formula and the number of years of earnings needed to reach the paid-up status. It would be relatively easy to analyze the impact of reforms that use different values for these parameters. For example, would retirement incentives be further reduced if both parameters were set at fifty?

A key component of the proposal analyzed by Goda, Shoven, and Slavov is that progressivity is based on average earnings in years with positive earnings rather than on average earnings regardless of whether earnings were positive. For practical purposes, the proposal defines positive earnings as earnings exceeding 5 percent of the earnings cap. This raises two issues. The first is practical. Holding lifetime income constant, the new proposal is more generous toward those who have more years with positive earnings. This creates incentives for individuals to shift earnings in order to attain this earnings threshold in each year. It would be useful to ascertain whether these incentives are strong enough that possibilities for gaming the system would become a serious concern. The second issue concerns the deeper theoretical point of whether income redistribution should be based on annual earnings or on lifetime earnings. As Liebman (2003) discusses, this issue is largely unresolved because it depends on how well each measure proxies for unobserved true ability. If, as seems plausible, both measures contain useful information about unobserved true ability, using a combination of both measures is optimal. Given that the majority of the redistribution taking place through the tax and transfer system is based on annual (or sometimes even monthly) income, having some redistribution based on a measure of lifetime earnings, as currently is the case with Social Security, may well be optimal.

The chapter raises the empirical question of whether individuals understand the implicit retirement incentives from the Social Security system and whether they respond to them. The sharp break in retirement incentives induced by already having thirty-five years of positive earnings can be exploited to estimate this response. David Seif, Jeffrey Liebman, and I are currently analyzing this, and preliminary results indicate that the retirement hazard rate starts to increase sharply as soon as individuals have thirty-five years of positive earnings. This suggests that Goda, Shoven, and Slavov's concern about these implicit retirement incentives is pertinent and that the reform proposal will cause people to retire later.

Overall, this chapter makes an important contribution to the debate about Social Security reform because it makes a compelling case that a relatively straightforward and plausibly politically viable adjustment to the Social Security benefit formula can drastically reduce incentives from Social Security to retire early without major redistributive consequences. A reduction of the implicit Social Security tax will produce a first-order welfare gain because the implicit Social Security tax comes on top of other distortions, most notably from income taxation, that already encourage early retirement.

References

Feldstein, Martin S., and Andrew A. Samwick. 1992. Social Security rules and marginal tax rates. *National Tax Journal* 45:1–22.
Liebman, Jeffrey B. 2003. Should taxes be based on lifetime income? Vickrey taxation revisited. Harvard University. Unpublished Manuscript.

Notional Defined Contribution Pension Systems in a Stochastic Context
Design and Stability

Alan J. Auerbach and Ronald Lee

2.1 Introduction

Around the world, pay-as-you-go (PAYGO) public pension programs are facing serious long-term fiscal problems due primarily to actual and projected population aging, and most appear unsustainable as currently structured. All strict PAYGO programs (i.e., those that do not incorporate sizable trust fund accumulations) can feasibly pay an implicit rate of return equal to the growth rate of gross domestic product (GDP; labor force growth plus productivity growth) once they are mature and in steady state. This rate of return is typically lower than the rate of return that can be earned in the market, either through low-risk bonds or through investment in equities. The programs' long-term fiscal problems relate to a misalignment between these low but feasible rates of return and promised rates of return that may once have been feasible but no longer are so. The tradi-

Alan J. Auerbach is the Robert D. Burch Professor of Economics and Law at the University of California, Berkeley, and a research associate of the National Bureau of Economic Research. Ronald Lee is a professor of demography and economics at the University of California, Berkeley, and a research associate of the National Bureau of Economic Research.

This research was supported by the U.S. Social Security Administration (SSA) through grant #10-P-98363-1-02 to the National Bureau of Economic Research (NBER) as part of the SSA Retirement Research Consortium (RRC). The findings and conclusions expressed are solely those of the authors and do not represent the views of SSA, any agency of the federal government, or the NBER. The authors gratefully acknowledge the excellent research assistance of Erin Metcalf and Anne Moore; the contributions of Carl Boe in the development of the stochastic forecasting model; comments from Ed Palmer, Jason Seligman, and Ole Settergren (none of whom is responsible for any remaining errors); participants in the NBER summer institute, the eighth annual RRC conference, and the October 2006 NBER Conference on Retirement Research; and support from Berkeley's National Institute on Aging (NIA) funded Center for the Economics and Demography of Aging. The research funded here builds on basic research funded by NIA grant R37-AG11761.

tional plans are mostly defined benefit and have been criticized for creating strong incentives for early retirement. More generally, there is a concern that the taxes that finance these programs distort labor supply incentives throughout life. Many also believe that these plans undermine motivations to save, and, because they are themselves unfunded, thereby reduce overall capital accumulation and consequently lead to lower labor productivity and slower growth.

Recently, a new variety of public pension program known as "notional defined contribution" or "nonfinancial defined contribution" (NDC) has been created and implemented by Sweden, with first payments in 2001. A number of other countries have introduced or are planning to introduce NDC plans, including Italy, Poland, Latvia, Mongolia, and the Kyrgyz Republic, and proposed new plans for France and Germany have NDC aspects (Legros 2003; Holtzmann and Palmer 2005).

The NDC programs differ in detail, but the basic principle is that they mimic defined contribution plans without actually setting aside assets as such plans do. Under an NDC program, a notional capital account is maintained for each participant. Balances in this account earn a rate of return that is declared by the pension plan each year, and notional payments into this account are made over the entire life history to mirror actual taxes or contributions. Together with the declared rate of return, these notional contributions determine the value of the account at any point in time. After a designated age such as sixty-two, a participant can choose to begin to draw benefits, which is done by using the account to purchase an annuity from the pension plan. The terms of the annuity will depend on mortality at the time the generation turns sixty-five (for example) and on a rate of return stipulated by the pension plan, which might be the same rate of return used in the preretirement accumulation phase.

The NDC plans are seen as having many potential advantages over traditional PAYGO systems, but our focus in this chapter is on just one of these potential advantages, stability. A plan of this sort appears structured to achieve a considerable degree of fiscal stability because the promised rates of return reflect the program's underlying PAYGO nature, rather than being market-based, and the annuity structure should buffer the system from the costs of rising longevity. Further, in the event that it begins to go off the tracks, a braking mechanism can be incorporated that automatically modifies the rate of return to help restore the plan to financial health. Given the political difficulties of making frequent changes in PAYGO pension programs, the attractiveness of an inherently stable system is clear.

In this chapter, we use a stochastic macro model for forecasting and simulating Social Security finances to examine the behavior of NDC-type public pension programs in the context of the U.S. demography and economy. Given the structure and strategy of the stochastic model, we can study the probability distribution of outcomes (benefit flows and rates of return) for generations (birth cohorts) of plan participants for the NDC program, as well as the overall financial stability of the NDC system. The next section of the chapter describes our stochastic forecasting model. In the following section, we describe in some detail the Swedish NDC program and our adaptation of it to U.S. economic and demographic conditions. We then provide simulations of this basic U.S. NDC plan, as well as variants incorporating modifications of two key attributes of the NDC plan, the method of determining rates of return, and the brake mechanism applied when the system appears headed for financial problems.

2.2   The Stochastic Forecasting/Simulation Model

The stochastic population model is based on a Lee-Carter (1992a,b) mortality model and a somewhat similar fertility model (Lee 1993; Lee and Tuljapurkar 1994). Lee and Carter model the time series of a mortality index as a random walk with drift, estimated over U.S. data from 1950 to 2003. This index then drives the evolution of age specific mortality rates and thereby survival and life expectancy. This kind of model has been extensively tested (Lee and Miller 2001) and is widely accepted (Booth 2006), and although we shall see that the probability intervals it produces for distant future life expectancy appear quite narrow, these intervals have performed well in within-sample retrospective testing.

In a similar way, a fertility index drives age-specific fertility, but in this case it is necessary to prespecify a long-term mean based on external information. We set the long-run mean of the total fertility rate equal to the 1.95 births per woman, as assumed by the Social Security actuaries (Trustees Report, 2004, henceforth TR04). The estimated model then supplies the probability distribution for simulated outcomes. Because it is fitted on U.S. data, the fertility model reflects the possibility of substantial baby boom and bust type swings.

Immigration is taken as given and deterministic, following the assumed level in TR04.

Following Lee and Tuljapurkar (1994), these stochastic processes can be used to generate stochastic population forecasts in which probability distributions can be derived for all quantities of interest. These stochastic population forecasts can be used as the core of stochastic forecasts of the finances of the Social Security system (Lee and Tuljapurkar 1998a,b; Lee, Anderson, and Tuljapurkar 2003). Cross-sectional age profiles of payroll tax payments and benefit receipts are estimated from administrative data. The tax profile is then shifted over time by a productivity growth factor that is itself modeled as a stochastic time series. The benefit age profile is shifted over time in more complicated ways based on the level of productivity at the time of retirement of each generation. The real rate of return on special issue Treasury bonds is also modeled as a stochastic time series, and used to calculate the interest rate on the trust fund balance. The long-run mean values of the stochastic processes for productivity growth and rates of return are constrained to equal the central assumptions of TR04, but the actual stochastically generated outcomes will not exactly equal these central assumptions, of course, even when averaged over a 100-year horizon.

The probability distributions for the stochastic forecasts are constructed by using the frequency distributions for any variable of interest, or functions of variables of interest, from a large number of stochastically generated sample paths, say 1,000, typically annually over a 100-year horizon. Essentially, this is a Monte Carlo procedure. The stochastic sample paths can equally well be viewed as stochastic simulations, and the set of sample paths can be viewed as describing the stochastic context within which any particular pension policy must operate.

The stochastic simulation model is not embedded in a macro model and, therefore, does not incorporate economic feedbacks, for example, to saving rates and capital formation, and hence to wage rates and interest rates. For some purposes, this would be an important limitation. However, the model has given useful results for the uncertainty of Social Security finances, and it should also give useful results in the present context. Once the stochastic properties of different policy regimes have been studied in this manner, it may be appropriate to extend the analysis to incorporate more general economic feedbacks in future work.

2.2.1   A Stochastic Laboratory: Simulating Statistical Equilibrium

To date, the stochastic Social Security method just described has been used solely for projections or forecasts, based on the actual demography and Social Security finances of the United States. However, it can also be used as a stochastic laboratory to study how different pension systems would perform in a stochastic context divorced from the particularities of the actual U.S. historical context with its baby boom, baby bust, and other features. This is the main strategy we pursue in this chapter because we are hoping to find quite general properties of the NDC systems. We build on the important earlier work by Alho, Lassila, and Valkonen (2005). This approach also enables us to avoid dealing initially with the problems of the transition from our current system to the new system. Instead, we will analyze the performance of a mature and established system in stochastic steady state. In later work, we hope to consider the transition and to account for the actual historical initial conditions such as the current age distribution as shaped by the baby boom.

The key feature of a stochastic equilibrium is that the mean or expected values of fertility, mortality, immigration, productivity growth, and interest rates have no trend, and the population age distribution is stochastically stable rather than reflecting peculiarities of the initial conditions. The basic idea is simple enough, but there are a number of points that require discussion, as follows.

1. Productivity growth and interest rates are already modeled as stationary stochastic processes with preset mean values, so these pose no particular problem.

2. Net immigration is set at a constant number per period, following the Social Security assumptions (TR04). We treat immigration as deterministic and constant.

3. Fertility is also modeled as a stationary stochastic process with a long-term mean value of 1.95 births per woman, consistent with TR04. This is below replacement level, so absent positive net immigration, the simulated population would decline toward zero and go extinct, with the only possible equilibrium population being zero. But with immigration, there is some population size at which the natural decrease given a TFR of 1.95 will be exactly offset by the net immigrant inflow, and this will be the equilibrium population. The same principle applies in a stochastic context.

4. According to the fitted Lee-Carter mortality model, the mortality level evolves as a random walk with drift. First, we note that unless the drift term is set to zero, mortality will have a trend. So in constructing our stochastic equilibrium population, we will project mortality forward, with drift, until 2100 and then set the drift to zero thereafter. This sets equilibrium life expectancy at birth to be about eighty-seven years. Second, we note that a random walk, even with zero drift, is not a stationary process. It has no tendency to return to an equilibrium level, but rather drifts around. Our strategy is simply to set the drift term to zero. This means that we cannot view the simulated process as truly achieving a statistical equilibrium, but this is unlikely to cause any practical problems. An alternative would be to alter the model to make it truly stationary by providing some weak equilibrating tendency, for example, replacing the coefficient of unity on the previous level of mortality in the process by 0.99.

5. We also need to generate an appropriate initial state for our system. We begin by constructing a deterministic stable population corresponding to the mean values of fertility and mortality for the given inflow of immigrants. Population size adjusts until the net inflow of immigrants is equal to the shortfall in births due to below-replacement fertility. We then start our stochastic simulation from this initial population, but we throw out the first 100 years. We keep the next 500 years of stochastic simulations as our experimental set. Figure 2.1 plots fifteen stochastic sample paths for the old age dependency ratio defined as population 67+ divided by the population twenty-one to sixty-six. Evidently, the simulations often show very pronounced long-term variations resulting from something like the baby boom and baby bust in the United States.

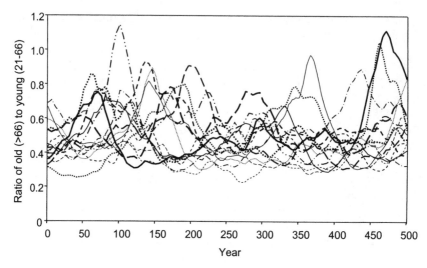

Fig. 2.1   Ratio of retirees to workers, 15 sample paths

6. For our policy experiments, we have created a single set of 1,000 sample paths or stochastic trajectories. We will examine the performance of different policies within the context of this single set of stochastic trajectories so that each must deal with the same set of random shocks, which makes their performances more comparable.

2.3   NDC System Design

As is well-known, the feasible internal rate of return for a PAYGO system with stable population structure equals the rate of growth of the population (which equals the rate of growth of the labor force, in steady state), plus the rate of growth of output per worker. Alternatively, this implicit rate of return simply equals the growth rate of GDP, provided that covered wages are a constant share of GDP. The NDC systems aim to mimic the structure of funded defined contribution systems while maintaining fiscal stability by using such an internally consistent rate of return (with due allowance for the nonsteady state context) rather than a market-based rate of return.

As under any pension system, an individual goes through two phases under an NDC scheme, corresponding roughly to periods of work and retirement. During the work phase, the individual's payroll taxes (T) are credited to a virtual account typically referred to as the individual's "notional pension wealth" (NPW). Like the individual account under an actual defined contribution plan, this account has a stated value that grows annually with contributions and the rate of return on prior balances; for an individual, this evolution is represented by:

(1) $$\text{NPW}_{t+1} = \text{NPW}_t(1 + r_t^i) + T_t,$$

where r_t^i is the rate of return credited to each individual's existing balances. Unlike the individual account balance under the defined contribution plan, NPW is only a virtual balance, and the rate of return is based on the system's internal growth rate. Once an individual retires, he or she receives an annuity based on the value of notional pension wealth at the time of retirement.

The Swedish system normally bases r^i on the contemporaneous rate of growth of the wages per worker, which we call g, rather than the total growth of wages, which would also account for the growth rate of the workforce, which we label n.[1] The notional accounts of individuals in Sweden also receive an annual adjustment for so-called inheritance gains, representing a redistribution of the account balances of deceased cohort members. That is, the rate of return to the cohort as a whole, which we denote r, equals g, where $r = g < r^i$.[2]

Upon retirement in the Swedish system, the individual's NPW is converted into an annuity stream based on contemporaneous mortality probabilities and an assumed real rate of return of 1.6 percent. Letting the superscript t denote the generation that reaches retirement age in year t, the annuity in year t for an individual retiring that year, x_t^t, may be solved for implicitly from the formula,

(2) $$\text{NPW}_t^t = \sum_{s=t}^{T}(1.016)^{-(s-t+1)}P_{t,s}^t x_t^t = x_t^t\sum_{s=t}^{T}(1.016)^{-(s-t+1)}P_{t,s}^t,$$

where NPW_t^t is the individual's notional pension wealth in the year of conversion, $P_{t,s}^t$ is the probability of survival from year t until year s, assessed in year t, and T is the maximum life span. In subsequent years, the individual's annuity level is increased or decreased according to whether the actual average growth of wages per worker, denoted $r_t = g_t$ in the preceding, exceeds or falls short of 1.6 percent. If wage growth continues at 1.6 percent, then the annuity level would remain constant in real terms throughout the individual's life. However, if the realized growth of wages per worker in year t were actually 1.3 percent, the annuity would be 0.3 percent lower in real terms in year $t + 1$ than in year t. If r were 1.3 percent in every year, the annuity would fall in real terms at a rate of 0.3 percent per year.

2.3.1 The Brake Mechanism

The system just described incorporates an adjustment mechanism aimed at keeping benefits in a range that can be supported by growth in the pay-

---

1. Our characterization of the Swedish system relies on several sources, including Palmer (2000) and Settergren (2001a,b).
2. Accounts in Sweden are also reduced annually to account for administrative costs. In our simulations, we ignore these adjustments and the underlying costs.

roll tax base. However, the adjustment is not perfect. First, although benefits are adjusted annually for changes wage growth, they are not adjusted after retirement to reflect changes in mortality projections. More important, the cohort rate of return r in the Swedish system is based on the growth rate of the average wage, g. While this approach might be more comprehensible from an individual worker's perspective, basing the cohort's rate of return instead on the growth rate of the covered payroll, $n + g$, would automatically take into account another determinant of the system's capacity to provide benefits, the growth rate of the workforce. Finally, as illustrated in the appendix using a simplified version of the NDC plan, even an NDC plan without these problems is not assured of annual balance if $n + g$ varies over time. This is in line with the analysis of Valdes-Prieto (2000), who observed that, under certain conditions, an NDC plan might be stable in a steady state, but will not be so in the short run.

Although it was anticipated by its designers that the Swedish system would nevertheless be quite stable, they added to the system a balance mechanism,[3] which we call a "brake," that would slow the growth rate of notional pension wealth and reduce the level of pension benefits in the event of a threat to the system's financial stability, as measured by a "balance ratio" b based on the system's conditions,

$$(3) \qquad\qquad b = \frac{F + C}{\text{NPW} + P}.$$

The numerator of the balance ratio is meant to account for the system's assets and is the sum of two terms. The first term in the numerator (F) equals the financial assets of the system (negative if the system has financial debt); the second term in the numerator (C) is a so-called contribution asset equal to the product of a three-year moving median of tax revenues and a three-year moving average of "turnover duration," which is the average expected length of time between the payment of contributions and the payment of benefits, based on current patterns. If the economy were in a steady state, the contribution asset would provide a measure of the size of the pension liability that contributions could sustain.

The denominator is the pension system's liability, equal to the sum of two components. The first component of the denominator (NPW) is aggregate notional pension wealth for generations not yet retired; the second component (P) is an approximation of commitments to current retirees, equal to the sum over retired cohorts of current annual payments to each cohort multiplied by that cohort's so-called economic annuity divisor, roughly the present value of their annuities calculated using the assumed 1.6 percent real return.[4]

---

3. The balance mechanism is described in Swedish Pension System (2005, 38–39).
4. For further detail, see Swedish Pension System (2005, 70).

This balance measure can be calculated entirely from observed values and does not involve any projected values. This has the advantage of reducing the risk of political manipulation, but a disadvantage in not taking advantage of all information available at the time in computing the contribution asset and the liability to current retirees, basing them simply on current conditions.

The balance ratio is not a perfect measure of the system's financial health. For example, the two components of the asset measure are based on inconsistent rate-of-return assumptions, the financial component being assumed to yield a market rate of return and the contribution asset being valued using the system's implicit rate of return. However, one would still expect a higher value of the balance ratio, in general, to be associated with a more viable system.

We refer to the Swedish balance mechanism as a "brake" because its effect is to prevent the excessive accumulation of debt, but not of assets; it applies only when the system is underfunded, as indicated by the balance ratio, but not when it is overfunded. It was understood when the system was designed that this potentially could lead to the accumulation of surpluses, but no formal mechanism was put in place to deal with this. One could imagine a system with a more symmetric brake that raises benefits and pension accumulations when the system is overfunded, and we consider such a system in the following.

For the Swedish system, the balance mechanism is activated only when the balance ratio b falls below 1.0 and stays in effect until a test of fiscal balance is satisfied. While the mechanism is active, two things happen each year. First, cohort pension wealth accumulates not at a gross rate equal to $(1 + g_t)$, but instead at a rate equal to $(1 + g_t)b_t$, where b_t is the balance ratio. Second, the gross rate of growth used to adjust the pension benefits of retirees is also set equal to $(1 + g_t)b_t$, meaning a greater likelihood of a real decline in pension benefits for any given cohort because real benefits grow at a gross rate of $(1 + g_t)b_t/1.016$. The balance mechanism remains in effect as long as the product of balance ratios from each year of the episode remains below 1.0. That is, if the balance ratio first falls below 1.0 in year t, then the balance mechanism continues to apply in year $s > t$ if $\Pi_{v=t}^{s} b_v < 1.0$. Once this product exceeds 1.0, the balance mechanism is taken off, with a new episode beginning the next time the balance ratio again falls below 1.0.

This design has several implications. First, because the balance mechanism is removed when the product of balance ratios first moves above 1.0, the balance ratio must exceed 1.0 in the year the balance ratio is removed. Second, as the balance ratio may stay below 1.0 for some time, there may be several years during the episode for which $b > 1.0$. Third, as mentioned in the preceding, the balance mechanism is asymmetric, in that it applies only when b first falls below 1.0; paths on which b starts above 1.0 and rises well above this level are subject to no external adjustment. Fourth, there may be recurrent episodes during which the balance mechanism is in effect. Fifth, while the balance ratio as defined in equation (3) can be negative (if financial debt exceeds the contribution asset), the balance mechanism is not meaningful for $b < 0$, for this would call for more than complete confiscation of pension wealth and benefits.

As to the logic of the test imposed to determine when the balance mechanism is removed, based on the product of balance ratios, this approach ensures that the balance mechanism has no long-run impact on the level of benefits. That is, the cumulative gross rate of return from the first year in which the brake applies, say t, through the year, say T, in which the product of the balance ratios reaches 1.0 and, hence, the brake mechanism is removed, is $(1 + g_t)b_t \cdot (1 + g_{t+1})b_{t+1} \cdot \ldots \cdot (1 + g_T) \cdot b_T = (1 + g_t) \cdot \ldots \cdot (1 + g_T) \cdot (b_t \cdot \ldots \cdot b_T) = (1 + g_t) \cdot \ldots \cdot (1 + g_T)$. Even though there is no impact on the long-run level of benefits, the brake mechanism has the capacity to reduce debt accumulation by keeping benefits below their regular long-run path for some time.

2.3.2   Adapting the NDC System to the U.S. Context

We have already outlined the basic structure of the Swedish NDC system, but there are various details to be specified in adapting the system to the U.S. context.

Contributions

What proportion of payroll is to be contributed? For comparability to our current Social Security system, we assume the Old-Age and Survivors Insurance (OASI) tax rate of 10.6 percent, applied to the fraction of total wages below the payroll tax earnings cap.

Rates of Return

Rate of return assumptions are required in two places in the NDC system, for use in accretions of notional pension wealth and in conversion of notional pension wealth into an annuity stream upon retirement. The Swedish plan sets the first of these rates equal to the growth rate of average wages, which should roughly equal the growth rate of productivity. It sets the second rate equal to 1.6 percent, taken to be the expected rate of productivity growth, and then adjusts annuities up or down in response to variations in the actual growth of the average wage. Sweden does not account for the growth rate of the labor force, but in principle it should be included because it is a component of the rate of return to a PAYGO system. Note that even if the growth rate of the labor force is not included, demography will still influence the outcomes for generations through the back door because if the system begins to go out of fiscal balance, then the brake will be applied.

For the U.S. system, we take the long-run mean rate of growth of the real covered wage to be 1.1 percent, following the Social Security assumption (TR04), as described in the following. We will refer to this interchangeably as the productivity growth rate or the growth rate of wages, g, although these are actually somewhat different concepts.[5] We have implemented NDC in two ways for the United States, once with rate of return based only on wage growth (g), and once with the rate of return based on both wage growth and labor force growth ($n + g$). These will presumably distribute risk in different ways across the generations. In stochastic equilibrium, population growth is near zero in any case, on average, but demographic change will certainly occur along simulated sample paths.

Annuity Calculations

We assume that annuitization of NPW occurs at age sixty-seven, the normal retirement age to which the U.S. system is currently in transition. We use the same rate of return for accumulations of NPW as in converting the account balance at retirement into an annuity stream. That is, we use either the growth rate of wages (g) or the growth rate of wages plus labor force ($n + g$) in both cases. As in the Swedish system, we set the pattern of the annuity stream to be constant in real terms, based on the growth rate and mortality projections at the time of the original annuity computation. Unlike the Swedish system, we use the actual growth rate (either g or $n + g$) as of retirement, rather than an assumed long-run value (in the Swedish case, 1.6 percent).

The annuity calculation can either be set once at the time of retirement, or it might be updated during the benefit period to reflect changes in the implicit rate of return, as is done in Sweden. We have programmed both possibilities, referring to one as "updating" and the other as "no updating." What mortality schedule is used to compute the annuitized income stream? Once again, this can be based on conditions at the time a generation retires (as is done in Sweden), or it can be revised during the benefit period, an approach that Valdes-Prieto (2000) refers to as a CREF-style annuity. We have done it both ways, bundled into the "updating" and "no updating" programs. Because we wish to determine the extent to which the NDC plan can be made stable, we present the results for the updating version in the following. However, the difference between the two versions is minor in our simulations, so the lack of updating for mortality experience in the actual Swedish system is unlikely to be a significant source of instability.

---

5. We note that the growth rate of productivity (output per hour of labor) may overstate the growth rate of covered wages, as is explicitly taken into account by the U.S. Social Security Administration. The growth rate of covered wages will be affected by changes in the supply of labor per member of the population of working age and by sex, both labor force participation and hours worked per participant, and by shifts in the population age distribution. It will also be affected by the proportion of compensation that is given in pretax fringe benefits.

The Brake

As explained earlier, the Swedish program has a brake but a limited "accelerator" that applies only until the impact of the brake on the level of benefits has been reversed. If surpluses begin to accumulate, there is no mechanism to raise benefits or reduce taxes relative to what is called for by the basic system. In our NDC program, we have incorporated this brake, but we also consider how much better it does than a simpler asymmetric brake that applies only when $b < 1$ (i.e., a brake mechanism without the Swedish system's provision for bringing benefits back to their long-run levels). In another version, we use a symmetric brake with an accelerator that raises the rate of return and raises current benefits when the fiscal ratio exceeds unity.

A second change we implement is in the design of the brake mechanism itself. As discussed in the preceding, the brake in the Swedish system multiplies the gross return implied by wage growth, r_t, by the current balance ratio of system assets to system liabilities. That is, when the brake is in effect, the adjusted net rate of return, r_t^a, is given by

$$(4) \qquad r_t^a = (1 + r_t)b_t - 1.$$

At low values of b, this mechanism implies a near confiscation of pension wealth, a not very desirable outcome if one is trying to spread fiscal burdens among generations. We, therefore, consider a generalized version of the balance mechanism in which equation (4) is replaced by:

$$(5) \qquad r_t^a = (1 + r_t)[1 + A(b_t - 1)] - 1,$$

where r and b are defined as before and $A \in [0,1]$ is a scaling factor. Setting $A = 1$ results in a brake like that in equation (4); when $A < 1$, full confiscation will result only when b reaches $1 - 1/A < 0$. Setting $A = 0$ eliminates the brake mechanism, and a positive value of A that is too small will still fail to provide adequate financial stability.

In the following simulations, we use a value of $A = 0.5$, meaning that the mechanism is well-defined for values of b above -1. This value of A was large enough to ensure that virtually none of the 1,000 trajectories, each 500-years long, ever encountered the lower bound on b for NDC type systems with $r = g$ (only 2 of 1,000 trajectories for the asymmetric brake case and 7 of 1000 for the symmetric brake case). Even for a much lower value of $A = .2$, the lower bound is basically irrelevant for trajectories with $r = n + g$ and binds along only relatively few trajectories for NDC systems with $r = g$ (15 for the asymmetric brake and 47 for the symmetric brake).

Initial Conditions

As discussed in the preceding, we start our simulations with a population structure based on a deterministic version of our demographic model, and then run the economy for a 100-year "presample" period to get a realistic distribution of demographic characteristics for the stochastic version of the model, which we then simulate over a period of 500 years.

We also use this initial 100-year period to establish the initial conditions for the NDC system. As of the beginning of the actual simulation period, and for each trajectory, we calculate each working cohort's NPW based on its earnings during the presample period and the relevant growth rates (g or $n + g$) used in compounding NPW accumulations. For each retired cohort, we calculate annuity values in the same manner. Finally, we assume an initial stock of financial assets equal to fifty times the average primary deficit in the first year of the model based on g with no brake. (This is roughly the level that would be needed to service the primary deficit while maintaining a constant assets-payroll ratio.)

Defining the Policy Scenarios

We simulate eight versions of the NDC system, differing as to whether the rate of return is based on the productivity growth rate, g; or the growth rate of wages, $n + g$; the type of brake used in attempting to achieve fiscal stability (none, Swedish, asymmetric, symmetric); and the strength of the factor, A, used to modify the brake adjustment.

In our projections, the mean rate of growth of the real covered wage is assumed to be 1.1 percent per year, following the assumptions of the Social Security trustees. The long-run growth rate of the projected population is close to zero in the stochastic equilibrium we generate, so the growth rate of covered wages is also about 1.1 percent per year. The internal rates of return for individual cohorts along any given trajectory of our stochastic projections should, therefore, tend to fluctuate around this central value if the system maintains financial stability.[6] In addition to considering the internal rates of return (IRR) under each NDC variant, we are also interested in the financial stability that each system provides. We measure financial or fiscal balance using the ratio of financial assets to payroll, where in the following figures a negative value indicates debt. Note that the numerator of this expression includes only financial assets, not the "contribution asset" that is used in computing the balance ratio.

2.4   Simulation Results

Consider first the performance of the NDC system based on $r = g$, roughly the Swedish approach without a brake mechanism. As shown in

6. The Social Security trustees' assumption about GDP growth is 1.5 percent (this is from TR04, where it results from 1.6 percent productivity growth, plus 0.2 percent growth in total employment plus the GDP deflator of 2.5 percent, minus the Consumer Price Index (CPI) deflator of 2.8 percent). But this is not in stochastic equilibrium, the population growth rate is not near zero, and the ratio of covered payroll to GDP is changing over time.

the first row of table 2.1, this system provides a mean internal rate of return of 1.07 percent, close to the rate of 1.1 percent for a system in which all variables are constant at their mean values. Note that the IRR is a highly nonlinear function of the variables so that the mean IRR across stochastic trajectories need not be close to the IRR of the means of the trajectories. The median IRR also equals 1.07 percent for this scheme. However, the need for a brake is quite evident from figures 2.2 and 2.3, the latter of which will be discussed in more detail below. These figures show the distribution of assets-payroll ratios for the system's first 100 years of operation. The median trajectory has essentially no accumulation of debt or assets. But, with no brake, some trajectories lead to accumulation of debt levels nearly forty times payroll, clearly an unsustainable level. Indeed, a debt-payroll ratio of

Table 2.1   **Average internal rates of return (IRR)**

Simulation	Mean IRR	Median IRR
NDC (g) no brake	.0107	.0107
NDC (g) Swedish brake	.0100	.0109
NDC (g) asymmetric brake, $A = 1$	.0093	.0105
NDC (g) symmetric brake, $A = 1$	.0122	.0130
NDC (g) symmetric brake, $A = .5$	.0106	.0130
NDC ($n + g$) no brake	.0110	.0113
NDC ($n + g$) Swedish brake	.0110	.0113
NDC ($n + g$) symmetric brake, $A = .5$	.0133	.0134

Source: Calculated from stochastic simulations described in text.
Note: NDC = notional defined contribution.

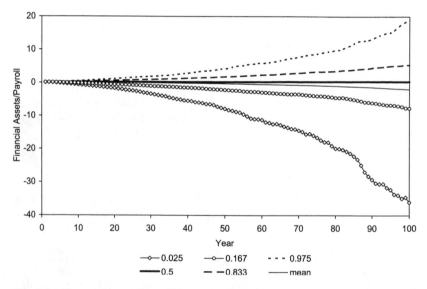

Fig. 2.2   Financial assets/payroll ($r = g$, no brake)

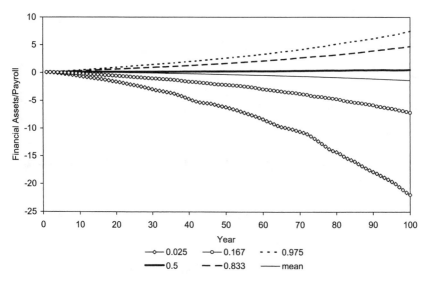

Fig. 2.3   **Financial assets/payroll ($r = g$, no brake, constant interest, growth rates)**

nearly 10 is present after 100 years in one-sixth of all trajectories, so this problem is not one limited to extreme draws from the distribution of outcomes. In addition, several trajectories involve substantial accumulation of assets relative to payroll.

Now consider the NDC system with the Swedish brake in place. As one would expect, imposing such a brake reduces the mean IRR, as shown in the second row of table 2.1. The median IRR, though, actually rises slightly.[7] As figure 2.4 shows, the lower tail of assets-payroll outcomes is raised, as also expected. Indeed, the Swedish balance mechanism is extremely successful in preventing excessive debt accumulation. After 100 years, the 2.5th percentile of the asset-payroll distribution is just –0.26, a debt-payroll ratio of just over one-quarter. But, even with the periods of acceleration that exist while it is in effect, the balance mechanism does little to restrain the accumulation of assets. Indeed, by cutting off the lower tail of the asset-payroll distribution, the balance mechanism raises both median and mean assets-payroll ratios so that both are substantially positive after 100 years. Indeed, even the 83.3rd percentile is slightly higher, as heading off debt makes the subsequent accumulation of assets levels more likely along a given trajectory.

This upward shift in the distribution of assets over time has an interest-

7. This result is possible because the brake mechanism has periods during which the growth rates of NPW accumulation and benefits are accelerated relative to the basic system without a brake. Thus, even though the brake mechanism is designed to reduce benefits overall while in effect, it may have distributional effects across cohorts that reduce the returns of cohorts with IRR already below the median, while raising the returns of those at the median.

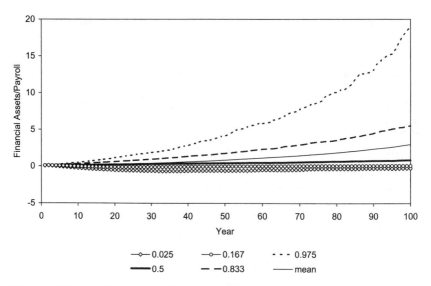

Fig. 2.4   Financial assets/payroll ($r = g$, Swedish brake)

ing impact on the distribution of IRR by cohort. Figure 2.5 shows this distribution for the Swedish brake just discussed, for all cohorts with complete lifetimes during the 500-year simulation period. For early cohorts, the lower tail of the distribution of IRR is quite low due to a chance of prolonged downward adjustment of NPW and benefits in the case of low rates of growth. Over time, the likelihood of such an outcome falls; with prior asset accumulation, even a series of bad draws with respect to the growth rate are less likely to drive the balance ratio below 1.0.

The Swedish balance mechanism is asymmetric, taking effect only once the balance ratio falls below 1.0. Once in effect, however, the Swedish mechanism does provide for "catch-up" periods of faster growth. A simpler mechanism would eliminate the catch-up phase and apply simply whenever $b < 1$. How different would this even more asymmetric system be from the Swedish system? That is, how significant is the catch-up phase of the Swedish balance mechanism? Figure 2.6 shows the asset accumulation pattern under this simple asymmetric brake. As one would expect, the distribution is shifted upward relative to the Swedish system, but only slightly. Consistent with this upward shift, the mean and median internal rates of return are a bit lower for this plan than for the Swedish system (compare the second and third lines of table 2.1). Thus, the Swedish system performs very much like a purely asymmetric brake, doing very well at avoiding debt accumulation but actually increasing the possibility of significant asset accumulation.

To limit asset accumulation in the presence of a brake, a symmetric

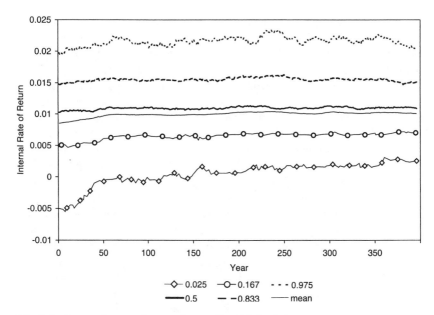

Fig. 2.5   Internal rates of return ($r = g$, Swedish brake)

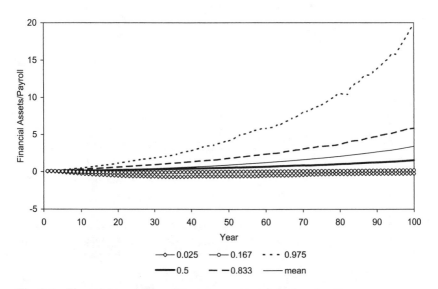

Fig. 2.6   Financial assets/payroll ($r = g$, asymmetric brake, $A = 1$)

brake mechanism is needed to increase accumulations and annuity benefits when the system's fiscal health is assured, not just to compensate for past periods of cutbacks. A symmetric brake would always be in effect, adjusting benefits and NPW up or down according to expression (4) or (5) regardless of whether b is below or above 1.0. Implementing a symmetric version of the brake leads to more generous benefits for some trajectories, and hence higher mean and median IRR, as the fourth row of table 2.1 shows. (It also eliminates the trend in internal rates of return seen in figure 2.5.) The distribution of assets-payroll ratios is similar for the lower tail as under the Swedish and asymmetric brakes, but the upper tail has been pulled down by the brake's symmetry, with the 97.5th percentile assets-payroll ratio just below 1.2 after 100 years. Further, both the mean and median assets-payroll ratios stay close to zero. Thus, the NDC system can be made to be quite stable financially, in both directions, by applying the brake not only when the balance ratio is too low but also when it is too high. This stability holds over the longer term as well, as shown in figure 2.7, which exhibits the distribution of assets-payroll ratios over 500 years for the symmetric brake scheme.

Another modification of the brake mechanism is in its strength rather than its symmetry. While rapid adjustment of benefits and NPW growth may provide stability, it may also concentrate the burdens of fiscal adjustment on relatively few cohorts. We plan to explore the questions of risk-sharing and distribution in subsequent research, but we can consider here

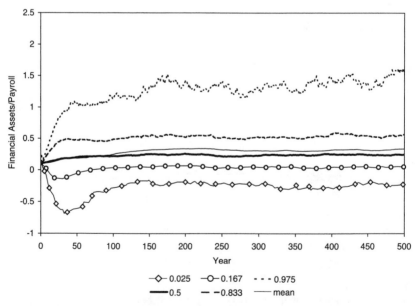

Fig. 2.7   Financial assets/payroll ($r = g$, symmetric brake, $A = 1$)

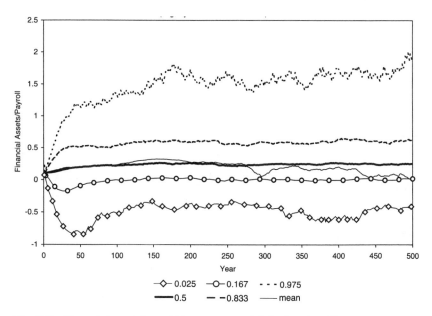

Fig. 2.8   Financial assets/payroll ($r = g$, symmetric brake, $A = .5$)

the impact of a more gradual adjustment process on the stability of the brake mechanism. Figure 2.8 shows the distribution of asset-payroll ratios when the brake is symmetric but the adjustment parameter, A, is set equal to 0.5 rather than 1. One can see from a comparison of figures 2.7 and 2.8 that more gradual adjustment does widen the distribution by about a third, but the impact is limited.

Another potential modification of the NDC system involves the computation of the rate of return for NPW accumulations and annuity computations. Even if the average population growth rate is zero, this growth rate can fluctuate, and with this fluctuation the ability of the NDC system to cover benefits. Thus, building population growth into the rate of return should provide greater system stability, ceteris paribus. Figures 2.9, 2.10, 2.11, and 2.12, and the last three rows of table 2.1, present assets-payroll distributions and IRR for NDC systems based on $r = n + g$ for the no-brake, Swedish-brake, and symmetric-brake ($A = 0.5$) variants.

The impact of this change in the method is most easily seen by comparing figures 2.9 and 2.10, the trajectory of debt under the NDC system with no brake and with $r = n + g$, and figures 2.2 and 2.3, the debt trajectory under the system with no brake and $r = g$. While the assets-payroll distribution still does not fully stabilize, its range is much smaller, especially in the lower tail. The (2.5, 97.5) range of outcomes is now (-2, $+8$) instead of (-35, $+19$). Still, a brake is needed to prevent eventual debt explosion along some paths, and the Swedish brake accomplishes this, as in the pre-

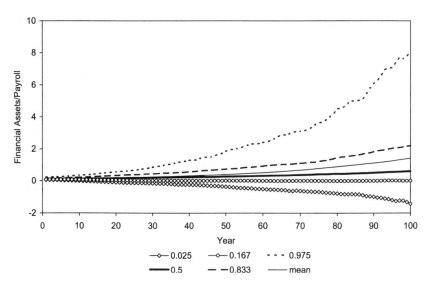

Fig. 2.9   **Financial assets/payroll ($r = n + g$, no brake)**

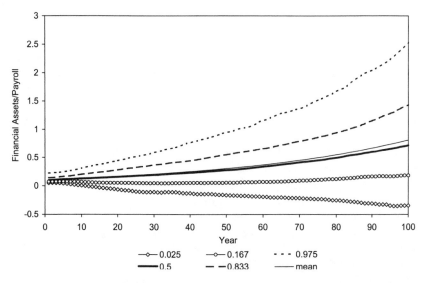

Fig. 2.10   **Financial assets/payroll ($r = n + g$, no brake, constant interest, growth rates)**

vious case of $r = g$. Again, basing pension calculations on $n + g$ rather than g also substantially reduces the variation in asset-payroll ratios, as one can see from a comparison of figures 2.4 and 2.11. Even though the upper range of the distribution has been lowered, though, a symmetric brake is still needed to stabilize the upside. Thus, even for the case of $r = n + g$, a

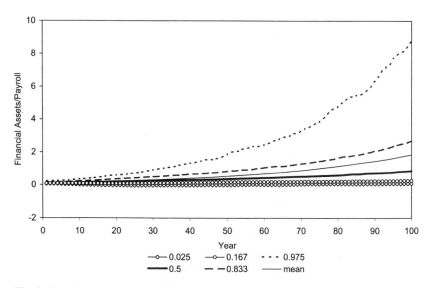

Fig. 2.11   Financial assets/payroll ($r = n + g$, Swedish brake)

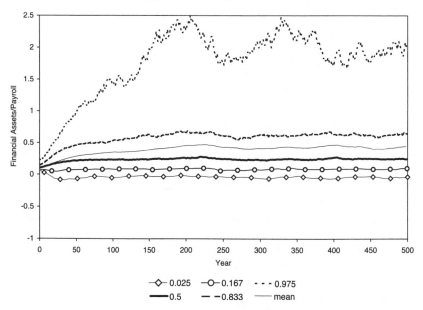

Fig. 2.12   Financial assets/payroll ($r = n + g$, symmetric brake, $A = .5$)

symmetric brake is a sine qua non for system stability in the very long run. Figure 2.12 shows the trajectory for the symmetric brake with $r = n + g$ and $A = 0.5$. As under the plan with $r = g$ pictured in figure 2.8, the distribution of outcomes is quite acceptable over even 500 years. A comparison of the two figures indicates that using $n + g$ in calculating the rate of return is particularly effective at preventing debt accumulation, a result that was also evident in the earlier comparisons.

2.4.1   Sources of Instability

As we have seen, the basic NDC system, even with Swedish-style net brake, is financially unstable. Even the NDC system based on setting the rate of return $r = n + g$ requires the application of a symmetric brake to head off substantial asset or debt accumulations on some trajectories. What is causing such instability? One can consider the impact of some sources of uncertainty by eliminating others from the simulations.

In our basic model, uncertainty arises from demographic and economic changes, the latter consisting of fluctuations in the interest rate and the rate of productivity growth.[8] These economic fluctuations, it turns out, are an important source of the NDC system's instability. Figures 2.3 and 2.10 present 100-year distributions of debt-payroll ratios for both versions of the NDC system (g and $n + g$) with no brake, corresponding to figures 2.2 and 2.9 and differing from the systems depicted in those figures only in that productivity growth and the interest rate are held constant at their mean values. With only demographic fluctuations present, these new figures show the distributions of asset-payroll ratios are substantially narrowed. Under the NDC(g) system, the (2.5, 97.5) percentile range at 100 years shrinks from (–35, +19) to (–22, +8); under the NDC ($n + g$) system, the same range shrinks from (–2, +8) to (–0.5, +2.5). Thus, even with the growth rate g incorporated in the rate of return used in the NDC system's calculations, this process does not come close to neutralizing fluctuations in that growth rate. Although these comparisons may seem to indicate that demographic fluctuations are an unimportant source of uncertainty relative to productivity growth and interest rates, other comparisons show the dramatic improvement in stability that results from including demographic change, n, in the system rate of return. For example, comparing figure 2.10 to figure 2.3 indicates that instability as measured by the width of the 95 percent range is narrowed by a factor of 10 in the $n + g$ system relative to the g system, and comparison of figure 2.9 to figure 2.2 indicates that this range narrows by a factor of 7 even when the economic variation is included as well. Clearly, both the economic and demographic variation are important sources of uncertainty in these NDC systems.

2.5   Conclusions

We have considered the financial stability of different variants of a system of notional defined contribution accounts, using demographic and

---

8. The interest rate matters because the NDC approach is not a pure PAYGO system. With nonzero values of financial assets, the rate of return on these assets matters.

economic characteristics of the United States. In subsequent work, we will consider other aspects of NDC systems, notably their ability to smooth economic and demographic risks among different generations. Among our findings are the following:

1. A system similar to that currently in use in Sweden, which bases rates of return on the growth rate of average wages and utilizes a brake to adjust the rate of return during periods of financial stress, ensures effectively against excessive debt accumulation but, very much like a simpler asymmetric brake, leads, on average, to considerable asset accumulation.

2. Only a symmetric brake, which raises rates of return during periods of financial strength, can avoid considerable accumulations of financial assets on some paths. The brake can be more gradual than under the Swedish system and still provide a stable distribution of outcomes.

3. An NDC system in which rates of return are based on total rather than per capita economic growth is inherently more stable than the basic NDC system, without reference to the brake mechanism in use.

4. A considerable share of the volatility in the financial performance of NDC systems is attributable to economic, rather than demographic, uncertainty.

Evidently, stochastic simulation of the system's finances can reveal aspects of its performance that are not otherwise obvious and can assist in improving system design. This promises to be a valuable use for stochastic simulation models of pension systems.

Appendix
Benefits and Taxes under a Simple NDC Plan

This appendix illustrates the relationship between benefits and taxes at a given point in time under a simple version of the notional defined contribution scheme in which the intrinsic rate of return is based on the growth rate of covered wages.

Consider the relationship between taxes and benefits at any given date t under a simplified version of an NDC system under which the rate of return used to accumulate notional pension wealth and to calculate annuities, r_t, is equal to the contemporaneous growth of covered wages. Taxes at time t are:

$$(A1) \qquad T_t = \tau(W_t^{t+1} + W_t^{t+2} + \ldots + W_t^{t+L}),$$

where W_t^{t+j} is covered wages in year t for the entire cohort that will retire j years hence, and L is the number of years that individuals work.

For simplicity, assume that each retired cohort receives in benefits the annual real return on its notional pension wealth of r_t so that the cohort's NPW will stay constant in real terms after retirement, and its annual payout is constant as well.[9] Then aggregate benefits at date t will equal:

(A2) $$B_t = r_t(\text{NPW}_t^t + \text{NPW}_{t-1}^{t-1} + \ldots),$$

where NPW_{t-j}^{t-j} is the notional pension wealth in the year of retirement for cohort retiring in year $t - j$. The notional pension wealth at retirement for cohort $t - j$ is:

(A3) $$\text{NPW}_{t-j}^{t-j} = \tau[W_{t-j-1}^{t-j} + W_{t-j-2}^{t-j}(1 + r_{t-j-1}) + \ldots$$
$$+ W_{t-j-L}^{t-j} \prod_{l=1}^{L-1}(1 + r_{t-j-l})].$$

Combining expressions (A2) and (A3) and comparing the resulting expression with expression (A1), we can see that a sufficient condition for taxes and benefits to be equal is that, for all k between 1 and L,

(A4) $$\tau W_t^{t+k} = \tau r_t \sum_{j=0}^{\infty} W_{t-j-k}^{t-j} \prod_{l=1}^{k-1}(1 + r_{t-j-l}),$$

or that taxes paid by workers k years away from retirement equal benefits attributable to earnings at the same age for all retirees.

We have assumed that r_s equals the growth rate of covered wages between dates $s - 1$ and s. If we assume in addition that this growth rate is shared by the entire age-wage distribution (i.e., that the relative age-distribution of covered wages remains fixed), then expression (A4) can be rewritten as:

(A5) $$W_t^{t+k} = r_t W_{t-k}^t \sum_{j=0}^{\infty} \prod_{m=1}^{j}(1 + r_{t-m})^{-1} \prod_{l=1}^{k-1}(1 + r_{t-j-l})$$
$$= r_t W_t^{t+k} \prod_{p=0}^{k-1}(1 + r_{t-k+p})^{-1} \sum_{j=0}^{\infty} \prod_{m=1}^{j}(1 + r_{t-m})^{-1} \prod_{l=1}^{k-1}(1 + r_{t-j-l})$$
$$\Rightarrow r_t \prod_{q=0}^{k-1}(1 + r_{t-1-q})^{-1} \sum_{j=0}^{\infty} \prod_{m=1}^{j}(1 + r_{t-m})^{-1} \prod_{l=1}^{k-1}(1 + r_{t-j-l}) = 1.$$

The last line of expression (A5) is satisfied if r is constant over time, which reflects the underlying consistency of using the growth of covered wages as a rate of return for the NDC system. If r varies over time, though, expression (A5) will generally not hold. For example, suppose $k = 1$, corresponding to wages in the year prior to retirement. Then the last line of (A5) reduces to:

---

9. This assumption implies that a cohort's benefits per capita grow as the cohort's population declines and indeed approaches infinity as the generation dies off, which is obviously unrealistic. We impose it here only for purposes of exposition.

(A6) $r_t(1 + r_{t-1})^{-1}[1 + (1 + r_{t-1})^{-1} + (1 + r_{t-2})^{-1} + \ldots] = 1.$

From this, we can see that if the current growth rate used to compute annuities, r_t, is greater (less) than the growth rates of covered wages during the accumulation phase, then the expression on the left side will be greater (less) than 1 and taxes on earnings for those in the year prior to retirement will be inadequate (more than adequate) to cover benefits for retirees based on earnings in the year prior to retirement. Although the results are more complicated for values of k > 1, the point is that variations in r over time can cause the NDC system to run deficits or surpluses, the variation being larger the larger is the variation in the growth rate of covered wages. This variation in deficits occurs even under the assumption of a fixed covered earnings age profile; relaxing this assumption adds yet another potential source of variation in the system's annual deficits.

References

Alho, Juha M., Jukka Lassila, and Tarmo Valkonen. 2005. Demographic uncertainty and evaluation of sustainability of pension systems. In *Non-financial defined contribution (NDC) pension schemes: Concept, issues, implementation, prospects,* ed. Robert Holtzmann and Edward Palmer, 95–115. Washington, DC: World Bank.

Booth, Heather. 2006. Demographic forecasting: 1980 to 2005 in review. *International Journal of Forecasting* 22 (3): 547–81.

Holtzmann, Robert, and Edward Palmer, eds. 2005. *Non-financial defined contribution (NDC) pension schemes: Concept, issues, implementation, prospects.* Washington, DC: World Bank.

Lee, Ronald. 1993. Modeling and forecasting the time series of US fertility: Age patterns, range, and ultimate level. *International Journal of Forecasting* 9:187–202.

Lee, Ronald, Michael W. Anderson, and Shripad Tuljapurkar. 2003. Stochastic forecasts of the Social Security trust fund. Report for the Social Security Administration, January. http://www.ssa.gov/OACT/stochastic/others.html.

Lee, Ronald, and Lawrence Carter. 1992a. Modeling and forecasting U.S. mortality. *Journal of the American Statistical Association* 87 (419): 659–71.

———. 1992b. Rejoinder. Journal of the American Statistical Association 87 (419): 674–75.

Lee, Ronald, and Timothy Miller. 2001. Evaluating the performance of the Lee-Carter approach to modeling and forecasting mortality. *Demography* 38 (4): 537–49.

Lee, Ronald, and Shripad Tuljapurkar. 1994. Stochastic population projections for the United States: Beyond high, medium and low. *Journal of the American Statistical Association* 89 (428): 1175–89.

———. 1998a. Stochastic forecasts for Social Security. In *Frontiers in the economics of aging,* ed. David Wise, 393–420. Chicago: University of Chicago Press.

———. 1998b. Uncertain demographic futures and Social Security finances. *American Economic Review* 88 (2): 237–41.

Legros, Florence. 2003. Notional defined contribution: A comparison of the French and German point systems. Paper presented at the World Bank and RFV Conference on NDC Pension Schemes, Sandhamn, Sweden.
Palmer, Edward. 2000. The Swedish pension reform model—Framework and issues. World Bank Pension Reform Primer Social Protection Discussion Paper no. 0012. Washington, DC: World Bank.
Settergren, Ole. 2001a. The automatic balance mechanism of the Swedish pension system—A non-technical introduction. *Wirtschaftspolitishe Blatter* (4/2001) 339–49. http://www.forsakringskassan.se/sprak/eng/publications/dokument/aut0107.pdf.
———. 2001b. Two thousand five hundred words on the Swedish pension reform. Paper presented at workshop on pension reform at the German Embassy, Washington DC.
Swedish Pension System. 2005. *Annual report.* Stockholm: Swedish Social Insurance Agency. http://www.fk.se/filer/publikationer/pdf/par05-e.pdf.
Valdes-Prieto, Salvador. 2000. The financial stability of notional account pensions. *Scandinavian Journal of Economics* 102 (3): 395–417.

Comment   Jeffrey Liebman

Notional defined contribution (NDC) systems are the latest fad in social security retirement system design, having been adopted in the past decade in Sweden, Italy, Poland, Latvia, and Mongolia. Additional countries are looking seriously at the NDC model. For example, there is currently a debate raging in China about the future of its social security system.

The Chinese pension law on the books says that China is implementing a funded defined contribution (DC) personal retirement account (PRA) system. Unfortunately, local governments responsible for collecting the revenues for the personal accounts have been diverting the funds to other uses—resulting in what is known as the "empty accounts" problem. Some western experts have been arguing that China should follow through with the setting up of funded accounts—that the establishment of clear property rights to the accounts will minimize the chance that local governments continue to misappropriate the funds (Feldstein and Liebman 2006). Other experts have argued that China should adopt an NDC system (Ahser et al. 2005)—an approach that would result in the accounts remaining permanently empty.

The fundamental features of an NDC system are that it is pay-as-you-go and that there is a transparent relationship between contributions and future benefits, with benefits defined by the accumulation of past payroll tax

Jeffrey Liebman is the Malcolm Wiener Professor of Public Policy at the John F. Kennedy School of Government, Harvard University, and a research associate of the National Bureau of Economic Research contributions at a given interest rate and with no redistribution from high earners to low earners. Indeed, assuming that the annuitization factors do not vary with the size of accumulated balances, such systems are actually regressive because high-balance individuals will, on average, live longer and receive payouts for more years, a perverse sort of redistribution that is offset in the U.S.-style defined benefit (DB) system by a progressive benefit structure.

The two potential advantages of the NDC approach relative to a traditional DB system result directly from the transparent link between contributions and benefits. First, there will be fewer labor supply disincentives. Part of the reduction in labor supply disincentives comes from the lack of redistribution from lifetime higher earners to lifetime lower earners in an NDC system. This component reflects a standard equity-efficiency trade-off and may or may not be desirable depending on one's tastes for redistribution. But another part comes from increasing workers' awareness of the marginal retirement benefits they earn per hour of work. If the complex benefit formulas of traditional DB systems cause workers to ignore the incremental benefits per hour of work and to instead perceive the Social Security payroll tax as a pure tax, then switching to an NDC system could improve labor supply incentives (a switch from a traditional DB system to a PRA system also has the potential to produce this improvement in labor supply incentives. See Auerbach and Kotlikoff 1987). With this channel, there is no offsetting loss of redistribution. Moreover, an NDC system avoids the kinds of retirement incentives that the Goda, Shoven, and Slavov paper (chapter 1 in this volume) documents.

The second potential benefit of the transparent link between contributions and payments is that it gives governments a way to resist pensioner demands for benefit increases. With an NDC system, the government can simply explain that people's benefits are what they deserve based upon their contributions. This consideration is said to have motivated Italy's adoption of the NDC approach.

What struck me as I read this excellent chapter by Auerbach and Lee is how far behind research on NDC systems is compared with research on PRA and traditional DB systems. While there has been some notable NDC research (Holtzmann and Palmer 2006; Valdes-Prieto 2000), countries such as Sweden have erred in designing some of the details of their NDC systems quite simply because the type of analysis done in this chapter was not available at the time the design choices were made.

That said, this chapter is not really about NDC systems at all. It is about the much broader topic of how one designs automatic stabilizers in pay-as-you-go social security systems, whether they are NDC systems or DB systems. The presence of an automatic stabilizer is not a fundamental feature of an NDC system.

In particular, the chapter studies four features of the Swedish NDC system that cause benefit levels to depend on realized economic and demographic conditions, thereby helping to keep the system in balance:

1. The rate at which tax payments are accumulated forward to determine a worker's notional account balance at retirement. In the Swedish system, this rate is based upon the growth rate of average wages.

2. The annuity factor for converting notional account balances to retirement income, a factor that is adjusted in the Swedish system based on contemporaneous mortality probabilities.

3. Postretirement adjustments to retirement benefit levels that occur based on the growth rate of average wages.

4. A braking mechanism that reduces benefits if the system's assets become too low relative to its liabilities.

Studying the stability of such a system requires a stochastic simulation model that incorporates both demographic (mortality and fertility) and economic (productivity growth and interest rate) factors and that is linked to a cohort-by-cohort model of social security finances. The authors are uniquely qualified to develop such a model. What they find when they do so is that the Swedish NDC system is not as stable as one might like, with the system accumulating large balances in a significant fraction of simulation runs and with later cohorts receiving higher rates of return than earlier ones. Auerbach and Lee show, however, that with two fairly simple modifications, the system can be made much more stable. First, Sweden accumulates contributions at the wage growth rate, but the authors show that NDC system are more stable if they accumulate benefits based on the sum of wage and population growth. The intuition behind this result is that it is the total earnings base, not just the average wage, that determines the level of benefits that can be supported with a given tax rate. Second, the braking mechanism in the Swedish system is an asymmetric one. Benefits are adjusted downward if the system becomes underfunded, but they are not increased when the system starts to accumulate assets. Auerbach and Lee show that a symmetric brake, applied continuously, leads to much greater stability. Because these modifications are straightforward to implement, it seems likely that the analysis in this chapter will lead rather quickly to improved system design by future adopters of NDC systems.

The payoffs to this research need not be limited to NDC systems. A similar set of stabilizers could be applied to the U.S. DB system, achieving the stability benefits illustrated in the Auerbach-Lee analysis without sacrificing the redistributive nature of the U.S. benefit formula:

1. The United States already implicitly accumulates contributions at the wage growth rate via the wage-indexing provisions of the average indexed monthly earnings (AIME) calculation.

2. It would be straightforward to have the U.S. primary insurance amount (PIA) formula include a multiplier to adjust annually for changes in longevity.

3. Similarly, postretirement benefit levels could be adjusted based not only on the Consumer Price Index (CPI) but also on wage and population growth rates.

4. A braking mechanism could be introduced in the United States.

I, therefore, suggest that the authors write a follow-up paper that simulates the effects of applying automatic stabilizers to the current U.S. system. Doing so would illustrate that it is possible to obtain the benefits of stabilization, while preserving redistribution based upon lifetime income. I would also suggest that the authors extend their analysis to include simulations in which the stabilization features work via adjustments to payroll tax rates, rather than solely via changes in benefit levels. It seems unlikely to be optimal to have all stabilization occur only on the benefit side.

References

Asher, Makul, Nicholas Barr, Peter Diamond, Edwin Lim, and James Mirrlees. 2005. *Social Security reform in China: Issues and options.* Policy Study of the China Economic Research and Advisory Programme. http://econ-www.mit.edu/files/691.

Auerbach, Alan, and Lawrence Kotlikoff. 1987. *Dynamic fiscal policy.* Cambridge, UK: Cambridge University Press.

Feldstein, Martin, and Jeffrey Liebman. 2006. Realizing the potential of China's social security pension system. *China Economic Times,* February 24, 2006.

Holtzmann, R., and E. Palmer, eds. 2006. *Non-financial defined contribution (NDC) pensions schemes: Concept, issues, implementation, prospects.* Washington, DC: World Bank.

Valdes-Prieto, Salvador. 2000. The financial stability of notional account pensions. *Scandinavian Journal of Economics* 102 (3): 395–417.

Reforming Social Security with Progressive Personal Accounts

John Geanakoplos and Stephen P. Zeldes

3.1 Introduction and Related Literature

In recent years, the United States has been engaged in a heated debate about whether to replace part of the current, defined benefit (DB) Social Security system with a system of defined contribution (DC) personal accounts. In 2005, President Bush gave speeches in numerous cities and towns advocating a reform that included these individual accounts. Both proponents and opponents of individual accounts have emphasized the stark differences between the current DB system and a system with individual accounts. The mechanics and outcomes of the two systems seem to be quite different, and their goals are usually presented as diametrically opposed.

Advocates of preserving the current system (predominantly Democrats) are committed to four core goals that stem from regarding Social Security as social *insurance:* (1) social security should redistribute wealth from those who have earned more over their whole working lives to those who have earned less, (2) different generations should share the risks of aggre-

John Geanakoplos is the James Tobin Professor of Economics at Yale University and an external professor at the Santa Fe Institute. Stephen P. Zeldes is the Benjamin Rosen Professor of Economics and Finance at the Graduate School of Business, Columbia University, and a research associate of the National Bureau of Economic Research.

We thank Ryan Chahrour, Theodore Papageorgiou, and Allison Schrager for research assistance, and Andrew Biggs, Jeffrey R. Brown, Jason Furman, Jeffrey Liebman, Deborah Lucas, Kent Smetters, and Salvador Valdes-Prieto for helpful comments and suggestions. This research was supported by the U.S. Social Security Administration (SSA) through grant #10-P-98363-1 to the National Bureau of Economic Research (NBER) as part of the SSA Retirement Research Consortium. The findings and conclusions expressed are solely those of the authors and do not represent the views of SSA, any agency of the federal government, or of the NBER.

gate shocks, (3) workers should be insured against inflation and long life with indexed life annuities, and (9) there should be limited opportunity for individuals to make mistakes that would lower their standard of living during retirement.

Advocates of shifting to a personal account system for Social Security (predominantly Republicans) base their support on a commitment to a set of core goals that stem from a desire for real social *security,* specifically (4) ownership by individuals of tangible assets that cannot be revoked by a future government, (5) transparency regarding accrual of those assets, so that workers know what they own, (6) market valuations of assets as they are accrued so that rational planning for retirement can take place outside of Social Security and so that (7) workers know how much their wages are being taxed or subsidized by the Social Security system, (8) equity-like returns on at least some of those assets, and (10) the opportunity for individuals to make choices about the allocation of assets in their portfolio.

Our purpose is to find common ground between these two approaches that preserves the core goals 1 to 8 of each, while compromising on portfolio choice 9 versus 10. We show that it is perfectly possible to convert Social Security into a system of personal accounts, with irrevocable ownership of market priced assets, while at the same time redistributing benefits based on lifetime income and sharing risks across generations. We call this system *progressive personal accounts.* Moreover, we envisage this system of progressive personal accounts automatically balancing the Social Security budget.

There are two crucial ingredients in progressive personal accounts. First, benefits would be awarded in the form of a new kind of derivative security that pays a worker a life annuity that is proportional to the economy-wide average labor earnings in his (statutory) retirement year. We call this security a *personal annuitized average wage* security, or PAAW. This security explicitly delivers payouts that achieve risk sharing across generations because retiree benefits move in lock step with worker wages. Second, PAAWs would be awarded based on worker contributions plus a government match that is more favorable for workers with low lifetime earnings. This variable match redistributes wealth, transferring benefits from those households with high realized lifetime earnings to households in the same generation that have low lifetime earnings.[1]

Opposition to personal accounts has arisen in part from the belief that personal accounts would necessarily violate desiderata 1 to 3. We show that on the contrary, progressive personal accounts are consistent with 1 to 3. Furthermore, we envisage active market trading in PAAWs, and thus a continuously evolving market price for PAAWs, giving PAAW owners a

---

1. Wealth redistribution from high lifetime earners to low lifetime earners can also be regarded as intragenerational risk-sharing.

market rate of return. We shall argue that progressive personal accounts also satisfy Republican goals 4 to 8. Thus, they provide a clear starting point for a bipartisan effort to reform and improve the current Social Security system.[2]

A growing number of countries have moved away from the pay-as-you-go type social security system still used in the United States. Some countries (e.g., Chile) have moved toward traditional individual account systems. Others (Sweden, Italy, and a number of other European countries) have adopted notional defined contribution accounts in which participants have "notional" account balances that earn a "notional" rate of return, typically tied to the growth rate of wages. While progressive personal accounts bear some relation to each of these, we argue that progressive personal accounts have a number of advantages. First, they retain the intra-generational redistribution/risk-sharing missing from both traditional personal accounts and notional accounts. Second, they retain intergenerational risk-sharing, which traditional personal accounts do not. Third, they provide account balances that correspond to market value and returns that are market rates of return, whereas notional accounts do not. For these reasons, progressive personal accounts would put the U.S. system back in the vanguard of managing lifetime financial security.

Our chapter proceeds as follows. We begin with a brief overview of the tax and benefit rules of the current system. Next, we define a PAAW as a security that pays its designee one inflation-corrected dollar for every year of his life after a fixed date t_R (the year he hits the statutory retirement age), multiplied by the economy-wide average wage at t_R. Personal annuitized average wage securities are, of course, new and unfamiliar securities, but they are not fundamentally different from a host of other derivative securities introduced by Wall Street in recent years. A household holding PAAWs is sharing risk with the next generation because higher wages for young workers in the future would imply larger PAAW dividends. The PAAWs also protect against long life and inflation because at retirement they turn into indexed annuities.

Having defined a PAAW, we next show that the Social Security benefits promised under the current system can be neatly summarized by the number of PAAWs a household is entitled to. The current system is akin to a system of personal accounts in which households accrue nothing until retirement and then (based on their lifetime earnings) suddenly accrue a large number of PAAWs that they can never sell. By specifying an accrual rule that enables households to accumulate PAAWs as they work, we show that it is possible to create a system of progressive personal accounts that

2. Of course, care must be exercised in the implementation, as there is a danger that support for progressive personal accounts might get transmuted during the political process into support for traditional personal accounts that hold only stocks and bonds and have no government match.

gives retired workers the same benefits as the current system and also gives them property rights over their PAAWs before retirement. At the very least, this demonstrates that there is no inherent contradiction between the current DB system and an appropriately structured personal account system.

We explicitly describe two accrual rules specifying how workers might acquire ownership of PAAWs over their working lives. Both lead to ownership of the same number of PAAWs at retirement as is promised by the current Social Security benefit formula. The "fastest" accrual rule allocates property rights over PAAWs at the fastest rate consistent with never having to take back a PAAW and reaching the current benefit formula at retirement no matter what earnings history materializes. Though the "fastest" accrual rule is the simplest, an alternative that we call the "straight line" accrual rule has the advantage that it makes the real tax or subsidy Social Security imposes on the worker wages more transparent.

Next we describe how a market in PAAWs could be developed. We argue that PAAWs could be pooled, similar to the way individual mortgages are pooled by the government agencies Fannie Mae and Freddie Mac, and then traded.[3] Investors would not buy individual PAAWs, but instead a pro rata share of a large pool of them. To eliminate adverse selection, and to guarantee a large, liquidly traded market, we would oblige all households to sell a small fixed percentage (e.g., 10 percent) of their newly acquired PAAWs into the pools. A liquid PAAWs market would establish a market price for PAAWs, bringing the added transparency that comes with reliable valuations of assets.

PAAWs are tangible assets and thus, once accrued, difficult to revoke (4). Their accumulation in personal accounts would make benefits already accrued completely transparent (5). Once PAAWs became reliably priced by the market, the government could even less easily expropriate the PAAWs held in personal accounts because households would know exactly how much money they were losing (4). Personal annuitized average wage security prices would enable individuals to compute a market value balance sheet to facilitate their financial planning (6). If the allocation of PAAWs per dollar of tax contributions followed the straight-line rule we describe later, then workers would quickly and easily see the true average match rate they faced (the percentage difference between the value of the additional PAAWs added to their Social Security accounts and the Social Security taxes they paid), and statements could provide information on the marginal match rate as well, giving the system much more transparency than it has now (7). And over long time periods (e.g., thirty years), the increase in wages and the stock market are highly correlated. Thus, over long horizons

---

3. Agency mortgage pools (in contrast to subprime mortgages) have been one of the most successful innovations in U.S. financial history.

PAAWs would earn equity-like returns (8), while in the short run being far less volatile than equities as the worker approaches retirement.[4]

We also point out some additional benefits of a market for PAAWs. A liquid PAAWs market would enable the government to observe the market value of its new promises and its accrued Social Security liabilities. We argue that market value is a better and less arbitrary measure of liabilities than actuarial value. Moreover, a market for PAAWs would likely lead to a watershed in advancing annuities markets and other retirement markets.

At the same time, by forcing personal accounts to retain 90 percent of their PAAWs, including those awarded by the government match, we ensure that benefits are very similar to those of the current system and that households with smaller lifetime earnings get proportionately higher benefits (1). The holding of PAAWs also embodies the Democrats' desire for intergenerational risk-sharing (2) and inflation-hedged life annuities (3). Of course, 90 percent is an arbitrary figure that could be negotiated. Republicans would tend to prefer more choice, and thus a lower number, and Democrats might prefer an even higher number.[5]

The last part of our chapter takes up the question of budget balance, at the household level and for the system as a whole. Since the current Social Security system contains no budget balance mechanism at either level, a progressive personal accounts system that mimics the contributions and payouts of the current system would not either. We describe the benefits of making Social Security self-balancing at the aggregate level and argue that these are particularly important for plans such as this one that lock in benefits by enhancing property rights on accrued benefits. We describe a system such that workers pay for their PAAWs with their Social Security taxes, augmented or reduced by a government match similar in spirit to that arising from the straight-line accrual rule under the current benefit rules. But we impose the constraint that the total value of Social Security taxes should be equal to the total value of PAAWs awarded.

To make the discussion concrete, and since PAAWs are not currently marketed, we undertake a back-of-the-envelope calculation of their value. We simplify the calculation considerably by assuming risk-neutrality and computing expected values of payouts, but in related work (Geanakoplos and Zeldes 2008), we treat valuation more thoroughly and specifically incorporate the effects of systematic market risk.

4. The fact that PAAWs earn equity-like returns does not imply that shifting to personal accounts (these or traditional ones) would raise overall rates of return on Social Security contributions. See Geanakoplos, Mitchell, and Zeldes (1998) and the discussion in section 3.4.

5. If the only source of market-traded PAAWs were sales from personal accounts, then the percent of PAAWs retained in accounts would need to be set low enough to lead to a liquid market in PAAWs. However, as we describe later, the government could instead issue extra individual PAAWs and sell them directly to pools in financial markets, leaving open the possibility that a liquid PAAW market could be created even with workers retaining 100 percent of their PAAWs.

Once we obtain estimated market prices for pooled PAAWs of every vintage, we can value accrued PAAWs and compare these numbers to the dollar contributions that generate the accruals. We define the government match for a household as the difference between the dollar value of extra PAAW accruals and the dollar value of the extra contributions generating those accruals, and the match rate as the match divided by the contributions. Depending on the accrual rule, this match rate may vary from year to year for the same household.

The match rates for any accrual rule that mimics the current system are non-zero for five reasons: (a) the current system is not self-balancing, that is, there is a disconnect between contributions and benefit rules, which Congressional interventions have often worsened; (b) the current pay-as-you-go system uses part of current contributions to pay off the legacy debt incurred by the early generations who received benefits far in excess of their contributions; (c) in the current system, the aggregate number of PAAWs accrued in any given year does not depend on the aggregate level of current Social Security contributions or on future wages, hence to the extent that current contributions are unusually low (high) and to the extent it can be foreseen that future wages will be much higher (or lower), accrued PAAWs will likely be worth more (or less) than contributions; (d) depending on the speed of accrual, households might get better or worse annual deals when they are young or old; (e) in the current system, households with low lifetime earnings receive more PAAWs per dollar of contributions.

There are a number of ways to make the system self-balancing, each of which will by necessity alter the risk-sharing (and match rates) built into the current system. We propose a mechanism that ensures aggregate fiscal balance "on the way in," that is, that sets the market value of annual aggregate accrued PAAWs equal to annual contributions, but that retains all the desiderata 1 to 8. This mechanism would eliminate reasons (a), (b), and (c) for nonzero household match rates, but retain reason (e), and possibly reason (d) as well. This is consistent with the principle that households making low lifetime contributions (because of low lifetime incomes) should get a positive government match, and households with high contributions should get a negative government match. Fiscal balance "on the way out" could be ensured by requiring the government, or the private sector, to use the Social Security trust fund to hedge Social Security liabilities.

As part of ensuring fiscal balance on the way in, we would first recognize the legacy debt of the current system by giving PAAWs to all workers and retirees according to what they have already accrued under the old rules. (Naturally what this amounts to requires explanation.) This would represent new explicit debt to the government. The government could finance future interest and principal payments both by issuing new Treasury debt (i.e., rolling over the debt) and by raising general taxes. In this way, the legacy debt would be removed from the Social Security system and be paid by all (current and future) entities subject to general taxes, like corporations and investors earning dividend income, and not just by workers. We calculate that this tax would amount to about 1 percent on all income. Then, every year from now on, households would have to pay for their own PAAWs with their Social Security contributions, except that the government match would redistribute contributions from workers with high lifetime earnings to those with low lifetime earnings. In the aggregate, the Social Security system would then be fully funded and automatically balanced "on the way in." We estimate that at the current time, workers would be able to afford to buy just about the same benefits that they are implicitly accruing in the current Social Security system. The 1 percent general tax would thus enable a Social Security system that was in balance now and that would automatically stay in balance "on the way in" in the future. Over time, of course, the market value of the outstanding PAAWs would diverge from their original price. The government would have to hedge this risk, or as we explain in the following, engage the private sector in doing so.

3.1.1 Related Literature

Our work is related to and builds on a number of other papers in the literature. Feldstein and Samwick (1992) and Cushing (2005) compute the implicit marginal tax rate of the current U.S. Social Security system. In the following, we show the relationship between their calculations of marginal tax rates and our calculations of marginal match rates. Geanakoplos, Mitchell, and Zeldes (1999) discuss alternative ways to compute accrued Social Security benefits, and Jackson (2004) describes a system of accrual accounting that he argues would more clearly describe Social Security's financial situation. Feldstein and Liebman (2002) analyze the redistributive features of an individual account plan with a two-tier contribution structure in which part of the inflows are proportional to earnings and part are lump-sum contributions. Vickrey (1947) and Liebman (2003) discuss the advantages of basing taxation on lifetime rather than annual income. Valdes-Prieto (2000), Borsch-Supan (2005), and Auerbach and Lee (2006) analyze notional DC systems, such as those adopted in Sweden and Germany, and the self-adjustment mechanisms built into them.

A number of papers have proposed the creation of related new financial securities. For example, Shiller (1993) proposes gross domestic product (GDP) linked securities, Blake and Burrows (2001) propose longevity or survivor bonds, and Bohn (2002) and Goetzmann (2005) propose aggregate wage-related securities. Valdes-Prieto (2005) advocates creating "pay-as-you-go securities" (which would securitize the part of future Social Security contributions that represents a net tax) and using them as a basis for Social Security reform.

3.2   The Mechanics of Progressive Personal Accounts

In this section, we first briefly describe how the current U.S. Social Security system works, that is, the tax and benefit rules. We then show that it is possible to create a system of individual accounts that exactly replicates the current system. This means that personal accounts can be compatible with progressivity and intergenerational risk sharing.

In the current system, the benefits received by Social Security contributors are based on a concave function of lifetime earnings, providing smaller increments in benefits with each additional dollar of lifetime earnings. While personal accounts as typically implemented eliminate this progressivity, we show that this need not be the case. Personal accounts can be made progressive simply by making annual PAAW accruals depend on the size of accumulated past accruals. Later in the chapter, we show that this is equivalent to providing a variable government match (positive or negative) where the size of the match depends on accumulated accruals to date.

Personal accounts, by virtue of being personal, would also seem to eliminate the intergenerational risk sharing that is built into the current system. In the current system, retiree benefits depend on the wages of the next generations of workers. As the young do better, so will the old, and vice versa. If the personal accounts hold stocks and bonds, it is quite possible that retiree benefits will move in the opposite direction from wages, at least for some cohorts. But there is no reason the personal accounts should be confined to traditional investment securities. We explain that by holding PAAWs, retirees will receive payouts that move in the same direction as the wages of the next generation of workers.

3.2.1   The Current System

We start by describing the current contribution and benefit *rules* for the U.S. Social Security system; we ignore adjustments that would have to occur in the event that the system is unable to meet its obligations. For simplicity, we focus on an individual who will be single and childless throughout life, who will not become disabled, and who will retire at the "normal retirement age" specified by Social Security.[6]

Program rules mandate that individuals and their employers together contribute 12.4 percent of all "covered" earnings, defined as earnings below the Social Security earnings cap (the annual earnings cap equaled $102,000 in 2008). No contributions are collected on earnings above the cap. Of the 12.4 percent, 1.8 percentage points are earmarked for disability coverage. In the analysis that follows, we ignore disability insurance

---

6. See section 3.2.3 for a sketch of how the analysis could be extended to include spouses and children (and their associated program benefits), as well as early or delayed retirement.

(DI) coverage, and, therefore, use a Social Security contribution rate of 10.6 percent.

The benefits under the current system are a function of the worker's lifetime "covered" earnings history. An important feature of the system is that it is "wage-indexed": (1) the earnings that enter the benefit function are individual earnings in any year divided by average economy-wide earnings in that year, (2) initial benefits upon retirement are scaled by average economy-wide earnings in the statutory retirement year, and (3) the earnings cap and the "bend points" defined in the following are adjusted so that their ratios to the average economy-wide earnings remain constant over time.[7] As a result, the system can be described more easily and clearly by defining a set of "relative" variables that are equal to the dollar amounts divided by average economy-wide earnings for the year. We define *relative earnings* for a worker in any year t as his current covered earnings for that year divided by average economy-wide earnings, and *average relative earnings* as the average of his highest thirty-five values of relative earnings.[8]

We can use these variables to describe the promised benefit structure of the current U.S. Social Security system. *Initial relative benefits* are defined by the concave function of average relative earnings given in panel A of figure 3.1. Initial relative benefits are equal to 90 percent of average relative earnings that are less than .24, plus 32 percent of average relative earnings between .24 and 1.35, plus 15 percent of average relative earnings between 1.35 and 1.99.[9]

A worker's initial dollar benefits (also referred to as the primary insurance amount or PIA) are paid at his statutory normal retirement age (NRA).

---

7. Average economy-wide earnings for a given year is the average across workers of annual labor earnings in that year. (We use the terms "labor income," "wage income," "labor earnings," "earnings," and "wages" interchangeably in this chapter). The SSA's measure of average economy-wide earnings is the average wage index (AWI). They compute the AWI sequentially, by first constructing a "raw earnings growth rate" $g(t)$, and using this to construct the next AWI level, that is, $\text{AWI}(t) = [1 + g(t)] \times \text{AWI}(t - 1)$. Various techniques have been used over time to construct the raw earnings growth rate. Since 1991, the SSA has calculated the "raw" growth based on employer-reported W-2 forms, summing all earnings (including amounts above the Social Security earnings cap), including deferred compensation, less distributions, and dividing by the total number of earners. From 1985 to 1990, the measure excluded deferred compensation and distributions. Prior to 1985, growth was calculated using earnings measurements provided by the Internal Revenue Service. Because the SSA has used varied methods to compute earnings growth, the current level of the AWI series does not equal the level of "raw" average earnings computed by the SSA. Under the current computation method, the AWI is about 4 percent larger than the "raw" series. See Clingman and Kunkel (1992), Donkar (1981), and SSA (2006). Benefits after retirement are indexed to the CPI.

8. We ignore for simplicity the program rule that, in calculating average earnings over a career, earnings prior to age sixty are indexed forward to age sixty wage levels using Social Security's *Average Wage Index,* while earnings from age sixty and after are included at their nominal levels. Our definition assumes all earnings are indexed.

9. The points at which the slope of the line change are referred to as "bend points." We ignore here the rule that individuals must earn income in a minimum of forty quarters in order to receive benefits.

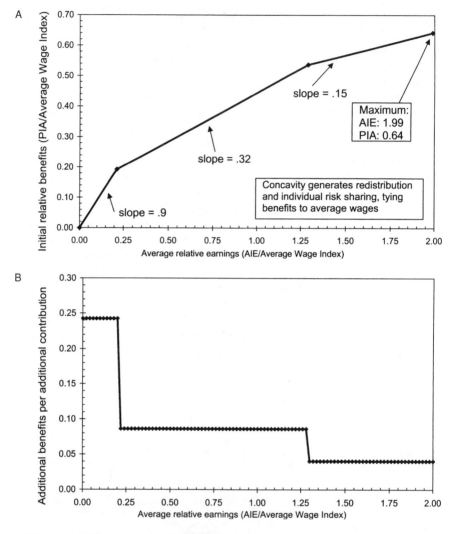

Fig. 3.1   Mechanics of current OASDI system: *A,* **Calculation of primary insurance amount (PIA);** *B,* **Additional benefits per additional contribution, measured in average wage units**

They are equal to initial relative benefits multiplied by average economy-wide earnings in that year. Benefits in subsequent years are indexed to the Consumer Price Index (CPI) so that individuals receive a constant stream of real benefits for as long as they live.

Another way of describing the initial relative benefit function is to say that by the end of their working lives, workers will fall into one of three life-time earnings categories and that the marginal benefit a worker receives per dollar contributed in taxes depends on his category. If a worker about to retire had increased his relative earnings in any one previous year by Δ, he would have made extra tax contributions of $\Delta \times 10.6$ percent (assuming a Social Security tax of 10.6 percent), measured in average wage units. (His contribution would be that number multiplied by the economy-wide average wage for the year). According to the formula just described, the worker thereby would have increased his lifetime average relative earnings by $\Delta/35$. For a worker with very low lifetime earnings, this would have increased his initial relative benefits by $.9 \times \Delta/35$, as in panel A of figure 3.1. For this worker, the extra initial benefit per additional contribution (measured in relative wage units is) $(.9 \times \Delta/35)/(\Delta \times 10.6$ percent$) \approx .24$. For a worker with somewhat higher lifetime earnings, the corresponding number is $(.32 \times \Delta/35)/(\Delta \times 10.6$ percent$) \approx .09$. For a higher earnings worker, the number is $(.15 \times \Delta/35)/(\Delta \times 10.6$ percent$) \approx .04$.[10] We present these marginal benefit brackets in panel B of figure 3.1.

Note that because benefits are determined by *relative* earnings, a temporary and proportional increase in the earnings of all workers in any year t will leave unchanged the benefits that those workers receive when they retire in year $t_R > t$. The benefits of individuals reaching the statutory retirement age in year t would be proportionately higher in year t and each year they live thereafter.

3.2.2 Defining New Securities—PAAWs

We define a personal annuitized average wage security or PAAW as a security that pays its owner one inflation-corrected dollar for every year of his life after a fixed date t_R (the year he hits the statutory retirement age R), multiplied by the economy-wide average wage at t_R. Personal annuitized average wage securities are tied to specific individuals (i) and to the year of the first payout on the security (t_R), and we use the notation PAAW(i, t_R) to capture this.

We also define two other securities that could help in the construction and pricing of PAAWs. First, we define a personal annuity unit, PANT(i, t_R), as a person-i-specific "year t_R annuity unit" as a security that pays one dollar in year t_R and one inflation-adjusted dollar in every subsequent year that the individual i is alive. Second, we define an average wage(t) security as a security with a single payout in year t equal to the average economy-wide earnings in that year. An alternative way of describing a PAAW is that it is a composite security that pays off one PANT(i, t_R) for every dollar paid in year t_R by the average wage(t_R) security.

A PAAW (as well as a PANT or an average wage security) is a derivative security, similar to countless others that have been created in recent years

---

10. This exercise assumes that the increase Δ in relative earnings occurred in one of the thirty-five highest relative-earnings years (otherwise, there would be no incremental benefit).

by Wall Street. Because the security is partly an annuity, it provides insurance for long life, paying every year until death. Furthermore, because the payment depends on the average wage at retirement, it creates risk-sharing across generations. If young workers are doing well and receiving high wages, the old will get higher payoffs from their PAAWs, and conversely.

3.2.3   Translating the Current System into an Equivalent DC System

We are now in a position to translate the current system into an equivalent DC system, that is, to show that by choosing a particular variable match, and restricting accounts to hold PAAWs, it is possible to create a system of progressive personal accounts that exactly mimics the promised taxes and payouts of the current system. Replicating the current system may not be the best way to implement individual accounts, but it serves as a starting point that allows one to compare and contrast the current system (translated into the language of DC) with the more standard DC systems typically proposed. We argue that this is an important step toward improving communication between the two sides of the current Social Security debate, potentially easing the political gridlock that has occurred in the United States.

In order to replicate the current system, workers would receive PAAWs in exchange for their Social Security contributions, which they would hold in their personal accounts; workers would be prohibited from selling them. Later we consider both the advantages and disadvantages of allowing workers to sell some of their PAAWs in exchange for other financial securities and also the advantages of observing a public market price for PAAWs.

To replicate the current system, workers and employers would (as in the current system) together contribute 10.6 percent of earnings up to the earnings cap. The government would credit each individual's account with a number of PAAWs; the exact number credited would depend (in a way to be specified) on current and past contributions. At the normal retirement age, each PAAW would pay off a dollar amount equal to the average wage in the economy in that year, and then in every subsequent year of life, the same inflation-indexed real payment.[11]

The current system redistributes from rich to poor on the basis of lifetime income, through the computation of benefits at the age of retirement. A natural question is whether we can replicate this redistribution in personal accounts, where the benefits are irrevocably owned by the account as they are earned, long before one's lifetime earnings can be measured. At first glance this seems impossible. But we show that by making new accru-

11. Equivalently, at retirement, each PAAW is transformed into a number of PANTs equal to the economy-wide average wage that year.

als depend on accumulated balances, as well as new contributions, we can indeed achieve the lifetime redistribution in the current system.

Computing Accrued Balances (Total and Incremental)

We define $PBAL_{it}$ to be the number of units of PAAWs(i, t_R) accrued by worker i as of year t. There are actually many rules for the accumulation of balances $PBAL_{it}$ that can replicate the current system. The simplest is to define $PBAL_{it}$ as the benefits worker i would be entitled to under the current system given his earnings history up through year t, and assuming all his future earnings were zero. Clearly with such a definition $PBAL_{it}$ can rise, but can never fall. There are other methods of accrual that also end with the same amount at retirement and never fall, but among them our definition accumulates balances most rapidly. We shall call it the fastest accrual rule. Later in this section, we examine a second accrual rule that we refer to as straight-line accrual.

Under the "fastest accrual rule" definition, progressive personal accounts can be described by simply changing the units on the axes in figure 3.1. These are presented in figure 3.2. For panel A of figure 3.2, the *Y*-axis is now relabeled as PBAL. For panel B of figure 3.2, the *Y*-axis is "additional PAAWs per additional contribution" and the *X*-axis is PBAL. (Because the PBAL function defined in panel A of figure 3.2 is strictly monotone in average relative wage, we can replace each average relative wage on the *X*-axis of panel B of figure 3.1 with the corresponding PBAL, giving panel B of figure 3.2.) Panel B of figure 3.2 shows the extra PAAWs divided by the extra contributions that together arise from working an additional hour (holding constant the number of years of work), as a function of how many PAAWs have already been accumulated. Additional PAAWs per additional contribution (measured in relative wages units) is a decreasing function of PBAL, falling from .24 to .09 to .04 as PBAL increases from less than .2 to more than .54.[12]

It might have seemed that our definition of $PBAL_{it}$ would need to be a function of all of worker i's relative wages before year t. But panel B of figure 3.2 makes clear that $PBAL_{it}$ can be rewritten as a function of just $(PBAL_{it-1}$, Contribution[t]), provided that for a contribution coming after the first thirty-five years, only the excess of that contribution over the thirty-fifth highest relative contribution to date counts toward PAAW accrual.

Personal annuitized average wage security accrual replicates the redistribution in the current system, and PAAW accrual is a function of (1) new contributions and (2) accumulated balances PBAL. This definition of PAAW accrual shows that we can award irrevocable benefits to young

---

12. In the current system, there is a ten-year vesting period, so we are referring here to workers in their eleventh year, or to workers in earlier years if we ignore the vesting requirement.

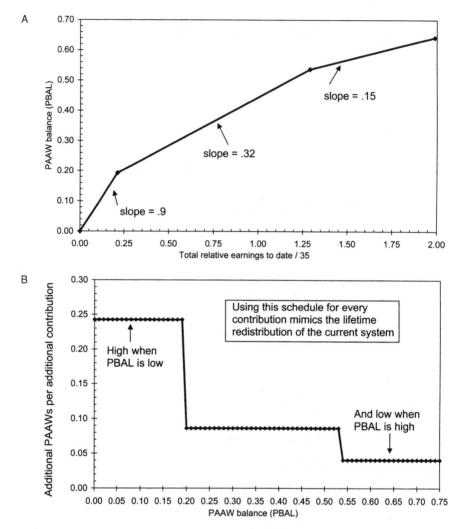

Fig. 3.2   Mechanics of PAAW system: *A,* **Calculation of PAAWs balance;** *B,* **Additional PAAWs per additional contribution, measured in average wage units**

workers and yet still make total benefits accrued at retirement depend on lifetime earnings.

We illustrate how this accrual works in four examples, based on different assumed age-relative earnings profiles. For worker 1 (the "economy-average" worker), we assume that earnings equal average economy-wide earnings in every year, that is, that relative earnings equal 1. For worker 2 (the "average-earner worker"), we assume relative earnings at each age equal average relative earnings at the same age for the cohort of men born

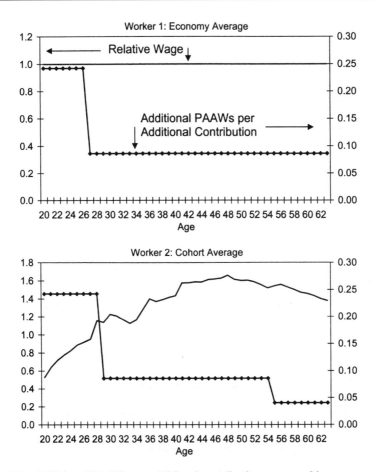

Fig. 3.3   Additional PAAWs per additional contribution, measured in average wage units

in 1937.[13] For worker 3 (the "low-earner" worker), we suppose that relative earnings equal one-half the relative earning of worker 2. For worker 4 (the "high-earner" worker), we assume that relative earnings are 1.5 times the relative earnings of worker 2. Our results are shown in figures 3.3 to 3.5.[14]

Figure 3.3 plots additional PAAWs per additional relative contribution against time, for each of the four workers. This can be interpreted as the extra PAAWs per unit of extra contribution that would accrue from working an extra *hour* (holding constant the number of years worked) now plotted

13. We are grateful to Seung An from the SSA for providing us with the data on average cohort earnings. These men earned more than the economy-wide average at every age over twenty-eight.
14. Although we have not done so, our approach could easily be extended to examine realizations of a stochastic earnings process.

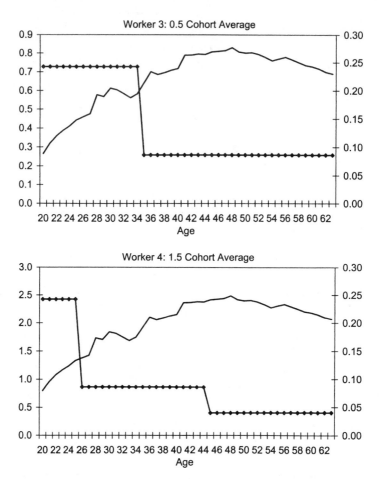

Fig. 3.3 (cont.)

against age. This graph shows how fast workers move along the schedule in panel B of figure 3.2. The average earner and the high earner both eventually move down to the .04 ratio, but the high-earner worker gets there sooner. The economy-average worker and the low-earner worker never earn enough to move all the way to the .04 ratio. (The economy-average worker starts at .24 ratio and ends in the .09 ratio. The low-earner worker does the same, but takes longer to get to the .09 ratio.) Notice that because in these profiles earnings in every year are among the highest thirty-five to date, marginal benefits never drop to zero.[15] Hence, on the margin, an additional contribution would yield the full additional benefit.

15. Note that it is purely by coincidence that worker 2 (cohort average) accumulates enough PAAWs to drop to the .04 ratio at exactly the same date that the worker has worked thirty-five years. Thus the drop after age fifty-four in figure 3.3 for worker 2 is unrelated to having worked thirty-five years at that point.

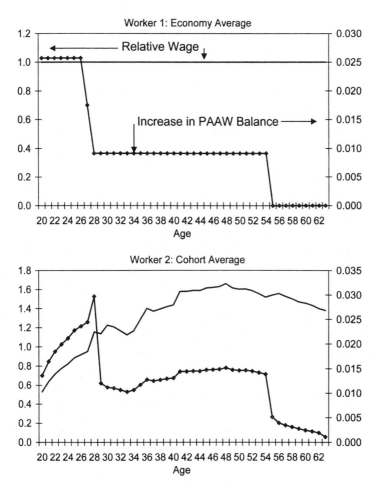

Fig. 3.4   **Change in PAAW balances**

Note that extra PAAWs are accrued due to increases in *relative* earnings (and contributions). If the earnings of all workers rise proportionately (due to either higher work hours or higher wages per hour), relative earnings remain unchanged and, therefore, workers will not accrue *any* additional PAAWs as a result of this change.

In figure 3.4, we illustrate the annual change in PAAW balances at each age for the four workers. These graphs measure absolute increments over the year, rather than the increment per unit of contribution as in figure 3.3. They, therefore, take into account the varying contributions due to the age profile of relative earnings. After year thirty-five, a large fraction of each contribution does not count toward accrual—all that counts toward accrual is the difference between relative earnings and the thirty-fifth highest relative earnings.

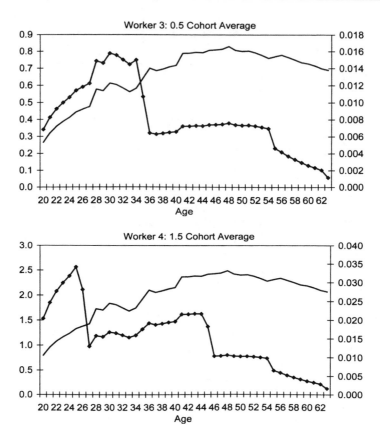

Fig. 3.4   (cont.)

Finally, in figure 3.5, we look at the level of accrued PAAW balances (PBAL) versus age. The average worker (worker 1) accumulates enough securities to receive about 44 percent of the average wage in his first year of retirement. The cohort average worker (worker 2) accumulates enough securities to receive almost 60 percent of the average wage in his first year of retirement. The fact that this is less than twice the 36 percent accumulated by the low-earner worker 3 (who earns half as much) illustrates again the redistribution in the system.

Incorporating Other Social Security Benefits and
Features into Progressive Personal Accounts

In the preceding analysis, we focused on single individuals with no children who retired at the normal retirement age with no chance of disability. We also ignored the requirement that only workers with forty quarters of positive earnings are eligible to collect retirement benefits. We could extend our analysis to incorporate these minimum work requirements, as

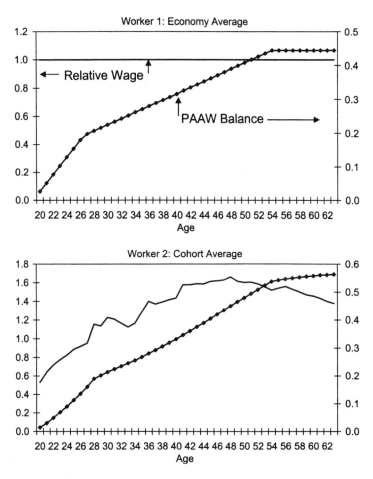

Fig. 3.5   PAAW balances (PBAL)

well as spousal benefits, survivor benefits, early or delayed retirement, and disability. For example, the accrual rules could be changed so that all PAAWs become vested only after forty quarters of work. In addition, spousal benefits could be implemented through the creation of a separate spousal account. To replicate the current system, the accrual of PAAWs in this account would depend on the current contributions of both the individual and the spouse, as well as the accumulated balances of each individual. The accounts would become vested only after ten years of marriage to match the requirement in the current system that divorced spouses must have been married for ten years or more to receive spousal benefits. Finally, individuals wishing to retire later than age t_R (the NRA) could be allowed to use their PAAW payouts in the years immediately following t_R to purchase additional PAAWs, and those wishing to retire earlier than age t_R

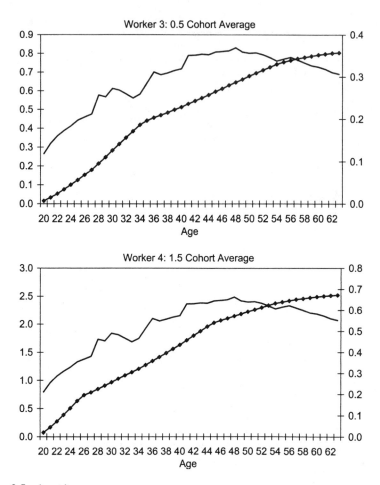

Fig. 3.5   (cont.)

could be allowed to sell some of their PAAWs to provide retirement income during the years prior to t_R. These transactions could occur at prespecified prices (to correspond to the current system) or at market prices.

The Assignment of Property Rights to Accrued Benefits

Under the current system, workers' future Social Security benefits are not protected with formal legal property rights. Congress can alter benefits, without regard to whether they have been implicitly accrued under the current system.[16] Our approach would formally split future benefits into

16. The 1935 Social Security Act stated "The right to alter, amend, or repeal any provision of this Act is hereby reserved to the Congress." The right of Congress to reduce or eliminate benefits that are scheduled to be paid as a result of previous Social Security contributions was reaffirmed by the 1960 Supreme Court decision on Fleming v. Nestor. See http://www .socialsecurity.gov/history/nestor.html for further details.

those accrued to date and those yet to be accrued, giving property rights and reduced political risk to the former but not to the latter. Workers would get periodic Social Security statements telling them their balance of PAAWs and their market value (assuming that there is a market for PAAWs, as we discuss in the following). This treatment would enhance the ability of individuals to plan for their retirement. It would also correspond more closely to the legal treatment of private and state and local DB pension plans.[17]

The assignment of property rights at the individual level leads to a natural choice of accounting method for the system as a whole: accrual accounting. Under this method, the present value of new accruals would be reported directly on the income statement of Social Security. This would make the present value costs of a legislative increase in Social Security benefits much more transparent than under the current system (see Jackson [2004] for a discussion of this and other advantages of accrual accounting). As we describe later in the chapter, the development of a liquid market in PAAWs would take this one step further by allowing the government to report the *market value* of new accruals (as opposed to an actuarial estimate of present value).

Assigning property rights to accrued benefits has potential disadvantages as well. In particular, it reduces the flexibility that future Congresses have to reduce benefits in response to unexpected shocks. To reduce this cost, we propose later in the chapter that the system be made self-balancing on a present value basis so that decreases in revenue and increases in system costs are automatically compensated for by decreases in accruals. We leave a full treatment of the advantages and disadvantages of assigning property rights to future work.

Alternative Accrual Rules

As mentioned in the preceding, there are alternative accrual rules under which the benefits of young individuals accrue less rapidly. The "fastest" accrual rule described in the preceding corresponds to the benefits an individual would end up with in the current system if he never worked again. For some purposes, such as considering a transition to a completely new system, this accrual rule may be overly generous. Young workers, even with maximal covered wages, accrue large numbers of PAAWs per contribution because their accrual is equivalent to a poor worker who had steadily earned very low relative wages all through his life. A worker whose average relative wage for the first s years is w would accrue $f[(w \times s)/35] = f[w \times (s/35)]$ PAAWs by the end of s years, where f is the initial relative benefits function, exactly equal to a worker who earned smaller re-

17. As in the current system, we would forbid the use of PAAWs held by workers in their private Social Security accounts as collateral for loans. This limitation on property rights is necessary in order to preserve Social Security savings for old age.

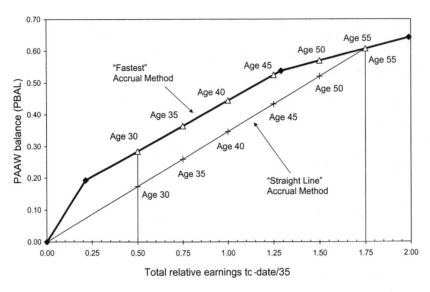

Fig. 3.6   PBAL under two accrual methods, for a worker with relative earnings of 1.75 for all ages

lative wages of $w \times (s/35)$ per year but worked all thirty-five years. We, therefore, consider a second accrual rule that we see as a natural alternative.

Instead of taking the sum of relative wages to date and dividing by 35, compute the average relative earnings to date, put this value into the initial relative benefits formula, and then prorate the benefits by the fraction of years worked to date (based on an assumed thirty-five-year work life). A worker whose average relative wage for the first s years is w would then accrue $f(w) \times (s/35)$ PAAWs by the end of these years. Because f is concave, with $f(0) = 0$, this second accrual is always smaller than the first, $f(w) \times (s/35) \le f(w \times s/35)$ for all $0 \le t \le 35$. Figure 3.6 shows the accruals by age under each rule for a hypothetical worker who always earns relative wages of 1.75 for the thirty-five years between the ages of twenty and fifty-five.

The second accrual method has the advantage of not treating high-wage young people as if they were poor. Also, as shown in figure 3.6, a worker who earned a steady relative wage all his life would accrue the same number of additional PAAWs each year, moving up the straight line. For this reason, we refer to this method as the "straight-line" accrual rule. Figure 3.7 plots the path (for each of our four workers) of accrued PAAW balances under this straight-line method and compares them to those under the fastest method.

This straight-line accrual method closely resembles that used by the Social Security board of trustees (2008) to calculate the *maximum transi-*

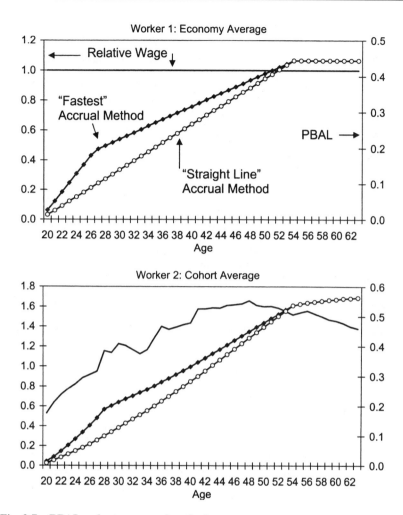

Fig. 3.7   **PBAL under two accrual methods**

tion cost measure of unfunded obligations.[18] The maximum transition cost measure is also the basis for Jackson's (2004) analysis of accrual accounting.

18. The *maximum transition cost* measure of unfunded obligations equals the present value of accrued Social Security benefits payable after the current date, minus the present value of taxes on future benefits minus the value of the trust fund. Accrued benefits of participants who are currently working are calculated in the same manner as disability benefits (Goss 1999), but then prorated by (age −22)/40 (see SSA 2007). Benefit calculations for the maximum transition cost measure exclude the lowest *n* years of relative earnings, where *n* equals the whole-number portion of min(5, years_worked/5). Our accrual rule is based on the highest thirty-five years of relative earnings, with no exclusions allowed if there are fewer than thirty-five years worked.

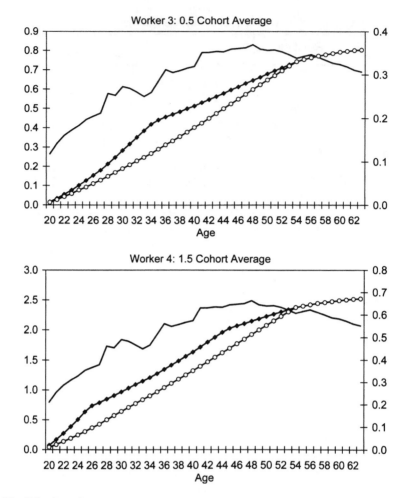

Fig. 3.7   (cont.)

3.2.4   PAAWs versus Notional Accounts

A growing number of countries, most notably Sweden, Italy, and Poland, have recast their social security systems as notional accounts. Participants in these systems make contributions to "notional" accounts, and the balances are legislated to earn an interest rate that is generally set as a function of wage growth. At retirement, balances are converted to a life annuity, based on cohort survival probabilities. These accounts are called "notional" because balances do not correspond to any underlying assets and returns are not those of a financial instrument. Notional accounts are by construction partially self-balancing (see Valdes-Prieto 2000; Auerbach and Lee 2006).

While PAAWs are similar in some ways to notional accounts, we think progressive personal accounts would represent a significant advance. First, because PAAW accrual is based on a redistributive, concave formula (modeled on the current system), progressive personal accounts would retain the intragenerational risk-sharing/redistribution of the current system, whereas notional accounts as typically implemented do not. Second, and more fundamentally, because PAAWs are bona fide securities, they can be traded and will have a market price (as we will describe more clearly in the next section). Therefore, with a system of PAAWS, the statement account balances would equal market value, and the statement returns would be market returns. In our view, the information conveyed by market balances and returns is much more useful to account owners and stewards of the Social Security system than the information conveyed by notional balances and returns.

3.3   Trading PAAWs

So far we have not allowed PAAWs to be traded or priced, and we have replicated the current DB system, including its intra- and intergenerational risk-sharing, with a system of progressive personal accounts. One difference is that this progressive personal accounts system would bestow property rights over benefits as workers accrue them, meeting one of the goals of the Republican push to reform Social Security. The use of PAAWs would also make the accrual of future benefits transparent, in contrast to the opaqueness of the current system.

The trading of PAAWs from individual accounts is a step that need not be taken. But if implemented in a measured way, it could provide further advantages.

3.3.1   The Benefits of a Market for PAAWs

The market price for PAAWs would provide important information to households, governments, and other market participants. First, a market price for pooled PAAWs would give people information about the market value of their own PAAWs, helping them with their financial planning decisions regarding saving and asset allocation. Second, a market value would make it more difficult for the government to take them, thus further enhancing property rights. Third, the price of PAAWs would allow households to compare the value of their tax contributions with the value of their accrued assets. Fourth, the price of PAAWs would give economists a reliable guide to the present value of the benefits promised by the Social Security system, a number that is currently quite controversial. It would also help in designing policies that make the system self-balancing. Fifth, the trading and pricing of PAAWs would enable the private sector to play a more significant role in Social Security, as we shall see. Sixth, as the pools of PAAWs mature, they turn into pools of individual annuities. As such, they become a form of survivor or longevity bond that provide a market guide to aggregate mortality probabilities.

There is another big indirect benefit from trading PAAWs. The Social Security system embodies a gigantic contingent obligation from the government. The economic system could be improved if a fraction of these obligations could be securitized and priced and made available as collateral for other obligations. PAAWs could be used as collateral for issuing further annuities. We believe this would have a salutary effect on the annuities markets and the reverse mortgage markets, which at the moment are hobbled by inefficiencies and adverse selection.

Until a few years ago, financial markets may not have been able to process these new securities. But given the recent advances in structured finance, Wall Street should now be ready for them.

3.3.2   Implementing the Trade of PAAWs via Pools

One way to ensure volume in the trading and pricing of PAAWs would be to require owners of the personal accounts to sell a fixed percentage of their new PAAWs each year and purchase other securities with the proceeds. Workers would not be allowed to spend the proceeds prior to retirement, nor would they be allowed to use balances in their Social Security accounts (PAAWs or other securities) as collateral for loans. They could either be required to purchase a specific basket of securities (for example a broad-based equity index fund) or allowed to choose the securities or baskets of securities that they wished to hold in their accounts.

As discussed in the preceding, portfolio choice is a dimension along which Democrats and Republicans typically disagree. Republicans see choice as beneficial, while Democrats see it as dangerous. Here, a compromise is conceptually easy to work out; one simply restricts the degree of choice available within personal accounts. By keeping the percentage of PAAWs sold each year to be rather low (say at 10 percent), personal account holders would not be able to put the bulk of their Social Security benefits at risk.

An alternative approach would be for individuals to retain 100 percent of their PAAWs, but for the government to issue extra individual PAAWs in proportion to those accrued that year and to sell these PAAWs directly to pools in financial markets. The government could use the proceeds of the sale to retire other, more traditional, forms of debt. Under this approach, the payouts from individual's accounts would continue to mimic those promised by the current system.

Personal annuitized average wage securities (and PANTs) are individual-specific securities, paying as long as the individual lives, so trading them presents many liquidity and adverse selection problems. They are thus analogous to individual mortgages, whose payments depend on the individual's decision to prepay or default (in which case the payoff also depends on the individual's home resale value). In the mortgage market, these problems have been overcome by the pooling of securities, and that is what we propose for PAAWs. Investors in the pool would not buy a single PAAW, but a pro rata share of all the PAAWs in the pool.[19]

Let us denote by Pool(t, t_R) the collection of all PAAWs issued in year t to workers whose statutory retirement year is t_R. This pool of PAAWs would consist of PAAWs(i, t_R) issued to over 3 million workers i. The prediction of PAAW payments for any one worker i is fraught with uncertainty, but the pool is much less uncertain in percentage terms.

Assume for now that the personal account owners would be required to sell exactly the 10 percent of their newly accrued PAAWs we spoke of in the preceding. These would be gathered into Pool(t, t_R), and then shares would be sold off to investors, exactly as in the mortgage market. A single price $\pi_t(t, t_R)$ per PAAW would emerge for each pool, even though the individual PAAWs (i, t_R) would pay off differently, depending on the idiosyncratic mortality of individual i. In the mortgage market, different homeowners, with different propensities to prepay or to default, sell their individual specific promises into pools. Shares in these pools are sold to the public. Investors are enabled to hold liquid shares, and they need only predict the average default rates or prepayment rates for the pools, not individual specific rates. The same would be true of pools of PAAWs. Investors would only need to predict average mortality rates, for example. The shares could be resold later at any time $s > t$ for price $\pi_s(t, t_R)$.

Once $s \geq t_R$, the pool of PAAWs effectively becomes a pool of PANTs. These pooled PANTs would be a form of survivor or longevity bond.[20] The current annuities market is so hobbled by adverse selection and thin markets that it is hard to obtain a market forecast about longevity. The gigantic mandatory saving plan created by Social Security provides a remarkable opportunity to improve this situation. The prices of the pools of PAAWs and PANTs would be an invaluable guide to private companies wishing to issue their own annuities, or reverse mortgages, making those markets more efficient. It would also provide information about longevity to private firms with DB pension obligations. Annuity providers and DB pensions could hedge their exposure to longevity risk by holding shares of pooled PANTs.

3.3.3   The Private Sector

Until now, we have imagined PAAWs as securities issued by the government to individuals, with a fraction tradeable in pools among the general

19. Rather than pooling all individuals together, one could imagine creating separate pools for men and women. All else equal, the price of the pool of women's PAAWs would be higher, due to women's higher life expectancy. To offset this, the government would likely want to set higher match rates for women.

20. For more on survivor or longevity bonds, see, for example, Blake and Burrows (2001) and the literature that followed.

public. But it is also possible that the private sector could issue a significant fraction, or even all, of the PAAWs. A firm issuing x percent of the total PAAWs $P(t, t_R)$ awarded in year t to workers reaching retirement age in year t_R would be responsible for delivering x percent of the benefits called for by that pool.[21] Firms would compete with each other, offering to take on the PAAW liabilities for the lowest price per PAAW. For every $s \geq t$, they would be required to keep a margin collateralizing their obligations, based on the price $\pi_s(t, t_R)$ of the tradable government PAAWs of the same vintage. Workers would receive PAAWs from the government and from private firms, but would only be allowed to sell the government issued PAAWs.[22] The collateral requirement would be set high enough to ensure that the privately issued PAAWs would be as secure as the government PAAWs. One could further imagine creating a second pool PrivatePool(t, t_R) of privately issued and tradable PAAWs in addition to the pool Pool(t, t_R) of PAAWs issued by the government.

3.4   Pricing PAAWs

To determine what the market price of a PAAW would be if it were traded, we will need to introduce a model.[23] We first examine the simplest model: one that assumes risk neutrality. We then sketch out the beginnings of how one might construct a model to compute pricing under risk aversion, leaving the implementation of this for ongoing work.

3.4.1   Pricing PAAWs Assuming Risk Neutrality

Under risk neutrality, the value of an individual PAAW depends on assessments of (1) the growth in average wages, (2) the future path of interest rates, (3) individual survival probabilities. For our calculations in the following we assume a long-run growth in average real wages of 1.1 percent and a long-run real interest rate of 3 percent.[24] We use the cohort life tables from Bell and Miller (2002) and assume for now that all individuals of the same age face the same conditional survival probabilities,[25] that is, that

---

21. One complication is that a firm would have to rely on the government to inform it when workers in the pool died. Information about deaths is also a requirement (and also sometimes a problem) for the current Social Security system.

22. To insure the safety of payments to retirees, the government could be held responsible for making any payments the private sector failed to make. This would provide the government with the incentive to set strong funding and collateral requirements.

23. Of course, once the market is thriving, one could simply observe market prices. But this still begs the question of how market participants would price PAAWs.

24. These equal the intermediate cost assumptions in the 2005 Social Security trustees report. The assumptions in the 2008 Trustees Report are virtually the same: growth in average real wages of 1.1 percent and real interest rate of 2.9 percent.

25. For the calculations presented, we used the survival probabilities for males born in 1980.

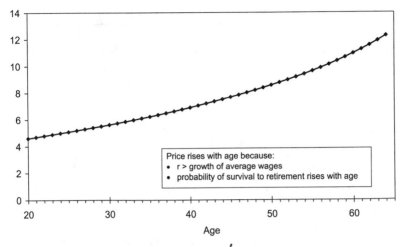

Fig. 3.8   **Projected market price of one PAAW, under risk neutrality, measured in average wage units**

there is no heterogeneity or private information about these probabilities.[26] Finally, we make the assumption that the individuals are fully rational and have the correct expectations of the average wage growth rate.

Based on these assumptions, we compute an estimate of the market price $\pi_s(2000, 2047)$, measured in average wage units. Figure 3.8 shows the estimated price of a PAAW across time (age) for individuals born in 1980, turning twenty in 2000, and hitting the statutory retirement age of sixty-seven in 2047. The market price of the PAAW, in date s average wage units, rises steadily as s approaches t_R, because (1) the probability of reaching the retirement age increases as any individual survives an additional year and (2) the real interest rate is greater than the growth in average real wages so that one year's less discounting has a bigger effect than the increasing value of a wage unit.

Next, for each of the four representative workers, we compute (see figure 3.9) the total projected market value of accrued PAAWs (measured in contemporaneous average wage units), that is, the product of PAAW balances at any date s and the price at date s of a PAAW $\pi_s(2000, 2047)$.[27] These rise over time, for example, to a value of 6.7 for the cohort-average worker, meaning that the value of accrued balances at retirement is expected to be 6.7 times average economy-wide wages.

---

26. With heterogeneity in survival probabilities, the price of a representative pool of PAAWs would not give a perfect signal to individuals about the market value of their individual future retirement cash flows.

27. Because we assumed that all workers have the same mortality, it follows that the prices of all accumulated PAAWs are the same, $\pi_s(t, 2047) = \pi_s(2000, 2047)$ for all $2000 \leq t \leq s$.

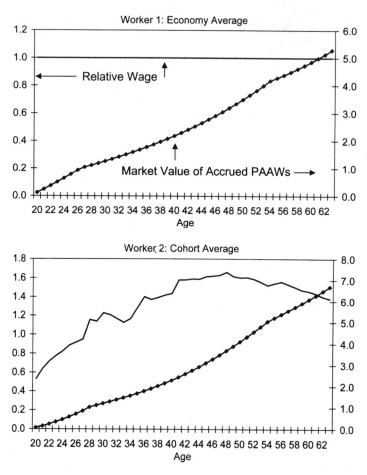

Fig. 3.9   Projected market value of accrued PAAWs, measured in average wage units

3.4.2   Allowing for Risk Aversion

Pricing PAAWs by assuming risk neutrality could easily be misleading. In ongoing work (Geanakoplos and Zeldes 2008), we are examining model-based pricing allowing for risk aversion. If PAAWs were a redundant security (i.e., the payoffs could be perfectly replicated by holding a basket of other traded securities), this would be a relatively straightforward task. For example, if the cash flows were always equal to the cash flows stemming from a certain number of shares of the S&P 500, plus a certain number of Treasury inflation protected securities (TIPS), then one could simply price PAAWs by looking at the market price of the shares of the S&P 500 and the investment needed to acquire the TIPS. Of course, it is not

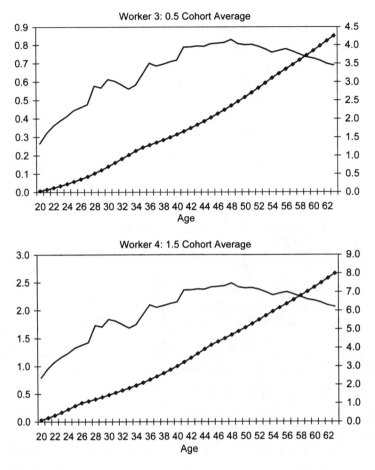

Fig. 3.9   (cont.)

possible to perfectly replicate PAAWs with securities that are currently marketed. An alternative approach (followed in Geanakoplos and Zeldes 2008) is to project the return on PAAWs onto the returns of currently traded securities and assume that the residual has price equal to zero.

   Goetzmann (2005) found that wage growth and stock returns are uncorrelated, or even slightly negatively correlated, over short periods of time. He concluded that stocks would not figure much in a replicating portfolio for wage-indexed liabilities. While this might be true for wage-indexed securities with very short maturities, this would not be so for wage-indexed securities with long maturities. Common sense suggests that over the long run, real wages and stock returns must be positively correlated. For example, a permanent drop in future productivity would likely lead to both lower future real wages and a lower future value of the stock market, compared to what they would have been otherwise. It is perfectly consistent that a rise in stock returns today does not signal a higher wage today, yet does make it more likely that wages in thirty years will be higher. Thus stocks would almost surely have a significant positive weight in the replicating portfolio at time t for PAAWs indexed to wages at time t_R much greater than t. As t approaches t_R, the replicating portfolio would change and stocks would drop out. In Geanakoplos and Zeldes (2008), we model this long-run correlation and use Monte Carlo derivative pricing methods to estimate the price of a PAAW.[28]

An alternative approach to pricing PAAWs directly would be to first estimate the prices of the two underlying securities—average wage securities and pools of PANTs, and then use these to price the composite PAAWs. There is a literature in financial theory indicating how, under certain conditions, it is possible to dynamically trade the portfolios of two securities to replicate the product of the securities.[29] We could apply this approach to obtain the price of PAAWs as a function of the prices of average wage bonds and pools of PANTs.

If the best replicating portfolio of currently traded securities leaves a residual that cannot be assumed to have price zero, then one has to use an alternative asset pricing model to assess the value of the residual. There are several models available for this purpose, and one would need to check that the price of the residual is robust, or at least that upper and lower bounds could be sensibly computed. We leave this for future work.

Risk and Return of PAAWs

As just discussed, in the long-run, wage growth is correlated with stock market growth. Hence, if PAAWs are priced in the market, they must offer equity-like returns in the long run.[30] But as workers age, and t approaches t_R, PAAW volatility becomes very low. For example, when $t = t_R - 1$, the only payoff uncertainty is over what next year's real wage will be. All future payoffs are determined by that same number and by aggregate mortality. By contrast, even if investors can be fairly confident of next year's dividends, they will be very uncertain about dividends in ten years, and stock

28. This follows the work of Lucas and Zeldes (2006), who use this type of approach to estimate the market value of private DB pension liabilities (projected benefit obligation [PBO] measures).

29. Amin and Bodurtha (1995) show how to price certain types of "quantos": contingent claims with a "quantity" or nominal cash flow determined by equity values in one currency but paid in another currency at a fixed rate. For example, the value of a first security, such as the Nikkei stock index, might determine the number of units of a second security, such as the U.S. dollar, that must be paid.

30. This is consistent with Geanakoplos, Mitchell, and Zeldes (1998). Equity-like returns are a feature of PAAWs securities, but not necessarily of Social Security as a whole. Achieving equity-like (or any market) returns for all of Social Security would first require eliminating its legacy debt, for example, by increasing taxes outside of Social Security to pay off the interest and principle of the legacy debt. See section 3.6.

prices at t_R are quite uncertain at $t = t_R - 1$. If personal accounts hold only PAAWs, it will never happen that two different cohorts retiring one year apart will get 20 percent different retirement benefits, as could easily happen if investors kept their money in stocks and sold them for annuities at retirement. Thus, PAAWs might turn out to be a more attractive investment vehicle than stocks for individuals planning for retirement.

3.5   The Government Match Rate (under Risk Neutrality)

Once PAAWs are priced, in any of the ways indicated in the preceding, we can compute the government "match" under the current Social Security system (which can be positive or negative, i.e., a subsidy or a tax) as the difference between the market value of PAAWs received and the value of the contribution. The average match rate is defined as $[\pi_t(t, t_R) \times (\Delta \text{PBAL})/$ annual contribution] -1 and captures the percentage by which the Social Security system is subsidizing (or taxing if negative) account contributions in each year. The marginal match rate is defined as $[\pi_t(t, t_R) \times$ (increment to PBAL per additional dollar of contribution)] -1, that is, the percent subsidy (or tax) for a marginal additional account contribution. The match rate of course depends on which accrual rule (fastest or straight line) we use.

Unlike most simple DC plans, the match rate is not constant across people or time. It depends on PBAL, the price of a PAAW, and the fraction of a contribution that "counts." The match rate can be positive or negative, but it can never be < -100 percent (i.e., balances cannot be taken away). Note that all of the redistribution related to these accounts occurs on the way in (i.e., as contributions are made); none of it occurs while funds are earning returns or when they are withdrawn.

Figures 3.10 and 3.11 show the average match rate and the marginal match rate, under the fastest accrual rule, for our representative workers, taking the price of PAAWs derived earlier from our risk neutral model. For the first thirty-five years of work, the average and marginal match rates are identical, with the exception of those rare years containing bend points. On average over the life cycle, the match rates are quite negative. This corresponds to the fact that the current system is primarily unfunded; current and future workers are paying for the benefits given to the initial generations starting in the 1940s who had not contributed much before getting benefits. Rather than getting low returns, as they would under the current system, workers receive negative matches on their contributions and then receive market rates of return on balances in their accounts.[31] The match

---

31. Consistent with Geanakoplos, Mitchell, and Zeldes (1998), this negative match combined with market returns corresponds to the lower-than-market rate of return received overall under the current system.

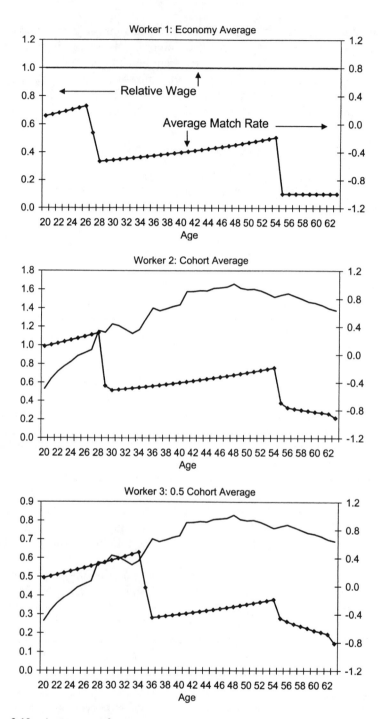

Fig. 3.10   Average match rate

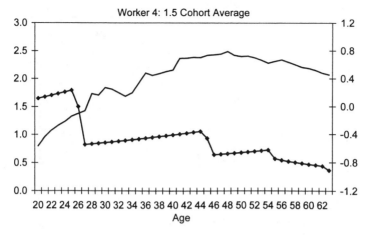

Fig. 3.10   (cont.)

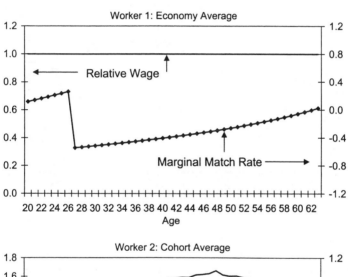

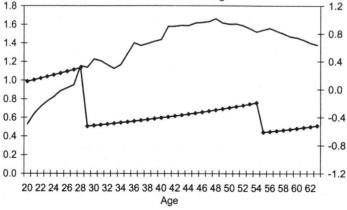

Fig. 3.11   Marginal match rate

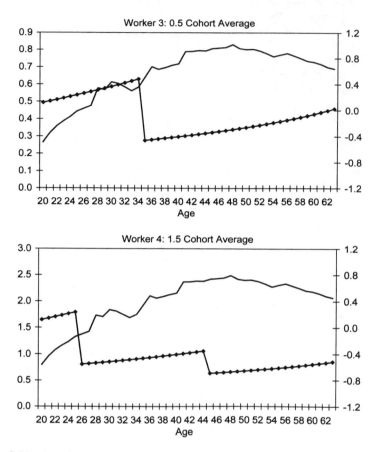

Fig. 3.11   (cont.)

rates are positive for young workers and negative for middle-aged and old workers. The average match rate is lower for the old for two reasons. First, under the rapid accrual rule, a given relative wage contribution generates less PAAWs the higher is PBAL, and PBAL rises with age, as we saw in figure 3.3. Second, the thirty-five-year averaging formula means that earnings in the thirty-sixth year and beyond accrue PAAWs only by the amount they exceed the thirty-fifth highest relative wage to date so that an extra year of work generates fewer additional PAAWs than it would if the worker had not yet worked thirty-five years. (This second effect is not relevant for the marginal match rate in figure 3.11 because relative wages in later years are greater than or equal to the thirty-fifth highest so that an extra hour of work generates the full PAAWs increment.) These factors are only partially offset by the fact that, as we saw in figure 3.8, the price of a PAAW rises with age.

We agree with our discussant Jason Furman about the importance of having our match rate inform each worker directly and simply about his incentives to work. Feldstein and Samwick (1992) estimated the implicit tax rate on labor income (or the extent of the work disincentive) due to the U.S. Social Security system, that is, the difference between the incremental contribution and the present value of the incremental lifetime benefits due to a dollar increase in current income.[32] They found it to be much higher for the young than for the old.[33] This might seem to contradict our generally declining marginal *match* rates in figure 3.11 (a positive match corresponds to a negative tax), but this is not the case because the marginal match rates in figure 3.11 do not give an accurate guide to the implicit marginal tax rate on labor income. Workers who want an accurate assessment of the incentive to work under the fastest accrual rule must make a more complicated dynamic calculation. Earning more when young may accrue many PAAWs (which the match rate reveals), but the resulting increase in PBAL lowers future match rates. Hence, for young workers the true incentive to work is much lower than the marginal match rate in figure 3.11 suggests.[34]

Under the assumption that relative wages do not vary too much over a worker's lifetime, the marginal match rate from our second accrual method—the "straight-line method"—is proportional to the implicit marginal tax rate on labor due to Social Security.[35] The marginal match rate under the straight-line method, therefore, conveys the correct incentive to work, without requiring any dynamic adjustment. Workers' account statements could include either the value of the marginal match rate directly or the inputs needed to compute it. The greater correspondence under this second accrual method between the match rate and the incentive to work represents an additional advantage of using the "straight-line" accrual instead of the "fastest" accrual method.

Figures 3.12 and 3.13 show the average and marginal match rates under this straight-line accrual method and compares them to those under the fastest accrual method. A worker with constant relative earnings (such as

32. When earnings are stochastic, as opposed to deterministic, computing the incentive to work becomes much more complicated because one needs to incorporate the different possible earnings paths and the slope of the benefit schedule and the marginal utility of consumption under each path. The Feldstein and Samwick calculations of the lifetime marginal tax rate of Social Security do not incorporate this uncertainty—their calculations simply assume that workers will end up on a specific segment of the PIA schedule with certainty.

33. Cushing (2005) showed that the decline largely disappears once one takes into account disability and survivor benefits.

34. We are grateful to Jason Furman for bringing the importance of this issue to our attention, thereby directing our focus toward the "straight-line" accrual rule.

35. Formally, the worker's average relative earnings to date must put the worker in the same bracket (the range across which the slope in panel A of figure 3.2 is constant) as his average relative earnings at the end of his career. Under this assumption, the implicit marginal tax rate from Social Security equals –1 times the marginal match rate from the straight-line method times the Social Security contribution rate. Note that the marginal incentive to work is the same under both accrual methods (while the marginal match rate is not).

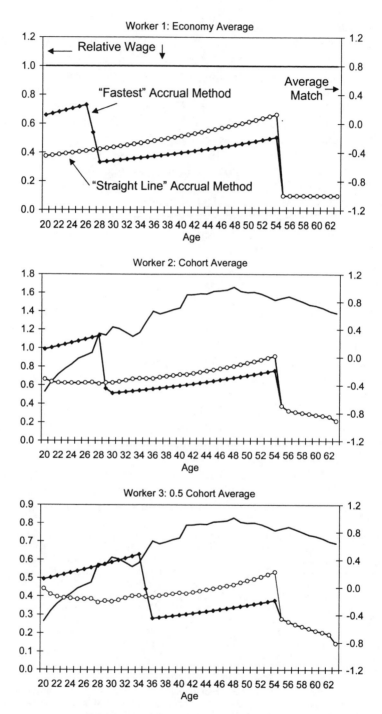

Fig. 3.12 **Average match rate under two accrual methods**

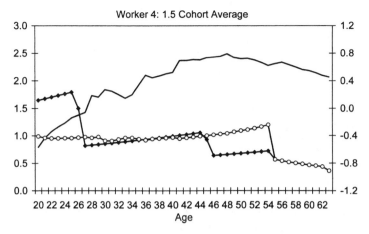

Fig. 3.12   (cont.)

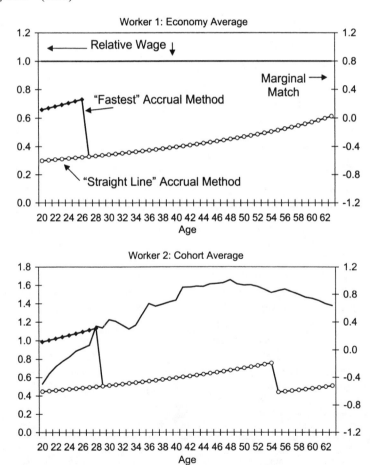

Fig. 3.13   Marginal match rate under two accrual methods

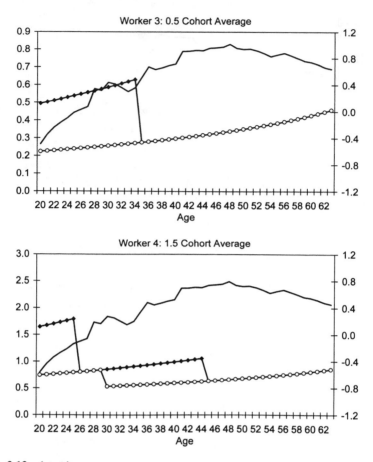

Fig. 3.13   (cont.)

worker 1) will get the same PAAW allocation per relative wage contribution all through his life (recall figure 3.6). Because PAAW values rise as a worker ages (and survives), the match rate is steadily increasing for this worker, that is, a worker who always earns the same relative wage will have increasing incentive to work an extra hour as he gets older.[36] The average match rate for the economy-wide average worker starts out around negative forty percent, meaning that for every dollar of contributions, he gets sixty cents of benefits. Because contributions are about 10 percent of

36. The assumption in footnote 35 holds for workers 1 and 3 in figure 3.13, and thus the marginal match rate under this accrual method exactly captures the true incentive to work. For workers 2 and 4, final average earnings turn out to be sufficiently higher than cumulative average earnings when young, to put workers in a higher panel A of figure 3.2 bracket than is used for computing the contemporaneous match rate. In this case, the annual match rate when young does not correspond to the incentive to work.

wages, this means he faces an average tax rate on wages of around 4 percent. Because the system is progressive, his marginal tax rate is higher than his average tax rate. As the worker ages, the tax eventually turns into a slight subsidy.

3.6   Incorporating Budget Balance Mechanisms into Progressive Personal Accounts

In this section, we show that our proposed system can be modified to incorporate a market-based aggregate self-correction mechanism. There is a variety of ways to do this. Here we focus on one in particular, in which we balance the system "on the way in," meaning that in any year the aggregate quantity of newly issued PAAWs is set such that their market value equals the aggregate value of new contributions. Assuming that we start with an initially balanced system (and we describe possible ways to transition to this), then the government should be able to optimally manage its portfolio to hedge its exposure and maintain balance "on the way out" as well.

3.6.1   Transition

The first step is to recognize that in a pay-as-you-go system, the early generations are given a huge windfall transfer. Retirees in the 1940s collected Social Security benefits even though they hardly made any contributions. Similarly, retirees in the 1950s collected benefits even though they had only contributed for ten or fifteen years, and so on.[37] In a pay-as-you go system, current and future generations of workers are called upon to pay off those transfers. But why should this debt overhang be borne by those least able to pay?

One approach would be to move rapidly to a new system by issuing "recognition PAAWs" to current workers and retirees to compensate for (i.e., recognize) past Social Security contributions. These would be obligations of the United States government, and not of future Social Security contributors. Goss, Wade, and Schultz (2008) calculate that the "maximum transition cost" (as of the beginning of 2007) would be $16.7 trillion. Ignoring risk adjustments, this provides an estimate of the market value of the required recognition PAAWs. There is no reason that the burden of this debt, created by the transfers to the early generations of Social Security beneficiaries, should be apportioned based solely on "covered" labor earnings. Payments of interest and principal on the recognition bonds would, therefore, come both from issuing new debt (i.e., rolling some of it over) and from taxes on all income, including labor income above the Social Security earnings cap and capital income. Using a back-of-the envelope calculation, we estimate that this burden would amount to about a 1 percent-

---

37. See Geanakoplos, Mitchell, and Zeldes (1999).

age point increase in the tax rates on personal income and corporate profits in perpetuity.[38]

Because the current system does not legally ensure property rights on accrued benefits, it might also be appropriate to give workers fewer recognition PAAWs than would be implied by the accrual rule chosen for new contributions. By making this reduction for current generations, the government would reduce the future tax rates it would have to levy on future generations. There is a compelling case for such a reduction. The current system of taxes and legislated benefits is not in fiscal balance, and the shortfall has to be borne by somebody. There seems no reason to exclude the current generations from bearing any of these costs. Under our plan, future workers would have to pay a tax on the order of 1 percent, or about 10 percent above their normal Social Security tax. It seems fair to ask the current generations to accept a 10 percent reduction in their Social Security benefits, especially because we will be locking in property rights to these benefits. If we thought current benefits were still too large, or that the resulting tax in perpetuity was still too high, we could reduce these benefits even more.

3.6.2   A Fully Funded Social Security System

Once this debt overhang is taken out of the Social Security system, there is no reason the system cannot operate in fiscal balance going forward, as a fully funded ("prefunded") system. We are thus led to propose a modification of the current benefits rules that has the virtue of balancing the system "on the way in." While the government match under a system that maintains "balance on the way in" will by necessity alter the redistribution/risk-sharing of the current system, we propose to keep such changes to a minimum.

The present value of the Social Security contributions a cohort makes under the current system is greater than the present value of the benefits mandated by current law. Thus workers could be made to buy their benefits via their contributions without having to increase contributions or reduce future benefits. We propose modifying the accrual rules so that in every year the market value of PAAWs awarded is just equal to the market

---

38. To obtain this estimate, we solve for the perpetual tax on personal income and profits that would be equal in present value to $16.7 trillion, the SSA Office of Actuary's estimate of the 2007 "maximum transition cost" measure of unfunded obligations (UO). In formula, we need to solve for t such that $(t \times Y)/(r - g) = \$16.7$ trillion, where t is the tax rate, r is the real interest rate, and g is the growth rate of income (GDP). This implies that $t = (UO/Y) \times (r - g)$. Based on the *2008 OASDI Trustees Report* long-term forecast, we assume a constant future real interest rate of 2.9 percent and future real income growth of 2.1 percent. Given combined 2007 personal income and corporate profits of about $13.3 trillion, our assumptions imply a tax burden of 1 percent. Note that these calculations do not incorporate any risk adjustment of the sort proposed in Geanakoplos and Zeldes (2008).

value of all Social Security tax contributions. This aspect is similar to what occurs with standard DC accounts.

There are many ways to structure the government match such that the overall budget balances on the way in. Here we focus on one simple possibility. For each year t, let the preliminary allocation of PAAWs be established exactly as in the current system described in the previous section, say under the straight-line method of accrual. Compute the total market value of this allocation in the PAAWs markets. Next, define λ_t as the ratio of total annual tax contributions in t to the market value of the preliminary PAAW allocation in the preceding.[39] The final allocation of PAAWs is set by multiplying the preliminary allocation by λ_t. This will result in an allocation of PAAWs that exactly balances the budget. The government match will then be the difference for each individual between the value of his final allocation of PAAWs and his tax contribution.

Once the legacy tax is taken out and the PAAWs are scaled up to equal current contributions, the government match rate looks much more generous. In figures 3.14 and 3.15, we display the average and marginal government match rates (respectively) that incorporate this budget balancing (for each accrual rule) for each of our four representative workers. Values for λ_t are calculated using the assumption that the cross-sectional age-income profile is flat (panel 1) or equivalent to the cohort-average time profile (panels 2 to 4.) Figure 3.14 shows that average match rates are generally above zero for the cohort-average worker under straight-line accrual. Note in figure 3.15 that, for straight-line accrual, marginal match rates are (weakly) less than average match rates, and typically below zero for all but low earners.[40]

This revised budget balance system will be similar to the current system, but it cannot replicate it exactly. For example, we noted that the aggregate accruals in any year of the current system are independent of the aggregate contributions during that year. In the budget balance system, the aggregate accruals would move dollar for dollar with contributions.

Another difference is that in this revised system, the quantity of PAAW accruals in a year depends on the market price of PAAWs in that year, whereas in the current system it does not. In the current system, the num-

39. To estimate λ_t in the following figures, we assume that cross-sectional income profiles correspond to the cohort profiles used in our figures. We then rescale wages so that the average wage in the cross-section is one, where the average is weighted by survival probabilities (to proxy for each age's proportion in the population). We use the contribution rates to calculate aggregate annual contributions for year t, and we use the accrual formula together with the market prices of PAAWs to calculate the aggregate market value of newly accrued PAAWs in year t. The ratio of these two values is λ_t.

40. The wedge between marginal and average match rates exists because workers earn additional benefits each year even if they have no additional earnings, which boosts the average match rate but not the marginal match rate. This wedge will exist for "straight-line" accrual with any concave benefit schedule.

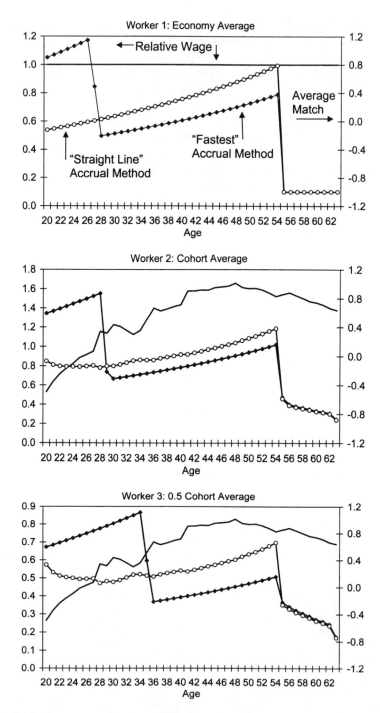

Fig. 3.14 Average match rates under automatic balance

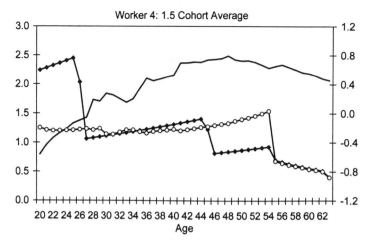

Fig. 3.14   (cont.)

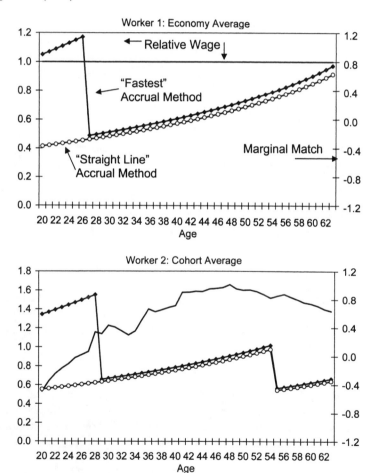

Fig. 3.15   Marginal match rates under automatic balance

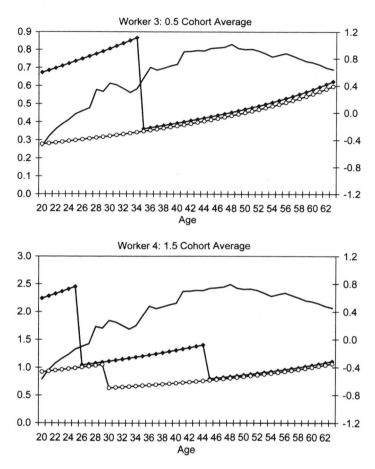

Fig. 3.15   (cont.)

ber of PAAWs a worker gets is independent of interest rates. In the budget balance system, when long-run interest rates fall relative to the long-run expected growth in wages, PAAW prices will rise, and workers will, therefore, get fewer PAAWs.[41]

3.6.3   Maintaining Balance Through Hedging

Because PAAWs promise future payments that are uncertain as of the time they are issued, their eventual value may diverge from their original price. Thus, a system in balance on the way in may fall out of balance later. So we suggest that there is a need for a hedging entity to keep the system in

41. A complete analysis of intergenerational risk sharing would have to take into account interest rate risk in addition to wage risk.

balance. One possibility is to create a government agency with this responsibility. Another complementary possibility would be to involve the private sector in issuing PAAWs that would be sold to households, that is, pay firms to take on the obligations. As described earlier, the private firms would, of course, need to be regulated and monitored to ensure that they fully collateralized their obligations. We leave a full description of this hedging for future work.

3.7   Conclusions and Future Research

We showed that it is possible to preserve the redistribution and risk-sharing of the current system in a system of progressive personal accounts, clarifying the link between contributions and benefits, and at the same time enhancing the property rights of the system. Along the way, we translated the current DB system into the language of DC—facilitating communication in the debate over individual accounts.

We developed a variable match approach to provide progressivity based on lifetime (rather than annual) income. This approach could also be used to modify standard personal accounts (holding traditional financial assets) or notional defined contribution accounts that have recently been adopted in a number of other countries.

We argued that it would be possible to create and trade pools of PAAWs, providing an estimate of the market value of each individual's account and opening up the possibility of allowing (limited) trade in accounts. These new markets could have a beneficial impact on the current annuities and reverse mortgage markets.

We emphasized the importance of making the Social Security system self-balancing by incorporating a market-based aggregate self-correction mechanism. We described one possible way to do this through "balancing on the way in" and system hedging.

This chapter lays the groundwork for our ongoing and future work in this area. In Geanakoplos and Zeldes (2008), we present a model for estimating PAAW prices under risk aversion, taking into account a long-run link between aggregate labor earnings and the value of the stock market. We then use these prices to calculate the market value of aggregate outstanding U.S. Social Security benefit promises. Our resulting estimates of the "maximum transition cost" measure of system obligations are significantly lower than those of the Social Security Administration, due to our incorporation of market risk into the discounting of future benefits.

In other work, we are trying to further improve the risk-sharing and redistribution features of our progressive personal accounts, and we are also examining alternative market-based self-correction mechanisms. We are working to spell out in more detail how our proposed market for PAAWs and related new securities would operate in practice. Finally, we hope to investigate the relevance of progressive personal accounts to private pension plans.

References

Amin, Kaushik I., and James N. Bodurtha, Jr. 1995. Discrete-time valuation of American options with stochastic interest rates. *Review of Financial Studies* 8 (1): 93–234.

Auerbach, Alan J., and Ronald Lee. 2006. Notional defined contribution pension systems in a stochastic context: Design and stability. NBER Working Paper no. 12805. Cambridge, MA: National Bureau of Economic Research, December.

Bell, Felicitie C., and Michael L. Miller. 2002. Life tables for the United States Social Security area 1900–2100. Actuarial Study no. 116. Washington, DC: Office of the Chief Actuary, Social Security Administration.

Blake, David, and William Burrows. 2001. Survivor bonds: Helping to hedge mortality risk. *Journal of Risk and Insurance* 68 (2): 339–48.

Bohn, Henning. 2002. Retirement savings in an aging society: A case for innovative government debt management. In *Ageing, financial markets and monetary policy,* ed. A. Auerbach and H. Herrmann, 139–81. New York: Springer.

Borsch-Supan, Axel. 2005. From traditional DB to notional DC systems: The pension reform process in Sweden, Italy, and Germany. *Journal of the European Economic Association* 3 (2–3): 458–65.

Clingman, Michael D., and Jeffrey L. Kunkel. 1992. Average wages for 1985–1990 for indexing under the Social Security Act. Actuarial Note no. 133. Washington, DC: Office of the Chief Actuary, Social Security Administration, September.

Cushing, Matthew J. 2005. Net marginal Social Security tax rates over the life cycle. *National Tax Journal* 58 (2): 227–45.

Donkar, Eli N. 1981. Average wages for indexing under the Social Security Act and the automatic determinations for 1979–81. *Actuarial Note* no. 103. Washington, DC: Office of the Chief Actuary, Social Security Administration, May.

Feldstein, Martin, and Jeffrey Liebman. 2002. The distributional effects of an investment-based Social Security system. In *Distributional aspects of Social Security and Social Security reform,* ed. M. Feldstein and J. Liebman, 263–326. Chicago: University of Chicago Press.

Feldstein, Martin, and Andrew Samwick. 1992. Social Security rules and marginal tax rates. *National Tax Journal* 45 (1): 1–22.

Geanakoplos, John, Olivia Mitchell, and Stephen P. Zeldes. 1998. Would a privatized Social Security system really pay a higher rate of return? In *Framing the Social Security debate: Values, politics, and economics,* ed. R. D. Arnold, M. J. Graetz, and A. H. Munnell, 137–56. Washington, DC: Brookings Institution.

———. 1999. Social Security money's worth. In *Prospects for Social Security reform,* ed. O. S. Mitchell, R. J. Meyers, and H. Young, Philadelphia: University of Pennsylvania Press.

Geanakoplos, John, and Stephen P. Zeldes. 2008. The market value of accrued Social Security benefits. Columbia University, Graduate School of Business. Unpublished Manuscript.

Goetzmann, William N. 2005. More Social Security, not less. Yale ICF Working Paper no. 05-05. New Haven, CT: Yale International Center for Finance.

Goss, Stephen C. 1999. Measuring solvency in the Social Security system. In *Prospects for Social Security reform,* ed. O. S. Mitchell, R. J. Myers, and H. Young, 16–36. Philadelphia: University of Pennsylvania Press.

Goss, Steve, Alice Wade, and Jason Schultz. 2008. Unfunded obligation and transition cost for the OASDI program. Actuarial Note no. 2007. 1. Washington, DC: Office of the Chief Actuary, Social Security Administration, February.

Jackson, Howell. 2004. Accounting for Social Security and its reform. *Harvard Journal on Legislation* 41 (1): 59–159.

Liebman, Jeffrey. 2003. Should taxes be based on lifetime income? Vickrey taxation revisited. Harvard University. Unpublished Manuscript.

Lucas, Deborah, and Stephen P. Zeldes. 2006. Valuing and hedging defined benefit pension obligations—The role of stocks revisited. Columbia University, Graduate School of Business. Unpublished Manuscript.

Shiller, Robert J. 1993. *Macro markets: Creating institutions for managing society's largest economic risks.* New York: Oxford University Press.

Social Security Administration. 2007. *Online Social Security handbook.* http://www.ssa.gov/OP_Home/handbook/.

Social Security Administration, Office of the Chief Actuary. 2006. *Average wage index.* http://www.ssa.gov/OACT/COLA/awidevelop.html.

Social Security Board of Trustees. 2008. *The 2008 annual report of the board of trustees of the Federal Old-Age and Survivors Insurance and Federal Disability Insurance Trust Funds.* http://www.ssa.gov/OACT/TR/TR08/.

Valdes-Prieto, Salvador. 2000. The financial stability of notional account pensions. *Scandinavian Journal of Economics* 102 (3): 395–417.

———. 2005. Securitization of taxes implicit in PAYG pensions. *Economic Policy* 20 (42): 215–65.

Vickrey, William. 1947. *Agenda for progressive taxation.* New York: Ronald Press.

Comment   Jason Furman

John Geanakoplos and Stephen P. Zeldes make an important analytic contribution to our understanding of the difference between defined benefit and defined contribution systems. But Geanakoplos and Zeldes' goal is not simply to make an analytic contribution but to forge a potential compromise between Republican supporters of individual accounts and Democratic opponents of them. As such, it is important to judge this chapter on whether it should—or would—form the basis of a future compromise.

Jason Furman is a senior fellow at the Brookings Institution.

Editors' note: This comment was prepared by Jason Furman based on the version of the paper presented at the conference in October 2006 when Jason Furman was a Senior Fellow at the Center for Budget and Policy Priorities. Due to his move to the White House National Economic Council in January 2009, Dr. Furman was unable to edit this comment to reflect the revisions undertaken by the authors in response to his comments. The editors have noted those places in the comment where Geanakoplos and Zeldes have revised their paper to address the concerns raised in this comment. The views expressed in this comment do not represent the views of SSA, any agency of the federal government, or of the NBER.

The Analytic Contribution

Geanakoplos and Zeldes' principal analytic contribution is to develop a general framework that makes it possible to express a defined benefit system in defined contribution terms. They develop a new set of securities, a mandatory savings rule, and a system of matching contributions that make it possible to use individual accounts to reproduce Social Security retirement benefits, including risk-sharing across generations and redistribution based on lifetime income. (The authors do not reproduce survivors or auxiliary benefits.)

Specifically, each year a person would be required to use 10.6 percent of his income (the amount that currently funds Old-Age and Survivors Insurance) to purchase a new type of security called a *personal annuitized average wage* security or PAAW. A PAAW initially pays the economy-wide wage in the year of retirement and then pays the same amount indexed for inflation every year until the death of the original recipient. This security matches two features of Social Security that are generally absent in defined contribution plans: a security whose payoff is linked to productivity and a real annuity.

Geanakoplos and Zeldes reproduce Social Security's lifetime redistribution by specifying a matching rule that can be positive or negative and would specify the number of PAAWs a person can buy per $1 of mandatory saving. The Geanokplos-Zeldes matching rule exploits the fact that the lifetime Social Security benefit formula can be rewritten as a the sum of a series of nonnegative functions of income received to date:

$$f(w_1, w_2, w_3, \ldots, w_T) = \sum_{t=1}^{T} g(w_1, \ldots, w_T) \text{ where } g(\cdot) \geq 0$$

As a result, specifying the appropriate matching rule is simply coming up with a function g that specifies the amount of PAAWs a worker receives as a function of their income earned to date. And the particular function is based on the additional retirement benefits a worker would get if he never worked again.[1] Specifically, worker i gets awarded PAAWs at time t that correspond to the three primary insurance amount (PIA) formula factors in the Social Security system, 0.90, 0.32, and 0.15. The amount of PAAWs you get thus shifts as your earnings to date, averaged over thirty-five years, move you through these three factors:

1. Editors' note: There are a variety of possible choices of the function g, each of which represent a different method for accruing benefits. Geanakoplos and Zeldes examine two: one that they call the "fastest" method and another that they call the "straight-line" method. Only the first of these methods was included in the original conference version of this paper, so Furman's comment focuses on this one. This fastest accrual method computes the benefits a worker would receive under the current system based on earnings to date, assuming that he never worked again. The incremental PAAWs awarded each year are chosen to replicate the incremental accrued benefits in that year.

$$\text{Get } 0.9 * \frac{1}{35}\left(\frac{w_{i,t}}{\overline{w}_t}\right) \text{ until Bend 1}$$

$$\text{Get } 0.32 * \frac{1}{35}\left(\frac{w_{i,t}}{\overline{w}_t}\right) \text{ until Bend 2}$$

$$\text{Get } 0.15 * \frac{1}{35}\left(\frac{w_{i,t}}{\overline{w}_t}\right) \text{ until maximum}$$

Get 0 thereafter

Having recast Social Security retirement benefits in terms of securities (which match the intergenerational risk sharing) and a matching rule (which matches the intragenerational redistribution), makes several helpful substantive points and provides the basis for moving forward analytically.

First, it shows that the essential difference between a defined benefit and a defined contribution plan is not the intergenerational risk-sharing, the intergenerational redistribution, or the intragenerational redistribution. You can have as much or as little of these features as you want either type of plan. This is the first step toward focusing the debate about accounts on some of the other genuine distinctions, many of them discussed in the following.

Second, recasting the existing Social Security system in terms of financial securities is a first step toward using alternative methods to analyze Social Security's current situation. For example, the Social Security Administration's Office of the Chief Actuary calculates the "maximum transition cost," which is the value of Social Security benefits incurred for work to date net of the balance in the trust fund. The actuaries estimated that this totaled $13.5 trillion as of the beginning of 2004. Geanakoplos and Zeldes provide an alternative framework for estimating the maximum transition cost by valuing the financial securities that are equivalent to the benefit promise. In their chapter, they just do this in the risk neutral case, which is equivalent to the actuaries' procedure. But in forthcoming work, they plan to extend these results to the case with risk aversion.

Finally, the Geanakoplos-Zeldes framework can flexibly be extended to examine other issues, like how to achieve robust solvency that ensures not just that Social Security is in long-run balance but also that it can stay in long-run when subjected to various shocks. The Geanakoplos-Zeldes chapter offers one version of a plan that would adjust the matching formula to ensure that the value of PAAWs that were distributed in any given year was equal to the payroll taxes collected in that year. Hopefully in future work Geanakoplos-Zeldes will be able to use some of the analytic machinery they develop to perform a welfare analysis of this approach as compared to alternative ways of achieving robust solvency.

Should Geanakoplos-Zeldes Be Adopted?

Helping us understand Social Security reform better is not the same as providing the basis for an actual Social Security plan. And in this regard, I am more skeptical. Geanakoplos-Zeldes appears to lose many of the potential benefits of accounts and in some cases even turn the virtues of accounts into vices.

The Geanakoplos-Zeldes plan has two distinct parts. The first part is a structure for the accounts. The second part is a mechanism for restoring balance. In effect, these two parts are separable—the account structure is compatible with alternative methods of achieving solvency, and their solvency proposal could be implemented without accounts or with more traditional accounts. The accounts proposal is more novel, and thus it is what I concentrate my comments on.

Accounts have several claimed advantages. Without passing judgment on whether these advantages are real or quantitatively important, how does the Geanakoplos-Zeldes plan do on them?

Reduced Labor-Leisure Distortions

One potential benefit of accounts is that by tying benefits more closely to contributions, they reduce labor-leisure distortions (the flip side of reduced redistribution). The Geanakoplos-Zeldes accounts, by design, reproduce all of the redistribution associated with the current system and, thus, all the distortions as well.

Diversification for Constrained Households

A second potential benefit of accounts is that they can help achieve diversification for households that are equity constrained due to liquidity constraints or the inability to use future Social Security benefits as collateral. The core Geanakoplos-Zeldes proposal to securitize Social Security benefits through PAAWs does nothing to change this situation because these benefits mimic traditional Social Security. The proposal to require people to sell 10 percent of their PAAWs to purchase traditional securities would achieve this goal, although this part of the plan is logically unrelated to the broader structure.

Improved Political Economy of Prefunding

Another potential benefit of accounts is that contributions would count as a reduction in the unified deficit, making it more likely that non-Social Security fiscal policies will not offset any prefunding in Social Security. The Geanakoplos-Zeldes plan might share this benefit with other accounts plans, although the extent could be minimized because the optics and budgetary accounting treatment of individual-specific securities like PAAWs might differ from more conventional securities. Moreover, the Geanakoplos-Zeldes plan, by design, does not actually have any prefunding.

Greater Transparency

Another potential benefit of accounts is that they can have greater transparency in terms of the link between contributions and benefits and the underlying financial status of the system. The Geanakoplos-Zeldes plan would have the advantage of providing a market estimate of the maximum transition cost, a number that is currently calculated by the actuaries. However, estimating conventional solvency criteria would still require projections about the evolution of matching rates and would not be reflected in a market price.

This gain for system transparency comes at a large cost in terms of reduced transparency for individual beneficiaries. There are serious optical issues and apparent cliffs in the formula. Some of these optical problems should not be held against the plan because they are simply making features of the current system more transparent, for example, the fact that the typical sixty-three-year-old will get zero PAAWs for his payroll contribution reflects the fact that a typical sixty-three-year-old today does not incur any additional benefits from his work.

More serious, however, is that the Geanakoplos-Zeldes plan introduces cliffs and sends misleading signals about marginal tax rates in a manner that does not correspond to today's Social Security system.[2] It might be hard to explain why a worker in the first year of a $500,000-a-year job will get a better matching rate than a worker in the thirtieth year of a $50,000-a-year job. There is some risk that labor-leisure decisions would be distorted by the signals the system sent. For example, an average earner at age thirty-two would get 100 PAAWs for each $1 contributed to the account (renormalizing the units). The following year, however, he would move into the new bracket and get only thirty-nine PAAWs for each $1 contributed to the account. This would appear to be a large increase in the marginal tax rate. In fact, it is just an artifact of the benefit calculation. The marginal rate on earnings at age thirty-two and age thirty-three—assuming the person plans to continue working until age sixty-five—are essentially the same. The problem arises because the apparent marginal rate in the Geanakoplos-Zeldes rule is correct only for someone who plans to never work again after that year, which, for the vast majority of workers, is the wrong thought experiment.

Figure 3C.1 generalizes this point. It shows the true marginal tax rates for a scaled medium earner who will work until age sixty-four. These are 10.6 percent initially (because the early years of work will be dropped from the benefit calculation) and then gradually fall, become negative, and then rise back up to 10.6 percent in the years before retirement. In contrast, the perceived marginal rates in the Geanakoplos-Zeldes plan (or the true marginal rates for someone deciding whether to continue working) follow a

2. Editors' note: This comment applies only to the "fastest accrual method," which was the method presented in the original conference version of the paper.

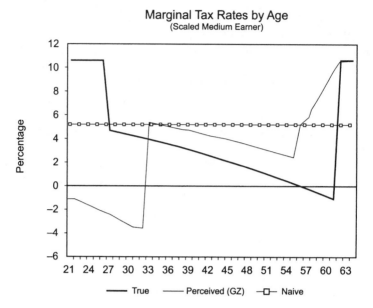

Fig. 3C.1   **Marginal tax rates by age (scaled medium earner)**

very different pattern. In fact, a naive person who considers the 5.3 percent employee share of the tax as their marginal rate will, in a mean-squared deviation sense, be closer to correct than someone who follows the matching rates under this proposal.[3]

Enhanced Ownership

The principal benefit of shifting from our current system to this form of accounts is, according to Geanakoplos and Zeldes, that it would replace Social Security's uncertain promise with a system with "irrevocable ownership of market priced assets." Set aside the question of whether this is a desirable goal—arguably with significant long-run fiscal challenges and uncertainty, you might not want policymakers to preserve the flexibility to adjust on a variety of other margins. Set aside also the observation that this goal could be achieved in other ways, for example, by enacting a constitutional amendment guaranteeing workers a legal property right in their accrued benefits.

The bigger question about this proposal, and virtually all accounts proposals, is would it achieve the stated goal of strengthening the ownership of benefits and reducing political risk? The answer is no—at least not any bet-

3. Editors' note: In the final version of their paper, Geanakoplos and Zeldes introduced the straight-line accrual method in order to address the problem that Jason Furman raised in his original critique above.

ter than the current system. Policymakers could directly "cut" benefits by imposing a tax on account withdrawals, perhaps rationalized as a recapture of the tax benefits associated with the accounts. While it is hard to imagine that it would be politically feasible to impose this retroactively on current retirees, it is equally hard to imagine a politically feasible benefit cut on current retirees. More politically feasible would be to impose a tax on account accumulations, effectively equivalent to phasing in a benefit reduction in the current system. Finally, policymakers could change the matching rule—in the extreme case letting a thirty-five-year-old worker keep all of his PAAWs but not granting him or her any new ones. This would be tantamount to a benefit cut of more than 50 percent. The political economy of these measures does not seem to differ materially from the political economy of cutting entitlements under the existing system: as indeed you would expect if people, or at least interest groups like the American Association of Retired Persons (AARP), are remotely rational.

Even if accounts succeeded in establishing a firmer property right with less political risk than current benefits, this effect would simply be undone elsewhere in the system. For example, if there was a large unforeseen shock, then the inability to alter Social Security benefits would result in larger adjustments in Medicare benefits. As long as any part of the fiscal system is discretionary, then it is impossible to lock in any pattern of inter- or intra-generational redistribution simply by removing discretion from one part of the system—the remainder of the system will just pick up the residual changes.

Downsides of Accounts

Finally, Geanakoplos and Zeldes avoid many of the downsides of accounts. But their specific proposal suffers rather acutely from very large administrative costs relative to the size of accounts. The marketable portion of their accounts is less than 1 percent of payroll, generally considered well below the minimally acceptable level. Moreover, the complicated individual-specific securities they create would themselves require substantially higher transactions cost than more traditional securities as owners of the

Table 3C.1   **Alternative views on Social Security**

Democrats	Republicans
Prefer more redistribution within lifetime (i.e., higher taxes and replacement rates)	Prefer less redistribution within lifetime (i.e., lower taxes and replacement rates)
Prefer more progressivity on the tax side (e.g., raise the taxable maximum)	Prefer more progressivity on the benefit side (e.g., means testing or progressive price indexing)
Hate anything called "accounts"	Love anything called "accounts"

bundles would need a mechanism to track the retirement and death of each of the many thousands of people named on the specific PAAWs.

Would Geanakoplos-Zeldes Form the Basis of a Future Compromise?

Finally, I end with a purely positive question: would I predict that Geanakoplos-Zeldes ultimately forms the basis of a future compromise. In a well-run world, the answer to this question would follow directly from the normative questions asked in the preceding. In the actual world, the answer is probably uncorrelated, but coincidentally also happens to be no.

The three most important differences between Democrats and Republicans are listed in table 3C.1, albeit in somewhat exaggerated and stylized form.

The Geanakoplos-Zeldes plan would be most feasible in a world populated by stupid Republicans and smart Democrats. The stupid Republicans would be so excited about something called "accounts" that they would miss the fact that this plan does very little to achieve most of the goals Republicans set for accounts. The smart Democrats would look past the optics of the accounts to discover that the system preserves intergenerational risk-sharing, a large forced savings component, and inflation-adjusted annuities—plus restores balance by paying for the entire long-run shortfall in Social Security through general revenues, ensuring both current benefit levels and a relatively progressive financing system. Without commenting on the two preconditions individually, I will just note I think it is unlikely that both of them hold simultaneously.

Future Work

Although not likely to be on the agenda in the near future, the Geanakoplos-Zeldes plan is an exciting analytic contribution. I look forward to future research building on their framework. In particular, the most intriguing suggestion in their chapter is a way to achieve robust solvency by matching the benefits incurred by workers in any given year with the payroll taxes paid by those workers in that year. It would be interesting to simulate this proposal and understand how it could be translated back into the language of the defined benefit system as a step toward evaluating whether it should indeed be the basis of a Social Security reform.

II

Retirement Plan Choice

Who Chooses Defined Contribution Plans?

Jeffrey R. Brown and Scott J. Weisbenner

4.1 Introduction

In recent years, numerous proposals have been forwarded to fully or partially replace the defined benefits provided by the U.S. Social Security system with personal retirement accounts (PRAs). A key feature of many personal account proposals, including those of the President's Commission to Strengthen Social Security and the plan forwarded by President Bush in 2005, is that participation in personal accounts would be voluntary. Individuals would be given the opportunity to choose whether to redirect some of their existing payroll taxes away from the current system and into PRAs. In exchange for the ability to participate in the personal accounts program, an individual would give up the right to some portion of the traditional Old-Age, Survivors, and Disability Insurance (OASDI) benefit, a feature that is commonly referred to as a "benefit offset." An interesting and difficult question is who would choose to participate in such a plan were it to be offered.

Jeffrey R. Brown is the William G. Karnes Professor of Finance at the University of Illinois at Urbana-Champaign, and a research associate of the National Bureau of Economic Research. Scott J. Weisbenner is an associate professor of finance at the University of Illinois at Urbana-Champaign, and a faculty research fellow of the National Bureau of Economic Research.

This research was supported by the U.S. Social Security Administration (SSA) through grant #10-P-98363-1-03 to the National Bureau of Economic Research (NBER) as part of the SSA Retirement Research Consortium. The findings and conclusions expressed are solely those of the author(s) and do not represent the views of SSA, any agency of the Federal Government, or of the NBER. We are grateful to the SSA for this support. We are also grateful to Dan Slack, Doug Steele, and other staff members at the State Universities Retirement System for their tireless efforts at providing us with the data for this project, as well as for helpful conversations and comments on the chapter. We thank Sarah Jackson for excellent research assistance.

Understanding participation is of more than academic interest. Participants in personal accounts would face a different risk and return profile of retirement benefits than would nonparticipants, and thus understanding who is most likely to participate might influence one's view of the individual welfare implications of reform. At an aggregate level, participation rates are a critical assumption in understanding the fiscal implications of Social Security reform proposals that involve a redirection of existing payroll tax revenue away from the trust funds and into personal accounts. For a given reform, high participation rates would increase the size of the transition cost that must be financed in the early years of a reform and, correspondingly, would result in larger reductions in pay-as-you-go expenditures in future years. When scoring reform proposals, the Social Security Office of the Chief Actuary typically handles this uncertainty by showing the financial implications of reform under several alternative assumptions, such as 100 percent, 67 percent, 50 percent, and 0 percent. The uncertainty about participation rates is apparent from the comparison of the administration and Congressional Budget Office (CBO) estimates of participation for the president's plan. In its analysis of the president's FY 2007 budget, the CBO estimated that approximately one-third of workers would sign up for the accounts under the President's plan, whereas the OMB projected a two-thirds participation rate (CBO 2006).

As important as participation rates are, there is very little useful guidance in the literature on how to estimate them. Unfortunately, the very large literature on 401(k) participation rates is of only limited use because the alternative to participating is entirely different in a 401(k) than in most Social Security reform proposals. If one chooses not to participate in the 401(k), the alternative is to take the compensation in the form of taxable wages. In such a case, the main trade-off is between current and future consumption. In contrast, in Social Security plans with a benefit offset, the individual would face a trade-off between two alternative methods of financing future consumption. For example, according to President Bush's 2005 proposal, for every dollar that an individual redirected into a personal account, he or she would have been required to give up a traditional benefit amount equal to the annuitized value of that one-dollar contribution accumulated at a 3 percent real rate of interest. Thus, if an individual were to receive an average real rate of return on the personal account balances in excess of 3 percent, then his or her retirement income would be higher due to having participated in the account. In contrast, if the individual's average real return fell below 3 percent, participation in the account would reduce retirement income. Thus, the decision of whether to participate in a Social Security PRA program has less to do with one's views about the relative value of consumption today versus in the future (which is the key decision in a 401[k] plan) and more to do with an individual's beliefs about expected financial market returns, mortality risk, financial and political risk, the value of choice, the value of inheritability, and so forth.

A better way to learn about potential participation rates in a PRA plan would be to analyze situations in which an individual worker has an explicit choice between a defined benefit (DB) and a defined contribution (DC) plan, holding job characteristics fixed. In most cases, however, individuals can only choose their pension type by choosing their employer, and it is quite clear that a firm's pension plan is but one element in a whole vector of characteristics that vary across jobs and firms. Thus, one can never be sure that the decision to work for an employer that offers a 401(k) instead of an employer that offers a DB plan reflects characteristics of the pension as opposed to numerous other differences across the employers. Alternatively, one could attempt to determine the worker characteristics that correlate with valuing DC over DB by looking at firms that switch pension type. Such plan conversions, however, may be driven more by firm level concerns, such as the costs of plan administration, than by employee preferences per se. Even if the cross-sectional variation in which firms choose to convert to a DC plan is correlated with employee preferences, it only tells us that some subset of employees valued this shift, not that all employees at the firm valued such a shift.

Finally, in an ideal world, one would wish to examine the DB versus DC choice in the absence of the confounding effects of the Social Security program itself. In most private-sector plans, even if individuals were given a DB versus DC choice, it would be for income that is above that which they expect to receive from Social Security in the first place. While there have been several studies that have been able to examine an explicit DB versus DC choice, including among employees at a large nonprofit firm (Yang 2005), among corrections officers in Michigan (Papke 2004), and among faculty in the North Carolina university system (Clark, Ghent, and McDermed 2006), employees in all three cases were also covered by the existing Social Security system. Given that the value of annuitization, for example, is a declining function of the fraction of wealth already annuitized, this may make individuals more likely to choose a DC if it is on top of the DB already provided by Social Security.

In this chapter, we make use of a unique data set of employees in the State Universities Retirement System (SURS) of Illinois. This sample has four key features that make it a particularly valuable environment for studying the DB versus DC plan choice. First, these employees are given an explicit choice between a DB and a DC plan, holding all job characteristics fixed.[1] Specifically, in their first six months of employment, employees are asked

---

1. As reported in Clark, Ghent, and McDermed (2006), the choice between a DB and a DC plan is a common feature of pension plans at public (but not private) universities.

to make a one-time, lifetime, irrevocable choice among three retirement plans: (1) a traditional formula-based DB plan; (2) a "portable DB plan," which is slightly less generous than the ordinary DB if one retires from the system, but more generous if they take an early lump-sum distribution; and (3) the "Self-Managed Plan" or SMP, which is a 100 percent self-directed DC plan. Individuals who fail to make an active choice within the first six months of employment are automatically defaulted into the traditional DB plan.

Second, because Illinois is one of several states that opted out of the Social Security system, wages that individuals earn from SURS-covered employment are not covered by Social Security, meaning that no OASDI payroll taxes are withheld and no OASDI benefits accrue based on these earnings.[2] Thus, unless an individual has substantial employment earnings outside of the SURS system, it will be SURS and not Social Security that will provide the primary source of income in retirement.

Third, the combined employer/employee retirement contributions to the SURS system are, at minimum, 14.6 percent of annual salary, which is larger than the payroll tax paid by those in the Social Security system. Therefore, the SURS system looms large as part of a participant's lifetime financial plan.

Fourth, the SURS data includes a diverse group of employees, including campus administrators, faculty members, clerical staff, individuals in the employ of university police and fire services, and others. Prior studies of the DB versus DC choice using state university employees (e.g., Clark, Ghent, and McDermed 2006; Clark and Pitts 1999) were limited to faculty members only, and thus it is more difficult to generalize the results to populations that are less highly educated. Our sample allows us the opportunity to more carefully examine how the DB versus DC decision might vary across broad education and occupation groups.

Along with these advantages come two limitations. First, unlike most proposals for having voluntary personal accounts as part of Social Security, the SURS system includes a third "hybrid" choice that adds an extra dimension of complexity to the analysis. Second, as will be discussed in more detail, the three SURS plans are not actuarially equivalent, and thus some care must be taken in applying the numerical estimates to an environment in which the choices are actuarially fair, as is the case in some (although not all) personal account proposals. On net, however, we believe this analysis is quite useful for illuminating key issues in the DB versus DC decision.

2. According to the U.S. Government Accounting Office (GAO; 2003), "historically, Social Security did not require coverage of government employees because they had their own retirement systems, and there was concern over the question of the federal government's right to impose a tax on state governments." Other states whose employees do not participate in Social Security include California, Colorado, Louisiana, Massachusetts, Ohio, and Texas, among others.

Using administrative data on the full universe of SURS-covered employees since the plan choice was first made available starting in 1998 and 1999, we analyze what types of employees are most likely to choose the DC plan over the portable or traditional DB plan. We have two major findings. First, despite the projections by SURS at the start of the program that a majority of new employees would actively select the SMP or portable plan, in fact, the majority of new employees never make any active pension choice, and thus are defaulted into the traditional plan. After the initial publicity surrounding the introduction of plan choice started to fade, the proportion of new employees not making a choice, and hence defaulting into the traditional plan, increased from 43 percent in 1999 to roughly three-fifths over the period 2001 to 2004.[3] Second, we find that approximately 15 percent of new employees choose the SMP, despite the fact that the SMP is likely an inferior choice due to plan parameters that make it less generous than the portable plan under reasonable assumptions. Interestingly, we find that individuals are more likely than average to choose the SMP if they are more highly educated (as proxied by being an academic employee as opposed to staff, as well as being at a university as opposed to a community college), have higher earnings, are married, and work at an institution where a higher fraction of other employees also chose the SMP. We attribute much of the selection of the SMP to framing effects in how the plan choices are communicated to new employees, but we discuss alternative explanations as well, including beliefs about political risk facing the DB and portable DB systems.

This chapter is structured as follows: Section 4.2 outlines the basic structure of the SURS system, including more details about each of the plan options and how the choices are made. Section 4.3 discusses the administrative data in more detail, including its strengths and limitations. In section 4.4, we outline our empirical methods and present some simple tabulations of plan choice. Section 4.5 reports more formal results. Section 4.6 concludes and sets forth several directions for subsequent research.

4.2 SURS Choices

4.2.1 Background on SURS and Allowance of Choice

As the name implies, the State Universities Retirement System of Illinois (SURS) is the retirement program for all employees of the Illinois state university and community college system. Established in 1941, SURS "serves over 70 employers in Illinois, including state universities,

---

3. There are a number of reasons that the pattern of plan choices may differ over time. For example, in addition to differences in press attention to the issues, stock market performance changed markedly over this period. Our administrative data do not allow us to disentangle these and other possible hypotheses.

community colleges, and state agencies. It employs more than 100 people in offices in Champaign and Chicago and provides benefit services to over 180,000 members throughout the world" (SURS Web site, June 19, 2006). "SURS covers all faculty and support staff of Illinois higher public education including universities, colleges, Class I community colleges, scientific surveys, and other related agencies" (SURS Traditional Defined Benefit Package, 1). There is a large range in the size of the employers, with several state agencies (e.g., the State Water Survey) having only a few new employees during our sample period, while the University of Illinois at Chicago and the University of Illinois at Urbana-Champaign together comprise about one out of every four new employees over this period.

As noted in the preceding, the employees include university, college or campus administrators, faculty members, administrative and clerical staff, individuals in the employ of university police, and others. In general, an individual will participate as long as their position requires them to work "continuously for at least one academic term or 4 months, whichever is less, and . . . employment is not temporary, intermittent, or irregular . . . SURS participation ends on the date you retire or terminate employment with a SURS-covered employer" (SURS Traditional Benefit Member Guide, 1). Eligibility does not extend to students regularly attending classes at a SURS-covered employer who are employed on a part-time or temporary basis for that employer, to J-1 or F-1 visa holders who have not yet established residency, or to current annuitants from SURS.

Social Security taxes are not withheld from SURS earnings, and SURS participants are not eligible for Social Security coverage based on their employment with a SURS-covered employer.[4] The State Universities Retirement System of Illinois withholds 8 percent of salary as an employee contribution to SURS. The state/employer contribution varies by plan, and will be described in more detail in the following.

Prior to 1998, all employees in the SURS system were covered by the traditional DB system. In the mid-1990s, however, pressure began building on the state legislature to offer a DC option to state employees. In 1997, the Illinois Legislature passed a law allowing participating employers to offer individuals a choice of three plans. The addition of a DC option was viewed as having three key benefits. First, it was believed that a DC plan would be more attractive to potential new employees. The SURS executive director at the time was quoted as saying "The legislation passed because universities were saying they needed it to attract people from other states."[5] Second, the creation of the SMP option was viewed as a cost-reduction

---

4. Participants hired after March 1986 are subject to withholding for Medicare.
5. Natalie Boehme, "University Workers Get Greater Choice in Retirement Planning," *The State Journal Register,* March 12, 1999, 39.

measure by the state, due to the fact that the state's contributions to the SMP are lower than the contributions required to fully fund benefits under the traditional DB option.[6] Finally, the shift was also promoted as a way to impose fiscal discipline on the state legislature. State Senator Peter Fitzgerald, a leading advocate of the switch, argued that the DC plan would force lawmakers to put the money up front so that employees could invest it, rather than offering promises of future benefits that the legislature had a history of underfunding.[7]

The next three subsections summarize the key features of each of the three pension options.

4.2.2 Traditional Benefit Package

This SURS DB retirement plan is the only one that was in place prior to 1998. As of the writing of this chapter, the traditional plan remains the default option for individuals who do not make an active plan designation within six months of their hire date (or specifically, the date that is received by SURS as the individuals' certification of employment.) Employees contribute 8 percent of pay, which is the same contribution rate as in the other two options. Of this 8 percent, SURS reports that 6.5 percent is designated to fund the normal retirement benefit, 0.5 percent is designated to fund automatic annual increases in retirement benefits, and 1 percent is designated to fund survivor benefits, although it is not clear how closely these reported designations match actuarial costs. Because all SURS-covered workers are employees of the State of Illinois, the employer contribution to SURS is a general state obligation. For participants in the traditional plan, SURS documents state "the State's share for a retirement annuity averages about 9.1 percent of the total earnings of all SURS participants in a Defined Benefit Plan" (SURS Traditional Benefit Member Guide, 2). This 9.1 percent figure is an oversimplification and most likely represents a lower bound on the average cost to the state. Indeed, for fiscal year 2007, the employer normal cost for the various benefits and expenses associated with the DB plan (which includes both the traditional and the portable plan) are approximately 10.8 percent of payroll.[8]

Benefits from the traditional plan are paid as life annuities. An individual is eligible to receive benefits at age fifty-five with at least eight years of service, age sixty-two with five years of service, or at any age with thirty years of service (if employment terminated after August 2, 2002). An individual must start receiving a retirement annuity no later than

6. Section 15-158.3 of the SURS governing statute requires an actuarial assessment of "the extent to which employee optional retirement plan participation has reduced the State's required contributions to the System . . . in relation to what the State's contributions to the System would have been . . . if the self-managed plan had not been implemented."

7. Don Thomson, "Fitzgerald Floats Trial Balloon to Change State Pension System to a 401(k) Plan," *Daily Herald,* January 14, 1997.

8. Based on personal communication with SURS, August 7, 2006.

April 1 of the year following the year he or she reaches age seventy and a half if he or she is not participating in SURS or another Illinois state system.

For most employees there are two formulas for calculating the retirement annuity.[9] For each individual, the benefit will be calculated each way, and the worker receives the larger of the calculated amounts.

The two formulas are:

1. *The General Formula:* For those retiring at age sixty after July 1997, the formula is:

Benefit = 2.2% × Years of Service × Final Average Earnings.

For nondisabled individuals with less than thirty years of service, there is an early retirement actuarial reduction of 0.5 percent for each month under age sixty. For retirement after August 2, 2002, retirement at any age—without reduction—is permitted if a member has thirty or more years of service.

2. *Money Purchase Formula:* For most individuals, the money purchase formula is equal to 6.5 percent of the employee's salary (6.5 percentage points of the 8 percent contribution is for the retirement benefit, excluding survivor and inflation adjustments), plus a 140 percent match by the State of Illinois, plus interest accumulated at a rate set by the SURS board all divided by a unisex annuity factor.

Both these approaches to calculating the benefit have numerous additional complexities that we do not expand on here in the interest of space. For example, there are special rules governing a supplemental minimum annuity guarantee, reversionary annuities to provide a spouse or dependent with higher income than the usual survivor benefits, and an additional formula that applies only to police officers and firefighters.

For all employees, the benefit is calculated under both methods (with one extra in the case of police and fire), and the individual receives the higher of these benefit amounts. In recent years, the majority of retirees have received the highest level of benefits under the money purchase formula. The only additional restriction is that, regardless of method, benefits in retirement cannot exceed 80 percent of final average pay (and some individuals have lower maximum pensions based on their termination date.) Benefits are automatically increased by 3 percent every January 1. There are also generous survivor benefits both before and after retirement. In particular, the benefit that comes out of these calculations is automatically paid as a joint and 50 percent contingent survivor annuity. If a single individual retires under the traditional plan, then in addition to receiving

9. A third option, known as the minimum annuity formula, is so rarely used that it is largely obsolete.   .

the calculated monthly benefit, he or she is entitled to a refund of 1/8 of his contributions plus interest.

The service credit is a key parameter in the calculation of one's benefits. In any academic year (from September 1 through August 31), an individual may earn no more than one year of service credit, and it is possible to earn fractional years of credit. A complex set of rules determines how service credits are affected by disability leave, sick leave, unused sick leave, prior service with other employers, military service, and other similar situations. A second key parameter is an individual's final average earnings (or "final rate of earnings"). This is basically the average earnings in the four consecutive academic years of service in which the individual's earnings were the highest. There are limitations on the rate at which earnings are permitted to grow year over year as part of this calculation.

While the traditional benefit package is quite generous relative to most private-sector plans, it is important to bear in mind that the SURS package must substitute for Social Security as well as a private pension. Indeed, the 2.2 percent formula multiplier is, if anything, a bit less generous than that in other public pension plans whose employees are not covered by Social Security. A recent study of public pensions (Ford 2005) indicates an average formula multiplier of 2.27 percent among such states (versus 1.95 percent average among public pension plans in states that are covered by Social Security). Of course, over the 2001 to 2005 period, approximately two-thirds of SURS retirees received benefits via the money purchase option, which means this benefit was higher than that calculated under the traditional formula.

In short, the traditional benefit package is a fairly generous pension plan for those who retire from the system. The major downside of this plan, however, is that it is not very generous for those who leave the system early and take a refund. Regardless of length of service, participants in the traditional benefit package who take a refund from the system upon terminating employment will receive their own contributions (equal to 8 percent of salary) plus a 4.5 percent interest rate. No employer or state contributions are refunded, even after the individual is vested. Many individuals who leave the system early would be better off leaving their contributions in the SURS system and claiming a benefit based on the money purchase formula.

In contrast to private-sector DB plans, the SURS benefits are not insured by the Pension Benefit Guarant Corporation (PBGC), and it is worth noting that the State of Illinois has massively underfunded its share of the pension obligations. As of March 31, 2006, the SURS investment portfolio (which covers both the traditional and the portable plan options) was valued at nearly $14.5 billion, but faced liabilities of over $21 billion, for a funding ratio of only 68 percent. In actuality, the funding problem is worse than these official statistics indicated because the liabilities are discounted using a high discount rate that reflects the expected return on plan assets rather than using a riskless rate of interest that would be appropriate given the constitutional guarantee of benefits to participants (discussed in the following). The degree of official underfunding is widely reported in the Illinois press, as well as in the regular participant newsletters sent out by SURS, and thus most participants are likely aware that there is political risk to their future benefits.

This political risk is, however, substantially mitigated by the fact that Article XIII, Section 5 of the Illinois Constitution states that "membership in any pension or retirement system of the State . . . shall be an enforceable contractual relationship, the benefits of which shall not be diminished or impaired." This "impairment clause," as it has come to be known, means that the legislature cannot reduce the generosity of the SURS benefit without a constitutional amendment. Nonetheless, uncertainty about the ability of the state to make good on its future funding obligations may lead some individuals to prefer the SMP. Indeed, as of July 1, 2005, the power to set the interest rate used in calculating benefits under the money purchase formula has been transferred from the SURS board to the state comptroller. In addition, the money purchase option was eliminated for employees starting after July 1, 2005. Such actions likely reinforce the belief that future benefits from SURS are not free from political risk.

4.2.3   Portable Benefit Package

The portable benefit package is a modified version of the traditional package. The first key difference is that if the person leaves the system early and takes a refund of his or her contributions, he or she has historically received a rate of interest that is substantially higher than the 4.5 percent provided by the traditional plan. Indeed, this effective interest rate (which, until June 30, 2005 was the same rate used to calculate retirement benefits under the money purchase option) has averaged over 8 percent for the past twenty years.[10] If an individual has at least five years of service and is thus vested, he or she also receives a full dollar-for-dollar match from the state. In short, for any individual who departs SURS service and takes a refund rather than leaving the money in the SURS system, the portable plan is far more generous than the traditional plan.

The second key difference is that the benefits from the portable plan are not as generous as the traditional plan if the individual retires from the system. In particular, for participants in the traditional plan, the monthly benefit amount is paid as a joint and survivor annuity. Single individuals under the traditional plan can take 1/8 of their contributions plus interest as

---

10. Since July 1, 2005, the state comptroller sets the effective interest rate for the money purchase option when calculating retirement benefit. The SURS board continues to set the effective interest rate for refund calculations. Since July 1, 2006, these rates have diverged.

a lump sum at retirement in lieu of the survivor benefits. In contrast, under the portable plan, the retirement benefit is a paid as a single life annuity, and married individuals must accept an actuarial reduction to convert it to a joint and survivor annuity.

There are other differences as well. For example, whereas participants in the traditional plan are required to annuitize their assets, portable plan participants do have the option to take a lump sum at retirement. Doing so, however, comes at the high cost of losing eligibility for retiree health benefits.

4.2.4   Self-Managed Plan (SMP)

The SMP is an entirely participant-directed defined contribution plan that invests a total of 14.6 percent of salary (8% employee and 6.6% employer) into retirement accounts.[11] Participants are able to choose from a variety of mutual funds and annuity contracts from the Teachers Insurance and Annuity Association-College Retirement Equities Fund (TIAA-CREF) and Fidelity. Upon full vesting after five years of service, the individual is entitled to a 100 percent refund of both employer and employee contributions, plus any investment gains or losses. Upon retirement, the individual is able to choose from a wide range of annuities (e.g., joint and survivor with 50 percent, 75 percent or 100 percent survivor benefits, and the option of ten-, fifteen-, and twenty-year period certain guarantees) or a lump sum. As with the portable plan, however, retirees must annuitize their full account balance in order to be eligible for retiree health benefits from the State of Illinois.

All of the educational information provided by SURS, including the instructional videos, the program guides and online information, guides new SURS participants through the plan choice by focusing on the distinction between DB and DC plans. A reasonable inference from this material, even by financially sophisticated employees, is that the traditional benefit package is the best choice for individuals who expect to retire from SURS covered employment, while the SMP option is a good choice for highly mobile employees (such as new, untenured faculty members) who value choice and are comfortable making their own investment decisions. The portable plan is largely presented as a modified version of the DB. Indeed, much of the material is structured so as to guide individuals down the DB versus DC path first and then discuss the portable versus traditional distinction only after one has gone down the DB path. Thus, many employees may be left with the general impression that the portable plan lies somewhere between the traditional and the SMP on nearly all dimensions.

---

11. The 6.6 percent rate has been the rate applied since the program's inception. Technically, this rate could rise slightly if SURS decides that the cost of providing disability benefits to SMP participants is less than 1 percent. It cannot rise beyond 7.6 percent, and indeed is unlikely rise to anywhere near this level due to the cost of paying disability benefits.

A more careful examination, however, suggests that the SMP may be an inferior choice, relative to the portable plan, for most employees, regardless of their expected employment longevity with a SURS employer. To understand its inferiority, it is useful to consider the benefits from these two options for individuals at different points in their careers.

First, consider an employee who leaves SURS employment and takes a lump-sum refund from the system. If they leave service prior to vesting (i.e., individuals with less than five years of service), the differences are small. In both cases, individuals receive their own 8 percent contributions. In the portable plan, the individual receives the SURS rate of interest, while in the SMP, they receive actual investment returns. After vesting, however, the differences are much larger. Under the portable plan, the individual also receives a full 8 percent match from the state, while in the SMP, the individual only receives 6.6 percent. Thus, for the SMP to be an optimal choice based solely on relative returns (i.e., ignoring political risk), the individual must expect to earn investment returns that are sufficient to exceed the rate of interest credited by SURS to the portable plan (which has averaged 8 to 9 percent nominal for the past twenty years), *plus* enough extra return to make up the 1.4 percent of salary shortfall in the state contribution rate. Assuming an 8 percent return for the portable plan, SMP participants must expect annual rates of return of 8.5 percent even with a thirty-year time horizon (those with a five-year time horizon must achieve an 11.2 percent average return).[12] Note that nominal returns of this level are substantially greater than what one should expect from a diversified stock/bond portfolio using historical U.S. data, let alone what one should expect if the equity premium going forward is lower than its historical realized value.

Second, consider an employee who retires from SURS. In this case, the employee receives the higher of the two methods of benefit calculation discussed in the preceding. Just focusing on the money purchase option, the individual must, as in the case of a refund, beat the 8 to 9 percent effective interest rate plus make up for the contribution shortfall. Furthermore, even if the effective interest rate were to decline in the future, the general formula provides a benefit floor equal to 2.2 percent of final average salary for each year of service. In short, for long-service employees, the SMP is an inferior choice to the traditional or the portable plans.

Thus, unlike the theoretical comparison between DB and DC provided by Bodie, Marcus, and Merton (1988), in which there is a constraint that the two plan types have equal costs to the employer, in the case of SURS, the required employer contributions to the SMP plan are significantly lower than that of the two DB options. Given this, and the resulting disad-

12. These calculations assume a 3 percent annual increase in salary and a fixed investment return from the SMP.

vantage of the SMP to the portable plan at all time horizons, it may be surprising that anyone chooses it. However, many of the differences just described, such as the difference in the match and the magnitude of the effective interest rate, are not easily discernable from the material provided by SURS. Further, as previously mentioned, the framing of the pension plan choice as first a decision between DB and DC, as opposed to a direct comparison of all three options simultaneously, may also help explain participation in the SMP. The SURS manual explicitly cites as a disadvantage of a DB plan that "members with short service, or those who expect to leave their job soon, will not earn a large benefit," while a key advantage of a DC plan is that "members can transfer balances to other defined contribution plans should they change employers" (SURS, *The Power of Choice,* http://www.surs.org/pdfs/power_of_choice.pdf, 5). However, while the portable plan is classified as a DB-type plan, members with short service are treated essentially the same under the SMP and portable plan options, with the accumulated balances of both allowed to be transferred to another plan if the worker changes employers (including employer contributions if vesting has occurred).

In addition to a simple lack of understanding of key plan parameters, there are other reasons that individuals may prefer the SMP option, despite its apparent financial disadvantages. These include concerns about political risk in the traditional and portable plans, arising from the fact that the State of Illinois has consistently underfunded the plans. While there is a state constitutional guarantee against the impairment of benefits for current state pension plan participants, the substantial underfunding of the plans may lead some participants to question the long-term ability of the state to make good on its pension promises. In contrast, the state contributions to the SMP are made immediately. Individuals may also have overly optimistic beliefs about future equity market returns that lead them to believe that their SMP investments can outperform the SURS rate of interest. Individuals may also simply place a high value on the ability to choose their investment portfolio. While we are not able to distinguish among these various reasons in the current administrative data, we are planning to address these issues in follow-on work using a survey of SURS participants.

Finally, another difference between the SMP and the other two plans (portable and traditional), is that employer contributions commence after the employee formally selects the SMP option and not when employment starts. In the portable and traditional plans, the participant receives credit back to the date of employment for both benefit calculation and refund purposes.[13] Thus, a four-month lag between the start of employment and

13. In this sense, it is as if the employer made contributions retroactively to the first day of employment. In reality, the state contributions are made on an aggregate, not individual, basis and are generally not made at the level that would be required for the plan to remain fully funded.

selecting a retirement plan will result in the worker losing four months of employer contributions in the SMP plan, but will result in no loss of employer contributions in the other two plans. This provides a financial incentive to make a quick decision if one is considering the SMP.

4.3   Data

The State Universities Retirement System of Illinois has provided us with rich data containing administrative records for the entire population of workers who have started working for a SURS-covered employer subsequent to that employer's offering of plan choice. The State Universities Retirement System of Illinois provided us with data on both (1) employees who had already been covered by SURS at the point in time at which their employer first began offering choice and (2) new employees who have joined the system since choice was first offered. We are confident that the new employee data is complete, that is, that we observe individuals who were given a choice, even if they subsequently left the system, became disabled, or died. With the preexisting employee data, however, we are not confident that we have a complete set of records of individuals who subsequently left the system. Therefore, we will focus our analysis on the "new employee" sample, where there are no concerns about sample selection. Fortunately, this is also the more interesting population to examine because their choice is not "contaminated" by the fact that they had significant prior service under the traditional plan. For preexisting employees who switched to the SMP at the time the new plans were initially adopted, they had to forfeit all prior employer contributions, which should have strongly tilted the decision against the SMP (although interestingly, a nontrivial number of individuals made this choice).

As such, our analysis focuses on those individuals that began service with a SURS-covered employer in 1999 or after. While most employers adopted the new choices at some point during the 1998 calendar year, we only know the year in which an employee began service with a SURS-covered employer, and not the month, so we are unable to determine which employees joining the system in 1998 joined the employer after adoption of the new plan options. By focusing on the 1999 or after sample, we are confident that we are examining the "postchoice" cohorts.

The universe of individuals beginning employment in 1999 or after (through 2004) consists of approximately 63,000 observations. However, SURS was unable to provide complete earnings records for the entire sample, and thus the sample size drops to just over 45,000 when we condition on observing earnings.[14]

---

14. Our measure of earnings is the reported earnings in the second year of employment. While we would have liked to use the respondent's first year of earnings, we were given actual

Table 4.1   Plan choice by start year

	Start year						
Variable	Total (1)	1999 (2)	2000 (3)	2001 (4)	2002 (5)	2003 (6)	2004 (7)
Made an active choice	0.443	0.569	0.497	0.421	0.394	0.396	0.402
Chose SMP	0.153	0.220	0.215	0.138	0.115	0.118	0.125
Chose portable	0.186	0.204	0.175	0.186	0.190	0.182	0.180
Chose traditional	0.104	0.146	0.107	0.096	0.089	0.096	0.097
Defaulted into traditional	0.557	0.431	0.503	0.579	0.606	0.604	0.598
No. of observations	45,303	6,596	7,187	8,649	7,975	7,158	7,738

Note: SMP = self-managed plan.

In table 4.1, we report the fraction of the population that makes each plan choice in each year of our 1999 to 2004 sample. Over the entire sample period, we see that slightly under half the sample (44 percent) made an active pension selection, while the majority (56 percent) were defaulted into the traditional benefits package. The fact that the default option draws such a large number of individuals could reflect either the power of the default itself, as one would expect given the evidence in this area (e.g., Madrian and Shea 2001; Choi et al. 2001), or it could simply reflect that a large number of individuals concluded that the traditional plan was the best choice and, therefore, just allowed SURS to default them into it. Another 10 percent of participants made an active choice into the traditional plan, bringing the total number of participants in the traditional plan to nearly two-thirds of the sample. Approximately 15 percent of the sample chose the SMP, while just under 19 percent chose the portable package.

A striking feature of the data is that the fraction of individuals accepting the default option has grown steadily over time, from 43 percent in 1999 to around 58 percent in 2001, where it has remained relative stable since. This time series pattern perhaps reflects the flurry of local press attention paid during the introduction of plan choice, which quickly subsided.

The fraction choosing the SMP also shows substantial changes over time. Specifically, in both 1999 and 2000, 22 percent of the sample chose

---

rather than annualized earnings during the first year. Thus, for many individuals who worked only part of the year, we observe only a fraction of their annual salary. We are unable to annualize the data because SURS did not provide us with the month that a person started employment. In addition to dropping observations that are missing earnings, we have experimented with several other approaches (including a dummy variable for missing along with its interaction with earnings, imputing each missing value with a predicted value, etc.) and found that our coefficient estimates were not terribly sensitive, which is not surprising given that the reason earnings is missing is not systematically correlated with plan choice. This is often called an "ignorable case" of missing data in the econometrics literature.

the SMP. These years came after a period of extremely high equity market returns, which peaked in early 2000. In 2001, the fraction choosing the SMP fell to only 13.8 percent and declined further to 11.5 percent in 2002. In contrast, while the SMP has seen a sharp decline in enrollment from 2000 to 2004, enrollment in the portable plan has remained relatively stable in the 18 to 19 percent range over the same period.

In table 4.2, we report summary statistics for a number of key variables. We first report classifications by occupation (academic, staff, or police), interacted whether the individual works for a university, community college,

Table 4.2   **Descriptive statistics**

			Plan choice			
Variable	Full sample (1)	Made active choice (2)	SMP (3)	Portable (4)	Traditional (5)	Defaulted into traditional (6)
Occupation						
Academic (university)	0.315	0.395	0.510	0.415	0.191	0.251
Staff (university)	0.218	0.237	0.159	0.242	0.345	0.202
Police (university)	0.003	0.002	0.001	0.003	0.005	0.004
Academic (community college)	0.233	0.179	0.190	0.143	0.229	0.275
Staff (community college)	0.151	0.141	0.108	0.152	0.170	0.159
Police (community college)	0.004	0.004	0.001	0.005	0.006	0.004
Other type of institution	0.077	0.042	0.032	0.042	0.055	0.104
Plan status						
Active	0.663	0.732	0.787	0.675	0.753	0.609
Disabled	0.003	0.003	0.002	0.004	0.004	0.003
Retired	0.000	0.000	0.000	0.000	0.000	0.000
Dead	0.001	0.000	0.000	0.000	0.000	0.001
Left with vested benefits	0.016	0.022	0.025	0.024	0.014	0.011
Left prior to vesting	0.317	0.243	0.186	0.297	0.228	0.377
Financial						
Earnings in $100,000s	0.241	0.318	0.390	0.303	0.237	0.180
Percentage time worked	0.722	0.803	0.799	0.838	0.745	0.659
Demographics						
Female	0.568	0.582	0.525	0.612	0.611	0.557
Single	0.262	0.340	0.306	0.401	0.280	0.200
Married	0.590	0.626	0.669	0.563	0.677	0.561
Age	41.5	42.2	41.9	40.9	45.0	40.9
Reciprocal service agreement	0.137	0.114	0.102	0.097	0.162	0.156
No. of observations	45,303	20,049	6,920	8,421	4,708	25,254

Note: SMP = self-managed plan.

or some other employer type. The single largest group, comprising just under one-third of the sample, are academic employees at state universities. Staff members at universities and academics at community colleges each contribute another 22 to 23 percent of the sample, while community college staff comprise 15 percent of the sample. Police account for less than 1 percent of the sample. Approximately 8 percent of the sample is employed by a state agency other than a university or community college.

Interestingly, only two-thirds of the participants in our sample are considered "active" SURS participants, meaning that they are still employed by a SURS-covered employer and thus making contributions. Most of the rest left SURS employment, while a trivial fraction of the sample had died or retired. Individuals who leave SURS service after five years are considered vested and thus eligible to receive state contributions along with their own if they choose the portable SMP plan, and thus we will control for this in our analysis.

A majority of new employees (57 percent) are women, and 59 percent of our sample is married.[15] The average age in the sample is just over forty-one years. Approximately 14 percent of the sample has "reciprocal service" from another state-administered pension plan, such as the State Teacher's Retirement System: this is an important control because these individuals may have a financial incentive to stay with the traditional plan due to rules that coordinate benefits across various public plans in the State of Illinois.

Average earnings in the sample are only $24,100 per year, but this figure includes part-time employees (which are over one-quarter of our sample). If we condition the sample on being considered a full-time employee, the average earnings are roughly $43,000 for an academic, $35,000 for a police officer, and $28,000 for staff. In addition to these covariates, we also know information about the individual's three-digit zip code and his or her campus, which we will use in some of the following specifications.

While our data are quite rich in many respects, they have the usual limitation of administrative data in that we do not know many potentially relevant demographic characteristics, such as health status, or non-SURS financial resources such as wealth, spousal earnings, or non-SURS earnings.

4.4   Unconditional Tabulations and Empirical Methods

When an individual joins a SURS-covered employer, there are four possible outcomes with respect to their pension choice:

---

15. For administrative reasons, marital status was missing for some of the individuals who accepted the default option. For these individuals, we imputed their marital status using a probit analysis on those individuals who took the default option and whose marital status was known.

1. The individual chose the self-managed plan.
2. The individual chose the portable benefits package.
3. The individual actively chose the traditional benefits package.
4. The individual made no active choice and was thus defaulted into the traditional benefits package.

Table 4.3 displays the retirement plan choices made across various groups based on occupation, plan status, and demographics. These unconditional tabulations suggest that academics at universities are more than twice as likely to enroll in the SMP (the DC plan) and are significantly less likely to actively select or be defaulted in to the traditional (DB) plan than are other employees. Those employees that left their job before vesting (i.e., in less than five years) are more apt to have made no pension choice and thus be defaulted into the traditional plan ex ante than are em-

Table 4.3   **Plan choice by group**

| | Plan choice | | | |
| | | | | Defaulted into traditional (4) |
Variable	SMP (1)	Portable (2)	Traditional (3)	
Occupation				
Academic (university)	0.247	0.245	0.063	0.445
Staff (university)	0.111	0.206	0.164	0.518
Police (university)	0.028	0.162	0.155	0.655
Academic (community college)	0.125	0.114	0.102	0.660
Staff (community college)	0.109	0.186	0.117	0.588
Police (community college)	0.035	0.227	0.157	0.581
Plan Status				
Active	0.181	0.189	0.118	0.512
Disabled	0.092	0.239	0.146	0.523
Retired	0.000	0.750	0.000	0.250
Dead	0.000	0.087	0.087	0.826
Left with vested benefits	0.239	0.277	0.092	0.392
Left prior to vesting	0.090	0.174	0.075	0.662
Demographics				
Female	0.141	0.200	0.112	0.547
Male	0.168	0.167	0.094	0.571
Married	0.164	0.168	0.113	0.555
Not married	0.134	0.216	0.089	0.561
Reciprocal service				
Yes	0.114	0.131	0.123	0.632
No	0.159	0.195	0.101	0.546

Note: SMP = self-managed plan

ployees who ended up staying with their employer or stayed long enough to be vested. This could reflect that, for this group of short-tenured workers, the pension choice is not viewed as being of much importance (i.e., differences in plan benefits are much more striking after vesting).

To more formally analyze these plan choices and their determinants, we follow two complementary approaches. First, we analyze a series of linear probability models to provide simple-to-interpret point estimates (marginal effects from probit models are similar). We define the dependent variable y_i in six different ways: (1) chose SMP, (2) chose portable, (3) chose or defaulted into traditional, (4) made any "active" choice (versus defaulting), (5) actively chose traditional, conditional on being in traditional, and (6) chose traditional, conditional on making an active choice. These will be explained in more detail in the following. We include a full set of control variables.

A second approach is to use a multinomial logit model, in recognition of the fact that the individual is choosing from among four distinct outcomes that do not have a natural ordering. In the multinomial logit model, we estimate a set of coefficients $\beta^{1(\mathrm{smp})}$, $\beta^{2(\mathrm{port})}$, $\beta^{3(\mathrm{trad})}$, and $\beta^{4(\mathrm{default})}$ corresponding to each outcome category, such that the probability of an individual choosing SMP is:

$$\Pr(y = 1) = \frac{e^{X\beta^1}}{e^{X\beta^1} + e^{X\beta^2} + e^{X\beta^3} + e^{X\beta^4}}.$$

To identify a multinomial model, it is standard to select one set of coefficients equal to zero so that the remaining set of coefficients measures the change relative to the base group. In our specifications, we will use as our base group those individuals who failed to make an active choice and thus defaulted into the traditional plan ($y = 4$) and thus set $\beta^{4(\mathrm{default})} = 0$.

Thus, the *relative* probability of choosing the SMP to defaulting into the traditional plan is:

$$\frac{\Pr(y = 1)}{\Pr(y = 4)} = e^{X\beta^{1(\mathrm{smp})}}.$$

Thus, the way to interpret the coefficients is that the exponentiated value of a coefficient is the relative risk ratio for a one unit change in the corresponding variable, where the risk is being measured is the "risk" of choosing SMP relative to taking the default option. The elements of X are the same as in the linear probability models. In our tables, we will report the relative risk ratios for ease of interpretation.

4.5   Results on Plan Choice

4.5.1   Who Chooses the SMP, Portable, and Traditional?

Table 4.4 reports results from six linear probability models. We begin in columns (1), (2), and (3) with an analysis of who chooses the SMP,

Table 4.4   Ordinary least squares estimate of plan choice

	Dependent variable					
Independent variable	SMP (1)	Portable (2)	Traditional (3)	Any active choice (4)	Choose traditional, given traditional (5)	Choose traditional, given choice (6)
Community college	-0.036***	-0.009	0.047***	-0.017**	0.025***	0.081***
	(0.006)	(0.006)	(0.008)	(0.008)	(0.007)	(0.012)
Other type of institution	0.006	-0.012	0.009	-0.008	-0.004	0.036**
	(0.008)	(0.009)	(0.012)	(0.013)	(0.008)	(0.018)
Staff	-0.097***	-0.032***	0.130***	0.053***	0.078***	0.188***
	(0.005)	(0.005)	(0.006)	(0.006)	(0.006)	(0.008)
Staff (community college)	0.064***	0.043***	-0.107***	0.043***	-0.063***	-0.169***
	(0.007)	(0.008)	(0.009)	(0.010)	(0.009)	(0.015)
Police	-0.231***	-0.076**	0.308***	-0.221***	0.034	0.336***
	(0.016)	(0.031)	(0.035)	(0.041)	(0.037)	(0.073)
Police (community college)	0.129***	0.152***	-0.282***	0.252***	0.039	-0.234**
	(0.022)	(0.045)	(0.048)	(0.056)	(0.053)	(0.093)
Disabled	-0.069***	0.015	0.054	-0.073*	-0.037	-0.021
	(0.023)	(0.037)	(0.040)	(0.043)	(0.043)	(0.056)
Retired	-0.183***	0.418*	-0.242	0.106	-0.369***	-0.260***
	(0.038)	(0.227)	(0.231)	(0.256)	(0.023)	(0.051)
Dead	-0.153***	-0.093	0.245***	-0.285***	-0.107*	0.236
	(0.020)	(0.059)	(0.063)	(0.083)	(0.063)	(0.229)
Left with vested benefits	-0.006	0.056***	-0.051***	0.000	-0.063***	-0.071***
	(0.016)	(0.017)	(0.018)	(0.018)	(0.021)	(0.019)
Left prior to vesting	-0.062***	0.000	0.061***	-0.091***	-0.052***	-0.010
	(0.004)	(0.004)	(0.005)	(0.005)	(0.005)	(0.008)
Earnings in $100,000s	0.299***	0.065***	-0.364***	0.339***	0.100***	-0.140***
	(0.011)	(0.010)	(0.012)	(0.012)	(0.015)	(0.012)

Percentage time worked	−0.027***	0.141***	−0.115***	0.144***	0.054***	−0.034**
	(0.007)	(0.008)	(0.009)	(0.010)	(0.009)	(0.015)
Female	0.004	0.042***	−0.047***	0.060***	0.033***	−0.008
	(0.003)	(0.004)	(0.004)	(0.005)	(0.004)	(0.006)
Married	0.029***	−0.032***	0.003	0.024***	0.047***	0.032***
	(0.005)	(0.005)	(0.006)	(0.006)	(0.007)	(0.006)
Age 15–19	0.047	−0.043	−0.003	−0.078	−0.080***	−0.354***
	(0.047)	(0.045)	(0.067)	(0.068)	(0.013)	(0.044)
Age 20–24	−0.017**	−0.055***	0.072***	−0.100***	−0.034***	0.008
	(0.008)	(0.011)	(0.012)	(0.014)	(0.011)	(0.029)
Age 25–29	−0.019***	0.003	0.016**	−0.035***	−0.027***	−0.038***
	(0.006)	(0.007)	(0.008)	(0.008)	(0.007)	(0.011)
Age 30–34	0.009*	−0.006	−0.003	−0.019***	−0.032***	−0.046***
	(0.006)	(0.006)	(0.007)	(0.007)	(0.007)	(0.009)
Age 40–44	−0.008	0.001	0.007	−0.004	0.003	0.012
	(0.006)	(0.007)	(0.008)	(0.008)	(0.008)	(0.010)
Age 45–49	−0.009	−0.005	0.014*	−0.003	0.014**	0.026**
	(0.006)	(0.007)	(0.008)	(0.008)	(0.008)	(0.011)
Age 50–54	−0.029***	0.001	0.028***	−0.005	0.025***	0.048***
	(0.006)	(0.007)	(0.008)	(0.008)	(0.008)	(0.011)
Age 55–59	−0.035***	0.006	0.029***	0.024***	0.068***	0.094***
	(0.007)	(0.007)	(0.009)	(0.009)	(0.009)	(0.013)
Age 60–64	0.011	−0.033	0.022	−0.035	−0.019	−0.004
	(0.018)	(0.024)	(0.027)	(0.032)	(0.031)	(0.050)
Age 65+	−0.054***	0.027	0.026	0.062**	0.106***	0.161***
	(0.014)	(0.020)	(0.023)	(0.026)	(0.025)	(0.041)
Reciprocal service agreement	−0.022***	−0.020***	0.043***	−0.025***	0.013**	0.063***
	(0.005)	(0.005)	(0.006)	(0.007)	(0.006)	(0.011)
Start year 2000	−0.015**	−0.028***	0.044***	−0.077***	−0.074***	−0.035***
	(0.007)	(0.007)	(0.008)	(0.008)	(0.009)	(0.010)

(continued)

Table 4.4 (continued)

Independent variable	Dependent variable					
	SMP (1)	Portable (2)	Traditional (3)	Any active choice (4)	Choose traditional, given traditional (5)	Choose traditional, given choice (6)
Start year 2001	−0.083***	−0.017***	0.103***	−0.137***	0.099***	−0.018*
	(0.006)	(0.006)	(0.008)	(0.008)	(0.009)	(0.010)
Start year 2002	−0.106***	−0.008	0.117***	−0.146***	−0.101***	−0.010
	(0.006)	(0.007)	(0.008)	(0.008)	(0.009)	(0.011)
Start year 2003	−0.114***	−0.013*	0.129***	−0.149***	−0.098***	0.010
	(0.006)	(0.007)	(0.008)	(0.009)	(0.010)	(0.012)
Start year 2004	−0.107***	−0.012*	0.122***	−0.141***	−0.098***	−0.003
	(0.006)	(0.007)	(0.008)	(0.009)	(0.010)	(0.012)
% made choice on campus	0.238***	0.492***	0.358***	0.356***	0.231***	0.018
	(0.078)	(0.078)	(0.058)	(0.047)	(0.059)	(0.076)
constant	0.207***	0.002	0.418***	0.194***	0.061***	0.203***
	(0.013)	(0.018)	(0.043)	(0.031)	(0.022)	(0.029)
Zip Code controls (3-digit)?	Yes	Yes	Yes	Yes	Yes	Yes
Adjusted R^2	0.1053	0.0446	0.1318	0.1305	0.0647	0.0811
No. of observations	45,303	45,303	45,303	45,303	29,962	20,049

Notes: Standard errors are in parentheses. SMP = self-managed plan.

***Significant at the 1 percent level.

**Significant at the 5 percent level.

*Significant at the 10 percent level.

portable, and traditional (whether by active choice or default) plans, re-spectively. Because an individual will ultimately be in one of these three plans, and being in one plan means not being in the other two, the coefficients across the three columns will add up to zero (within rounding). Consistent with the simple tabulations presented in table 4.3, the results clearly indicate strong differences by occupation (which, in this setting, is a good proxy for educational attainment and perhaps financial sophistication). When one accounts for all of the interaction terms, we find that, relative to an academic at a university, staff members at a university are 9.7 percentage points less likely to choose the SMP, academics at a community college are 3.6 percentage points less likely to choose the SMP, and staff members at a community college are 6.9 percentage points less likely to choose the SMP. These effects are quite large given the baseline SMP participation rate of only 15 percent. Relative to other occupation groups, academics at universities are much less likely to be enrolled in the traditional plan. This is very much consistent with many academics' uncertainty surrounding their long-term future at a university (i.e., the tenure decision) when these retirement plan decisions are made (recall the traditional plan is particularly attractive for employees likely to have a long stay with their employer). For example, staff members at a university are 13 percentage points more likely to be enrolled in the traditional plan than are academics (with the difference much more muted when one focuses on staff and academics at community colleges). Part of the community college effect might also be driven by the fact that many community colleges in Illinois are heavily unionized, and the faculty unions tend to be "pro-DB."

Benefits for police officers under the portable and traditional plans are more generous than those for other employees due to the existence of a fourth option for calculating benefits that applies only to police and fire employees. Consistent with this, police officers at a university are 23.1 percentage points less like to participate in the SMP, while police officers at a community college are 10.2 percentage points less likely to do so.

There is evidence that there is a correlation between the ex post employment duration and the ex ante retirement plan choices. For example, those individuals that ended up leaving the firm before vesting were more likely to enroll in the traditional plan (the default option). For a worker that leaves SURS before vesting, the choice of retirement plan has little economic consequence. However, workers that ex post left the SURS system, but with sufficient tenure to obtain vesting, were much less likely to have chosen the traditional plan. Recall that workers who leave their SURS employer after vesting and opt for a refund of their retirement plan balance receive both employee and employer contributions under the SMP or portable plans, but relinquish employer contributions under the traditional plan. Thus, assuming some foresight in employment duration, the coefficients on the "left with vesting" and "left without vesting" variables are sensible given the pension plan rules in place.

Higher-income workers are more likely to enroll in the SMP or portable plans, at the expense of enrollment in the traditional plan—a $10,000 increase in earnings corresponds to a nearly 3 percentage point increase in the probability of choosing the SMP, a 0.7 percentage point increase in the probability of choosing portable, and a 3.6 percentage point decline in enrollment in the traditional plan. To the extent that income may proxy for greater financial sophistication (similar to being an academic at a university), greater financial sophistication is associated with a higher likelihood of selecting the DC plan. Females are more likely to pick the portable plan than males, and married individuals are more likely to pick the SMP than single. Both younger and older individuals seem less likely to select the SMP and are instead more apt to enroll in the traditional plan (but perhaps for different reasons given that the traditional is also the default option).[16] As expected, individuals with prior service in another system with reciprocity are more likely to be enrolled in the traditional plan.

We also observe how the plan choice varies over time, holding fixed other characteristics. The time series trends presented in table 4.4 are very similar to the unconditional trends documented in table 4.1. We find that SMP participation rates in 2001 to 2004 are significantly lower than the rates in 1999 to 2000. These effects are quite large: holding all other covariates fixed, an individual joining the plan in 2003 was 11 percentage points less likely to choose the SMP than was an individual who joined SURS in 1999. This is consistent with the possibility that SMP participation rates are influenced by equity market performance in prior years. There is very little time trend in take up of the portable plan from 1999 to 2004, all of the decrease in SMP selection is attributable to an increase in enrollment in the traditional plan (mainly through default).

Finally, "Percent on campus" indicates what fraction of the campus population chose the same option as the individual. This is defined by taking the total number of employees on that campus at the time the individual began employment who chose the SMP option, for example, and dividing it by the total number of campus employees (excluding individual i). We find a strong positive relation for all the pension plan decisions, indicating the possibility of either peer effects (e.g., an individual is more likely to choose the SMP if others on the campus also did so), human resources effects (e.g., the HR officer gives common advice to all new employees on that campus), or sorting effects from more general sorting of individuals across campuses based on unobserved (to the econometrician) characteristics that are correlated with pension plan choice.

In unreported results, we further explore peer effects. In the spirit of

16. The omitted age group in the regression is thirty-five to thirty-nine.

Duflo and Saez (2002, 2003), we also include the percent of academics making a particular choice and the percent of staff making a choice. We then interact these two campuswide measures with whether the individual is an academic or staff. This enables us to test whether academics are more influenced by the decisions of fellow academics as opposed to staff, and vice versa. We find, across all of the pension choices, that the choice of a given academic is highly correlated with that of other academics on campus, but is uncorrelated with that of staff on campus, with the reverse also holding.

To summarize, we find that the SMP (DC plan) is most likely to be chosen by individuals who are highly educated (e.g., university academics) and have higher incomes, while the traditional plan (DB plan) is most likely to be chosen by less-educated individuals with lower incomes. In essence, the SMP is disproportionately chosen by the very group that one would likely expect to be the most financially sophisticated. It is ironic, that, as explained in section 4.2, a close examination of this plan suggests that it may be inferior to the portable plan in most states of the world. While we plan to do more research on this subject, our initial hypothesis is that most participants are making a more general "DB versus DC" decision and that the SMP may indeed be rationally preferable to the traditional plan for most of these employees. The failure to choose the portable plan instead, however, may be due to the difficulty of understanding the relative advantages of the portable plan, particularly given the manner in which this complex information is provided to new participants. Other possibilities include that individuals are overconfident in their ability to earn high returns through the SMP or that individuals are concerned about political risk in the portable or DB system.[17]

4.5.2   Active versus Passive Choice

The results in column (3) combine individuals who actively chose the traditional plan and those who were defaulted into it. This distinction is worth further consideration, as these may represent two very different populations. In column (4) we use as our dependent variable whether the individual simply made any active choice (including SMP, portable, or traditional) as opposed to passively accepting the default. The complement of this dependent variable is defaulting into the traditional option (and thus the coefficients from a "default" regression will simply be the negative of those displayed in column [4]). Consistent with earlier results, we find that more-educated individuals (academics, university employees) and those with higher earnings are more likely to make an active plan choice, as are women and married individuals. As noted earlier, the overall fraction of ac-

17. Indeed, the recent decision by the legislature to shift decision-making authority over the setting of the effective interest rate in the future is one manifestation of political risk.

tive decision making declined substantially over the period, falling by 15 percentage points between 1999 and 2003.

In columns (5) and (6), we examine individuals who made an active choice to go with the traditional plan, even though an active choice was not necessary to achieve the traditional plan outcome. In column (5), we limit the sample to those in the traditional plan and are thus analyzing active versus passive traditional plan participants. We can clearly reject that these two groups are the same. Conditional on ending up in the traditional plan, it is actually community college employees and staff members who are most likely to have actively made this choice. Higher earners, women, and married individuals are also more likely to have made this active choice, while younger people are more likely to have ended up in the traditional plan by default. In sum, the population of defaulters is "different" both from the general population of those that made an active pension choice as well as those that actively selected the same plan as the default option (i.e., the traditional plan).

In column (6), we explore how those who actively chose the traditional plan differ from other individuals who made active choices (dropping those who defaulted). The patterns are largely as expected based on earlier results.

4.5.3   Campus/Employer Fixed Effects

As stated earlier, the framing of the pension plan choice as a discussion of DB versus DC, as opposed to simultaneously comparing all three plans (SMP, portable, and traditional) may obfuscate the benefits of the portable plan (particularly relative to the SMP). Of all the more than sixty campuses/employers covered by SURS, one would expect or hope that the employees of SURS itself, the organization that makes and administers the pension plan rules, would be best informed of the pros and cons of all three retirement plan. Focusing on employers with at least twenty-five new hires over the period 1999 to 2004 (there are a handful of employers with very few new hires), we find that only 19 percent of the sample chooses the portable option. In contrast, we find that 49 percent of new employees working directly for SURS chose the portable plan. Not only is this the largest fraction of any employer, but it vastly exceeds the 27 percent of new employees choosing the portable plan at the next highest employer. Only 5 percent of SURS employees select the SMP, the fourth lowest among all employers, compared to 15 percent for the whole sample. Also, 90 percent of SURS employees make an active choice (i.e., only 10 percent default into a choice), which is again the highest proportion by far across the employers covered by SURS. This evidence is consistent with our hypothesis that the SMP, once its details are understood, is inferior to the portable plan. It also suggests, more generally, that there may be important employer effects influencing plan choice.

More formally, in specifications not reported, we have further included employer indicator variables in our regression specifications. While we are no longer able to identify some of our campuswide variables in these specifications (such as community college and its interactions, or the percent choosing the same option) because of a very little time series variation in these variables, we do find that the campus variables are jointly significant, with a p-value of 0.000, even in a regression that already controls for three-digit zip codes. This clearly suggests that there are strong campus effects, although it does not allow us to definitively distinguish whether it is driven by peer effects, human resource effects, or sorting effects.[18]

4.5.4 Multinomial Logit Results

A limitation of the ordinary least squares (OLS) specification is that they limit us to examining one choice at a time. In reality, individuals can choose from the entire menu of actions upon joining a SURS-covered employer. Specifically, there are four distinct actions an individual can take, as noted earlier. In table 4.5, we introduce a multinomial logit specification to examine this choice. By treating the default option as our base category, we report the relative risk ratio of our key covariates for each of the other three possible outcomes. In interpreting the coefficients, recall that what matters is whether the risk ratio is greater than or less than 1.0. For example, the relative risk ratio of 0.744 for community college in column (1) means that an employee of a community college is only 74.4 percent as likely to choose the SMP over the traditional plan than is an employee of a university. Note that unlike the earlier table, all of the columns in table 4.4 are from the same regression. Column (1) reports the risk ratio for the SMP versus the default option, column (2) for portable versus the default option, and column (3) for actively choosing the traditional plan versus accepting the default option.

The direction and significance of most of the effects are consistent with what we found using the series of linear probability models. Specifically, relative to university employees, those that work for a community college are less likely to choose the SMP or portable plan and more likely to actively choose the traditional plan. Employees at other employer types are less likely to make any active choice, meaning that they are much more likely to accept the default. Relative to academic employees, staff are also less likely to choose the SMP or portable options and more likely to actively choose the traditional plan. Police officers, particularly those at universities, are substantially less likely to take the SMP or portable option.

Individuals who subsequently leave employment for any reason (disability, retirement, death, or leaving prior to vesting) are significantly less

---

18. All of the patterns in coefficients in table 4.4 also hold in the employer fixed effect regression.

Table 4.5   Multinomial logit estimate of plan choice

	Plan choice[a]		
Independent variable	SMP (1)	Portable (2)	Traditional (3)
Community college	0.744***	0.788***	1.349***
	(0.036)	(0.037)	(0.080)
Other type of institution	0.447***	0.469***	0.552***
	(0.037)	(0.029)	(0.040)
Staff	0.432***	0.722***	1.957***
	(0.018)	(0.025)	(0.089)
Staff (community college)	1.674***	1.460***	0.564***
	(0.113)	(0.085)	(0.040)
Police	0.061***	0.400***	1.520*
	(0.032)	(0.096)	(0.383)
Police (community college)	3.852**	3.683***	1.067
	(2.595)	(1.144)	(0.363)
Disabled	0.458**	0.931	0.715
	(0.142)	(0.207)	(0.188)
Retired	0.000***	5.167	0.000***
	(0.000)	(7.164)	(0.000)
Dead	0.000***	0.280*	0.407
	(0.000)	(0.212)	(0.302)
Left with vested benefits	0.985	1.392***	0.634***
	(0.103)	(0.136)	(0.089)
Left prior to vesting	0.498***	0.927**	0.615***
	(0.019)	(0.028)	(0.024)
Earnings in $100,000s	11.116***	4.319***	2.243***
	(0.958)	(0.348)	(0.246)
Percentage time worked	1.231***	3.145***	1.644***
	(0.080)	(0.195)	(0.122)
Female	1.175***	1.426***	1.262***
	(0.035)	(0.039)	(0.043)
Married	1.401***	0.970	1.517***
	(0.056)	(0.034)	(0.074)
Age 15–19	1.037	0.536	0.000***
	(0.789)	(0.397)	(0.000)
Age 20–24	0.429***	0.613***	0.641***
	(0.068)	(0.059)	(0.085)
Age 25–29	0.765***	0.953	0.753***
	(0.044)	(0.044)	(0.050)
Age 30–34	1.029	0.908**	0.713***
	(0.046)	(0.038)	(0.042)
Age 40–44	0.932	0.996	1.029
	(0.046)	(0.046)	(0.060)
Age 45–49	0.934	0.968	1.101*
	(0.048)	(0.047)	(0.064)
Age 50–54	0.799***	0.990	1.192***
	(0.044)	(0.050)	(0.069)
Age 55–59	0.804***	1.081	1.567***
	(0.050)	(0.060)	(0.095)

Table 4.5   (continued)

	Plan choice[a]		
Independent variable	SMP (1)	Portable (2)	Traditional (3)
Age 60–64	1.214	0.771	0.887
	(0.303)	(0.156)	(0.161)
Age 65+	0.598**	1.302	2.181***
	(0.127)	(0.213)	(0.325)
Reciprocal service agreement	0.812***	0.809***	1.187***
	(0.038)	(0.035)	(0.056)
Start year 2000	0.765***	0.693***	0.598***
	(0.036)	(0.033)	(0.033)
Start year 2001	0.424***	0.639***	0.483***
	(0.021)	(0.029)	(0.026)
Start year 2002	0.332***	0.645***	0.463***
	(0.017)	(0.030)	(0.026)
Start year 2003	0.307***	0.606***	0.477***
	(0.017)	(0.029)	(0.027)
Start year 2004	0.337***	0.617***	0.471***
	(0.018)	(0.030)	(0.027)
Pseudo R^2	0.0871		
No. of observations	45,303		

Notes: Standard errors are in parentheses. SMP = self-managed plan.
[a]Default into Traditional plan is the omitted category.
***Significant at the 1 percent level.
**Significant at the 5 percent level.
*Significant at the 10 percent level.

likely to have been SMP participants. Those who left SURS employment with vested benefits were much more likely to have chosen the portable plan.

Higher earners and those with full-time status are less likely to default and more likely to choose each of the active plans, with the earnings effect strongest for the SMP. In general, women are more likely to make an active choice, as are married individuals. Individuals under the age of thirty are far less likely to make any active choice, while those over fifty are less likely to choose the SMP, but more likely to actively choose the traditional plan.

To put all these findings together, it is useful to consider a few stylized individuals and what our results suggest about their choices:

- Young, single, male low earners with less job attachment to the SURS employer (both in terms of percent time worked in terms of whether they subsequently leave) are extremely likely to accept the default option.
- High earning, well-educated, married professors in their thirties with

the strongest attachment to their employer are disproportionately likely to choose the SMP plan, and to a slightly lesser extent, the portable plan.

- Older, part-time, married, female, community college staff members with above-average earnings are disproportionately likely to actively choose the traditional plan.

4.6   Conclusions and Future Directions

This chapter has provided novel evidence about what types of workers are most likely to choose DC plans. We find that, even in an environment where choosing the pure DC plan may not be the best financial decision, individuals are more likely to choose the DC option if they are high earners, well-educated, married, in their thirties, with strong attachment to their employer. These finding suggest that these "educated, high-earning, young professionals" have a strong preference for DC plans, even when the financial terms are unfavorable. For example, among the 650 individuals in our sample who are full time, age thirty to thirty-nine, academics at a university, married, have earnings in excess of $50,000, and are still active employees as of spring 2006, 52 percent of them chose the self-managed plan (versus 15 percent in the sample as a whole). This is despite the fact that an individual would need to earn a nominal rate of return of approximately 9 percent to 12 percent per year (which is, at current inflation rates, substantially higher than the 3 percent real rate in President Bush's Social Security proposal) in order for the SMP to be preferred to the portable plan. Using Robert Shiller's (2005) methodology, we estimate that even using what most would consider rather high historical equity returns in the market, no cohort of individuals between 1871 and 2004 would be able to achieve these returns by following a life-cycle portfolio strategy over their full working lives.

This analysis raises fascinating questions as to *why* individuals who, by most observables, appear to be highly capable individuals make what appear to be suboptimal choices. We speculate that there are at least five reasons why they may do so. First, participants may simply have difficulty processing the complex information that they are provided when making this choice, due either to time constraints or some form of bounded rationality. Second, the information provided by SURS may not be optimally designed to facilitate meaningful comparisons between the self-managed plan and the portable benefits package. This might lead some employees to mistakenly believe that the self-managed plan is the most generous plan for individuals who leave SURS employment early in their career. Third, individuals may understand the rules, but may simply suffer from overconfidence in their investment abilities or have unrealistically high expectations about future risk-adjusted equity market returns. Fourth, individuals may have either rational or irrational beliefs about the degree of political risk in the traditional or portable benefit plans, arising due to the chronic underfunding problem facing the SURS system. Fifth, individuals may simply place a very high value on choice for its own sake. In future research, we intend to explore these alternative hypotheses using a survey of current SURS participants.

References

Bodie, Zvi, Alan J. Marcus, and Robert C. Merton. 1988. Defined benefit versus defined contribution pension plans: What are the real trade-offs? In *Pensions in the U.S. economy,* ed. Zvi Bodie, John Shoven, and David Wise, 139–62. Chicago: University of Chicago Press.

Choi, James, David Laibson, Brigitte Madrian, and Andrew Metrick. 2001. For better or for worse: Default effects and 401(K) savings behavior. NBER Working Paper no. 8651. Cambridge, MA: National Bureau of Economic Research, December.

Clark, Robert L., Linda S. Ghent, and Ann A. McDermed. 2006. Pension plan choice among university faculty. *Southern Economic Journal* 72 (3): 560–77.

Clark, Robert L., and M. Melinda Pitts. 1999. Faculty choice of a pension plan: Defined benefit vs. defined contribution. *Industrial Relations* 38:18–45.

Congressional Budget Office (CBO). 2006. An analysis of the president's budgetary proposals for fiscal year 2007. Washington, DC: CBO.

Duflo, Esther, and Emmanuel Saez. 2002. Participation and investment decisions in a retirement plan: The influence of colleagues' choices. *Journal of Public Economics* 85:121–48.

———. 2003. The role of information and social interactions in retirement plan decisions: Evidence from a randomized experiment. *Quarterly Journal of Economics* 118:815–42.

Ford, William, 2005. 2004 comparative study of major public employee retirement systems. Madison, WI: Wisconsin Legislative Council, December.

Madrian, Brigitte, and Dennis Shea. 2001. The power of suggestion: Inertia in 401(k) participation and savings behavior. *The Quarterly Journal of Economics* 116:1149–1525.

Papke, Leslie. 2004. Pension plan choice in the public sector: The case of Michigan State employees. *National Tax Journal* 57 (2, Part 1) 329–39.

Shiller, Robert J. 2005. The life cycle personal accounts proposal for Social Security: An evaluation. Yale ICF Working Paper no. 05-06. New Haven, CT: Yale International Center for Finance.

U.S. Government Accounting Office (GAO). 2003. Social Security: Issues relating to noncoverage of public employees. Statement of Barbara D. Bovbjerg before the Subcommittee on Social Security, Committee on Ways and Means, House of Representatives. GAO-03-710T. Washington, DC: GPO.

Yang, Tongxuan. 2005. Understanding the defined benefit versus defined contribution choice. Pension Research Council Working Paper no. 2005-04. Philadelphia: The Wharton School, University of Pennsylvania.

Comment   Brigitte C. Madrian

The purported goal of this chapter is to analyze employee preferences over a defined benefit versus a defined contribution retirement plan in a way that would inform such a choice in a Social Security system with a voluntary defined contribution component. The authors note that looking at participation rates in employer-sponsored defined contribution plans for guidance may not be very informative because the choice between participating or not in such a plan is a tradeoff between current versus future consumption, whereas the decision to allocate part of one's Social Security contributions to a defined contribution account is a trade-off between how to fund future consumption. To assess preferences for being in a defined benefit versus a defined contribution plan, the authors look to the 1998 introduction of a defined contribution option in the Illinois State University Retirement System which had traditionally offered only a defined benefit pension plan. Unfortunately, the results of their analysis are largely uninformative about the preferences that individuals might have for diverting part of their Social Security contributions to a defined contribution account, for reasons that I will outline below. Although the authors are largely unsuccessful in achieving their primary aim, they nonetheless document many interesting patterns that speak more generally to how individuals make decisions. These will also be discussed below.

There are several reasons why the analysis of the natural experiment in this chapter is largely uninformative on the question of individual preferences for a defined contribution component to Social Security. First, the natural experiment allows employees to choose between three options: a "traditional" defined benefit plan, a "traditional" defined contribution plan (the self-managed plan or SMP), and a portable defined benefit option that shares some features of both a defined benefit and a defined contribution plan but that is largely branded to employees as a modified defined benefit plan. Using the fraction of employees who choose the defined contribution SMP plan in this context as an indicator of preferences for a defined contribution option in the Social Security system is problematic as doing so requires assuming that the presence of the portable defined benefit option is irrelevant to the choice between the traditional defined benefit and the SMP plan. It is, however, highly unlikely that the fraction of employees choosing the defined contribution SMP plan is unaffected by whether the portable defined benefit option is available.

Second, the natural experiment analyzed in the chapter gives individu-

Brigitte C. Madrian is the Aetna Professor of Public Policy and Corporate Management at the John F. Kennedy School of Government, Harvard University, and a research associate of the National Bureau of Economic Research.

als an all-or-nothing choice: employees are wholly committed to one of the three options. They cannot choose to have part of their contributions allocated to the defined benefit plan and part allocated to the SMP. In contrast, the personal account proposal of President Bush's Commission to Strengthen Social Security does not give individuals an all-or-nothing option; rather, individuals are only allowed to redirect a part of their Social Security contributions to a personal account. Thus, the overall portfolio risk associated with choosing the defined contribution SMP plan in the natural experiment is very different from that of choosing to participate in a personal account under Social Security.

Third, employer contributions to the defined benefit plan in the natural experiment are higher than are employer contributions to the defined contribution SMP plan. Thus, the choice between the plan in the natural experiment is not only between the defined benefit versus defined contribution characteristics of the plans, but also in the effective level of compensation that employees receive under the two plans.

Fourth, an important component of the benefits received upon retirement is retiree health insurance, but the receipt of retiree health insurance is contingent upon actually choosing to annuitize benefits under the defined contribution SMP plan or the portable defined benefit plan. This makes the traditional defined benefit plan more attractive than would be the case if employees had a preference to take a lump sum at retirement rather than to annuitize (as might be the case for employees with a shorter life expectancy). The choice in the natural experiment thus confounds preferences over a defined benefit versus a defined contribution plan with preferences over annuitization and retiree health insurance.

Finally, the results in the chapter suggest that even in the absence of any bias from the four factors described above, employees in the natural experiment probably do not well understand the choices that they face as many fail to make any choice at all and are defaulted into the traditional defined benefit plan as a result. In this context, it is very difficult to infer much from employee preferences at all. If the default plan had been different, it is likely that the fraction of employees in each of the plans would have been very different (see, for example, Madrian and Shea 2001; Choi et al. 2004). A more informative natural experiment would have required all employees to make an active decision about which plan to participate in (Carroll et al. 2005).

If we cannot learn much about actual preferences over participation in a defined contribution plan from the analysis of the natural experiment in the chapter, what can we learn? The chapter corroborates existing evidence on the importance of defaults in saving plans and other outcomes (Madrian and Shea 2001; Choi et al. 2004; Yang 2005). The authors find that 56 percent of employees overall are defaulted into the defined benefit plan. Furthermore, the authors find that the fraction of employees defaulting into the defined benefit plan is much higher after the initial marketing blitz associated with the plan change has subsided, which is consistent with results about the importance of the default investment option under the private account component of the Swedish Social Security system (Palme, Sundén, and Söderlind 2007). While some of these defaulted employees probably did have preferences over the traditional defined benefit plan, it is likely that many did not. The key piece of evidence supporting this contention is that employees who defaulted into the traditional defined benefit plan have the highest rate of departure prior to being vested, and yet this plan is arguably the worst plan for those employees who leave with short tenure.

The chapter also provides some very intriguing evidence on how complexity impacts decision-making outcomes. Employees of the State University Retirement System who arguably have or have access to the most information and expertise on the relative merits of the three plans make very different elections than other employees in the system. Only 10 percent of these employees are defaulted into the defined benefit plan (versus 56 percent overall). Forty-nine percent actively elect the portable defined benefit plan (versus 19 percent overall), and only 5 percent choose the defined contribution SMP plan (versus 15 percent overall). The chapter finds, perhaps not surprisingly, that employees who are likely to find the choice between the three plans the most complicated, namely, younger and lower-income employees, are more likely to be defaulted into the traditional defined benefit plan. Surprisingly, the group most likely to elect the defined contribution SMP plan, the academic staff at universities, are presumptively more financially literate than most other employees even though the chapter makes the case that the portable defined benefit plan ought to dominate the SMP plan for almost everyone. The familiar axiom, a little knowledge is a dangerous thing, may very well be true here. The results are certainly in line with those of Choi, Laibson, and Madrian, (2006); Beshears et al. (2006); and Duflo et al. (2006) that complexity may lead individuals to make suboptimal savings choices.

Collectively, these results raise as many questions as they answer and provide many avenues for future research. If the default matters for outcomes, and one default is not predominantly the best for most employees, how should the Illinois State University Retirement System choose its default pension plan? If employees were forced to choose among the plans, which plan would they actually choose? If employees were provided with either better or different information about the plan options, how would their choices change? If the outcomes observed depend on factors such as which plan is the default and how information is presented, can we really hope to learn anything about employee preferences, and if so, what conditions would need to prevail?

References

Beshears, John, James J. Choi, David Laibson, and Brigitte C. Madrian. 2006. Simplification and saving. NBER Working Paper no. 11920. Cambridge, MA: National Bureau of Economic Research.

Carroll, Gabriel D., James J. Choi, David Laibson, Brigitte C. Madrian, and Andrew Metrick. Optimal defaults and active decisions. Forthcoming. *Quarterly Journal of Economics.*

Choi, James J., David Laibson, and Brigitte C. Madrian. 2006. Reducing the complexity costs of 401(k) participation through quick enrollment™. NBER Working Paper no. 11979. Cambridge, MA: National Bureau of Economic Research.

Choi, James J., David Laibson, Brigitte C. Madrian, and Andrew Metrick. 2004. For better or for worse: Default effects and 401(k) savings behavior. In *Perspectives on the economics of aging,* ed. David A. Wise, 81–126. Chicago: University of Chicago Press.

Duflo, Esther, William Gale, Jeffrey Liebman, Peter Orszag, and Emmanuel Saez. 2006. Saving incentives for low- and middle-income families: Evidence from a field experiment with H&R Block. *Quarterly Journal of Economics* 121 (4): 1311–46.

Madrian, Brigitte C., and Dennis F. Shea. 2001. The power of suggestion: Inertia in 401(k) participation and savings behavior. *Quarterly Journal of Economics* 116(4): 1149–87.

Palme, Mårten, Annika Sundén, and Paul Söderlind. 2007. How do individual accounts work in the Swedish pension system? *Journal of the European Economic Association* 5 (2-3): 636–46.

Yang, Tongxuan. 2005. Understanding the defined benefits versus defined contribution choice. Pension Research Council Working Paper no. 2005-04. Philadelphia: The Wharton School, University of Pennsylvania.

5

The Importance of Default Options for Retirement Saving Outcomes
Evidence from the United States

John Beshears, James J. Choi, David Laibson, and
Brigitte C. Madrian

If transaction costs are small, standard economic theory would suggest that defaults should have little impact on economic outcomes. Agents with well-defined preferences will opt out of any default that does not maximize their utility, regardless of the nature of the default. In practice, however, defaults can have quite sizeable effects on economic outcomes. Recent research has highlighted the important role that defaults play in a wide range of settings: organ donation decisions (Johnson and Goldstein 2003; Abadie and Gay 2004), car insurance plan choices (Johnson et al. 1993), car option purchases (Park, Jun, and McInnis 2000), and consent to receive e-mail marketing (Johnson, Bellman, and Lohse 2003).

This paper summarizes the empirical evidence on defaults in another

John Beshears is a PhD candidate in business economics at Harvard University. James J. Choi is an assistant professor of finance at Yale School of Management, and a faculty research fellow of the National Bureau of Economic Research. David Laibson is the Harvard College Professor of Economics at Harvard University, and a research associate of the National Bureau of Economic Research. Brigitte C. Madrian is the Aetna Professor of Public Policy and Corporate Management at the John F. Kennedy School of Government, Harvard University, and a research associate of the National Bureau of Economic Research.

We thank Hewitt Associates for their help in providing the data analyzed in this and several previous papers that form the foundation for the arguments advanced in this chapter. We are particularly grateful to Lori Lucas and Yan Xu, two of our many contacts at Hewitt Associates. We acknowledge individual and collective financial support from the National Institute on Aging (NIA) through grants R01-AG021650 and T32-AG00186 and the U.S. Social Security Administration (SSA) through grant #10-P-98363-1 to the National Bureau of Economic Research (NBER) as part of the SSA Retirement Research Consortium. The opinions and conclusions expressed are solely those of the authors and do not represent the opinions or policy of NIA, SSA, any other agency of the U.S. Federal Government, or the NBER. Laibson also acknowledges financial support from the Sloan Foundation.

Chapter 5 was originally published as "The Importance of Default Options for Retirement Saving Outcomes: Evidence from the USA" in *Lessons from Pension Reform in the Americas,* edited by Stephen J. Kay and Tapen Sinha. Published by permission of Oxford University Press.

economically important domain: savings outcomes. The evidence strongly suggests that defaults impact savings outcomes at every step along the way. To understand how defaults affect retirement savings outcomes, one must first understand the relevant institutions. Because the empirical literature on how defaults shape retirement savings outcomes focuses mostly on the United States, we begin by describing the different types of retirement income institutions in the United States and some of their salient characteristics. We then present empirical evidence from the United States and other countries, including Chile, Mexico, and Sweden, on how defaults influence retirement savings outcomes at all stages of the savings life cycle, including savings plan participation, savings rates, asset allocation, and postretirement savings distributions. Next we examine why defaults have such a tremendous impact on savings outcomes. And, finally, we consider the role of public policy toward retirement saving when defaults matter.

5.1   Retirement Income Institutions in the United States

There are four primary sources of retirement income for individuals in the United States: (1) Social Security payments from the government, (2) traditional employer-sponsored defined benefit pension plans, (3) employer-sponsored defined contribution savings plans, and (4) individual savings accounts that are tied neither to the government nor to private employers. We will briefly describe each of these institutions in turn.[1]

The Social Security system in the United States provides retirement income to qualified workers and their spouses. While employed, workers and their firms make mandatory contributions to the Social Security system. Individuals are eligible to claim benefits when they reach age sixty-two, although benefit amounts are higher if individuals postpone their receipt until a later age. Individuals must proactively enroll to begin receiving Social Security benefits, and most individuals do so no later than age sixty-five. The level of benefits is primarily determined by either an individual's own or his or her spouse's earnings history, with higher earnings corresponding to greater monthly benefit amounts according to a progressive benefits formula. Benefits are also indexed to the cost of living and tend to increase over time because of this. They are paid until an individual dies, with a reduced benefit going to a surviving spouse until his or her death.

On average, Social Security replaces about 40 percent of preretirement income, although this varies widely across individuals. Replacement rates tend to be negatively related to income due to the progressive structure of the benefits formula. Benefits are largely funded on a pay-as-you-go basis, with the contributions of workers and firms made today going to pay the

---

1. See the Employee Benefit Research Institute (2005) for a more detailed discussion of the U.S. retirement income system.

benefits of currently retired individuals who worked and paid contributions in the past. There is no private account component to the U.S. Social Security system, although this is something that has received a great deal of discussion in recent years.

Traditionally, the second largest component of retirement income has come from employer-sponsored defined benefit pension plans. These plans share many similarities with the Social Security system. Benefits are determined by a formula, usually linked to a worker's compensation, age, and tenure. Benefits are usually paid out as a life annuity, or in the case of married individuals, as a joint-and-survivor annuity, although workers do have some flexibility in selecting the type of annuity or in opting instead for a lump-sum payout.

Because traditional defined benefit pension plans are costly for employers to administer and because they impose funding risk on employers, there has been a movement over the past two decades away from traditional pensions and toward defined contribution savings plans. There are now more than twice as many active participants in employer-sponsored defined contribution savings plans as in defined benefit pension plans, with total assets in defined contribution plans exceeding those in defined benefit plans by more than 10 percent (U.S. Department of Labor 2005).

These defined contribution savings plans come in several different varieties. The most common one, the 401(k), is named after the section of the U.S. tax code that regulates these types of plans. The typical defined contribution savings plan allows employees to make elective pretax contributions to an account over which the employee retains investment control. Many employers also provide matching contributions up to a certain level of employee contributions. The retirement income ultimately derived by the retirees depends on how much they elected to save while working, how generous the employer match was, and the performance of their selected investment portfolios. At retirement, benefits are usually paid in the form of a lump-sum distribution, although some employers offer the option of purchasing an annuity. Relative to traditional defined benefit pension plans, defined contribution savings plans impose substantially more risk on individuals while reducing the risks faced by employers.

The final significant source of retirement income comes from personal savings accounts that are not tied to an employer (or the government). There are many different ways that individuals can save on their own for retirement, but one particular vehicle, the Individual Retirement Account (IRA) is very popular because it receives favorable tax treatment. After IRAs were first created, the primary source of funding came from direct individual contributions. Over time, however, restrictions have been placed on the ability of higher-income individuals to make direct tax-favored contributions, and the primary source of IRA funding has shifted to rollovers—transfers of assets from a former employer's defined contribution savings plan into an IRA. In general, individuals employed at a firm with a defined contribution savings plan that has an employer match would find that savings plan more attractive than directly contributing to an IRA. Direct IRA contributions largely come from individuals whose employers do not sponsor a defined contribution savings plan, individuals who are not eligible for their employer's savings plan, or individuals who are not working.

The relatively low Social Security replacement rate (compared to other developed countries) in conjunction with the recent shift toward defined contribution savings plans and IRAs in the United States has spurred much of the research interest into how defaults and other plan design parameters affect savings outcomes. With individuals bearing greater responsibility for ensuring their own retirement income security, understanding how to improve their savings outcomes has become an important issue both for individuals themselves and for society at large.

5.2 The Impact of Defaults on Retirement Savings Outcomes: Empirical Evidence

We now turn to the evidence on how defaults affect retirement savings outcomes, discussing first the effect of institutionally specified defaults, then "elective" defaults—mechanisms that are not a pure default, but that share similar characteristics with the institutionally chosen defaults, in terms both of their structure and of their outcomes.

5.2.1 Savings Plan Participation

In a defined contribution savings environment, savings plans—whether they are employer-sponsored, government-sponsored, or privately sponsored—are only a useful tool to the extent that employees actually participate. Recent research suggests that when it comes to savings plan participation, the key behavioral question is not whether individuals participate in a savings plan, but rather how long it takes before they actually sign up. The most compelling evidence on the impact of defaults on savings outcomes comes from changes in the default participation status of employees at firms with defined contribution savings plans.

In most companies, savings plan participation requires an active election on the part of employees. That is, if the employee does nothing, the default is that the employee will not be enrolled in the savings plan ("standard enrollment"). An alternative but less widely used approach is to enroll employees in the savings plan automatically, requiring an active election on the part of employees to opt out of participation.[2] This simple change in

2. In a recent survey of large U.S. employers, Hewitt Associates (2005) reports that 19 percent of companies used automatic enrollment in their 401(k) plans in 2005, up from 7 percent in 1999. In another survey, the Profit Sharing/401(k) Council of America (2005) reports that 8 percent of firms overall have automatic enrollment, but that the likelihood of having automatic enrollment was much higher in large than in small firms (24 percent versus 1 percent).

the default participation status that applies to employees who do nothing has a dramatic impact on participation outcomes.

To illustrate the effect of automatic enrollment on both participation and other savings outcomes, we present the experience of a medium-sized U.S. chemicals company (Company A). This particular firm has a standard defined contribution savings plan: employees can direct up to 15 percent of pay into the plan; employee contributions are matched dollar for dollar up to 6 percent of pay; and employees have seven investment options from which to choose. This company is interesting to consider because it actually implemented automatic enrollment in two different ways for three different groups of employees.

Company A initially adopted automatic enrollment in December 2000 with a default contribution rate of 3 percent of pay. The first group of employees affected was new hires going forward, which is how automatic enrollment is most commonly implemented. This firm, however, also applied automatic enrollment to previously hired employees who were not then participating in the plan. In October 2001, the company then increased its default contribution rate to 6 percent of pay, a change that applied only to new hires going forward.

Figure 5.1 shows the impact of automatic enrollment on the participation rates of new hires at Company A. For employees hired and observed prior to automatic enrollment, savings plan participation is low initially and increases slowly with employee tenure. Under automatic enrollment, however, participation jumps to approximately 95 percent of employees once it takes effect (between one and two months after hire in this firm) and increases only slightly thereafter. At low levels of tenure, the difference in participation rates under the standard enrollment and automatic enrollment regimes is substantial, with a difference of 35 percentage points at three months of tenure. As participation increases with tenure under standard enrollment, this difference diminishes but remains sizeable even after a considerable period of time; for example, at twenty-four months of tenure, employees under automatic enrollment have a participation rate more than 25 percentage points higher than that of employees hired prior to automatic enrollment. The impact of automatic enrollment when applied to existing nonparticipants is no less dramatic, as shown in figure 5.2. These differences are borne out in other firms as documented in Madrian and Shea (2001), Choi et al. (2002, 2004a,b) and the Vanguard Group (2001).

Most firms with automatic enrollment have adopted a relatively low default contribution rate, typically 2 to 3 percent of pay (Profit Sharing/401(k) Council of America 2005). The reason commonly cited for the low rate is a concern that more employees will opt out of the savings plan with a higher default contribution rate. The experience of Company A as shown in figure 5.1 suggests that this concern may be unfounded. The participation rate under automatic enrollment is virtually identical with either a low

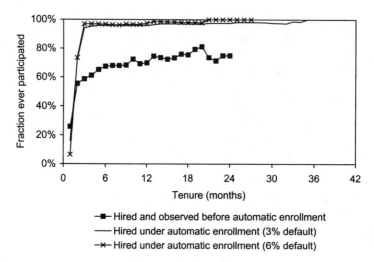

Fig. 5.1   Automatic enrollment for new hires and savings plan participation: Company A

Source: Authors' calculations.

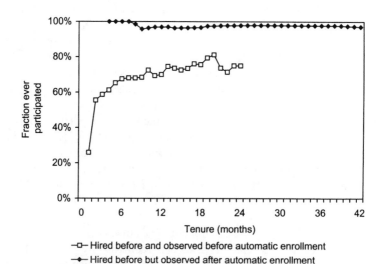

Fig. 5.2   Automatic enrollment for existing nonparticipants and savings plan participation: Company A

Source: Authors' calculations.

3 percent contribution rate or a higher 6 percent contribution rate, a result corroborated for other firms in Choi et al. (2004a,b). This finding should not in fact be much of a surprise, as employee contributions up to 6 percent of pay receive a generous dollar-for-dollar employer match at this firm. Most employees should thus have a strong incentive to contribute at least this amount to the savings plan (even if automatically enrolled at the lower 3 percent default contribution rate!).

5.2.2 Savings Plan Contributions

While automatic enrollment is effective in getting employees to partici-pate in their employer-sponsored savings plan, it is less effective at moti-vating them to make well-planned decisions about how much to save for re-tirement. Consider, for example, the distribution of contribution rates in figure 5.3 for employees at Company A hired under automatic enrollment at a 3 percent default contribution rate (the black bars) versus that of em-ployees hired under automatic enrollment at a 6 percent default contribu-tion rate (the gray bars). The sample under both default regimes in figure 5.3 is restricted to employees with the same level of tenure so that the re-sults are not confounded by differences in the time that employees have had to move away from the default.

The distributions of contribution rates are strikingly different for the two regimes. Under the 6 percent default regime, only 4 percent of em-ployees have a 3 percent contribution rate; 49 percent of employees have a 6 percent contribution rate (the default); and fully 79 percent of employees

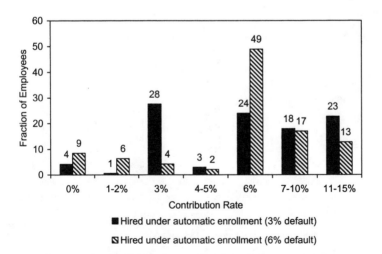

Fig. 5.3   Automatic enrollment for new hires and the distribution of 401(k) contri-bution rates: Company A (15–24 months tenure)
Source: Authors' calculations.

have a contribution rate at or above the 6 percent match threshold. In contrast, under the 3 percent default regime, 28 percent of employees are contributing at the default 3 percent contribution rate (a sevenfold increase relative to the 6 percent regime), while only 24 percent are contributing 6 percent of pay (half the fraction in the 6 percent regime). Sixty-five percent of employees overall are at or above the match threshold under the 3 percent regime, which is 14 percentage points lower in the 6 percent regime despite the very strong financial incentives to contribute at least 6 percent of pay due to the generous employer match.

The influence of the 3 percent default contribution rate is somewhat smaller in Company A than in other companies documented in the existing literature on automatic enrollment (Madrian and Shea 2001; Choi et al. 2002, 2004a,b). This circumstance is likely due to the extremely generous employer match at Company A, which provides a stronger incentive for employees at this firm relative to those at other firms to take action and increase their contribution rate to the match threshold. But clearly, the default contribution rate still has a sizeable impact on the savings outcomes of employees hired under automatic enrollment at Company A.

This impact is even more apparent if we examine the distribution of contribution rates for employees who were subject to automatic enrollment after being hired. Recall that employees who were not currently participating in the 401(k) plan were subject to automatic enrollment in December 2000 unless they specifically elected to opt out. Figure 5.4 compares the distribution of contribution rates for employees who were not subject to automatic enrollment in December 2000 because they had already elected

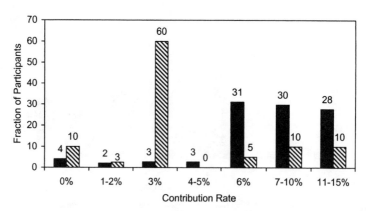

■ Initial participation before automatic enrollment

☒ Initial participation after automatic enrollment or never participated

Fig. 5.4   Automatic enrollment for existing hires and the distribution of 401(k) contribution rates: Company A (25–48 months tenure)
Source: Authors' calculations.

to participate in the 401(k) plan (the black bars) with that of employees who were subject to automatic enrollment with a 3 percent default contribution rate (the gray bars). Among employees who elected to participate in the 401(k) plan before automatic enrollment, only 3 percent chose a 3 percent contribution rate, 31 percent chose to contribute at the 6 percent match threshold, and fully 89 percent of these employees were contributing at or above the match threshold. In contrast, among employees subject to automatic enrollment, 60 percent are contributing at the 3 percent automatic enrollment default, while only 5 percent are at the 6 percent match threshold, and 25 percent are at or above the match threshold.

The comparison between the two groups of employees in figure 5.4 is not as clean as that in figure 5.3—we might expect the employees who were subject to automatic enrollment by virtue of the fact that they had not yet enrolled in the 401(k) plan to be different from more savings-motivated employees who were not subject to automatic enrollment. Nonetheless, the fraction of those subject to automatic enrollment at the 3 percent default contribution is large indeed. The general tenor of these results—the impact of the default contribution rate on the distribution of savings rates, both for new hires and for existing employees—has been corroborated for other firms in Madrian and Shea (2001) and Choi et al. (2002, 2004a,b).

5.2.3   Asset Allocation

Just as automatic enrollment tends to anchor employee contribution rates on the automatic enrollment default contribution rate, it also tends to anchor employee asset allocations on the automatic enrollment default asset allocation. This is shown for Company A in table 5.1, which gives the fraction of participants with any balances in the default fund, all balances in the default fund, and the combination of having all balances in the default fund along with the default contribution rate (the default automatic enrollment asset allocation in Company A is a money market fund). The

Table 5.1   Automatic enrollment and asset allocation outcomes: Company A (%)

	Hired after automatic enrollment (15–24 months tenure)		Hired before automatic enrollment (25–48 months tenure)	
	3% default contribution rate	6% default contribution rate	Participated before automatic enrollment	Participated after automatic enrollment
Any balances in default fund	33.8	46.5	9.9	86.1
All balances in default fund	25.6	39.5	1.4	61.1
100% default fund				
+ default contribution rate	18.1	32.6	0.0	52.8

Source: Authors' calculations.

employee groups shown are the same as those in figure 5.3 (columns 1 and 2) and figure 5.4 (columns 3 and 4).

Consider first the asset allocation of employees who were hired and initiated savings plan participation before automatic enrollment (column 3) and who were thus not subject to automatic enrollment. None of these employees is saving at the automatic enrollment default contribution rate of 3 percent in conjunction with an asset allocation entirely invested in the automatic enrollment default fund. Only 1 percent have all of their assets wholly invested in the default fund at any contribution rate. Finally, only 10 percent have any of their assets invested in the default fund. In general, investment in the automatic enrollment default fund is not widespread among employees who had to elect participation in the Company A savings plan actively.

For those employees who were subject to automatic enrollment because they had not initiated participation in the Company A savings plan by December 2000, the picture is very different. A whopping 86 percent of these participants have some of their assets allocated to the default fund (compared to 10 percent for their counterparts not subject to automatic enrollment), with 61 percent having everything invested in the default fund (compared to 1 percent for those not subject to automatic enrollment). Over half have retained both the default contribution rate of 3 percent and a 100 percent asset allocation in the default fund.

For employees subject to automatic enrollment as new hires, the impact of the default fund on asset allocation outcomes is not quite as stark as that for existing but nonparticipating employees subject to automatic enrollment, but it is nonetheless clear (columns 1 and 2). Between 34 percent and 47 percent of these participants have something invested in the default fund, and between 26 percent and 40 percent have everything invested in the default fund. Interestingly, the default investment allocation is much more prevalent among those hired with a 6 percent default contribution rate than for those hired with a 3 percent default contribution rate. The likely explanation has to do with the incentives for moving away from the automatic enrollment defaults. Employees hired with the 3 percent default contribution rate have two reasons to change their savings parameters: first, to choose a higher contribution rate to fully exploit the employer match and, second, to choose a nondefault asset allocation. For employees hired with a 6 percent default contribution rate, the first of these motives is missing and the cost/benefit calculation for making any change shifts toward doing nothing.

The automatic enrollment default asset allocation is not the only type of default that affects employee portfolio outcomes. As noted earlier, most organizations in the United States that offer a defined contribution savings plan match employee contributions to some extent. In most of them, the employer matching contributions are invested in the same manner as the employee's own contributions. In many large publicly traded companies, however, the match is directed into employer stock, sometimes with restrictions on when employees can diversify their matching balances out of employer stock, and sometimes not.[3] Choi, Laibson, and Madrian (2005b, 2007) document a strong flypaper effect when it comes to matching contributions that are directed into employer stock: the money sticks where it lands, even when employees are free to diversify.

A final example of how savings outcomes are impacted by a default asset allocation comes from the defined contribution component of different social security systems. Cronqvist and Thaler (2004) study the asset allocation outcomes of participants in the Swedish social security system and find that despite heavy advertising encouraging Swedes to actively elect their own asset allocation at the time that private accounts were instituted, one-third of the investments of those who were initially enrolled were directed to the default fund. After the initial rollout, when advertising was much diminished, the contributions of over 90 percent of new participants were invested in the default fund. Similarly, Rozinka and Tapia (2007) report that in Chile, over 70 percent of participants have retained the default fund.

5.2.4   Preretirement Cash Distributions

Another phase in the retirement savings accumulation process is changing jobs. When savings plan participants in the United States leave their employment, they may request a cash distribution, a direct rollover of savings plan balances into a new employer's savings plan, or a rollover of plan balances into a qualified individual savings account (e.g., an IRA). If terminated employees do not make an explicit request, the default treatment of those balances depends on how large their accounts are. For balances in excess of $5,000, balances remain in the former employer's savings plan by default. For balances below the $5,000 threshold, employers have the option to compel a cash distribution.[4] Anecdotally, most employers choose the cash distribution option as their default for terminated employees with balances under $5,000. Choi et al. (2002, 2004a,b) document the important relationship between balance size and the likelihood that terminated employees receive a cash distribution. In an analysis of data from four differ-

---

3. See Choi, Laibson, and Madrian (2005b) for evidence that allowing employees to diversify out of a match directed into employer stock has only a small effect on asset allocation outcomes relative to not being able to diversify the match at all. Because the companies that offer employer stock tend to be larger firms, 35 percent of participants in 401(k) plans have an investment menu that includes employer stock (Even and Macpherson 2004) even though only 10 percent of plans offer employer stock (Mitchell and Utkus 2003).

4. Beginning in January 2005, the threshold at which employers can compel a cash distribution for terminated employees will fall from $5,000 to $1,000. For balances between $1,000 and $5,000, employers will have two options absent other direction from the affected participants: retain the balances in their savings plan or roll over the balances into an IRA.

ent firms, they find that more than 70 percent of terminated employees with small account balances receive a cash distribution, the default for employees with balances below $5,000, whereas less than one-third of terminated employees with larger account balances receive a cash distribution. This can have important implications for whether these balances continue to be saved or whether they are consumed. Previous research suggests that the probability of receiving a cash distribution and subsequently rolling it over into an IRA or another savings plan is very low when the size of the distribution is small. Instead, these small distributions tend to be consumed.[5] When employers compel a cash distribution and employees receive an unexpected check in the mail, the path of least resistance is to simply consume the proceeds.

5.2.5   Postretirement Distributions

The final part of the retirement savings process is that of decumulation. There is ample reason to believe that the type of retirement income distributions received by older individuals from their retirement plans impacts economic outcomes. For example, Holden and Zick (2000) find that incomes for older widows fall by 47 percent following the death of their husbands, moving 17 percent of these women into poverty. Presumably, it would be possible to devise a retirement income stream that does not propel one spouse into poverty when the other one dies.

The actual decumulation options that are available to older individuals vary widely across different types of retirement income vehicles. For example, in the U.S. Social Security system, payments do not begin until individuals actively sign up to begin receiving them, but there are no options when it comes to the structure of the benefits. Recipients essentially receive an inflation-protected life annuity that is based on an individual's own earnings history and potentially that of his or her spouse. For married couples, Social Security payments fall subsequent to the death of one partner, but the surviving spouse continues to receive some benefits.

In a typical employer-sponsored defined benefit savings plan in the United States, retired individuals have more options. Married individuals can take their retirement income as a single annuity or as a joint-and-survivor annuity with a lower monthly benefit amount. In addition to these different annuity options, some employers also offer the choice of a lump-sum payout.

The options in an employer-sponsored defined contribution savings plan are different still. In some companies, the only choice is a lump-sum

---

5. Poterba, Venti, and Wise (1998) report that the probability that a cash distribution is rolled over into an IRA or another employer's savings plan is only 5 to 16 percent for distributions of less than $5,000. The overall probability that a cash distribution is rolled over into an IRA or another employer's savings plan or invested in some other savings vehicle is slightly higher at 14 to 33 percent.

distribution. In others, the employer may retain the account balances, giving individuals the option to take periodic and variable distributions. In still others, the employer may facilitate the purchase of annuities through a private provider.

Just as in the retirement income accumulation phase, defaults also matter for the retirement income decumulation phase. The most telling evidence comes from a government-mandated change in the annuitization options that traditional defined benefit pension plans must offer their beneficiaries. The U.S. regulatory framework established for pensions in 1974 required that the default annuity option offered to married pension plan participants be a joint-and-one-half-survivor annuity. Married beneficiaries could, however, opt out of this default, choosing a single life annuity with higher monthly benefits during the retired worker's lifetime. In 1984, these regulations were amended to require the notarized signature of the spouse if a retired worker decided to opt for a single life rather than the joint-and-survivor annuity.

Holden and Nicholson (1998) document the effect of this change in the default annuity option on the annuitization outcomes among married men with traditional employer-sponsored pensions. Before the institution of the joint-and-survivor default in 1974, they calculate that less than half of married men elected the joint-and-survivor option. After the move to the joint-and-survivor default, they estimate an increase in joint-and-survivor annuitization among married men of over 25 percentage points. It is not clear how much of this shift is due to the change in the default among retirees at firms that offered both the single life option and the joint-and-survivor option before the regulatory mandate, and how much is due to the increased availability of joint-and-survivor annuities at firms that were not previously offering them. Saku (2001), however, examines only the impact of the 1984 amendment that requires explicit spousal consent to opt out of a joint-and-survivor annuity. By this time, all firms would have been offering joint-and-survivor options to their pension beneficiaries. He finds an increase in joint-and-survivor annuitization of 5 to 10 percentage points following this strengthening of the default. One might expect much larger effects from its initial implementation so that the 25 percentage-point effect estimated by Holden and Nicholson (1998) is likely mostly attributable to the change in the default annuity option rather than an increase in the provision by employers of joint-and-survivor annuities.

5.2.6 Elective Defaults

The evidence presented so far all pertains to defaults that specify the savings outcome that will occur if individuals take no action. There are, however, some interesting examples of employer attempts to improve savings outcomes through the use of affirmative savings elections that exploit features of some of the defaults discussed in the previous sections. For lack of a better term, we refer to these as *elective defaults,* although this does stretch the typical usage of the word "default."

One particularly successful elective default is the contribution rate escalator popularized by the Save More Tomorrow (SMarT) plan of Benartzi and Thaler (2004). With a contribution escalator, participants elect to have their savings plan contribution rate increase in the future if they take no further action; in other words, they opt into a default of increasing contributions. The striking results of the first experiment with such a contribution escalator, in which employees signed up for future contribution rate increases of 3 percentage points per year, are reported in Benartzi and Thaler (2004) and Utkus and Young (2004). At the company studied, employees who elected the contribution escalator feature saw their savings plan contributions increase by 10.1 percentage points over four years, from 3.5 percent to 13.6 percent of pay. In contrast, employees who did not sign up for the contribution escalator but who instead elected to adopt immediately a savings rate recommended to them had higher initial contribution rates but increased their savings plan contributions by only 4.4 percentage points over four years, from 4.4 percent to 8.8 percent of pay. Other companies that have subsequently incorporated a contribution escalation feature into their savings plans have also seen increases in employee contribution rates (Utkus 2002). Such contribution escalators are an interesting way to capitalize on the widespread savings plan inertia documented thus far. They are also something that could be easily incorporated as a proper savings plan default.

Choi, Laibson, and Madrian (2005c), Beshears et al. (2006), and Hewitt Associates (2003) study another elective default dubbed Quick Enrollment. Quick Enrollment operates by giving employees an easy way to elect a preselected contribution rate and asset allocation from among the many other options that are available within an employer's savings plan. Figure 5.5 shows the impact of Quick Enrollment on savings plan participation at two different firms (see Choi, Laibson, and Madrian 2005c). At Company B, new hires were given Quick Enrollment forms at orientation allowing them to check a box to be enrolled in their firm's savings plan at a 2 percent contribution rate with a preselected asset allocation (50 percent in a money market fund and 50 percent in a stable value fund). Participation rates for employees with four months of tenure tripled under Quick Enrollment, from 9 percent of new hires to 34 percent. At Company C, nonparticipating employees at all levels of tenure were mailed postage-paid Quick Enrollment response cards allowing them to check a box to be enrolled in their firm's savings plan at a 3 percent contribution rate allocated entirely to a money market fund. Relative to the enrollment trends of nonparticipants a year prior to the mailing, savings plan participation four months later more than doubled, from 6 percent of nonparticipants enrolling to 16 percent. A different implementation of Quick Enrollment at Company B

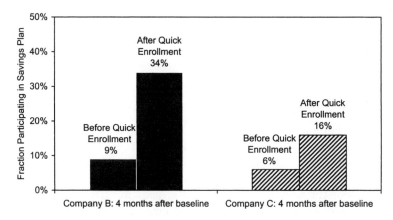

Fig. 5.5   Quick Enrollment and savings plan participation: Companies B and C
Source: Choi, Laibson, and Madrian (2005c).

directed toward existing nonparticipants allowed them to choose any contribution rate allowed by the plan with the same preselected asset allocation previously described. Fully 25 percent of nonparticipants signed up
for the savings plan over a four-month period following this version of
Quick Enrollment (Beshears et al. 2006).

Beyond its effects on savings plan participation, the impact of Quick Enrollment on other savings outcomes is interesting because, like automatic
enrollment, Quick Enrollment induces a heavy clustering of enrollees at
the employer-selected default contribution rate and asset allocation. At
Company B, no savings plan participants affirmatively elected the Quick
Enrollment default asset allocation prior to the implementation of Quick
Enrollment. Among those participants offered Quick Enrollment at the
new hire orientations, 60 percent have the Quick Enrollment default asset
allocation. Among those who enrolled in the savings plan when Quick Enrollment was offered to existing nonparticipants, 91 percent have the
Quick Enrollment default asset allocation. The picture is similar at Company C, where only 6 percent of participants prior to Quick Enrollment
affirmatively elected the Quick Enrollment default asset allocation. In contrast, between 75 percent and 91 percent of existing nonparticipants who
were offered Quick Enrollment and became participants have the Quick
Enrollment default asset allocation.

The impact of Quick Enrollment on contribution rates is equally striking. At Company B, the fraction of new hires at the Quick Enrollment default contribution rate of 2 percent of pay increased from 1 percent of employees before Quick Enrollment to 14 percent of employees after Quick
Enrollment. At Company C, the fraction of newly participating employees
at the Quick Enrollment default contribution rate of 3 percent increased
from less than 1 percent of employees before Quick Enrollment to 12 per-

cent of employees after Quick Enrollment. In both companies, the fraction of savings plan participants at the Quick Enrollment defaults (as opposed to the fraction of employees overall) is much higher because the participation rates among the impacted groups are relatively low.

5.3   Explaining the Impact of Defaults on Retirement Savings Outcomes

The substantial evidence presented in the preceding section of this chapter on the impact of defaults on savings outcomes is interesting for (at least) three reasons: first, in most of the examples cited, switching from one default to another resulted in very different savings outcomes even though the change in the default did not affect the menu of savings options available to individuals; second, none of the defaults proscribed employees from effecting a different savings outcome; and third, the direct transaction costs (filling out a form, or calling a benefits hotline) for making savings plan changes were generally small.[6]

If direct transaction costs are not a plausible explanation for the persistence of savings plan defaults, then what factors are? In this section of the chapter, we consider three alternative explanations: (1) procrastination generated by the complexity of the decision-making task, (2) procrastination generated by present-biased preferences, and (3) a perception of the default as an endorsement for certain savings outcomes. Madrian and Shea (2001) discuss some alternative explanations, but these three strike us as the most plausible given the existing empirical evidence.

5.3.1   The Complexity of Making a Nondefault Savings Plan Election

There are several sources of complexity involved in making an optimal savings plan decision. Consider, for example, the array of participation options in a typical defined contribution savings plan. Individuals must first choose what fraction of compensation to contribute to their savings plan, which in a typical plan would be anything from 1 to 15 percent of compensation (in some plans even higher contribution rates are allowed). They must then choose how to allocate that contribution among the available fund options. In a plan with ten funds and a maximum contribution rate of 15 percent, the number of different savings plan options is immense.

For some employees, a second source of complexity is learning how to evaluate the myriad savings plan options. Surveys of financial literacy consistently find that many individuals are not well-equipped to make complicated financial decisions. For example, in a recent survey of defined contribution savings plan participants, John Hancock Financial Services (2002) reports:

---

6. See Choi, Laibson, and Madrian (2005a) for evidence on the magnitude of some of these direct transaction costs.

- 38 percent of respondents report that they have little or no financial knowledge.
- 40 percent of respondents believe that a money market fund contains stocks.
- Two-thirds of respondents do not know that it is possible to lose money in government bonds.
- Respondents, on average, believe that employer stock is less risky than a stock mutual fund.

Given these results, it should not be surprising that two-thirds of these respondents also report that they would be better off working with an investment advisor than managing retirement investments solo.

The psychology literature has documented a tendency of individuals to put off making decisions as the complexity of the task increases (Tversky and Shafir 1992; Shafir, Simonson, and Tversky 1993; Dhar and Nowlis 1999; Iyengar and Lepper 2000). Evidence supporting the notion that the complexity of the asset allocation task leads employees to delay savings plan enrollment comes from a recent study by Iyengar, Huberman, and Jiang (2004). They document a strong negative relationship between the number of funds offered in a 401(k) plan and the 401(k) participation rate: having an additional ten funds in the fund menu leads to a 1.5 to 2 percentage point decline in participation, a result that holds even among firms with a relatively low number of funds. One suspects that this would also act as a deterrent to making asset allocation changes after the initial participation decision has been made.

A likely reason that savings plan participation is so much higher under automatic enrollment than with an opt-in enrollment mechanism is that automatic enrollment decouples the savings plan participation decision from the contribution rate and asset allocation decision. The initial participation decision is simplified from one that involves evaluating myriad options to a simple comparison of two alternatives: nonparticipation (consumption or saving outside of the savings plan) versus participating at a prespecified contribution rate with a prespecified asset allocation. Furthermore, Madrian and Shea (2001) and Choi et al. (2004b) find that automatic enrollment has its largest impact on participation for those workers who generally have the least amount of financial sophistication—the young and those with low levels of tenure (who would have less knowledge about their own particular savings plan). These are workers for whom the complexity of the participation decision would be a greater deterrent to enrolling in the savings plan under an opt-in regime.

Quick Enrollment works in much the same way as automatic enrollment, simplifying the participation decision by giving individuals a predetermined contribution rate and asset allocation bundle(s) that need only be compared to nonparticipation. The effect of Quick Enrollment on participation, however, is not as great as that of automatic enrollment, suggesting that the participation increases under automatic enrollment are due to more than just the simplification of the decision-making task.

5.3.2   Present-Biased Preferences and Procrastination

Recent research in behavioral economics has fingered another reason for the observed persistence in savings plan outcomes—individual problems with self-control (Laibson, Repetto, and Tobacman 1998; O'Donoghue and Rabin 1999; Diamond and Koszegi 2003). As the adage goes, why do today what you can put off until tomorrow? O'Donoghue and Rabin (1999) propose a model in which, under certain conditions (specifically, naïveté about time-inconsistent preferences), individuals may never reallocate their portfolios away from poor-performing investments even when the direct transactions costs of doing so are relatively small. A similar type of argument can be made for delays in savings plan enrollment. The possibility of the latter is suggested by the fact that savings plan participation rates prior to automatic enrollment in Company A and other firms that have been studied (Madrian and Shea 2001; Choi et al. 2002, 2004a,b) never exceed those under automatic enrollment, even at very high levels of tenure. It is also suggested by the substantial fraction of automatic enrollees at Company A who remained at the relatively low 3 percent default contribution rate two years after hire despite a 100 percent employer match on contributions up to 6 percent of pay. Additional corroborating evidence comes from Choi, Laibson, and Madrian (2005a), who document that even among older workers with very high average levels of tenure, roughly half fail to exploit the full match in their employer-sponsored savings plan, leaving matching contributions equal to roughly 1.3 percent of pay unclaimed (in companies without automatic enrollment).

5.3.3   The Default as an Endorsement

Default options may also influence outcomes if individuals perceive the default as an endorsement of a particular course of action (an endorsement effect). The lack of financial sophistication on the part of many individuals discussed in the preceding may lead them to search for advice without necessarily knowing the best place to find it. Because employer-sponsored savings plans are supposed to be run for the benefit of employees (that, after all, is why they are referred to as "employee benefits"), some individuals may incorrectly perceive that an employer-specified default must be in the best interest of the firm's employees.[7]

There are several pieces of evidence consistent with the notion that em-

---

7. While this may be true for some employer-specified defaults, in general, firms weigh other issues such as cost and legal liability in their selection of defaults, not only the potential benefit to employees.

Table 5.2   Automatic enrollment and asset allocation outcomes of employees not subject to automatic enrollment: Company D (%)

	Hired before automatic enrollment and initiated participation before automatic enrollment	Hired before automatic enrollment but initiated participation after automatic enrollment applied to newly hired employees
Any balances in default fund	13.3	28.9
All balances in default fund	2.3	16.1

Source: Taken from Madrian and Shea (2001, figures IVb and IVc)

ployees perceive defaults in part as some sort of advice or recommendation from their employer. The first comes from companies who have implemented automatic enrollment for only new hires going forward. In these companies, none of the employees hired before automatic enrollment are directly affected (that is, none of them are automatically enrolled), but some of them will have affirmatively elected to participate in the savings plan before automatic enrollment was instituted for anyone, whereas others will have affirmatively elected to participate only after automatic enrollment was implemented for new hires going forward. Madrian and Shea (2001) show that the fraction of assets allocated to the automatic enrollment default investment fund is more than three times as high for the latter group as it is for the former (see table 5.2).[8] Interestingly, Madrian and Shea do not find similar evidence for the contribution rates elected by these two groups of employees: those employees hired before automatic enrollment but who enroll in their savings plan only after automatic enrollment are not substantially more likely to choose the automatic enrollment default contribution rate than are their counterparts who enrolled in the savings plan before automatic enrollment. That the endorsement implicit in the automatic enrollment defaults is more important for asset allocation outcomes than for contribution rate outcomes is consistent with the notion that employees are much more uncertain about choosing an appropriate asset allocation than about choosing an appropriate contribution rate (or, at least, about choosing a contribution rate that garners the full employer match).[9]

Further evidence on the endorsement effect under automatic enrollment

8. The data for Company D in table 5.2 comes from Madrian and Shea (2001). This company implemented automatic enrollment with a 3 percent default contribution rate invested wholly in a money market fund. The match threshold at this firm was 6 percent.

9. Choi, Laibson, and Madrian (2005c) discuss in greater detail reasons why the asset allocation task may be more complicated for employees than the decision about how much to contribute to the savings plan.

comes from the savings outcomes of employees hired under automatic enrollment who choose to move away from the automatic enrollment default. These individuals have overcome the forces of inertia and have taken action. Even so, their asset allocation continues to be much more heavily invested in the automatic enrollment default fund than that of employees hired prior to automatic enrollment (Madrian and Shea 2001; Choi et al. 2004b). Table 5.3 illustrates this tendency for employees at Company A and Company D. The first column in table 5.3 shows the importance of the automatic enrollment default asset allocation for employees hired before automatic enrollment (and, for company A, employees who elected to participate before automatic enrollment). The fraction of these employees with anything in the default fund is 10 percent in Company A and 18 percent in Company D. The fraction with everything invested in the default fund is lower still: 1 percent at Company A and 5 percent at Company D. In contrast, those employees hired under automatic enrollment who have made an active election to move away from the automatic enrollment default, changing either their asset allocation or their contribution rate or both, are much more heavily invested in the automatic enrollment default despite having incurred the transactions costs of changing the parameters of their savings plan participation. Among automatic enrollees who have made a change from the automatic enrollment default, the fraction with any balances in the default fund is 19 percent at Company A, and 71 percent at Company D, much higher than for the employees hired before automatic enrollment. The proportional differences for those with everything in the automatic enrollment default fund are greater still. Clearly, the default fund exerts an impact on the asset allocation of employees hired under automatic enrollment even after these employees have elected to make

Table 5.3   Automatic enrollment and asset allocation outcomes of employees not at the automatic enrollment default asset allocation and contribution rate: Companies A and D (%)

	Hired before automatic enrollment	Hired after automatic enrollment but not at the default asset allocation and contribution rate
Company A		
Any balances in default fund	9.9	19.4
All balances in default fund	1.4	9.3
Company D		
Any balances in default fund	18.2	71.3
All balances in default fund	5.2	30.8

Sources: Authors' calculations for Company A and Madrian and Shea (2001, table VII) for Company D.

a change. A final piece of evidence on the endorsement effect of savings plan defaults comes from the fraction of employee contributions invested in employer stock in companies where employer stock is included in the fund menu. Benartzi (2001), Holden and VanDerhei (2001), and Brown, Liang, and Weisbenner (2006) all find that when the employer directs matching contributions into employer stock, the fraction of the employee's own contributions allocated to employer stock is higher than when the match is allocated according to the employee's direction.

5.4   Designing Public Policy When Defaults Matter

There are many goals associated with public policy. When it comes to retirement saving, politicians, economists, and other social planners would largely agree that if governments are to sponsor costly social welfare programs for individuals who are impoverished, they should also promote institutions that provide sufficient income to individuals when retired in order to reduce the reliance on costly social welfare programs. Because of the risks that defined benefit retirement income schemes impose on employers (through defined benefit pensions) and governments/taxpayers (through Social Security), there has been a broader trend toward defined contribution savings schemes through both private and government-sponsored institutions (e.g., 401(k) savings plans in the United States and the social security systems in Sweden and Chile). But if defaults have the potential to significantly impact savings outcomes in these types of schemes, what types of defaults should public policy encourage, especially if individuals have heterogeneous savings needs? In this section, we discuss first some of the conceptual issues associated with thinking about an "optimal" default. We then give some examples of public policy and defaults in practice, both those that seem sensible from the standpoint of promoting better savings outcomes and those that do not.

5.4.1   Is There an "Optimal" Default?

Choi et al. (2005) model the choice of an optimal default savings plan enrollment mechanism from the perspective of a social planner interested in maximizing individual welfare. In this model, defaults matter for three key reasons. First, individuals face a cost for opting out of the chosen default. Second, this cost varies over time, creating an option value to waiting for a low cost period to take action. Third, individuals with present-biased preferences may procrastinate in their decision to opt out of the default, even in a low cost period, if they believe that they are more likely to do so in the future. Three different potential enrollment defaults emerge from the model: automatic enrollment, requiring an affirmative participation election (opt-in), and requiring employees to actively make a decision so that there is, in essence, no default (but all employees must bear the immediate transactions costs of deciding what to do). Choi et al. (2005) refer to this latter outcome as the "active decision" approach. Which of these enrollment regimes is optimal varies according to the parameters in the model.

The conditions under which each of these approaches to savings plan enrollment is likely to be optimal, from both a theoretical and a practical standpoint, are discussed in greater detail in Choi et al. (2005), but we briefly describe them here. Defaults tend to be optimal when there is a large degree of homogeneity in individual preferences and when decision makers have limited expertise. In the case of a firm with an employer match, if most employees would prefer to be saving at the match threshold, then automatic enrollment with a default contribution rate equal to the match threshold is likely to be optimal. Requiring an affirmative participation election, on the other hand, is likely to be optimal if most individuals share a preference not to be participating in the savings plan[10] or if individuals have very heterogeneous preferences and little tendency to procrastinate. Requiring an active decision is more appropriate when individual heterogeneity implies that one choice is not ideal for everyone, but individuals do have a tendency to procrastinate.

Although requiring the use of an active decision as an alternative to selecting a default is uncommon in the context of savings plans, Choi et al. (2005) study the effect of just such an approach on savings plan outcomes in one firm. They find that requiring employees to make an active decision leads to substantially higher initial participation rates than those achieved under an opt-in enrollment regime without any perverse effects on the distribution of contribution rates such as is observed with mechanisms like automatic enrollment or Quick Enrollment.

For the purposes of this chapter, the important point of the modeling effort in Choi et al. (2005) is that there is no single optimal savings plan enrollment mechanism—the optimal default depends on parameters in the model, which are likely to vary across both institutions and individuals. More generally, the framework for thinking about an optimal savings plan enrollment mechanism can be used to think about how sensible other types of economic defaults are likely to be. We turn now to a few specific examples related to savings.

5.4.2   For Better and for Worse: Public Policy and Defaults in Practice

There are many interesting examples of how public policy both encourages and discourages better savings plan outcomes, some that have already been mentioned and others that have not. The first is the legislative mandate that, in defined benefit pension plans, the default payout option for

---

10. This could be true in a firm with a largely low-income workforce that has a high social security replacement rate, or in a firm with a generous defined benefit pension as the primary source of retirement income.

married individuals is a joint-and-survivor annuity. As discussed earlier, this mandate resulted in a sizeable increase in the fraction of married defined benefit pension recipients with joint-and-survivor annuities. This mandate, which was a matter of public policy rather than a matter of choice for pension plan providers, was adopted in order to improve the financial security of widows after their husbands' deaths. Whether it was successful at this objective has not been examined. However, Johnson, Uccello, and Goldwyn (2003) show that those married individuals who have opted out of this default appear to have had economically sound reasons for doing so, such as having a spouse with either his or her own source of retirement income or a shorter life expectancy than the pension beneficiary.

In the context of thinking about an optimal default, there are three particularly interesting aspects of this joint-and-survivor annuity default. The first is that there are actually two different default annuities: one for single individuals (a single life annuity) and the joint-and-survivor annuity for married individuals. Opt-in versus opt-out savings plan enrollment mechanisms, on the other hand, are blanket defaults that apply to everyone (unless individuals opt out). Clearly there is a need to think more carefully about the potential role of more nuanced defaults that apply only to some individuals in certain situations. The second interesting feature of the joint-and-survivor annuity default is that the decision to accept the default or to opt out of it is irrevocable—once made it cannot be reversed. The third interesting feature, an extension of the second, is that because the annuitization outcome is irreversible, individuals cannot forever delay the decision about what type of annuity is most appropriate—any opt-out decision must be made before the pension beneficiary can start receiving pension income. These two features reduce the scope for procrastination due to present-biased preferences. Individuals for whom a single-life annuity is better face strong incentives to take action to express those preferences quickly. This consequence shares some similarities with the active decision approach to savings plan participation discussed in the preceding. Although there is a default (in contrast to the active decision approach discussed in the preceding), it is structured in such a way as to provide strong incentives to take action immediately for those individuals who desire to opt out.

Overall, many features of the joint-and-survivor annuity default seem to work well. The one drawback, perhaps, is that for most individuals, understanding annuity options is no less complicated than understanding asset allocation. Annuity providers are continuing to develop a rich set of annuity products, some of which may be more appropriate to particular individuals than the one-sized joint-and-survivor default specified for married pension beneficiaries. The complexity of evaluating the different annuity products available in the market likely means that any default will significantly influence realized outcomes simply because of the endorsement effect.

Another interesting default to consider from a public policy perspective is the composition of the default investment fund in the defined contribution component of various social security systems. In contrast to the default asset allocation chosen by most employers that have automatic enrollment in the United States, which tends to be a single mutual fund, some countries such as Sweden, Chile, and Mexico have selected a default which is a portfolio of different types of financial assets. For example, in Sweden, the default includes exposure to domestic and international equities, bonds, and the money market.[11] Moreover, it is well diversified against geographical, industrial, and asset market shocks, and it comes with a relatively low expense ratio of approximately 0.16 percent. Although it is difficult to say whether the Swedish social security system could have chosen a better default asset allocation, Cronqvist and Thaler (2004) show that the portfolio performance of those in the default fund exceeded that of individuals who opted out of the default and selected their own asset allocation. On this metric, the default would seem to have been relatively well chosen.

The default investment portfolios in the Chilean social security system and in the defined contribution component of the Mexican social security system are interesting for another reason—in both countries the default investment fund for older workers differs from that for younger workers (Rozinka and Tapia 2007). In Chile, there are three different default asset allocations, one for workers below age thirty-five, a second for men aged thirty-six to fifty-five and women aged thirty-six to fifty, and a third for men aged fifty-six and older and women aged fifty-one and older. The Chilean default funds differ in their relative exposure to equities (both foreign and domestic) and fixed income securities, with the default portfolios holding fewer equities and more bonds as participants age. This pattern of equity versus bond holding is certainly consistent with what many financial planners would recommend. In Mexico, the default funds differ largely in the type of fixed income investments that they hold. In contrast to the Swedish default asset allocation, the defaults in both Chile and Mexico are heavily weighted toward domestic securities. In Mexico, there are no foreign investments in the default funds; in Chile, the highest foreign investment exposure is 34 percent in the default fund for younger workers (Rozinka and Tapia 2007). This is in contrast to Sweden, in which two-thirds of the default portfolio is non-Swedish stocks, and probably represents inadequate geographic diversification in the Chilean and Mexican defaults.

Another interesting default to consider from a policy perspective is the

---

11. The specific asset allocation as reported in Cronqvist and Thaler (2004) is Swedish stocks (17 percent), non-Swedish stocks (65 percent), inflation-indexed bonds (10 percent), hedge funds (4 percent), and private equity (4 percent).

treatment of savings plan balances following employee termination. This default shares one feature with the default annuity options just discussed. Rather than having a single blanket default option, the default outcome depends on the size of the terminated employee's account balance: balances less than $5,000 are sent to individuals as a cash distribution unless individuals direct the employer to roll over the balances into another qualified savings plan, whereas balances more than $5,000 are retained by the employer unless individuals direct otherwise. However, as previously noted, there is significant leakage from the retirement system for employees with account balances below the $5,000 threshold.

Policymakers in the United States reached an interesting compromise to deal with this issue of leakage. The cash distribution default is costly for employees because it reduces their long-term retirement accumulations, but retaining small account balances is costly for employers because of the fixed costs associated with retaining individual accounts. The public policy compromise applies to the accounts of terminated employees with balances greater than $1,000 and less than $5,000. For these accounts, employers cannot compel a cash distribution. Rather, they can keep the accounts (as was being done all along for accounts of greater than $5,000), or they can roll the accounts over into qualified individual savings plans (e.g., an IRA). Employers retain the option to compel a cash distribution for accounts under $1,000 although they could change the default for these accounts as well and roll the balances into an IRA. Because this change has not taken effect at the time of this writing, it is too early to assess the outcome, but it at least seems like an example of public policy promoting better savings outcomes. There is a catch, however: the regulations pertaining to the default fund associated with these automatic IRA rollovers make it highly unlikely that any employer will pick anything other than an extremely conservative default fund (e.g., a money market fund). Thus, it is likely that the majority of $1,000 to $5,000 account balances will be rolled over into an IRA following employee termination, where they will languish over time earning a rate of return that barely keeps pace with inflation. Public policy on this aspect of the default could probably do better.

Another area in which public policy could do better is with employer matches made in the form of employer stock. As already noted, employer matching contributions made in employer stock tend to stick where they land, which imposes greater financial risk on employees—first, because their retirement savings portfolio itself is not well diversified and, second, because much of the risk to their retirement savings portfolio is correlated with the risk to their labor income. Unfortunately, many employees do not seem to understand these risks. The John Hancock Financial Services (2002) Eighth Defined Contribution Plan Survey finds that savings plan participants on average rate employer stock as less risky than an equity mutual fund. Similarly, Benartzi et al. (2004) find that only 33 percent of savings plan participants believe that their employer stock is riskier than a diversified stock fund, whereas 39 percent believe it is equally risky and 25 percent believe it is safer. Furthermore, 20 percent of respondents say they would prefer $1,000 in employer stock that they could not diversify until age fifty to $1,000 that they could invest at their own discretion.

One could view public policy in this area as neutral: the government leaves companies to run their savings plans as they see fit, and some establish a match in which contributions are directed into employer stock. But contrast the approach here with the regulation of defined benefit pension plans, in which employer stock holdings are limited to no more than 10 percent of total plan assets, or to the rather proactive joint-and-survivor annuity default. Public policy could certainly greatly reduce the amount of employer stock held in defined contribution savings plans, either by precluding employer stock as an investment option altogether or by simply mandating that matching contributions be defaulted to the asset allocation selected by the employee.

5.5 Conclusion

This chapter has demonstrated the tremendous influence that defaults exert on realized savings outcomes at every stage of the savings life cycle: savings plan participation, contributions, asset allocation, rollovers, and decumulation. That defaults can so easily sway such a significant economic outcome has important implications for understanding the psychology of economic decision making. But it also has important implications for the role of public policy toward saving. Defaults are not neutral—they can either facilitate or hinder better savings outcomes. Current public policies toward saving include examples of both.

References

Abadie, Alberto, and Sebastien Gay. 2004. The impact of presumed consent legislation on cadaveric organ donation: A cross-country study. *Journal of Health Economics* 25 (4): 599–620.
Benartzi, Shlomo. 2001. Excessive extrapolation and the allocation of 401(k) accounts to company stock. *Journal of Finance* 56 (5): 1747–64.
Benartzi, Shlomo, and Richard H. Thaler. 2004. Save More Tomorrow™: Using behavioral economics to increase employee saving. *Journal of Political Economy* 112 (S1): S164–S187.
Benartzi, Shlomo, Richard Thaler, Stephen Utkus, and Cass Sunstein. 2004. Company stock, market rationality, and legal reform. University of Chicago, Graduate School of Business. Mimeograph.

Beshears, John, James J. Choi, David Laibson, and Brigitte C. Madrian. 2006. Simplification and Saving. Harvard University. Mimeograph.

Brown, Jeffrey R., Nellie Liang, and Scott Weisbenner. 2006. 401(k) matching contributions in company stock: Costs and benefits for firms and workers. *Journal of Public Economics* 90 (6–7): 1315–46.

Choi, James J., David Laibson, and Brigitte C. Madrian. 2005a. $100 bills on the sidewalk: Suboptimal saving in 401(k) savings plans. NBER Working Paper no. 11554. Cambridge, MA: National Bureau of Economic Research.

———. 2005b. Are empowerment and education enough: Underdiversification in 401(k) plans. *Brookings Papers on Economic Activity,* Issue no. 2:151–98. Washington, DC: Brookings Institution.

———. 2005c. Reducing the complexity costs of 401(k) participation: The case of quick enrollment. Harvard University, Working Paper.

———. 2007. Mental accounting and portfolio choice: Evidence from a flypaper effect. Yale University, Working Paper.

Choi, James J., David Laibson, Brigitte C. Madrian, and Andrew Metrick. 2002. Defined contribution pensions: Plan rules, participant choices, and the path of least resistance. In *Tax policy and the economy,* Vol. 16, ed. James Poterba, 67–114. Cambridge, MA: MIT Press.

———. 2004a. For better or for worse: Default effects and 401(k) savings behavior. In *Perspectives in the Economics of Aging,* ed. David A Wise, 81–121. Chicago: University of Chicago Press.

———. 2004b. Employees' investment decisions about company stock. In *Pension design and structure: New lessons from behavioral finance,* ed. Olivia Mitchell and Stephen Utkus, 121–37. Oxford, UK: Oxford University Press.

———. 2005. Optimal defaults and active decisions. NBER Working Paper no. 11074. Cambridge, MA: National Bureau of Economic Research.

Cronqvist, Henrik, and Richard H. Thaler. 2004. Design choices in privatized social security systems: Learning from the Swedish experience. *American Economic Review Papers and Proceedings* 94 (2): 424–28.

Dhar, Ravi, and Stephen M. Nowlis. 1999. The effect of time pressure on consumer choice deferral. *Journal of Consumer Research* 25 (4): 369–84.

Diamond, Peter, and Botond Koszegi. 2003. Quasi-hyperbolic discounting and retirement. *Journal of Public Economics* 87 (9–10): 1839–72.

Employee Benefit Research Institute. 2005. The U.S. retirement income system. Washington, DC: Employee Benefit Research Institute. http://www.ebri.org/pdf/publications/facts/0405fact.pdf.

Even, William E., and David A. Macpherson. 2004. Company stock in pension funds. *National Tax Journal* 56 (4): 299–313.

Hewitt Associates. 2003. *Increasing participation through quick enrollment.* Lincolnshire, IL: Hewitt Associates.

———. 2005. *Survey highlights: Trends and experience in 401(k) plans 2005.* Lincolnshire, IL: Hewitt Associates.

Holden, Karen C., and Sean Nicholson. 1998. Selection of a joint-and-survivor pension. Institute for Research on Poverty Discussion Paper no. 1175-98. Madison, WI: University of Wisconsin, Madison.

Holden, Karen C., and Kathleen Zick. 2000. Distributional changes in income and wealth upon widowhood: Implications for private insurance and public policy. In *Retirement needs framework,* 69–79. SOA Monograph M-RS00-1. Schaumburg, IL: Society of Actuaries.

Holden, Sarah, and Jack VanDerhei. 2001. 401(k) plan asset allocation, account balances, and loan activity in 2000. *ICI Perspective* 7 (5): 1–27.

Iyengar, Sheena S., Gur Huberman, and Wei Jiang. 2004. How much choice is too much?: Contributions to 401(k) retirement plans. In *Pension design and structure: New lessons from behavioral finance,* ed. Olivia Mitchell and Stephen Utkus, 83–95. Oxford, UK: Oxford University Press.

Iyengar, Sheena S., and Mark Lepper. 2000. When choice is demotivating: Can one desire too much of a good thing? *Journal of Personality and Social Psychology* 79:995–1006.

John Hancock Financial Services. 2002. *Eighth defined contribution plan survey: Insight into participant investment knowledge & behavior.* Boston: John Hancock Financial Services.

Johnson, Eric J., Steven Bellman, and Gerald L. Lohse. 2003. Defaults, framing and privacy: Why opting in-opting out. *Marketing Letters* 13 (1): 5–15.

Johnson, Eric J., and Daniel Goldstein. 2003. Do defaults save lives? *Science* 302:1338–39.

Johnson, Eric J., John Hershey, Jacqueline Meszaros, and Howard Kunreuther. 1993. Framing, probability distortions, and insurance decisions. *Journal of Risk and Uncertainty* 7 (1): 35–53.

Johnson, Richard W., Cori E. Uccello, and Joshua H. Goldwyn. 2003. Singe life vs. joint and survivor pension payout options: How do married retirees choose? Washington, DC: The Urban Institute.

Laibson, David I., Andrea Repetto, and Jeremy Tobacman. 1998. Self-control and saving for retirement. *Brookings Papers on Economic Activity,* Issue no. 1:91–196.

Madrian, Brigitte C., and Dennis F. Shea. 2001. The power of suggestion: Inertia in 401(k) participation and savings behavior. *Quarterly Journal of Economics* 116 (4): 1149–87.

Mitchell, Olivia, and Steven Utkus. 2003. The role of company stock in defined contribution plans. In *The pension challenge: Risk transfers and retirement income security,* ed. Olivia Mitchell and Kent Smetters, 33–70. London: Oxford University Press.

O'Donoghue, Ted, and Matthew Rabin. 1999. Procrastination in preparing for retirement. In *Behavioral dimensions of retirement economics,* ed. Henry Aaron, 125–56. Washington DC: The Brookings Institute.

Park, C. Whan, Sung Y. Jun, and Deborah J. MacInnis. 2000. Choosing what I want versus rejecting what I do not want: An application of decision framing to product option choice decisions. *Journal of Marketing Research* 37 (2): 187–202.

Poterba, James M., Steven F. Venti, and David A. Wise. 1998. Lump sum distributions from retirement savings plans: Receipt and utilization. In *Inquiries in the economics of aging,* ed. David A. Wise, 85–105. Chicago: University of Chicago Press.

Profit Sharing/401(k) Council of America. 2005. *48th Annual Survey of Profit Sharing and 401(k) Plans.* http://www.psca.org/DATA/48th.html.

Rozinka, Edina, and Waldo Tapia. 2007. Survey of investment choice by pension fund members. OECD Working Papers on Insurance and Private Pensions no. 7. Paris: Organization for Economic Cooperation and Development. http://www.oecd.org/dataoecd/39/1/37977416.pdf.

Saku, Aura. 2001. Does the balance of power within a family matter? The case of the Retirement Equity Act. IGIER Working Paper no. 202. Milan, Italy: Innocenzo Gasparini Institute for Economic Research.

Shafir, Eldar, Itamar Simonson, and Amos Tversky. 1993. Reason-based choice. *Cognition* 49 (1–2): 11–36.

Tversky, Amos, and Eldar Shafir. 1992. Choice under conflict: The dynamics of deferred decision. *Psychological Science* 3 (6): 358–61.

U.S. Department of Labor, Employee Benefits Security Administration. 2005. *Private pension plan bulletin.* http://www.dol.gov/ebsa/PDF/2000pensionplanbulletin.pdf.
Utkus, Stephen P. 2002. A recent successful test of the SMarT program. Valley Forge, PA: Vanguard Center for Retirement Research.
Utkus, Stephen P. and Jean A. Young. 2004. Lessons from behavioral finance and the autopilot 401(k). Valley Forge, PA: Vanguard Center for Retirement Research.
The Vanguard Group. 2001. Automatic enrollment: Vanguard client experience. Valley Forge, PA: The Vanguard Group.

Comment   Jeffrey R. Brown

This chapter provides powerful evidence about a deceptively simple idea: "defaults matter." The chapter nicely summarizes the large and growing literature (the lion's share of which was authored by various combinations of the current authors) about the power of default options to influence a wide range of behaviors related to retirement security.

Specifically, the authors provide evidence about how defaults influence behavior along every major dimension of the financial planning process related to retirement, including: (1) the decision of whether to participate in a 401(k) plan; (2) how much to contribute, conditional on participating; (3) what portfolio allocation to choose for those contributions; (4) what to do with the money when one leaves an employer; and (5) how to withdraw the money at retirement.

The foundation for this chapter is a large set of individual research projects that analyze a variety of natural or designed experiments to determine the effect of default options on individual behavior. To varying degrees, the underlying studies are individually compelling. Taken as a whole, the combined evidence is undeniable and overwhelming.

After providing this careful review of the existing evidence, the authors then explore several potential explanations for why defaults have such a strong effect on individual behavior, in contrast to the standard neoclassical model. These explanations include the following:

1. There are low average levels of financial literacy. Many studies indicate that most U.S. citizens are unable to correctly answer fairly basic questions about investment characteristics, such as whether a money market fund holds stocks or whether an individual employer's stock is more or less risky than a diversified stock fund.

Jeffrey R. Brown is the William G. Karnes Professor of Finance at the University of Illinois at Urbana-Champaign, and a research associate of the National Bureau of Economic Research.

2. Individuals view the default option as an endorsement, that is, as implicit investment advice from the plan sponsor.

3. Defaults provide a shortcut through the tremendous complexity facing individuals trying to make these decisions on their own.

4. Individuals are biased toward the present, and defaults help them to circumvent procrastination.

My suspicion is that all of these factors matter both individually and in combination. Nonetheless, the logical next step in this literature is to determine the relative importance of these factors and whether that ranking is the same in all contexts. Understanding the underlying determinants is of more than academic interest—it is also important for assessing whether there are other interventions that may influence behavior and possibly lead individuals to make more active decisions that may improve individual welfare.

The role of default options is particularly important in the context of retirement planning for at least two reasons. First, developing an optimal life-cycle savings and investment plan is extremely complex, particularly when one accounts for the many sources of uncertainty that one faces (e.g., earnings, rates of return, inflation, health status, medical expenditures, and longevity). The advice of "experts" is not necessarily the solution to the complexity problem, given the numerous and conflicting sources of investment advice available in the marketplace. Second, unlike many other contexts where one can "learn by doing," the opportunity to learn from one's mistakes is limited in this context. The reason is that an individual may not realize their mistakes until it is too late to fix them. For example, it does one little good to learn at age seventy that they should have saved more at age fifty.

The authors suggest that the alternative to a default option is to enforce an active decision. My view differs in a subtle way: even with active decision enforcement, there is still a default option. The default is to simply accept whatever penalty or punishment is meted out for a failure to actively decide. More important than the semantics is that the active decision enforcement approach still does not overcome some of the problems that led to the power of defaults in the first place, such as problems associated with a lack of knowledge or the inability of some to grapple with the complexity of the choice set. Thus, my own conclusion from this chapter and the underlying literature is that there is always a default option (although it is not always well-specified) and that intelligent policy design must, therefore, pay careful attention to the behavior that the default will engender.

Perhaps out of modesty, the authors do not discuss in this chapter just how influential and pervasive the idea that "defaults matter" has become in policy circles over the past few years. For example, only in current decade has it become standard for analyses of Social Security personal account reform proposals to explicitly distinguish whether participation in the personal accounts is on an "opt-in" or an "opt-out" basis, largely because policymakers and analysts now understand that this distinction will likely lead to significantly different participation rates. As another example, the Pension Protection Act, which was signed into law in August 2006, includes numerous changes to the nation's pension laws that are designed to pave the way for employers to adopt "automatic enrollment" in 401(k) and similar plans. In a related effort, the Department of Labor proposed new regulations in September 2006 that will set the framework that plan sponsors must work within when determining the investment portfolio that individuals can be defaulted into when they are automatically enrolled in a 401(k) plan. There is little question in my mind that the academic literature on the power of defaults has helped generate a tremendous (and largely bipartisan) enthusiasm for "automatic enrollment" approaches in the discussion of retirement policy in the United States.

Looking to the future, the one area of this body of work that has received the least attention, at least relative to its importance to overall retirement security, is the payout phase. The importance of this area is underscored by the large literature exploring the large potential welfare gains from annuitization. A basic empirical fact about the private pension system in the United States is that the vast majority of 401(k) plans do not even offer plan participants an option to annuitize their accounts at retirement. In other words, the current default option is to leave wealth in an unannuitized form. My normative judgment (which has been influenced by the annuities literature) is that this is a suboptimal default option because it leaves individuals suboptimally exposed to longevity risk.

Designing an annuitized default option for the payout phase poses a more difficult policy challenge than most other aspects of the retirement planning process, however, because of the "irreversible" nature of most existing annuity products. For example, we know that there will always be some individuals for whom an annuity is not an attractive option, such as those who are terminally ill or those with very strong bequest motives. If these individuals are automatically annuitized at retirement, their welfare could be substantially reduced if there is no way for them to undo the annuity contract once they have entered into it. This makes the downside risk of being defaulted into an annuity much larger than the downside of being automatically enrolled into a 401(k) plan, which can easily be reversed if the individual later decides to do so.

These difficulties, however, should not lead one to think that "no annuitization" is the better default. For example, one could imagine designing a default with two features. First, make the annuitization gradual, or laddered, such as by converting 20 percent of the account balance into an annuity each year for five years. In addition to helping to smooth out asset price and interest rate fluctuations, such an approach gives an individual the opportunity to opt out of the annuity on at least part of their wealth. If a person had 20 percent of their wealth automatically annuitized, this would "focus the mind" on the benefits and costs of doing so. At that point, if they realize that full annuitization is not optimal, they can avoid it on the remaining 80 percent of wealth. A second feature would be to allow a limited period of reversibility, such as 6 months after annuitization. Reversibility would allow individuals an opportunity to "undo" the annuitization if they were opted in and subsequently realized they did not want this. Keeping the time period short would limit the selection costs and administrative costs that such an approach would impose on the system.

In summary, the body of evidence discussed in this chapter makes it clear that default options matter at nearly every step in the financial planning process. Going forward, the research agenda in this area should seek to distinguish between the alternative hypotheses for *why* defaults matter. With this knowledge in hand, policymakers and plan designers will be able to more finely tune the policy levers that may increase average welfare of plan participants.

III

Reducing Financial Market Risk in Personal Retirement Accounts

6

Reducing the Risk of Investment-Based Social Security Reform

Martin Feldstein

Many governments around the world—including Australia, Britain, Sweden, Mexico, China, Chile—have shifted from pure pay-as-you-go (PAYGO) tax financed Social Security pensions to plans that rely in whole or in part on investments in stocks and bonds. There is now active discussion about the desirability of doing so in the United States. The Clinton administration came close to proposing such a plan. President Bush established a bipartisan presidential commission to advise on detailed aspects of such a plan and, after his reelection in 2004, reiterated his intention to introduce legislation to change Social Security in this way.

Any consideration of introducing an investment-based component into Social Security immediately raises the issue of the risk associated with uncertain asset returns. Some individuals would welcome the opportunity to achieve a higher return on their Social Security contributions, even if that entails accepting additional market risk. Others would be reluctant to subject their retirement income to the uncertainty of investment returns. More generally, individuals differ in the extent to which they would accept additional risk in exchange for higher returns.

This chapter presents a new market-based approach to reducing the risk of investment-based Social Security that could be tailored to individual

Martin Feldstein is the George F. Baker Professor of Economics at Harvard University, and former president of the National Bureau of Economic Research.

This chapter is a report on a project that is exploring alternative ways of dealing with the risk in investment-based Social Security pension plans. I am grateful to Eugene Soltes and Xuan Qin for the calculations in this chapter. The research was supported by the U.S. Social Security Administration (SSA) through grant #10-P-98363-1 to the National Bureau of Economic Research (NBER) as part of the SSA Retirement Research Consortium. The opinions and conclusions expressed are solely those of the author and do not represent the opinions or policy of SSA, any agency of the federal government, or of the NBER.

risk preferences. With this new form of risk reduction, substituting an investment-based personal retirement account (PRA) for the traditional pure PAYGO plan could achieve both a significantly higher *expected* retirement income and a very *high probability* that the investment-based annuity would be at least as large as the PAYGO benefit. A key feature of the approach developed here is a guarantee that the individual would not lose any of the real value of each year's PRA savings and might be guaranteed to earn at least some minimum real rate of return.

In one example of such a plan that is presented later in this chapter, I examine the effect of replacing the current 12.4 percent PAYGO tax with a mixed plan that has a 6.2 percent PAYGO tax and 6.2 percent annual PRA savings. This new mixed plan, when fully phased in, would have the following desirable characteristics:

- The median value of the combined retirement income (i.e., the sum of the PAYGO benefit and the PRA annuity) would be 147 percent of the traditional PAYGO benefit.
- There would be a 95 percent probability that the combined retirement income (the PAYGO benefit and the PRA annuity) exceeds the traditional PAYGO benefit.
- There would be less than 1 chance in 100 that the combined retirement income would be less than 96 percent of the traditional PAYGO benefit.
- Each year's PRA saving would be guaranteed to earn at least a 1 percent real rate of return between the time that it is saved and its value at age sixty-six (and generally substantially more). I, therefore, refer to this as a "Nose Lose" plan.
- The variable annuity purchased at age sixty-six would have a similar "No Lose" feature, that is, a guaranteed real rate of return of at least 1 percent.

Section 6.1 of the chapter discusses alternative approaches to risk reduction in investment-based Social Security plans. Section 6.2 summarizes a private market approach to risk reduction that I reported on in an earlier paper. Section 6.3 presents the idea of the "No Lose" plan, developed in the current chapter, in which private markets provide a guarantee based on Treasury inflation protected bonds. Simulation results for these alternative plans are then presented and discussed in sections 6.4 and 6.5 where the distribution of the combined pension income of the mixed plan (PAYGO plus PRA) is compared to the projected "benchmark" benefits of the current pure PAYGO plan. An alternative approach that permits tailoring the risk distribution to individual preferences by using the purchase and sale of equal value (i.e., self-financing) derivatives is analyzed in section 6.6. Section 6.7 shows the effect of lowering the combined PAYGO and PRA cost as a way of modeling the adjustment that would be needed to deal with the aging of the population without the large rise in the payroll tax that would otherwise be required.

6.1 Alternative Approaches to Risk Reduction

The risk borne by retirees in an investment-based plan can be thought of as the variability of the retirement income or as the probability that the retirement income will fall substantially short of the current-law PAYGO benefits. In previous papers, Elena Ranguelova, Andrew Samwick, and I assessed the magnitude of the risk in a pure investment-based plan and evaluated the effects of some of the ways of reducing that risk (Feldstein, Ranguelova, and Samwick 2001; Feldstein and Ranguelova 2001b).

One way in which the investment risk to individual retirees could, in principle, be reduced would be for the government to accumulate the investment in a single national fund. The government could use the investment returns from this fund to finance defined benefits, making up any shortfall with tax revenue or government borrowing. Such a central fund involves problems of its own that lie beyond the scope of this chapter.[1] I will assume, therefore, that the investment-based plans are all structured through PRAs. In all of these plans, individuals or their employers contribute to their PRAs during their working years and receive an annuity at retirement. The accumulated assets of individuals who die before reaching retirement age are assumed to be bequeathed according to the instructions of the deceased.

Strategies for reducing the risk of investment-based PRA plans involve various forms and mixtures of the following four approaches:

1. Restrictions on the investment assets
2. A mixed system that combines PAYGO benefits and investment-based annuities
3. Government guarantees
4. Market-based guarantees

I will comment now on each of these.

All actual and proposed investment-based plans *restrict the assets* in which the PRAs can be invested. These restrictions generally preclude investing in individual stocks by requiring that equity investments be limited to broadly diversified mutual funds. Asset restrictions may also set maximum fractions of the portfolio or of new saving that can be invested in equities. The analysis in this chapter considers the effect of using Treasury Inflation-Protected Securities (TIPS) to introduce a risk-free real return as a component of the PRA investment.

While some countries have opted for a pure investment-based plan (e.g.,

---

1. See my discussion of these problems in Feldstein (2000).

Chile and Mexico), most countries have chosen *a mixed system that combines PAYGO benefits and investment-based annuities.* The three proposals analyzed by the President's Commission were of this form. The current analysis will focus on plans in which traditional PAYGO benefits provide half of the benefits projected in current law with additional benefits provided by the PRA annuity.

In our earlier papers, Elena Ranguelova, Andrew Samwick, and I analyzed a variety of *government guarantees.* A typical guarantee would stipulate that the government would supplement the income of retirees if the combined annual annuity payment fell below some level. To avoid the moral hazard problem of inducing individuals to take excessive risk, the government supplement would be based on the return on a "standard portfolio" like a 60:40 mix of the Standard and Poors 500 and the Lehman bond index. To make individuals cost-conscious about the annuity provider, the guarantee might take the form of allowing the individual to keep some fraction of the investment-based annuity (say 25 percent) and then supplementing the annuity if the remaining portion does not reach some level.

Our earlier analysis showed that providing a guarantee that individuals will receive at least as much as the benefits projected in current law (the "benchmark benefits") would impose relatively little risk on future taxpayers. Nevertheless, critics of such plans worry that guarantees could be modified in the future to create expensive new entitlements. The current study, therefore, focuses on guarantees that could be provided by private financial markets.

6.2   A Private Market Solution: Accumulated Pension Collars

A specific proposal for a private market guarantee based on a system of puts and calls is presented in Feldstein and Ranguelova (2001a). That paper analyzed the potential experience of an individual who contracts at age twenty-one to deposit a fraction of his or her earnings each year in a PRA with the funds invested in a 60:40 portfolio of stocks and bonds. The accumulated funds are used at age sixty-six to finance a variable annuity invested in the same asset mix. This PRA investment is combined with a traditional PAYGO system that provides benefits equal to two-thirds of the projected "benchmark" benefits. The individual augments this combination with a put contract that provides that the sum of the PAYGO benefit, and the annual PRA annuity would be at least as large as the benchmark benefit, that is, that the PRA annuity would be at least equal to one-third of the benchmark benefit. The put contract would be part of the package provided by the seller of the PRA investment. To finance the cost of this put, the individual in effect sells a call that gives the buyer of the call any PRA annuity payments in excess of an amount that makes the value of the call equal to the value of the put. In short, the guarantee is based on purchasing a zero-cost "collar," that is, a combination of puts and calls of equal value.

Although this collar approach to guaranteeing that the combination of the PRA annuity and the PAYGO benefit would at least equal the benchmark benefit is conceptually interesting, it is not an operationally feasible strategy in practice because it requires individuals at the time that they enter the labor force to know the future path of their earnings. Only with this knowledge can they contract the amounts that they will save and calculate the size of the future PAYGO benchmark benefit.

6.3   An Annual Contract "No Lose" PRA Plan

The current analysis, therefore, develops an alternative approach to a market-based guarantee that could be implemented in practice. The key to this is that the guarantee is purchased each year based on that year's PRA savings. The basic contract would guarantee the individual a "No Lose" investment, that is, that the real value of the PRA account at age sixty-six will be at least equal to the amount that the individual contributed during each year of his or her working life. More specifically, the amount saved in each year would be guaranteed to retain at least its real value by age sixty-six. Such a guarantee could be provided by the firm that manages the PRA product (i.e., the mutual fund, bank, insurance company, etc.). The PRA legislation might require the PRA manager to offer such an option. Alternatively, the offer of such options might be voluntary. Similarly, individuals might be free to accept such an option only if they want or might be required to select such a guarantee on all or part of their PRA saving. We do not examine these issues but show the effect of such a guarantee on the possible levels of retirement income relative to the traditional PAYGO benefit.

The simplest way to achieve such a No Lose PRA account would be to combine TIPS (which have a guaranteed real return) with equities. The fraction of the annual PRA saving that would have to be invested in TIPS to guarantee that the annual PRA saving would retain its real value by age sixty-six depends on the age of the saver and the rate of return on the TIPS of the relevant maturity. For example, if the saver is twenty-one years old and the real return on TIPS is 2 percent, a $1,000 PRA saving would be divided between $410 in TIPS and the remaining $590 in equities. The 2 percent real return and the forty-five-year investment period imply that the $410 would accumulate to $1,000 at the initial price level by age sixty-six. Even if the equity portion became completely worthless, the PRA account would be worth the initial $1,000 real dollars.[2]

At older working ages, there are fewer years for the TIPS to accumulate

2. The supply of TIPS created by the Treasury is already being supplemented by privately issued inflation protected bonds issued by several financial firms. (See *Wall Street Journal,* July 28, 2004, D1.) The no-risk character of those bonds could be enhanced by requiring that the issuers have appropriate guarantees backed by capital. An appropriate derivatives market in long-term inflation options could facilitate the expansion of this private market.

and, therefore, a larger fraction of the initial saving must be invested in TIPS. For example, a forty-year-old would have to invest $598 out of each $1,000 of new saving in TIPS to guarantee the $1,000 value of the account at age sixty-six with the remaining $402 invested in equities.

In practice, of course, the value at age sixty-six of the annual PRA saving would be worth substantially more than the guaranteed amount because the equity portion of the account would add substantial value. Consider, for example, the forty-year-old. The $598 in TIPS would be worth $1,000 at age sixty-six. If the $402 in equities earned a 7 percent real return (approximately the average historic real return over the past half century), the $402 would grow to $2,335, making the total value of that year's account $3,335, more than three times the guaranteed amount.

When the individual reaches age sixty-six, all of the forty-five annual PRA accounts would be combined to provide a single PRA retirement fund. The individual could then buy a conventional fixed rate annuity or a variable annuity. Alternatively, the No Lose approach could be continued in the annuity phase of the retirement plan. The annuity provider could offer a guarantee that the annual annuity payments would be at least as large as the individual's retirement fund could purchase with a zero real return. The annuity provider could achieve this guarantee with the appropriate mix of TIPS and equities. The expected return would, of course, again be much larger than the guaranteed minimum.

There is an alternative way of achieving a zero real return during both the accumulation phase and the annuity phase. The individual in each working year could purchase a real annuity with a guarantee that the return on the funds saved in that year would provide at least as large a real annuity starting at age sixty-seven as would be available with a zero real rate of interest during both the accumulation and annuity phases. This "lifetime contract" has more funds invested in equities during the annuity phase than the "two stage" process that guarantees the accumulated value at age sixty-six and then uses that to buy the annuity with the zero real return guarantee.

This approach can be easily modified to increase the guarantee from a zero real return (No Lose) to a 1 percent real rate of return. For a forty-year-old, $1,000 saved in a PRA would grow at a 1 percent real rate of return to a real $1,295 at age sixty-six. To guarantee at least this amount at age sixty-six by using TIPS with a 2 percent yield would require purchasing $774 of TIPS. The reduction in the equity investment from $402 (in the zero real guarantee case) to $226 with a 1 percent real guarantee shows the nature of the trade-off between risk reduction and return reduction. If the $226 earned the historic average of 7 percent, it would grow to $1,312 by age sixty-six, making the total value of the account $2,607. This compares with an expected value of $3,335 with a zero real guarantee.

6.4 Simulating the Distribution of PRA Investment Outcomes

We simulate the distribution of the accumulated pension assets at age sixty-six in a fully phased-in plan on the basis of the means, variances, and covariances of the returns on equities measured by the Standard and Poors 500 from 1946 to 2003 and on bonds by the Lehman corporate bond returns for 1973 to 2003. The mean log real returns are 6.9 percent for equities and 4.4 percent for corporate bonds. We subtract 40 basis points from the mean returns to reflect potential administrative costs.[3]

The distributions of pension incomes are based on 10,000 simulations for each plan that we study. Each simulation begins by drawing a mean rate of return for the proposed mix of stocks and corporate bonds during the individual's lifetime. This mean is drawn from a normal distribution with a mean equal to the estimated mean from the sample of observations and a standard deviation that equals the standard error of that mean. Conditional on this mean, we draw eighty annual rates of return corresponding to the potential returns at ages 21 through 100. These returns are assumed to be normally distributed and serially independent.[4] The TIPS are assumed to deliver a sure real return of 2 percent.[5]

Each of the annual PRA accounts evolves in this way to age sixty-six. At that point, we aggregate the individual accounts and purchase a variable annuity. The annuity is subject to a No Lose guarantee that the annual benefits are at least as large as would be achieved with a zero real return. Alternatively we calculate the "lifetime contract" annuities based on a guaranteed real annuity from each year's PRA saving, which are then added together during the annuity phase.

6.5 Comparison of Alternative PRA Pensions Relative to the PAYGO Benchmark

Our basic analysis compares the retirement annuities produced by different PRA plans with the level of benefits associated with the PAYGO plan with a 12.4 percent payroll tax. For the sake of specificity, we consider an individual who earns $25,000 at age twenty-one and whose earnings then rise at 2 percent a year in real terms to $60,950 at age sixty-six. We assume that the benefits at age sixty-seven are then 40 percent of the earnings

3. Actual variable annuity plans like TIAA-CREF have lower cost despite marketing expenses.
4. See Feldstein and Ranguelova (2001b) for a detailed description of the simulation approach and the relation between the parameters of the log returns and the corresponding parameters in levels.
5. The actual return on TIPS currently (November 2004) varies between 0.8 percent at five years and 2.1 percent at twenty-five years. Our analysis does not vary the TIP return by maturity. This return has varied over time. Six months earlier it was 1.1 percent at five years and 2.25 percent at twenty-five years.

Table 6.1   **Guarantee based on combination with Treasury inflation-protected securities (TIPS); (frequency distribution of combined pension income relative to benchmark pay-as-you-go benefits with benchmark $T = 12.4$); ($T = 6.2$ $S = 6.2$)**

Real rate of return guarantee	0.01	0.05	0.10	0.30	0.50	0.70	0.90
None	0.74	0.93	1.08	1.71	2.61	4.38	10.28
Two-stage guarantee							
No lose ($r > 0$)	0.90	0.99	1.06	1.36	1.80	2.66	5.73
No lose ($r > 1$)	0.96	1.01	1.05	1.22	1.47	1.94	3.58
Lifetime contract guarantee							
No lose ($r > 0$)	0.82	0.91	1.00	1.43	2.14	3.58	8.62
No lose ($r > 1$)	0.90	0.95	1.01	1.27	1.69	2.57	5.63

Notes: Combined pension income at age 77 based on PAYGO equal to 0.5 benchmark benefit and personal retirement accounts invested in equities with TIPS to achieve the return guarantee. Benchmark based on pay-as-you-go with $T = 12.4$.

at age sixty-six. Although a 40 percent replacement rate is standard for an individual with a median level of lifetime income, 40 percent is higher than such an individual would receive in retirement benefits at the $60,950 level of immediate preretirement income. The 40 percent replacement is intended as a rough approximation to the combined effects of pre-sixty-seven mortality, benefits for a retired spouse, survivor benefits, and so on.[6]

The first row of table 6.1 shows the relative benefit distribution corresponding to a mixed plan with a tax rate of 6.2 percent and a PRA saving rate of 6.2 percent. All of the PRA funds are invested in equities (the Standard and Poors 500) with no guarantee. The PAYGO part of the plan, financed with a 6.2 percent tax rate, would provide benefits equal to half of the benchmark level. The data show that with no guarantee, the mixed plan with a pure equity PRA investment produces a median combined benefit equal to 2.61 times the benchmark.[7] There is only a 1 percent chance that the combined benefit would be less than 74 percent of the benchmark. Some individuals with low risk aversion might prefer to have no guarantee, accepting the risk of a low combined benefit in order to have a chance to get a high combined benefit and secure in the knowledge that the PAYGO benefit will provide 50 percent of the benchmark benefit.

Others, however, would be prepared to sacrifice some of the potential

6. All of the calculations of relative benefits for this representative individual do not depend on the specific level of income.
7. This is higher than the ratios reported in earlier studies with Ranguelova and Samwick because those studies used a PRA investment equal to 60 percent equities and 40 percent debt.

high return in order to reduce the risk of relatively low benefits. Row (2) of table 6.1 shows the effect of the No Lose plan with a guarantee that the annual real return would be at least zero. The PRA funds are invested in a mix of equities (the Standard and Poors 500) and TIPS; there are no corporate bonds. The calculation is based on the two-stage approach: the TIPS are selected to guarantee a No Lose accumulation (zero real return) to age sixty-six, and the accumulated funds are then used to buy a variable annuity invested in a combination of equities and TIPS selected to give a minimum zero ex ante real return.

Note first that the median ratio of the combined benefits to the benchmark pure PAYGO benefits is 1.80. That is, there is an even chance that the combination of the reduced PAYGO benefits and the PRA annuity will be at least 80 percent more than the basic benchmark PAYGO benefit. Note next that the 5th percentile in the distribution of the combined benefits corresponds to 99 percent of the benchmark benefits. There is thus only one chance in twenty that the combined benefits will be less than 99 percent of the benchmark benefits. There is thus only one chance in twenty that the combined benefits will be less than 99 percent of the benchmark benefits. Even at the extreme 1 percent level, the combined benefits would be 90 percent of the benchmark level. In short, the No Lose option offers a level of benefits that is likely to be substantially higher than the benchmark benefit in the pure PAYGO system, and that involves only a very small risk of receiving less than 90 percent of that benchmark benefit.

Note also that there is a significant chance with this No Lose plan of receiving a great deal more than the benchmark benefit. The 70th percentile in the relative distribution corresponds to combined benefits equal to more than twice the benchmark benefit; a combined annuity equal to 266 percent of the benchmark benefit corresponds to about 100 percent of the individual's peak preretirement income. Similarly, there is one chance in ten (i.e., the 90th percentile) that the combined income would be more than five times the benchmark benefit, equivalent to more than twice the peak preretirement income.

Selecting a guarantee of a 1 percent real return during both the accumulation and annuity phases instead of the zero percent reported in the second row of table 6.1 does little to reduce the small risk at the 1st and 5th percentiles and lowers the combined benefits above that level. The implications of the 1 percent real return guarantee are shown in row (3) of table 6.1. Comparing rows (2) and (3) shows that the combined income ratio at the 90th percentile declines from 5.7 times the benchmark benefit to about 3.6 times the benchmark. The combined median income falls from 180 percent of the benchmark to 147 percent of the benchmark benefit, still a substantial gain relative to the current law.

In exchange for these lower payouts at the middle and top of the distribution, the 1 percent real guarantee provides only slightly better protection against lower levels of combined retirement incomes. There is only a 1 percent risk that the combined benefit would be more than 4 percent below the benchmark level, not very different from the 10 percent with the $r > 0$ guarantee.

Rows (4) and (5) are based on lifetime return guarantees instead of the two-stage approach reported in rows (2) and (3). The individual during each working year contributes to a PRA annuity plan that promises to pay a positive rate of return during both the accumulations and annuity phases. If an individual dies before retirement age, the accumulated fund is paid as a bequest. This lifetime return guarantee approach keeps a larger share of funds invested in equities, thereby increasing both the risk and the expected return. Comparing the two $r > 0$ guarantees (rows [2] and [4]) shows that the lifetime guarantee approach raises the median benefit from 1.8 times the benchmark to 2.14 times the benchmark. The 90th percentile rises from 5.73 times the benchmark to 8.62 times the benchmark, but the 1st percentile declines from 90 percent of the benchmark to 82 percent.

None of the five distributions clearly dominates. A distribution with higher upside potential also has a greater probability of a low benefit. Individuals with different degrees of risk aversion will, therefore, have different preferences among these three options. One way to represent these preferences is by the expected utility of the different options using a constant relative risk aversion utility function. We do expected utility calculations for individuals for constant relative risk aversion (CRRA) values of 1 through 5 at ages sixty-seven, seventy-seven, eighty-seven, and ninety-seven and then combine these with weights reflecting survival probabilities to these ages. The expected utility calculations, therefore, do not take into account the value of the bequests that might occur under these different plans.

We find that the No Lose option with a zero guaranteed return (row [2]) is preferred to the less risky 1 percent guarantee for every CRRA value between 1 and 5, a not surprising result in light of the distribution of returns shown in table 6.1. More surprising, however, is that the No Guarantee option (row [1]) is preferred to the No Lose zero return option of row (2) for every CRRA value between 1 and 5. Because there is a substantial risk of a quite low combined benefit, this suggests that the upside gain potential outweighs this risk even for those with high risk aversion.

With the lifetime contract approach (rows [4] and [5]), the zero real return guarantee is again preferred to the 1 percent guarantee for all CRRA values, just as it is for the two-stage approach. Comparing the two different ways of achieving the zero real return guarantee shows that the expected utility is higher with the lifetime guarantee for CRRA values up to 3.5, presumably because it permits more risk-taking. Even with that greater risk-taking implied by the lifetime contract approach, individuals continue to prefer the no guarantee option (row [1]) to either of the lifetime contract options.

In the overall comparison of the No Guarantee and the four different guarantees shown in table 6.1, the expected utility comparisons show that No Guarantee is preferred for all of the CRRA values up to 5.0. The lifetime contracts and the 1 percent negative return are dominated.

Finally, a calculation comparing the expected utility of these five plans to the expected utility of the pure PAYGO benefit that pays 100 percent of the benchmark shows that for all of the risk aversion values between 1 and 5, the investment based plans are preferred to the pure PAYGO plan.

6.6 Tailoring the Guarantees to Individual Preferences with Zero-Cost Collars

It is possible to extend the range of options in a way that could make a guarantee plan preferable to the No Guarantee option. More specifically, using a combination of puts and calls in which the cost of the put is financed by selling a call, that is, a zero-cost collar, allows different ways of shaping the two tails of the distribution, depending on how the put and call are specified. In this way, the risk protection can be tailored to different groups of PRA participants.

To see why this might be a preferred option, consider row (2) of table 6.1. These figures show that with the No Lose real return guarantee the individual has a 10 percent chance of getting a retirement income equal to almost six times the benchmark benefit. Although such a large windfall would no doubt be welcome, a risk averse individual might be willing to forego some of that very high end possibility for a reduced risk of relatively low benefits and improved distribution of outcomes in the first 50 percent of the probability distribution.

One way to achieve that alternative distribution would be to buy a put option that guarantees a real return of at least zero and to finance the cost of this put by selling a call option that gives its buyer *all* of the value above some cumulative real rate of return. Such a put-call strategy that caps the upside rate of return in order to purchase a put that guarantees at least a zero real return would have a different distribution of combined pension incomes than a zero real return guarantee achieved with TIPS (because that does not put a cap on the maximum possible rate of return.)

This strategy can be extended to consider zero-cost collars that guarantee other minimum positive or negative real rates of return. On the basis of some preliminary analysis, the analysis here focuses on zero-cost collars for minimum real returns of zero and minus 1 percent.

Table 6.2 compares the distributions shown in table 6.1 for the no guarantee option (row [1]) and the zero real return option achieved with TIPS (row [2]) to the distributions using puts to guarantee minimum returns of zero (row [3]) and minus one (row [4]) financed by selling calls on all of the returns above the level needed to finance those puts.

Table 6.2   Guarantee based on zero-cost collar (frequency distribution of combined pension income relative to benchmark pay-as-you-go benefits with benchmark $T = 12.4$); ($T = 6.2$ $S = 6.2$)

Real rate of return guarantee	0.01	0.05	0.10	0.30	0.50	0.70	0.90
None	0.74	0.93	1.08	1.71	2.61	4.38	10.28
Two-stage guarantee Using TIPS							
No lose ($r > 0$)	0.90	0.99	1.06	1.36	1.80	2.66	5.73
Zero-cost collar guarantee							
No lose ($r > 0$)	0.94	1.01	1.13	1.56	1.81	1.85	1.86
$r > -1$	0.99	1.08	1.23	1.73	2.00	2.06	2.06

Notes: Combined pension income at age 77 based on PAYGO equal to 0.5 benchmark benefit and personal retirement accounts invested in equities with Treasury inflation-protected securities (TIPS) or zero-cost collar to achieve the return guarantee. Benchmark based on pay-as-you-go with $T = 12.4$.

It is clear that a risk averse individual might well prefer a collar strategy with a minimum guarantee of minus 1 percent return to the TIPS zero return guarantee or to no guarantee at all. With this collar strategy, there is only a 1 percent chance of receiving less than the benchmark benefit. The benefit is higher at each point in the distribution up to at least the 50th percentile. At the 90th percentile, the individual forsakes the one-in-ten chance of a benefit that is more than five times the benchmark (and, therefore, more than twice maximum preretirement income) but still can anticipate a benefit that is twice the benchmark.

This is borne out by the expected utility calculations. In a mixed system with a 6.2 percent PAYGO tax and a 6.2 percent PRA saving rate, an individual with CRRA less than or equal to four will prefer to invest their PRA in equities with no guaranteed return. But with a higher degree of risk aversion, the individual prefers to forego the potential high return for a minimum return of at least minus one percent.

There are, of course, other collars that might be preferred to this. For example, one possible strategy would sell a call that pays (say) 50 percent of the equity returns above some level and use the proceeds of that call option to buy a put that guarantees at least a minus 1 percent real return.

6.7   Lower Cost Mixed Plans: Limiting the Tax Increase

A primary goal of Social Security reform is to avoid the large increase in the tax rate that will result from the aging of the population if there is no program change. The Social Security actuaries estimate that the existing benefit rules would require raising the tax rate in the PAYGO system by about 50 percent, from 12.4 percent to about 18.6 percent.[8] An advantage of the investment-based approach is that it is possible to finance the benefits implied by the existing benefit rules with a lower future cost.

A useful way to analyze the implication of the long-run demographically caused increase in the cost of producing the benefits in a pure PAYGO system is to consider the impact on benefits of cutting the PAYGO tax by one-third with a pure PAYGO system. A pure PAYGO system with a tax rate equal to two-thirds of the current PAYGO 12.4 percent, that is, an 8.3 percent combined tax rate, would show the one-third decline in benefits relative to the currently projected "benchmark" benefits that would be occur as a result of the demographic change. In contrast, a mixture of a PAYGO tax and a PRA contribution that totals 8.3 percent would show the extent to which it is possible to reduce the benefit shortfall with no increase in the total cost when the system is fully phased in.

Analysis of such a mixed plan with a 4.15 percent PAYGO tax and a 4.15 percent PRA saving rate showed that the expected benefit would exceed the current benefit but that there would be a significant probability that benefits would be less than 75 percent of the benchmark benefit.

The current section, therefore, presents results for a plan that reduces costs by 20 percent instead of by the one-third needed to stabilize the implied tax rate. One way to interpret this would be as the net effect of reducing the payroll tax by one-third (from 12.4 percent to 8.3 percent, to stabilize the implied future tax rate) and dividing this between a PAYGO portion of 4.96 percent and a carve-out to PRA accounts of 3.35 percent supplemented by individual PRA contributions of an additional 1.61 percent, bringing the total to 9.92 percent or 80 percent of the current 12.4 percent.[9] This would be equivalent to a future cost increase from 12.4 percent to 14.9 percent (instead of the 18.6 percent rate implied by the 50 percent cost rise that would occur with a pure PAYGO system) with 2.5 percent of payroll paid as an individual contribution on top of the tax.

Table 6.3 shows results similar to table 6.1 except that the PAYGO and PRA costs have now both been reduced to 80 percent of what they were in table 6.1. Consider first the results for the No Guarantee plan in line (1). The median level of the benefits in this probability distribution is still substantially higher than the benchmark distribution: 2.09 times the benchmark.

At the 10th percentile, the new low-cost strategy with no guarantee produces a combined benefit equal to 86 percent of the benchmark. But at the 1st percentile, the combined benefits in the low-cost plan are only 59 per-

---

8. The calculation is more complex because of disability benefits that are now financed as part of the 12.4 percent.

9. The individual contribution could be induced on a voluntary basis by making the carve-out transfer to the PRA account conditional on the additional individual contribution. Making the individual contribution the "default option" would increase the participation rate.

Table 6.3   **Low cost mixed plans (Frequency distribution of combined pension income relative to benchmark pay-as-you-go benefits with benchmark $T = 12.4$); ($T = 4.96\ S = 4.96$)**

Real rate of return guarantee	0.01	0.05	0.10	0.30	0.50	0.70	0.90
None	0.59	0.74	0.86	1.37	2.09	3.50	8.22
Two-stage guarantee							
No lose ($r > 0$)	0.72	0.79	0.85	1.09	1.44	2.13	4.58
No lose ($r > 1$)	0.77	0.81	0.84	0.98	1.17	1.55	2.86
Lifetime contract guarantee							
No lose ($r > 0$)	0.65	0.73	0.80	1.15	1.71	2.87	6.89
No lose ($r > 1$)	0.72	0.76	0.81	1.02	1.35	2.06	4.50
Zero-cost collar guarantee							
No lose ($r > 0$)	0.75	0.81	0.90	1.25	1.45	1.48	1.49
$r > -1$	0.79	0.86	0.98	1.39	1.60	1.65	1.65

Notes: Combined pension income at age 77 based on PAYGO benefits equal to 0.4 benchmark benefit and personal retirement accounts invested in equities with Treasury inflation-protected securities or zero cost collars to achieve the return guarantee. Benchmark based on pay-as-you-go with $T = 12.4$.

cent of the benchmark, a level that some would consider an uncomfortably high level of risk.

The second and third rows of table 6.3 show how much the risk can be reduced by introducing guaranteed annual rates of return in a two-stage plan. A No Lose annual guarantee of a real return greater than zero raises the combined benefit at the 1st percentile from 59 percent of the benchmark to 72 percent of the benchmark. The price of this risk reduction is a decline in the relative combined benefits starting at about the 10th percentile. Thus, at the 30th percentile, the combined benefit declines from 137 percent of the benchmark to 109 percent. At the median, the drop is from 2.1 times the benchmark to 1.44 times benchmark. The prospect for very high gains falls even more.

Giving up more of the upside benefits by requiring at least a 1 percent real return on each year's PRA savings improves the very low probability ratios only slightly and reduces the combined benefits at all higher percentiles. Row (3) of table 6.3 shows that an annual guarantee of $r > 1$ raises the 1st percentile only from 0.72 with $r > 0$ to 0.77. Higher points on the distribution show the kinds of benefit decreases associated with these small risk reductions.

Rows (4) and (5) of table 6.3 repeat these calculations for the lifetime annuity plans. Because these involve a generally larger equity proportion in the PRA account, they have higher risk than rows (2) and (3).

The last two rows of table 6.3 use a collar to reduce risk by guaranteeing a minimum return of at least minus 1 percent on each year's savings and finance that put option by selling returns above a rate of return with an equal Black-Scholes value. This zero-cost collar has the effect of limiting the maximum benefit to 1.65 times the benchmark but uses this limit to raise the low probability level to 98 percent of the benchmark at 10 percent and 79 percent at the 1 percent level.

The implication of table 6.3 is that a mixed system with a cost that is 20 percent lower than the cost required with a pure PAYGO plan, when combined with a zero-cost collar that gives up the possibility of very high benefits in order to reduce the risk of low benefits, could provide benefits that are likely to be substantially higher than the current law benchmark and that have only a very small probability of being less than the current law benchmark. More specifically, using a zero-cost collar that guarantees that the real return on each year's saving is not less than minus 1 percent implies a median benefit equal to 1.6 times the benchmark and that there is only once chance in 10 that the benefit would be less than 98 percent of the benchmark and only one chance in one hundred that it would be less than 79 percent of the benchmark.

The expected utility ranking of the alternatives in table 6.3 imply that individuals with a CRRA value up to 4.0 would prefer to have no guarantee, while those with higher risk aversion prefer the collar approach with a guarantee of minus one. Those with a higher risk aversion would prefer the collar approach with a guarantee of minus 1 percent.

The final calculations, presented in table 6.4, show the implication of dealing with demographic change with a system that, when fully phased in, is purely investment-based with no PAYGO component. More specifically, we assume that the accumulation is based on annual saving of 9.92 percent of payroll, which is fully invested in equities except to the extent that a guarantee is provided by the use of TIPS or zero-cost collars.[10] With no guarantee, this pure investment-based plan has a 1 percent probability of a benefit that is less than 38 percent of the benchmark and a 5 percent probability that the benefit is less than 68 percent of the benchmark. A TIPS-based two-stage strategy that guarantees that each year's saving will have a positive real return substantially reduces this risk, raising the 1 percent level to 64 percent of the benchmark and the 5 percent level to 79 percent of the benchmark.

The risk can be reduced even more by the zero-cost collar that guarantees a real return of at least minus 1 percent on each year's saving by giving up any prospect of returns that would produce a benefit equal to more than

---

10. A method of transition from the existing PAYGO system to a pure investment-based system in a way that does not require more than an additional 2 percent of payroll each year during the transition (equal to less than 1 percent of gross domestic product [GDP]) is presented in Feldstein and Samwick (1998).

Table 6.4   Low cost pure investment plans (frequency distribution of combined pension income relative to benchmark pay-as-you-go benefits with benchmark $T = 12.4$); ($T = 0$ $S = 9.92$)

Real rate of return guarantee	0.01	0.05	0.10	0.30	0.50	0.70	0.90
None	0.38	0.68	0.93	1.94	3.38	6.21	15.65
Two-stage guarantee							
No lose ($r > 0$)	0.64	0.79	0.90	1.37	2.08	3.46	8.36
No lose ($r > 1$)	0.74	0.81	0.88	1.16	1.55	2.31	4.92
Lifetime contract guarantee							
No lose ($r > 0$)	0.50	0.65	0.80	1.50	2.62	4.93	12.99
No lose ($r > 1$)	0.64	0.72	0.81	1.23	1.90	3.31	8.21
Zero-cost collar guarantee							
No lose ($r > 0$)	0.70	0.81	1.01	1.69	2.09	2.16	2.17
$r > -1$	0.79	0.93	1.16	1.97	2.41	2.49	2.50

Notes: Combined pension income at age 77 based on no PAYGO benefits and personal retirement accounts invested in equities with Treasury Inflation-Protected Securities or zero cost collars to achieve the return guarantee. Benchmark based on pay-as-you-go with $T = 12.4$.

2.5 times the benchmark. With this collar, there is only a 1 percent risk of benefits that are less than 79 percent of the benchmark. The 5 percent risk level corresponds to 93 percent of the benchmark, and the 10 percent risk level is 116 percent of the benchmark.

An explicit expected utility calculation implies that with a CRRA value equal to 2.5 or less, the individual would prefer the pure equity investment with no guarantee. With CRRA values with 3 or more, the individual would choose the zero-cost collar with the guaranteed real return of at least minus 1 percent. The progression as risk aversion increases is thus from a more-risky to a less-risky approach.

For each CRRA value, the expected utility of the pure investment based plans with the 9.92 percent of payroll saving and with the utility maximizing guarantees exceeds the expected value with mixed system with taxes and PRA contributions of 4.46 percent of payroll. Additional calculations would be needed to consider the path of transition before deciding whether the extra cost in the transition to a pure investment-based system is justified by the higher level of long-run expected utility.

Two other expected utility calculations are worth mentioning. In the mixed plans with PAYGO taxes equal to PRA saving and with no guarantees, the expected utility of PRA investments that are 100 percent in equities exceeds the expected utility of PRA investments divided between equities and corporate debt in the ratio of 60 to 40. In contrast, in a pure investment-based plan with no PAYGO component, the 100 percent equity investment is preferred only by individuals with low risk aversion (CRRA values up to 3.0) with the 60:40 stock bond portfolios preferred by individuals with higher CRRA values.

6.8   A Concluding Comment

This chapter has described the risks implied by a mixed system of Social Security pension benefits with different combinations of PAYGO taxes and PRA saving. The analysis showed how these risks can be reduced by using alternative guarantee strategies. The first such strategy uses a blend of equities and TIPS to guarantee at least a positive real rate or return on each year's PRA saving. The second is an explicit zero-cost collar that guarantees an annual rate of return by giving up all returns above a certain level. One variant of these guarantees uses a two-stage procedure: a guaranteed return to age sixty-six and then a separate guarantee on the implicit return in the annuity phase. An alternative strategy provides a combined guarantee on the return during both the accumulation and the annuity phase.

Simulations are used to derive the probability distributions of retirement incomes relative to the "benchmark" benefits specified in current law. Calculations of expected utility show that these risk reduction techniques can raise expected utility relative to the plans with no guarantees. The ability to do so depends on the individual's risk aversion level. This underlines the idea that different individuals would rationally prefer different investment strategies and risk reduction options.

There are, of course, other ways that both types of guarantee could be modified that might produce higher expected utility. One line of research that should be considered is alternative designs of the puts and calls in the zero-cost collars. Another approach would allow adjustments in the portfolio composition during the accumulation or annuity phase based on the performance of the investments to that point.

References

Feldstein, Martin. 2000. Comment on Peter Diamond's "Administrative costs and equilibrium charges with individual accounts." In *Administrative aspects of investment-based Social Security reform,* ed. J. Shoven, 162–69. Chicago: University of Chicago Press.

Feldstein, Martin, and Elena Ranguelova. 2001a. Accumulated pension collars: A market approach to reducing the risk of investment-based Social Security reform. In *Tax policy and the economy.* Vol. 15, ed. J. Poterba, 149–66. Cambridge, MA: MIT Press.

———. 2001b. Individual risk in an investment-based Social Security system. *American Economic Review* 91 (4): 1116–25.

Feldstein, Martin, Elena Ranguelova, and Andrew Samwick. 2001. The transition to investment-based Social Security when portfolio returns and capital profitability are uncertain. In *Risk aspects of investment-based Social Security reform,* ed. J. Y. Campbell and M. Feldstein, 41–90. Chicago: University of Chicago Press.

Feldstein, Martin, and Andrew Samwick. 1998. The transition path in privatizing Social Security. In *Privatizing Social Security,* ed. M. Feldstein, 215–64. Chicago: University of Chicago Press.

Comment   David W. Wilcox

Martin Feldstein has probably done more than any other person to highlight the urgent need to reform our Social Security system and the potential benefits of putting the system on an investment-based foundation. In addition, he has personally conducted a goodly fraction of the seminal research in this area and inspired others to undertake much of the rest. To state the obvious, this conference volume—like many of its predecessors in this subject area—would not have come to fruition without his efforts, and the research careers of many of the participants at this conference would not have been nearly so rich without his beneficial influence. When the nation finally confronts the imperative of reforming the system, much of the thinking surrounding the ensuing debate will have been shaped directly or indirectly by Feldstein. For all of this, we owe him an enormous debt of gratitude.

This chapter continues in the tradition of his pushing the research frontier forward. In earlier work with Ranguelova and Samwick, Feldstein proposed the idea of limiting the financial risk associated with participation in personal retirement accounts (PRAs) by having the government provide an explicit guarantee.[1] Although the probability of a draw on taxpayer resources struck the authors as relatively low and the associated costs in those cases seemed manageable, the idea was criticized, partly on the apprehension that once a government guarantee had been agreed to in principle, no matter how limited in its original form, the guarantee might be enhanced over time, ultimately becoming a considerable new burden on taxpayers.

David W. Wilcox is a deputy director of the Division of Research and Statistics of the Federal Reserve Board.

The views expressed in this comment are those of the author and are not necessarily shared by the Board of Governors of the Federal Reserve or by the other members of its staff. I am grateful to many colleagues for helpful comments on an earlier version of these remarks.

1. See, among others, Feldstein, Ranguelova, and Samwick (2000).

This chapter proposes an elegant remedy for that critique. Feldstein notes that the objective of risk reduction can be achieved entirely through market-mediated means. For example, a PRA investor who wants to be guaranteed a minimum real return of zero percent can have each year's contribution invested in a mixed portfolio of Treasury Inflation-Protected Securities (TIPS) and equities. The TIPS ensure that the guaranteed minimum return will be paid, while the equities provide the potential for upside risk. When participants are young, the fraction to be invested in TIPS is relatively small; as participants age, the fraction to be invested in safe securities rises. Similarly, as Feldstein notes, participants could limit their downside risk by contracting for "zero-cost collars." Under this approach, participants would, in effect, purchase put options to eliminate their downside risk and sell call options to finance the insurance. Both approaches have the great virtue of never involving the government as guarantor; they also recognize and operationalize the important idea that there is no need to impose a one-size-fits-all type of approach in an investment-based Social Security system; individuals clearly differ in their attitudes toward risk and their ability to bear it, and policymakers ought to contemplate the possibility of allowing them to choose a PRA structure that is tailored to suit their own attitudes and situations.

The fundamental idea behind these market-based approaches is appealing, creative, and convincing: Feldstein has demonstrated that market-based mechanisms can be devised to sharply limit the risks associated with participation in a PRA—mechanisms that keep the government at two steps' remove, and so substantially alleviate concerns about an implicit contingent liability. Accordingly, my remaining comments are organized in two sections. In the first, I note two important methodological questions that are raised by Feldstein's paper. In the last section, I note some of the other issues, aside from portfolio diversification and the associated financial risk, that will likely figure in the debate as to whether individual accounts should be part of the inevitable future reform of Social Security.

Two Questions

The conclusion that PRAs would be welfare-enhancing depends on the treatment of transition costs and the specification of a welfare function, among many other factors. This section examines issues related to both factors. The issues are framed as questions because I do not know the answers and hope to encourage others to work on them.

Question #1: How Should Transition Costs Be Addressed
in Analyses of Fully Funded Systems?

In the long run, a sustainable pay-as-you-go Social Security system can pay a rate of return equal to the rate of growth of the population, n, plus the rate of growth of productivity, p. By contrast, in a world free of random variation, a fully funded system—whether administered on a centralized basis with a trust fund or a decentralized basis with a system of personal retirement accounts—can pay a riskless rate of return equal to r^*. Standard models predict that utility-maximizing individuals living in a stochastic environment will not choose a portfolio that delivers the riskless rate but will instead accept some risk as the price of a higher expected return, which I will denote as r. In this chapter, Feldstein compares plans delivering $n + p$ to plans delivering various versions of r and concludes that most people would be happier with the latter than the former.

As is well known by now, thanks especially to papers by Geanakoplos, Mitchell, and Zeldes (1998, 1999), there is no inherent rate-of-return inefficiency in a pay-as-you-go Social Security system. Policymakers chose to confer above-market rates of return on the first generations to participate in Social Security; the inexorable consequence of those decisions is that all subsequent generations, taken as a whole, must experience a below-market return on their participation. The issue of how best to distribute the burden of paying for the net benefit conferred on early participants is an open question, but there is no debating the fact that someone will pay.

This chapter compares the status quo pay-as-you-go system to a fully phased-in investment-based system. In so doing, it leaves aside the transition costs that would necessarily be associated with paying off the unfunded liability built up under the current system. In light of the uncertainty about how those transition costs will ultimately be borne, it is fair to ask how they should best be reflected in an analysis like this one. Two approaches present themselves immediately; I have no doubt that these do not exhaust the range of possibilities, but they illustrate that the underlying issue can be addressed.

One way to take the transition costs into account would be to build on the central insight of the papers by Geanakoplos, Mitchell, and Zeldes (1998, 1999), that a pay-as-you-go-system does not suffer from any rate-of-return inefficiency. Accordingly, households in the aggregate should be indifferent between the current pay-as-you-go system and the investment-based alternative provided the PRA is invested entirely in TIPS. In the Social Security Trustees' Report for 2006, population is assumed to grow about 0.3 percent per year in the long term (that is, between 2040 and 2080), productivity is assumed to grow 1.7 percent per year, and government bonds are assumed to pay a 2.9 percent real rate of return. Thus, in the world of the trustees' projections, the necessary indifference condition could be achieved by adjusting the assumed rates of return on TIPS and stocks downward by 90 basis points.

Another way to take the transition costs into account would be to regard the analysis in the chapter as providing part of the overall answer and augment it with an analysis of the welfare consequences of the investment-based approach for the generations that bear the transition cost. A complete apples-to-apples analysis could be produced by calculating the welfare gain or loss of *all* future generations, recognizing both that the transition costs are front-loaded relative to the benefits thereof and that all subsequent generations would presumably benefit from the shift to full funding.[2]

Under either approach, if the model is calibrated appropriately, PRAs will exhibit no welfare advantage over the pay-as-you-go system if households are required to invest the PRAs entirely in TIPS. Once that constraint is relaxed, however, many households will prefer PRAs because, as usual, a certain amount of additional equity risk will be seen as desirable given the higher expected rate of return.[3]

Question #2: What Welfare Function Should Be Used
to Evaluate the Results of the Simulations?

The CRRA utility function used to conduct the welfare analysis in this chapter yields counterfactual predictions on at least two issues of immediate relevance to the desirability of an investment-based approach to Social Security reform:

- If CRRA were the right utility function and the coefficient of relative risk aversion were between one and five, the equity premium would not have been declared a puzzle (Mehra and Prescott 1985). Put differently, if everyone had the utility function posited in this chapter, post-WWII returns on stocks and bonds would have had markedly different empirical properties.
- If CRRA utility were the right utility function, then—as my colleague Sean Campbell has recently pointed out—the reduction in the volatility of real activity that seems to have occurred around the early- to mid-1980s would have been accompanied by a proportionate reduction in the volatility of asset prices, but it was not (Campbell 2005).

The analysis in the chapter would be considerably more compelling if it used a utility function capable of generating the posited distribution of asset returns. Thanks to some relatively recent research, that objective appears to be achievable.[4]

---

2. Feldstein and Liebman (2002b) undertake an analysis of this sort and show that a transition to an investment-based Social Security system increases the present discounted value of consumption of all current and future generations provided the marginal product of capital exceeds the discount rate applied to the future consumption.

3. Some households will be indifferent to the constraint on portfolio holdings because they will adjust the composition of their non-Social Security portfolio to offset any change in the composition of their Social Security portfolio.

4. For example, the habit-based utility function proposed by Campbell and Cochrane (1999) can account for the behavior of the equity premium over the postwar period and, as demonstrated by Sean Campbell (2005), it can also account for the failure of the Great Moderation in real activity to be reflected in the volatility of equity returns.

Other Considerations Relevant to the Evaluation of PRAs

If the current pay-as-you-go system and an investment-based system are put on the same footing, and ignoring any lifetime wage insurance that might be provided through the current system but not by simple versions of individual accounts like the one studied here, the representative worker will be indifferent between the two systems if constrained to invest only in the risk-free asset, but will strictly prefer the investment-based approach if allowed to invest part of his or her portfolio in risky assets. What other considerations should policymakers take into account as they consider this extremely important decision? The issue is not easy because serious arguments can be made on both sides. The following strike me as some of the most important of those arguments. First, as to the arguments *in favor* of individual accounts:

- *Personal accounts are naturally self-sustaining.* Under a system of personal accounts, promised benefits can never exceed available resources because the only promise in a defined contribution (DC) structure is that each beneficiary will receive the proceeds of his or her own account. No solvency crisis can occur under such a structure; the parameters of such a system never need to be adjusted to put the system back on a sustainable trajectory. By contrast, in a defined benefit (DB) structure, the parameters can—and, as demonstrated by present experience, do—get out of alignment with what is sustainable. Moreover, the structure is not inherently self-correcting; unless self-correcting mechanisms have been built into the structure (such as, for example, indexing the retirement age to longevity), overt decisions must be taken to bring the system back into sustainability. In practice, these decisions can be delayed long past the time when they should be made.
- *A system of personal accounts is more credible as a vehicle for ensuring that "saving" for retirement actually adds to the capital stock.* A plausible argument can be made that the current system—while generating $1.9 trillion in apparent saving since 1983 in the form of trust-fund accumulation—has generated little or no real government saving.[5] This argument runs as follows: if, since 1983, Congress and the president have set their fiscal objectives in terms of the unified budget (for example, they might have been aiming to produce a balanced unified budget), then the Social Security surpluses that have been run during that time have served only to facilitate larger non-Social Security deficits than would have occurred otherwise. In other words, the saving that should have been used to prepare for future retirements has

---

5. To be sure, counterarguments can be made as well; see, for example, Diamond and Orszag (2003).

been dissipated. A system of individual accounts might be more likely to preserve such saving for its intended use. If contributions into the accounts are scored against the concept of the budget around which the political conversation revolves—a plausible but not certain hypothesis—then those resources might be seen as having been "taken off the table," and policymakers might be driven to choose a tighter fiscal policy than under the current system. In other words, *apparent* saving through the Social Security system would translate one for one into government saving. Whether that government saving would be transmitted into national saving would depend on whether the added saliency of the personal accounts would cause personal saving to decline. Unfortunately, the issue of whether Social Security surpluses actually contribute to government saving is of diminishing importance with each passing year because the time when Social Security surpluses will turn into deficits is drawing nearer.[6] Beginning roughly a decade from now, a fiscal policy anchored on the unified surplus or deficit will be more restrictive than one anchored on the balance excluding the current operations of the Social Security system.

• *A system of personal accounts might impress upon individuals that they have a responsibility for their own financial security in retirement.* A system of individual accounts might foster a greater sense of individual responsibility. In turn, that sense of individual responsibility could contribute to an enhanced popular appreciation of how important it is for individuals to behave in ways that are favorable to growth over time.

• *A system of personal accounts would open to everyone the opportunity to bear some equity risk.* For some individuals, failure to participate in equity ownership, no doubt, represents a rational decision grounded in considerations such as greater-than-average riskiness of own labor income, greater-than-average aversion to risk, and so forth. For others, however, it probably reflects considerations (such as high transactions costs or basic ignorance about investing in the stock market) that a system of personal accounts could help overcome. The magnitude of any welfare gain that would result from breaking down these market imperfections is difficult to estimate.

• *A system of personal accounts could reduce the price of risk and in so doing could induce entrepreneurs to undertake a riskier set of investment projects. Assuming risk is associated with return, the result could be an economy with somewhat greater aggregate risk but also somewhat faster average growth.* If a system of personal accounts induces additional

6. According to the 2006 Social Security Trustees' Report, Old-Age, Survivors, and Disability Insurance (OASDI) costs (benefits plus administrative expenses) will first exceed tax revenues in 2017; costs are projected to exceed overall OASDI income (including interest on assets held in the trust fund) starting in 2027.

demand for risky securities, it should also cause a reduction in the price of risk. Confronted with a lower price of risk in financial markets, entrepreneurs could, over time, choose to undertake a riskier portfolio of investment projects. To my knowledge, no empirical basis exists for judging whether any such shift would be important quantitatively or negligible.

Now as to some of the considerations militating *against* introduction of individual accounts:

- *Personal accounts could come to represent a major new liability for the federal government.* Over time, a system of individual accounts would inevitably create wave after wave of "notch babies"—cohorts retiring with noticeably lower accumulated assets despite having similar earnings histories. Policymakers would face enormous political pressure to insulate beneficiaries from the consequences of their investment decisions and the vagaries of the market. The contingent liability associated with any such move could represent a significant new fiscal burden. Given that no Congress can credibly restrict the actions of future Congresses, it is hard to see how the issue of the implicit put can be avoided entirely.[7]
- *In their simplest forms, personal accounts leave at best limited scope for sharing risks, either within or across generations.* The current system is intended to provide a measure of social insurance: It provides insurance against lifetime earnings risk by providing a higher replacement rate for low-income workers than for high-income workers; it provides insurance against disability; and it provides insurance against early death, in the form of survivors benefits for children of deceased workers, widows and widowers with minor children, as well as widows and widowers of retired workers. The current system also has the scope to smooth risks across generations; in principle, this could include not only demographic risks but also financial risks. While some of these features could be built into a system of individual accounts, they are not inherent in the simplest versions of PRAs.
- *Social Security may not be an appropriate vehicle for financial risk-taking.* Social Security is intended to provide a foundation for financial security in retirement, but was never intended as more than that. Under current law, Social Security promises a replacement rate of about 42 percent for a typical worker near the middle of the earnings distribution, but the current system is not sustainable. Assuming that resources into the system are capped at the current 12.4 percent of payroll, revenues will be sufficient to pay only about 70 percent of

7. Kent Smetters (2001) has emphasized the enormous cost of explicit government guarantees.

current-law benefits by the middle of this century. Assuming revenue of 12.4 percent of payroll, a sustainable replacement rate is probably in the neighborhood of 28 percent. Personal-finance professionals conventionally advise aiming to accumulate enough resources to provide an overall replacement rate of about 75 to 80 percent in retirement. Thus, by the middle of this century, workers should be aiming to replace about 50 percent of preretirement income out of some combination of employer pension benefits and personal saving. Even a very-risk-tolerant individual could probably satisfy his or her appetite for equity-risk exposure even if prevented from holding *any* equity risk through the Social Security system.

- *Relative to the current Social Security system, personal accounts could prove a costly means of transferring resources.* In 2003, the cost of administering the current Social Security system amounted to about 1 percent of benefits paid. If the costs of an investment-based system can be limited to 30 basis points per year, benefits over a forty-year career would be reduced by about 6 percent, or roughly six times as much as under the current system. Estimates on the order of 30 basis points are based on the idea of modeling an investment-based system on the federal Thrift Saving Plan. However, such analysis has been heavily criticized as too optimistic.[8] Based on the costs of administering private plans in the United States and the experience of foreign countries with privatized systems, some analysts have suggested that annual costs in the neighborhood of 1 percent per year are more realistic. Costs in this range would reduce annual benefits by about 20 percent—a very sizable reduction in efficiency compared to the current system.[9]

- *A system of personal accounts might turn out to be significantly more regressive than suggested by simple simulations.* The labor force attachment of lower-income individuals is much more tenuous than that of higher-income individuals. This can have important implications for the distributional characteristics of a system of personal accounts. If low-income workers have relatively more spells of unemployment, they will experience relatively smaller account accumulations than would be indicated by simulations based on hypothetical "steady

---

8. For example, Francis Cavanaugh, the first executive director of the federal Thrift Saving Plan, is quoted in the *Washington Post,* March 3, 2005, as follows: "There's no way they can do this without an enormous federal subsidy. . . . This has to do with workability, no matter how one feels about it philosophically, and it's not workable." He also characterized the 30 basis point estimate referred to in the text as "ridiculously optimistic." See http://www.washingtonpost.com/wp-dyn/articles/A2367-2005Mar2.html.

9. Related concerns are that a system of PRAs might give rise to much greater "leakage" of retirement saving during the preretirement years and that the introduction of PRAs might cause individuals to choose to annuitize too little of their Social Security resources, leaving themselves overexposed to the risk of outliving their resources.

earners" whose earnings follow smooth trajectories over their working careers. Feldstein and Liebman (2002a) conduct simulations of this type using real-life earnings histories and demonstrate that this concern can be addressed by a small change in the contribution or benefit rule.[10]

One consideration difficult to categorize as either a pro or con is the scope for participants in a system of PRAs to tailor their asset holdings to their risk tolerances and individual circumstances. If all individuals are fully rational, this scope for choice will obviously be utility-increasing. If at least some individuals are not fully rational, choice will be a mixed bag. The behavioral economics literature is replete with examples of individuals engaging in nonrational financial decision making.

Concluding Remarks

In demonstrating that the financial risk associated with participation in PRAs can be substantially mitigated through market-based mechanisms—leaving government more convincingly out of the picture—this chapter takes a significant step forward. The analysis suggests that workers would strongly prefer a fully funded investment-based system over the current pay-as-you-go system. The margin of preference would obviously be narrower if the costs of achieving full funding had been taken into consideration; an important question is how much narrower. Future research should address that question. It should also attempt to extend Feldstein's analysis to models that provide realistic accounts of why some individuals do not currently invest in equities and realistic accounts of why the decision making of other individuals seems to be so heavily influenced by factors (such as default settings) that should be irrelevant according to conventional theory. Aside from the welfare consequences of broadening the menu of available investment vehicles, myriad other issues, both pro and con, should also figure into the debate over whether to adopt a system of individual accounts.

References

Campbell, John Y., and John J. Cochrane. 1999. By force of habit: A consumption-based explanation of aggregate stock market behavior. *Journal of Political Economy* 107 (2): 205–51.
Campbell, Sean D. 2005. Stock market volatility and the great moderation. Federal Reserve Board, Finance and Economics Discussion Series no. 2005:47. Washington, DC: Federal Reserve Board.
Diamond, Peter, and Peter Orszag. 2003. *Saving Social Security: A balanced approach.* Washington, DC: Brookings Institution.

10. See Feldstein and Liebman (2002a).

Feldstein, Martin, and Jeffrey Liebman. 2002a. The distributional effects of an investment-based Social Security system. In *The distributional aspects of Social Security and Social Security reform,* ed. M. Feldstein and J. Liebman, 263–326. Chicago: University of Chicago Press.

———. 2002b. Social Security. In *Handbook of public economics.* Vol. 4, ed. A. Auerbach and M. Feldstein, 2245–2324. Amsterdam: Elsevier.

Feldstein, Martin, Elena Ranguelova, and Andrew Samwick. 2000. The transition to investment-based Social Security when portfolio returns and capital profitability are uncertain. In *Risk aspects of investment-based Social Security reform,* ed. J. Y. Campbell and M. Feldstein, 41–90. Chicago: University of Chicago Press.

Geanakoplos, Jean, Olivia Mitchell, and Stephen P. Zeldes. 1998. Would a privatized Social Security system really pay a higher rate of return? In *Framing the Social Security debate: Values, politics, and economics,* ed. R. D. Arnold, M. J. Graetz, and A. H. Munnell, 137–56. Washington, DC: Brookings Institution.

———. 1999. Social Security's money's worth. In *Prospects for Social Security reform,* ed. O. Mitchell, R. J. Myers, and H. Young, 79–151. Philadelphia: University of Pennsylvania Press.

Mehra, Rajnish, and Edward C. Prescott. 1985. The equity premium: A puzzle. *Journal of Monetary Economics* 15 (2): 145–61.

Smetters, Kent. 2001. The effect of pay-when-needed benefit guarantees on the impact of Social Security privatization. In *Risk aspects of investment-based Social Security reform,* ed. J. Y. Campbell and M. Feldstein, 91–112. Chicago: University of Chicago Press.

7

Pricing Personal Account Benefit Guarantees
A Simplified Approach

Andrew Biggs, Clark Burdick, and Kent Smetters

7.1 Introduction

A number of proposals to introduce personal accounts to the Social Security program contain provisions that would guarantee account holders against relatively poor investment performance that would make their total benefits fall below the level scheduled under current law. Such protections are attractive to account participants, who would gain the financial and other potential advantages of personal accounts without the principal downside risk of relatively poor investment performance.[1] However, given the size of Social Security benefit entitlements and the potential risk of market investment, guarantees constitute a significant contingent liability to whomever would be providing the guarantee, whether it be the private markets or the government. For that reason, it is important to fully evaluate the potential costs of guaranteeing private investments against market risk.

Although some academic researchers, most notably George Pennacchi

Andrew Biggs is a resident scholar at the American Enterprise Institute. Clark Burdick is an economist in the Division of Economic Research, Office of Policy, at the U.S. Social Security Administration. Kent Smetters is an associate professor of insurance and risk management at The Wharton School, University of Pennsylvania, and a research associate of the National Bureau of Economic Research.

Smetters's research was supported by the U.S. Social Security Administration (SSA) through grant #10-P-98363-1-03 to the National Bureau of Economic Research (NBER) as part of the SSA Retirement Research Consortium. The opinions and conclusions expressed are solely those of the authors and do not represent the opinions or policy of SSA, any agency of the federal government, or of the NBER. The authors thank Steve Goss, Olivia Mitchell, David Pattison, and George Pennacchi for many helpful comments but maintain sole responsibility for any remaining errors or inaccuracies.

1. Examples of potential advantages are portfolio choice, inheritability, clear property rights, and so on.

(1999) and Mari-Eve Lachance and Olivia Mitchell (2003), have shown considerable interest in the market cost of benefit guarantees, most policy analysis has tended to focus on the expected or mean cost of personal account benefit guarantees. An expected cost approach evaluates the probabilities of various outcomes and reports back the average or "expected" cost of a guarantee provision.

Expected costs provide valuable information, but do not reflect the greater valuation placed by the market on losses relative to the expected value of the losses. Indeed, the Congressional Budget Office (2006a, 18) has recently shown that the total cost of a benefit guarantee, including the associated cost of market risk, could be as much as three times larger than its expected cost. A so-called risk-neutral valuation provides such market information and thus may be useful to policymakers. This chapter demonstrates how a model for calculating the expected cost of a benefit guarantee can easily be modified to present the market price of personal account guarantees as a supplement to expected cost valuations.

We begin with a discussion of proposals to incorporate personal retirement accounts (PRAs) into Social Security and why some proposals have included guarantees against adverse investment outcomes. We also discuss the current actuarial analysis of Social Security personal account guarantees, which reports the expected cost of such a guarantee.

We then outline a simple method for producing a market-priced cost estimation of a guarantee against relatively poor investment performance. It is first shown for a simple example of a stock purchase to illustrate that it produces results equivalent to the Black-Scholes model. We then outline how such an approach could be useful in evaluating guarantees for personal accounts, where using an explicit Black-Scholes approach can be cumbersome.

We illustrate our approach using a Social Security reform proposal from Senator John Sununu (R-NH) and Representative Paul Ryan (R-WI). This proposal would introduce personal accounts investing from 5 to 10 percent of wages, depending upon the worker's earnings level. At retirement, individuals would receive either the proceeds of their personal account or their currently scheduled benefit, whichever was greater. Thus, this plan effectively guarantees that accounts would produce benefits no lower than those scheduled for the current program.

We first construct a simple model to estimate the expected cost of the benefit guarantee in the Ryan-Sununu proposal. This model is calibrated to roughly replicate the expected cost estimates produced by the SSA Office of the Chief Actuary (OACT). We then make a simple alteration to this model to produce a risk-neutral estimate of the guarantee cost. Estimates of the market cost of the guarantee using a risk-neutral valuation derived from our preferred approach, a stochastic modeling exercise that uses carefully calibrated Monte Carlo simulations, are similar to the results of the simple model.

It is worth noting that in our simple model, a number of variables are not modeled stochastically, including wage growth and inflation. Hence, any correlation between career-length wage growth and market returns is precluded. We also exclude the possible effects of the presence of a guarantee on portfolio allocations over time. While these issues are important for the consideration of the costs of any guarantee, be it from the expected cost or market-price perspective, they do not weigh on the choice between these two perspectives.

We close with a discussion of outstanding issues regarding personal account guarantees.

7.2   Types of Benefit Guarantees

The Social Security program is projected to experience financial strains as the baby boom generation retires and the population ages. Social Security's Trustees project that the program cost will begin to exceed tax revenues in 2017 and that its trust fund will be exhausted in 2040. At that point, the program would be capable of paying around 74 percent of scheduled benefits, with larger reductions in future years (Social Security Administration 2006).

A number of proposals to reform Social Security for the future have incorporated PRAs, similar to simplified individual retirement accounts (IRAs) or 401(k) accounts. Under personal account plans, individuals would invest part of their existing payroll taxes, additional contributions, or tax credits funded by general revenues into accounts holding portfolios of stocks, corporate bonds, and government bonds. At retirement, the proceeds of the account would augment or replace benefits paid from the traditional program.

Personal accounts invested in equities will tend to increase average retirement benefits for workers choosing to participate. This is one of the principle reasons advocates favor personal accounts: the higher expected benefits they provide would generally cushion against reductions in traditional benefits that could be used to balance the program's finances. Critics charge that expected value analysis ignores risk. While people might do better by holding a personal account most of the time, they could actually do worse.

In response, over the years a number of Social Security proposals have contained guarantees against adverse market outcomes. A number of different types of guarantees are possible, including guarantees of minimum rates of return on account savings, guarantees against retiring in poverty, and so on. However, almost all actual reform proposals have guaranteed current law scheduled benefits.[2] That is, a worker with a personal account (or spouses or widows receiving auxiliary benefits based upon that worker's earnings) would be guaranteed at retirement a benefit at least as high as those scheduled under current law, or more if the account balance could provide it.[3]

7.3   Current Practice: Expected Costs

The expected cost of a Social Security reform proposal's guarantee against market risk can be estimated based upon assumptions regarding the expected rate of return and standard deviation of portfolios held in personal accounts. From these assumptions, the mean and distribution of account balances (and the annuities they can purchase) is estimated (or approximated) relative to the guaranteed level, which is generally current law scheduled benefits. From this distribution the percentage of accounts falling short of the guaranteed level is calculated, as well as the average amount by which such accounts fall short. The average shortfall across all outcomes (or across the entire distribution), which is, therefore, also the average payment to satisfy the guarantee, represents the expected average cost of the guarantee. Projected across the retiree population, an aggregate expected cost of the guarantee can be calculated.

7.3.1   Advantages of Expected Cost Analysis

The expected cost of a guarantee is useful for budgeting, which is a primary use of actuarial analysis of current law Social Security and alternative proposals. The expected cost constitutes a "best guess" of what a guarantee will cost in a particular year. The 1990 Federal Credit Reform Act requires that the future costs of certain guarantees, although not personal account guarantees explicitly, be recorded on the budget. The costs of these guarantees are also typically recorded on an expected value basis (with some exceptions) using discount rates and procedures provided by the Office of Management and Budget.

2. All current proposals containing guarantees would ensure that individuals receive at least the benefit scheduled under current law. However, it is also possible to provide rate of return guarantees for accounts. These could be relevant for proposals that "offset" traditional benefits based upon contributions to accounts compounded at a given rate of interest. A guarantee of that interest rate on account contributions would ensure that account holders receive no less in total benefits than had they not participated in an account. While scheduled benefit guarantees and rate of return guarantees differ in form, they are analytically similar. Simply put, a scheduled benefit guarantee merely guarantees that an account produce a return sufficient to purchase an annuity equal to the portion of scheduled benefits that would not be payable from the traditional program under the plan. This implicit return would be different for each individual, but there is no fundamental difference between the two approaches.
3. Even aside from protecting against market risk, this is a relatively generous guarantee for younger individuals given that under current law, benefits would be cut significantly from scheduled levels once the trust funds became exhausted (which is currently projected to occur in 2040).

7.3.2   Disadvantages of Expected Cost Analysis

For expected cost analysis to be a useful guide for policymakers, however, the underlying risk must be fairly diversifiable from the government's perspective. A diversifiable risk is both small and uncorrelated with the other risks in the economy, including the tax base. Under these conditions, the classic Arrow-Lind theorem (1970) showed that the government should essentially be indifferent to risk and, therefore, discount future risky liabilities by the risk-free rate. An analogous result appeared in the Capital Asset Pricing Model and related work around the same time (Borch 1962).

The government might be able to diversify some risks better than the private sector if private markets are "incomplete" in at least one of two ways. First, some households in the economy might be underexposed to market risks, perhaps due to various fixed costs associated with investing (Abel 2001) or myopia. Exposing these households to market risks, maybe with personal accounts containing little or no overhead costs, could potentially increase their welfare (Diamond and Geanakoplos 2003; Campbell et al. 1999).

However, a guaranteed benefit backed by the government undermines some of this risk sharing and instead transfers risk to workers by increasing their risk of tax increases. Unlike financial markets, though, the government cannot distinguish between workers who are willing to take this risk and those who are not. Some workers might be more tolerant to additional risk because of their preferences or if their human capital returns (wages) are minimally correlated with stock market returns. Spreading this risk indiscriminately throughout the entire economy could actually harm households. Indeed, given the low investment fees now being charged by the private sector, the government could presumably improve risk sharing using guarantees only if many households are myopic or uneducated about saving and investment.

Second, the government might be able to diversify risk across generations because it is impossible for the private sector to write risk-sharing contracts with the unborn (Bohn 2003). A benefit guarantee would naturally shift resources from older retirees to younger workers through the tax system. In essence, younger workers would get exposure to the stock market risk of the preceding generation, something that they could not do directly through capital markets. Connecting generations in this manner, therefore, could improve risk-sharing.[4]

---

4. Social Security benefit guarantees could be limited by trust fund solvency, such that if the program became insolvent the guarantee would not be honored. However, the Ryan-Sununu proposal examined here and some other Social Security proposals contain provisions for transfers of general tax revenue as needed to maintain solvency, implying that that guarantee would be honored even if the program required additional non-Social Security resources to do so.

However, this argument requires that the human capital returns (wages) of younger workers are not sufficiently correlated with the stock returns of the preceding generation. This assumption is difficult to test at a generational level because there are only three or four unique data points at such low frequency. Nonetheless, while the associated standard errors are large, the data seem to suggest that human and physical capital returns are highly correlated, at around 0.8. In the context of the neoclassical model, that means that low frequency shocks can mainly be traced to changes in productivity rather than depreciation. While a correlation of 0.8 might still leave some room for shifting capital risk from older retirees to younger workers, it could also mean that the optimal direction of risk-sharing is just the opposite: from younger workers to older retirees (Smetters 2003).

It is true that markets do not currently offer options of the duration necessary to guarantee lifetime accumulations in personal accounts. Moreover, the vast size of the guarantees necessary for Social Security guarantees make it unlikely the market alone could provide them. For this reason, it might be argued that pseudomarket prices are not relevant to guarantees that would most likely be offered by the government. However, this ignores the fact that government itself does not truly bear risks so much as spread them among the various parties who provide resources to or receive resources from the government. Hence, the market cost of risk remains relevant in evaluating the economic impact of a guarantee, even if private markets are not used to hedge the associated risk.

In summary, the consensus in the academic literature is that it is unlikely that the government has much, if any, advantage in risk-sharing relative to the private market. Moreover, even if the government did have an advantage, especially between generations, it is not obvious that the optimal direction of risk shifting is from older retirees to younger workers, as implicit in a benefit guarantee.

As a result, policymakers arguably should not treat risk much differently than individual investors who consider both expected outcomes and risk. For instance, an individual deciding his own 401(k) investment strategy would not focus solely on expected outcomes. Rather, he or she would consider that stocks, bonds, and other investments offer combinations of risk and return. Moreover, periods of low returns from a risky asset are likely to be correlated with poor outcomes in other areas, such as labor income.

7.4   Risk-Neutral Valuation

A risk-neutral valuation of a guarantee reflects the potential market cost for insuring against the underlying risk, which could augment expected cost analysis of this risk. For these reasons, academics and government agencies are increasingly calculating market valuations of contingent liabilities of the government.[5] Risk-neutral methods are a common approach for estimating the market price of transfers of risk.

To be sure, the expression "risk neutral" might be a bit confusing at first glance because it seems to indicate an indifference to risk. The rather arcane expression reflects the assumed efficiency of capital markets, that is, that they are complete. In this case, the private-market cost that might be charged for a benefit guarantee can be priced using no-arbitrage relationships with private-market assets, riskless transactions that do, however, reflect the premium over expected cost that is demanded by markets to cover the risk.

A simple example illustrates the differences between an expected cost and a risk-neutral cost valuation. Consider a provision in which personal accounts were invested in stocks and the government guaranteed account holders against any returns below the long-term average for stocks. In exchange, the government reclaimed or "clawed back" any returns above that long-term average. Assuming a normal distribution of returns, the reclaimed returns above the average should be sufficient to compensate account holders for returns below the average. Thus, the expected cost of such a guarantee is zero.

Financial markets, however, would charge a significant premium for such a guarantee because it guarantees the equity premium, that is, the difference between average equity returns and the risk-free rate paid by government debt. In fact, ignoring additional administration charges, the cost of this guarantee would be exactly equal to the equity premium itself. Investors, therefore, would be exactly indifferent between investing in government bonds versus investing in equities and purchasing a guarantee.

By the Hans Stoll put-call parity relationship, this type of guarantee can be decomposed into two transactions: give investors a put option that allows them to sell the stock at an exercise or "strike price" implied by its expected return, while requiring investors to sell a call option allowing the government the right to buy the stock at the same strike price. Because the strike price exceeds the price implied by appreciation of the stock at the *risk-free* rate, the underlying put option would be much more valuable than the call option. The two options would have equal value only if the strike price were tied to the risk-free rate, which is much less than the expected return to equities.

7.4.1   Black-Scholes

The Black-Scholes option pricing formula is probably the easiest way to compute the cost associated with put and call options using the no-arbitrage approach. The Black-Scholes price of a call option is equal to

---

5. Pennacchi (1999), Lachance and Mitchell (2003), and the Congressional Budget Office (2006a) apply risk-neutral methods to individual accounts. The Congressional Budget Office (2004, 2006b) applies risk-neutral methods to federal loan guarantees.

$$C_0 = S_0 N(d_1) - Xe^{-rt}N(d_2),$$

where

$$d_1 = \frac{\ln(S_0/X) + (r + \sigma^2/2)T}{\sigma\sqrt{T}}$$

and

$$d_2 = d_1 - \sigma\sqrt{T}$$

and

C_0 = the call option price
S_0 = the purchase price
$N(d)$ = the probability that a random draw from a standard normal distribution will be less than the value d
X = the exercise price
e = the base of the natural log function (2.71828)
r = the riskless rate of return
σ = the standard deviation of the log of gross portfolio returns
T = the length of the option, or the time until maturity

Then, the put-call parity relationship implies that the put option price is equal to

$$P = C_0 + PV(X) - S_0 = C + Xe^{-rt} - S_0,$$

where P equals the put option price, and $PV(X)$ equals the present value of the exercise price. It is worth noting that the expected return on the asset plays no role in the formula: the option price is derived solely from the volatility of the asset and the riskless return. A more detailed discussion can be found in Ingersoll (1987).

7.4.2 General Risk-Neutral Valuation

The Black-Scholes formula, though, does not easily accommodate investments that are made and accumulated in personal accounts over numerous working years. The Black-Scholes formula would treat contributions made to personal accounts in each year separately. A Social Security benefit guarantee, though, would be applied to the accumulation of assets over many years. For an investment in any given year, the Black-Scholes formula would not recognize the amount of past accumulations.

More general risk-neutral methods pioneered by Cox and Ross (1976), however, can easily accommodate this added complexity. Our approach follows Hull (2002):

1. Sample a random path in a risk-neutral world: generate a return path based upon the *risk-free* rate of return and the standard deviation of annual returns on the *risky* asset.

2. Calculate the payoff from the guarantee: if the end balance is below the guaranteed level, the payoff is positive.

3. Repeat steps 1 and 2 to get many samples of the payoff in a risk-neutral world.

4. Calculate the mean of the sample payoffs to get an estimate of the expected payoff in a risk-neutral world.

5. Discount the expected payroll at the risk-free rate to get an estimate of the value of the guarantee.

Multiple contribution dates can be easily incorporated in Steps 1 and 2.

In anticipation of where we are headed, expected cost analysis in essence already follows Steps 1 to 5 with one difference in Step 1: the random path is generated using a rate of return larger than the risk-free rate to incorporate some expected equity returns. Simply reducing this parameter to the risk-free rate would allow a correctly specified expected cost model to calculate the market value of the underlying risk.

Consideration of these steps reveals an additional advantage offered by a risk-neutral valuation. In addition to providing a market cost estimate, a risk-neutral valuation is generally considered less subjective and potentially more accurate than an expected cost approach.[6] Notice that an expected cost analysis requires knowledge or a forecast of expected equity returns in addition to all of the information required for a risk-neutral valuation. Hence, a risk-neutral valuation requires less uncertain, and potentially subjective, information. Merton (1980) discusses some of the difficulties in estimating the equity premium (or equivalently the expected return on equities).

7.4.3   Comparison of the Two Approaches

For a large number of simulated paths and a *single* contribution date, the Black-Scholes formula and the more general approach outlined in the preceding should produce the same value for a benefit guarantee.

To illustrate, consider an individual who purchases $100 of stocks, with an expected return of 6.5 percent above inflation and a historical standard deviation of annual returns of 20.6 percentage points.[7] He or she intends to hold these stocks for ten years, with an expected end balance of $187.71. ($100 × 1.065^{10}) However, he or she wishes to purchase a guarantee that he or she can sell his stocks for no less than that amount ten years hence.

Using the Black-Scholes formula, the cost of a put option guaranteeing that $100 of stocks purchased today can be sold for $187.71 in ten years

---

6. The authors are especially grateful to George Pennacchi for pointing this out.

7. Notice than an annual standard deviation of stock returns of 20.6 percent implies a sigma, or volatility, of 19.17 percent. That is the parameter sigma in the Black-Scholes option pricing formula refers to the standard deviation of the log of gross returns and not the annual standard deviation of returns.

time would be $51.94. This is an expensive guarantee, equal to over half the initial purchase price and 28 percent of the guaranteed end balance.

The alternate approach, outlined in the preceding, stochastically generates a number of outcomes, with the initial purchase price compounded at the riskless 3 percent rate of return and varying with the historical 20.6 percent standard deviation for stocks. Due to the lower assumed rate of return, the mean end balance after ten years of 500,000 simulations equals $134.47, with a standard deviation of $93.16. Of the end balances, 79 percent are below the guaranteed value of $187.71, with an average shortfall (including instances of no payout) of $71.47. The present value of this shortfall is $53.18, a difference of only 2 percent from the value derived with Black-Scholes. This difference is primarily due to sampling variation; increasing the number of sample paths would reduce the difference even more.

Repeating this exercise but accumulating balances using the expected annual return to equities of 6.5 percent rather than the risk free rate as the mean for the simulations generates much different results. The average balance in 500,000 simulations becomes $187.45 with a standard deviation of $124.73. The average shortfall across simulations is $44.74, which has a present value of $33.29. This $33.29 represents the expected cost of the guarantee under an expected cost approach. Clearly the risk-neutral cost of $53.18 is a much better estimate of the market cost of $51.94 implied by the Black-Scholes option pricing formula. The expected cost approach underestimates the market cost by 36 percent.

The advantages of the more general approach become more apparent when applied to Social Security personal accounts. In this case, the government is not providing a guarantee that a single purchase made on one date can be sold for a given price at a stated later date. Rather, individuals make a number of purchases throughout their lifetimes, on an annual or more frequent basis, the compounded sum of which must be sufficient to purchase an annuity equal to their scheduled Social Security benefits.

7.5 A Simple Risk-Neutral Valuation Model for Benefit Guarantees

This section develops a simple model to show how risk-neutral valuation can be used to estimate the market value of the underlying risk associated with a benefit guarantee. Our model first attempts to replicate the expected cost of Social Security guarantees as projected by the SSA's Office of the Chief Actuary. It then alters the parameters as outlined in the preceding to estimate a risk-neutral cost for an identical guarantee. This model is designed solely for illustrative purposes. The technique outlined in the preceding could easily be applied to more detailed microsimulation models, though with an increase in computation time.

To illustrate, we make these calculations for the Social Security reform proposal from Senator John Sununu (R-NH) and Representative Paul Ryan (R-WI). While several other reform plans include guarantees, the Ryan-Sununu proposal is relatively simple in its construction, making for ease of modeling, and has been scored by OACT, thereby providing a baseline to ensure that the simple model roughly replicates existing expected cost estimates (Goss 2005).

7.5.1   Ryan-Sununu Proposal

Once phased in, individuals under the Ryan-Sununu plan would have personal accounts investing 10 percent of taxable earnings up to $10,000 (indexed with wages from 2006) and 5 percent of taxable wages above that level. Accounts are assumed to be invested in a portfolio consisting of 65 percent stocks and 35 percent corporate bonds, with annual administrative costs equal to 0.25 percent of assets managed. Stocks are projected to earn 6.5 percent above inflation and corporate bonds 3.5 percent, for an expected return net of administrative costs of 5.2 percent above inflation.

At retirement, individuals would receive either the annuitized value of their PRA balance or their currently scheduled benefit, whichever was greater.[8] This guarantee effectively entails supplementing personal account balances that fall short of the level needed to purchase an annuity equal to current law scheduled benefits.

For the purposes of calibrating our model, we simulate individuals who spend a full working lifetime under the Ryan-Sununu proposal. This eliminates the need to model implementation provisions contained in the plan for individuals spending only part of their careers with personal accounts.

7.5.2   Outline of Our Model

We base our model on the stylized scaled earner patterns produced by SSA's Office of the Chief Actuary (Clingman and Nichols 2005). Scaled earners have a typical hump-shaped life-cycle pattern of earnings from age twenty-one through age sixty-four. These earnings patterns are derived from a longitudinal sample of historical earnings records and are commonly used to simulate the effects of changes to the benefit formula and the introduction of personal retirement accounts upon individuals. These earnings profile exhibit the typical inverted U-shaped pattern over the life cycle. A medium-scaled earner would begin his or her working career with earnings below the national average wage, have earnings above the national average in middle age, and then have declining relative earnings as he or she neared retirement. With the exception of the maximum wage

---

8. In fact, individuals would be required to purchase an annuity with their PRA balance providing benefits equal to those scheduled under current law. If the PRA balance exceeded the annuity cost, extra funds could be withdrawn as a lump sum. If the PRA balance was not sufficient to purchase the required annuity, the guarantee provision would supplement the PRA balance to the necessary level.

worker, scaled earners at higher or lower earnings levels follow the general pattern of the medium-scaled earner, though at different absolute levels of earnings. We consider five different scaled earnings patterns, plus a steady earner at the maximum taxable wage:

- Very low: lifetime earnings at the 13th percentile of the distribution.
- Low: lifetime earnings at the 27th percentile.
- Medium: lifetime earnings at the 57th percentile.
- High: lifetime earnings at the 82nd percentile.
- Maximum taxable wage: lifetime earnings at the 100th percentile.

Applying these scaling factors against the average wage index projected by the Social Security Trustees, we can produce simulated earnings and account contributions.

For each worker type, a projected personal account balance is calculated consistent with OACT methods, in which annual account contributions are compounded at the projected geometric mean return for the assumed account portfolio, minus administrative costs.[9] Expected account balances at age sixty-five are converted to annuities based upon mortality and interest rate projections from the Social Security trustees.

The key statistic for this model's distribution of account balances is the coefficient of variation of final account balances, that is, the standard deviation of account balances divided by the mean balance. In lieu of a stochastic simulation, the variation in total account balances in retirement is estimated as the summed variation of account investments made in each year. Using a medium-scaled earnings pattern, account contributions for each year are calculated and individually compounded to age sixty-five at the mean expected return for the portfolio. The sum of these compounded annual contributions equals the expected account balance at retirement. Based upon the standard deviation of annual returns, the standard deviation of returns from the year a contribution is made through retirement is calculated for each year's contribution. An end balance is calculated for each year's contribution at the mean return minus the standard deviation of holding period returns; the sum of these balances represents the account balance at 1 standard deviation below the mean. The difference between this end balance and the end balance calculated at the expected return is the standard deviation; relative to the expected end balance, this difference is the coefficient of variation.

We calculate these values for the Ryan-Sununu default portfolio of 65 percent equities and 35 percent corporate bonds. The geometric mean returns are 6.5 percent and 3.5 percent, respectively, based upon standard Office of the Actuary projections. The standard deviations of returns and

---

9. The OACT also projects guarantee costs on a basis of an all-bond portfolio, as well as occasionally based upon a higher-yield assumption.

covariances between returns are from the 2006 Ibbotson yearbook (Ibbotson Associates 2006). The standard deviation of annual stock and corporate bond returns is taken to be 20.2 percent and 8.5 percent, respectively, and the correlation between them 0.19. Based upon the preceding method and these assumptions, the coefficient of variation for a personal account holding the Ryan-Sununu portfolio would be 50 percent.

Scheduled benefits at age sixty-five are calculated for each worker type. However, the Ryan-Sununu proposal guarantees all scheduled benefits, including auxiliary benefits paid to spouses and other eligible family members. The SSA Modeling Income in the Near Term (MINT) model projects that in 2050, auxiliary benefits will make up roughly 5 percent of total benefits paid to individuals of retirement age.[10] For that reason, scheduled benefits in 2050 are adjusted upward by 5 percent in an attempt to account for this provision.

Based upon scheduled benefits, expected account balances, and the distribution of account balances, we calculate the percentage of accounts for each worker type that could be expected to fall short of scheduled benefits and the size of the typical guarantee payment needing to be made.[11]

The next step is to convert benefits and guarantee estimates for each of these stylized workers into an approximation of costs covering the full population. This is accomplished using figures from OACT showing the percentage of individuals in the population who are best represented by each stylized worker type.

7.5.3   Calculation of the Expected Cost of Guarantee

Table 7.1 reports that 20.7 percent of the retiree population has average indexed monthly earnings (AIME) closest to those of the stylized very low earner; 22.4 percent closest to the low earner; 27.1 percent closest to the medium earner; 20.8 percent closest to the high earner; and 8.9 percent closest to the maximum wage earner.

The expected guarantee payment and scheduled benefit for each worker type are multiplied by the weighting factor. The sum of weighted guaran-

10. Calculations by SSA Office of Policy staff.

11. Note that correlation between market returns and wage growth could reduce personal account guarantee costs by a more mechanical route. Under current law, initial Social Security benefits are indexed to the growth of wages. If lifetime wage growth and market returns tend to be correlated, then individuals with low market returns would also tend to have low scheduled benefits, thereby reducing the cost of a personal account guarantee. Preliminary calculations (not shown here) by one author indicate that if working lifetime wage growth and market returns are perfectly correlated, the expected cost of a personal account benefit guarantee would decline by roughly one-quarter versus if lifetime wage growth and market returns are uncorrelated. If the correlation were 0.5, guarantee costs would decline by roughly one-eighth. Note, however, that this issue does not touch on the question of whether the expected cost or risk neutral valuation best expresses the value of the contingent liability to the guarantor. Rather, if correlation between wage growth and market returns is assumed, either an expected cost or a risk-neutral model should account for it.

Table 7.1   Calculation of expected guarantee costs for individuals retiring at age 65 in 2050

Earnings level	Very low	Low	Medium	High	Maximum
Average wage (wage indexed to present; US$)	8,516	15,329	34,065	54,112	72,342
Percentile of earnings distribution	13.4	27.1	57.4	82.1	100.0
Percent of workers closest to stylized worker	20.7	22.4	27.1	20.8	8.9
Scheduled benefits (US$)	9,808	12,832	21,138	28,024	34,568
Adjusted scheduled benefits (US$)	10,347	13,538	22,301	29,565	36,469
Expected annuity from personal account (US$)	9,969	15,031	31,545	38,273	64,245
Standard deviation of personal retirement account annuities (US$)	4,985	7,516	15,773	19,137	32,123
Percentage of account holders accessing guarantee	53	42	28	32	19
Average guarantee payment (US$)	1,859	1,917	2,185	3,292	2,707
Average guarantee payment as percentage of average benefits	18	14	10	11	7
Weighted value of benefits (US$)	2,142	3,032	6,043	6,150	3,246
Weighted value of average guarantee payment (US$)	385	429	592	685	241
Guarantee cost as percentage of total benefits	11.3				

Source: Authors' calculations.

tee payments is then expressed as a percentage of the sum of weighted benefit payments. Under these calculations, expected guarantee payments would equal roughly 11.3 percent of total benefits to new retirees in 2050.

According to the OACT analysis of the Ryan-Sununu proposal, expected guarantee costs in 2050 would equal $190.3 billion (in $2004). This amount is equal to 13.3 percent of total OASI costs in 2050, based upon projections from the 2004 Social Security trustees report. Thus, our simple model's estimates appear sufficiently close to proceed to the next step of converting the expected cost of the guarantee to the risk-neutral cost.

To repeat, this model is not intended to replicate existing results with precision, particularly as parameters used may be different. Nevertheless, as a calibrated replication of current results, it gets close enough to projected costs to illustrate the effects of the modified parameter input we propose here.

7.5.4   Calculation of the Market Cost of the Underlying Risk

Now that we confirmed that our model produces an estimate of the expected costs of a benefit guarantee that is roughly consistent with existing estimates, we then alter the model in order to estimate guarantee costs on a risk-neutral basis. The single change to the model's inputs is that the mean account balance is now produced by compounding account contributions at the rate of return projected to be earned by the Social Security trust funds rather than the expected return from the stock-corporate bond portfolio used in estimating expected guarantee costs. However, as detailed in the preceding the distribution of account balances expressed through the coefficient of variation remains the same as with the risky portfolio.[12]

The merit of this approach is that this conversion consists solely of altering the distribution of account balances at retirement from one based upon the expected return to one based upon the riskless return. That is, expected PRA balances at retirement are lower, but all other parameters remain the same. Thus, as detailed in table 7.2, projected end balances compounded at the bond rate are considerably lower than when compounded at the expected return, equaling roughly 60 percent of the expected account balance.

As expected, compounding returns at a lower rate of return increases the proportion of account holders whose balances require access to the guarantee and the size of the average guarantee payment. The guarantee cost relative to total benefits rises from 11.3 percent under expected cost valuation to 28.2 percent under risk neutral valuation, a factor of 2.5. If these proportions held true throughout the seventy-five-year scoring period, the present value expected guarantee cost of slightly over $2 trillion would rise to almost $5 trillion.

7.5.5   Change in Portfolio Composition

In proposals that allow for portfolio choice, it could be expected that inclusion of a benefit guarantee would alter the average portfolio allocation of account holders. In essence, the account holder is given two things of value: a cash allotment to be invested in the account and an implicit put option against losses relative to a given baseline. The present value of the account contribution is the same regardless of what it is invested in. The value of the option, however, rises with the volatility of the chosen portfolio. For that reason, rational account holders would tend to increase the share of

12. Note that the choice as the riskless rate of the projected return on the Social Security trust funds, whose special issue assets earn interest rates equal to the average of medium- and long-term government bonds in the market, will produce lower projected guarantee costs than a short-term bond rate, which might be more accurately described as riskless.

Table 7.2   Calculation of expected guarantee costs for individuals retiring at age 65 in 2050 (risk-free return)

Earnings level	Very low	Low	Medium	High	Maximum
Average wage (wage indexed to present; US$)	8,516	15,329	34,065	54,112	72,342
Percentile of earnings distribution	13.4	27.1	57.4	82.1	100.0
Percent of worke0rs closest to stylized worker	20.7	22.4	27.1	20.8	8.9
Scheduled benefits (US$)	9,808	12,832	21,138	28,024	34,568
Adjusted scheduled benefits (US$)	10,347	13,538	22,301	29,565	36,469
Expected annuity from personal account (US$)	6,071	9,072	15,879	23,181	37,768
Standard deviation of personal retirement account annuities (US$)	3,036	4,536	7,940	11,591	18,884
Percentage of account holders accessing guarantee	92	84	79	71	47
Average guarantee payment (US$)	4,215	4,519	6,744	7,593	5,796
Average guarantee payment as percentage of average benefits	41	33	30	26	16
Weighted value of benefits (US$)	2,142	3,032	6,043	6,150	3,246
Weighted value of average guarantee payment (US$)	873	1,012	1,828	1,579	516
Guarantee cost as percentage of total benefits	28.2				

Source: Authors' calculations.

stocks in their account portfolios in response to a benefit guarantee. The option value of the account would be maximized if invested solely in stocks.

While limits on portfolio allocations could be implemented to control for such effects in personal account plans, the Ryan-Sununu proposal does not limit the guarantee contingent upon holding a specified portfolio. Initially three portfolios would be offered, with equity components of 50, 65, and 80 percent, respectively, with the remainder held in corporate bonds. Once account balances reached $2,500 (in 2005 dollars), additional investment options would be available through private investment companies.

To illustrate the potential cost effects of changing portfolio allocations on guarantee costs, we repeat our preceding calculations for the Ryan-Sununu proposal but assume a portfolio of 100 percent stocks. Changing to an all equity portfolio does not alter any parameters other than the coefficient of variation of PRA annuities, which rises from 50 percent under the default 65-35 portfolio to 61 percent with all stocks. Doing so increases the risk-neutral cost of the Ryan-Sununu guarantee from 32.4 percent of total benefits to 33.9 percent. This relatively modest increase is due to the fact that the default portfolio already contains 65 percent equities, so the variance of outcomes does not increase a great deal.

However, larger costs are possible if account holders choose to vary their portfolios to "time the market." This could potentially increase costs further depending upon how this timing affected the variability of account portfolios. One advantage of the approach we introduce here is that if the effects of variable portfolio allocations are modeled for the purposes of calculating the expected cost of a personal account guarantee, those effects would be similarly treated in calculating the market cost of such a guarantee. That is, the change to parameter inputs we introduce to convert expected cost projections to risk-neutral valuations is not contingent upon modeling variability of account portfolios.

7.5.6   Alternate Calculations

As a check on the simple model presented in the preceding, we recalculate risk-neutral guarantee costs using a stochastic model, which is a preferred methodology for such an exercise. Nominal earnings profiles are created beginning in 2006 using the AWI and standard scaled earner profiles for very low, low, medium, and high earners. An additional nominal earnings profile is created for maximum earners who earn the taxable maximum in each year. We create earnings profiles for each of the thirty-one age cohorts who work a full forty-four years (ages twenty-one to sixty-four) between 2006 and 2079. Each of these cohorts is assumed to retire at age sixty-five in the years 2050 to 2080.

For workers at each age, nominal account contributions are calculated consistent with the Ryan-Sununu specifications. Nominal contributions are converted to constant 2004 dollars using the Consumer Price Index (CPI) assumptions from the 2004 Old-Age, Survivors, and Disability Insurance (OASDI) trustees' report. The real contributions are then accumulated at stochastic real annual rates of return less administrative costs equal to 25 basis points (0.25 percent). The stochastic real gross rates of return are generated from independently and identically distributed (i.i.d.) lognormal random variables to form 10,000 rate of return paths, each path representing the seventy-four years from 2006 through 2079. The lognormal rates of return are calibrated to have an expected value in levels equal to the OACT assumptions for the annual return on a PRA portfolio invested 65 percent in stocks and 35 percent in corporate bonds.[13] The standard deviation of the stochastic rates is assumed to equal 12.59 percent, the historical standard deviation of annual returns for a portfolio invested 65 percent in the S&P 500 with dividend reinvestment and 35 percent in a AAA corporate bond index.[14]

The accumulation of real (constant 2004 dollars) contributions at real annual rates of return results in a distribution of real final PRA balances for each of the 31 cohorts in the year they turn 65. The distribution of PRA balances for each cohort is then compared with the cost of purchasing an inflation indexed annuity that pays the age sixty-five retirement benefit in that and all subsequent years. The guarantee is a one-time "top up" payment made to individuals in the year of their retirement whenever their final PRA balance is insufficient to purchase the current law benefit annuity.

For each type of worker, the expected cost of the guarantee is approximated simply as the arithmetic mean of the guarantee payments across the 10,000 stochastic simulations. An aggregate expected cost estimate is produced by expressing the guarantee cost as a percentage of current law scheduled benefit payments (the cost of the inflation indexed annuity) and weighting this cost for each type of worker by the population percentage most closely resembling that type of worker.[15]

Given this procedure for producing expected cost estimates for a benefit guarantee, obtaining a market-cost estimate, or risk-neutral valuation, is remarkably easy. To produce a market-cost estimate, we follow exactly the same procedure described in the preceding, except that the stochastic rates of return are calibrated to have an expected value equal to the real new issue rate of 2.9 percent for government bonds issued to the OASDI trust funds as assumed in the 2004 trustees' report.[16] Importantly, the variance of the stochastic rates of return is unaltered from the value used in producing the expected cost estimate in the preceding. That is, the expected return of the PRA portfolio is altered, but the assumed variability of the portfolio is not.

Everything else proceeds exactly as before. Real PRA contributions are

13. We also calibrated the stochastic rates to have a geometric mean equal to the Commission to Strengthen Social Security (CSSS) assumptions, but those results are not reported here.

14. Historical data for the S&P 500 and the AAA-rated corporate bond index from 1914 through 2005 were obtained from the Total Return Database of Global Financial Data Inc.

15. Note that this relies on a cohort measure of benefit cost and not on a calendar year measure as is generally reported in the OASDI trustees' report. For a fully phased-in system of guaranteed personal accounts, there should be little difference between the guarantee cost as a percentage of cohort benefits and as a percentage of calendar-year benefit payments.

16. In 2004, the OASDI trustees assumed a nominal new issue rate of 5.8 percent and inflation of 2.8 percent annually under alternative II implying a real new issue rate of 2.92 percent. We use the new issue rate for trust fund assets assumed in the 2004 OASDI trustees' report as a proxy for the risk-neutral rate of return.

Table 7.3   **Risk neutral average guarantee payment as percent of average scheduled benefit (2050)**

	Very low	Low	Medium	High	Maximum
Stochastic model	41	34	32	27	17
Analytic model	41	33	30	26	16

accumulated at the stochastic risk-neutral rates, and the resulting distribution of real PRA balances is compared with the same inflation indexed annuity cost as before. Guarantee payments are again determined, but unlike before, the arithmetic average of these payments across all 10,000 simulations is now an approximate market cost for the guarantee. That is, the average guarantee payment using the stochastic risk-neutral rates approximates what an individual would pay in a competitive insurance market to purchase the benefit guarantee that ensures a minimum annual benefit equal to current law scheduled benefits.

Table 7.3 presents results from the stochastic model compared to those from the analytic model outlined in the preceding. In each case, the guarantee cost is represented as a percentage of average benefits for each worker type. These percentages are weighed to approximate costs for the full population.

As reported in the preceding, the analytic model calculates the risk-neutral guarantee cost for the Ryan-Sununu proposal in the year 2050 as 28.2 percent of total OASI benefits in that year. Using the same general method as the analytic model but inputs from the stochastic model generates an estimated risk neutral guarantee cost in 2050 of 29.6 percent of OASI benefits. Note, however, that the stochastic model does not contain an adjustment for auxiliary benefits. When that adjustment is dropped from the analytic model, the risk-neutral cost then declines to 25.8 percent of total OASI benefits. While neither model is a substitute for a full simulation against a representative population, they produce results roughly consistent with each other.

7.6 Conclusions

Once an appropriate model is constructed to calculate the expected cost of a guarantee, a change of a single parameter of that model enables the analyst to calculate the risk neutral guarantee cost as well. Our preferred approach uses a stochastic model to estimate the market value of the guarantee, but the risk-neutral price based on the analytic perspective turns out to be similar for the proposal modeled. From a practical perspective, the risk-neutral guarantee costs allows for greater information to be provided to policymakers with relatively little additional research cost.

References

Abel, Andrew B. 2001. The effects of investing Social Security funds in the stock market when fixed costs prevent some households from holding stocks. *American Economic Review* 91 (1): 128–48.
Arrow, Kenneth J., and Robert C. Lind. 1970. Uncertainty and the evaluation of public investment decisions. *American Economic Review* 60:364–78.
Bohn, Henning. 2003. Intergenerational risk sharing and fiscal policy. University of California, Santa Barbara. Mimeograph.
Borch, Karl H. 1962. Equilibrium in a reinsurance market. *Econometrica* 30: 424–44.
Campbell, John Y., Joao F. Cocco, Francisco J. Gomes, and Pascal J. Maenhout. 1999. Investing retirement wealth: A life-cycle model. NBER Working Paper no. 7029. Cambridge, MA: National Bureau of Economic Research.
Clingman, Michael, and Orlos Nichols. 2005. Scaled factors for hypothetical earnings examples under the 2005 trustees report assumptions. Actuarial note no. 2005.3. Office of the Chief Actuary, Social Security Administration, September. http://www.ssa.gov/OACT/NOTES/ran3/an2005-3.html.
Congressional Budget Office. 2004. Estimating the value of subsidies for federal loans and loan guarantees. CBO Study. Washington, DC: CBO, August.
———. 2006a. Evaluating benefit guarantees in Social Security. Background Paper. Washington, DC: CBO, March.
———. 2006b. Valuing the student loan consolidation option. Background Paper, Washington, DC: CBO, October.
Cox, John E., and Stephen A. Ross, 1976. The valuation of options for alternative stochastic processes. *Journal of Financial Economics* 3:145–66.
Diamond, Peter, and John Geanakoplos. Social Security investment in equities. *American Economic Review* 93 (4): 1047–74.
Goss, Stephen C. 2005. Estimated financial effects of the Social Security Personal Savings Guarantee and Prosperity Act of 2005. Office of the Chief Actuary, Social Security Administration, April. http://www.ssa.gov/OATC/Solvency/RyanSununu_20050420.html.
Hull, John C. 2002. *Options, futures, and other derivatives.* 5th ed. Upper Saddle River, NJ: Prentice Hall.
Ibbotson Associates. 2006. *Stocks, bonds, bills, and inflation: 2006 yearbook.* Chicago: Ibbotson Associates.
Ingersoll, Jonathan. 1987. Option pricing theory. *The New Palgrave: A Dictionary of Economic Theory and Doctrine.* New York: Macmillan.
Lachance, Marie-Eve, and Olivia Mitchell. 2003. Guaranteeing individual accounts. *American Economic Review* 93 (2): 257–60.
Merton, Robert C. 1980. On estimating the expected return on the market: An exploratory investigation. *Journal of Financial Economics* 8:323–61.
Pennacchi, George G. 1999. The value of guarantees on pension fund returns. *Journal of Risk and Insurance* 66 (2): 219–37.
Smetters, Kent. 2003. Trading with the unborn. NBER Working Paper no. 9412. Cambridge, MA: National Bureau of Economic Research.

Social Security Administration. 2006. *2006 annual report of the Board of Trustees of the Federal Old-Age and Survivors Insurance and Disability Insurance trust funds.* Washington, DC: GPO.

Comment   George G. Pennacchi

This chapter by Andrew Biggs, Clark Burdick, and Kent Smetters makes two simple but very important points. First, if one has a model that can compute the expected cost of a personal retirement account (PRA) guarantee, then with a couple of changes in parameter values, the model can also compute the market cost of the guarantee. Second, knowledge of the guarantee's market cost is critical for determining sensible policy.

I agree wholeheartedly with these two results. In these comments, I will offer more intuition for the chapter's findings and add arguments for why policy should be guided by market costs and not expected costs. I will close with some suggestions for improving estimates of the market cost of PRA guarantees.

Biggs, Burdick, and Smetters construct a simple model that is calibrated to roughly replicate the Social Security Administration Office of the Chief Actuary's (OACT) expected cost of the Ryan-Sununu PRA guarantee. For a PRA invested 65 percent in stocks and 35 percent in bonds and assuming the expected real returns on stocks and bonds are 6.5 percent and 3.5 percent, respectively, they calculate that the guarantee's expected cost in 2050 equals 11.3 percent of total Social Security Old-Age and Survivors Insurance (OASI) costs. The expected cost in 2050 of the same guarantee computed by OACT's model is 13.3 percent of total OASI costs.

Having shown that their model is comparable to that of the OACT, they consider what would be the market cost of the same Ryan-Sununu guarantee, rather than its expected cost. Their computation of market cost is based on standard asset pricing methodology that accounts for the systematic (priced) risks inherent in stock and bond returns. Specifically, they take the identical model that was used to compute the expected cost of a PRA guarantee and alter two parameter inputs. Rather than setting the expected real returns on stocks and bonds equal to their physical (actual) values of 6.5 percent and 3.5 percent, respectively, they set them equal to their risk-neutral values, which for both is assumed to equal a risk-free real

George G. Pennacchi is a professor of finance at the University of Illinois.

This research was supported by the U.S. Social Security Administration (SSA) through grant #10-P-98363-1-03 to the National Bureau of Economic Research (NBER) as part of the SSA Retirement Research Consortium. The findings and conclusions expressed are solely those of the author and do not represent the views of the SSA, any agency of the federal government, or of the NBER.

return of 2.9 percent.[1] With this simple change, they find that the PRA guarantee's market cost in 2050 equals 28.2 percent of total OASI costs.

Intuitively, it is not surprising that the market cost of this long-dated guarantee is almost two and one-half times its expected cost. The guarantor bears undiversifiable or systematic risk because equity losses (and to a lesser extent bond losses) over a long horizon would tend to occur following several years of economic recession. This is precisely the scenario when the guarantor would least prefer to fund claims on PRA losses. A market cost for the guarantee that exceeds its expected cost reflects the market compensation for this systematic risk.

Because the systematic risk of a PRA guarantee derives from the systematic risk premiums of the stocks and bonds in the PRA portfolio, a mathematically equivalent way of adjusting for this risk is to simulate scenarios of stock and bond returns using their risk-neutral expected returns, not their physical expected returns. Specifically, the correct market cost is found by simulating all security returns assuming that their expected return equals that of a short-maturity, risk-free, real return, such as the yield on a short-maturity Treasury Inflation-Protected Security (TIPS). This lowers the simulated returns of the PRA portfolio because they grow, on average, at the 2.9 percent risk-free rate rather than the portfolio's 5.45 percent physical rate. Hence, more of these randomly simulated risk-neutral PRA returns result in a claim on the guarantor, thereby increasing the guarantee's cost.

The preceding description points to an advantage of valuing guarantees based on their market, rather than expected, costs. Estimates of market costs involve less subjectivity compared to estimates of expected costs. Computing market costs requires knowledge of the real return on a short-maturity, inflation-indexed bond. This real return is practically observable and can be accurately measured from TIPS yields. In contrast, calculating expected costs requires knowledge of the physical expected returns on each of the securities in the PRA portfolio. Determining these expected returns over the life of the guarantee is more subjective, largely because it is not clear how they should be estimated. As discussed in Merton (1980), it is quite difficult to accurately estimate the expected returns on equities from their realized (historical) returns.[2] Such an exercise becomes even more

1. This implies a risk-neutral expected PRA return (before administrative costs) of 2.9 percent compared to a physical expected return of $(0.65 \times 6.5\% + 0.35 \times 3.5\%) = 5.45\%$. The paper's 2.9 percent return is based on the real return that nominal government bonds issued to the OASDI trust funds are expected to earn. Theoretically, this real return should be set to the real yield on a short-maturity, inflation-indexed government bond. Doing so may lead to a risk-neutral real return somewhat lower than 2.9 percent and result in a 2050 market cost slightly higher than what the paper calculates.

2. Equity variances and covariance can be estimated relatively more accurately. The accuracy of variance-covariance estimates improves with the frequency at which returns are sampled, whereas the accuracy of expected return estimates increases with the return sample's observation period. It may take an observation period of fifty years or more to obtain an accurate estimate of a stock's expected return, assuming its expected return is constant over time.

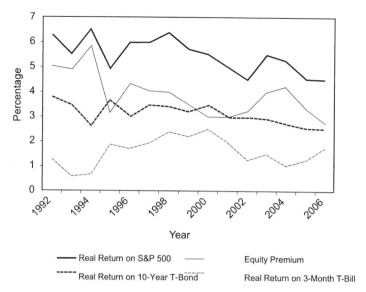

Fig. 7C.1   Survey of Professional Forecasters median 10-year forecasts

difficult if one (realistically) assumes that expected equity returns vary over time.

Survey evidence suggests that real expected equity returns are time varying and that the *equity risk premium,* defined as the difference between the expected return on equity and the short-maturity, risk-free interest rate, has been falling. Figure 7C.1 gives the median forecasts of the real returns on stocks, bonds, and bills, as well as the equity risk premium, from the Survey of Professional Forecasters (SPF) for the years 1992 to 2006.[3] Except for the real return on Treasury bills, these median forecasts have tended to decline over this fifteen-year period. In particular, the median forecast for the equity premium was 5.0 percent in 1992, peaked at 5.85 percent in 1994, and is now down to 2.75 percent. Further, the current median forecast for the real return on stocks over the next decade is 4.5 percent, which is 200 basis points lower than the OACT's assumed real return of 6.5 percent. An implication is that the OACT's estimate for the expected cost of a PRA guarantee is understated.

The SPF can be used to illustrate the subjectivity in determining the equity risk premium (and equity expected returns). Figure 7C.2 plots each of the individual forecasters' estimates of the ten-year horizon equity premium. It is clear that there is wide cross-sectional variation in what these

3. The Federal Reserve Bank of Philadelphia has conducted the Survey of Professional Forecasters since 1990. It was previously carried out by the American Statistical Association and the National Bureau of Economic Research beginning in 1968. In recent years, approximately thirty professional economic forecasters have participated in this survey. See Croushore (1993) for details.

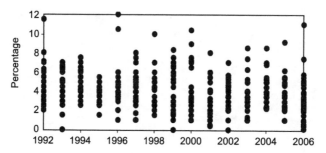

Fig. 7C.2   Survey of Professional Forecasters' individual equity premium forecasts

professional forecasters believe will be the average excess return on stocks over the next decade. This suggests much potential disagreement among reasonable individuals as to the appropriate expected return estimates to use in calculating the expected cost of a PRA guarantee. Consequently, the potential for political manipulation of PRA guarantees costs is greater when they are based on expected costs rather than market costs that do not require knowledge excess expected returns.

Another reason for valuing PRA guarantees using market, rather than expected, costs is that policy based on expected costs can lead to large economic distortions. All else equal, expected costs of PRA guarantees are lower the greater is the systematic risk of the PRA portfolio. Specifically, consider two PRA portfolios having the same real return variance, but different systematic risk. The market costs of a PRA guarantee would be the same for these two portfolios, but their expected costs would differ. The portfolio with greater systematic risk, and, therefore, a greater systematic risk premium (excess expected return), would have a lower expected cost. Thus, policy based on expected costs produces an incentive for choosing PRA portfolios that are highly procyclical. An implication is that the government would face large guarantee claims following several years of economic recession, a time when government budget deficits would already be large. Raising taxes or further increasing the government's debt during such a scenario would be especially painful to current and future taxpayers. This incentive to amplify the magnitude of business cycles is avoided by use of market costs.[4]

Related to how a PRA guarantee should be valued is the issue of how it should be funded. Suppose that a premium that covered the cost of a PRA's guarantee was deducted from the account balance. Then based on the previous logic, setting premiums equal to the expected cost of the guarantee would induce individuals to choose a portfolio with excessive systematic risk. This moral hazard incentive is avoided by setting the premium equal

4. Other government guarantee programs that charge premiums equal to expected costs may also be subject to moral hazard that results in excessive systematic risk. Pennacchi (2006) describes how this distortion arises when bank deposit insurance premiums are based on expected, rather than market, costs.

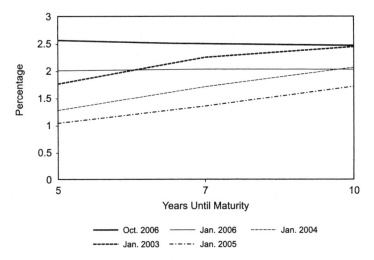

Fig. 7C.3   Term structures of TIPS yields

to the guarantee's market cost. However, while a policy of market cost premiums avoids distortions, it may be politically problematic. Charging a premium above the guarantee's expected cost means that the government guarantor would profit, on average, even though this profit reflects fair compensation to taxpayers for their exposure to systematic risk. To the financially unsophisticated, it might appear that the government is over-charging for PRA guarantees.

A potential solution is to avoid explicit premiums but constrain PRA investment allocations along the lines proposed in Feldstein (2005). This involves investing a portion of the PRA portfolio in assets that pay risk-free real returns (TIPS) until the portfolio's guaranteed return is obtained. Under this portfolio restriction, the PRA guarantee is implicitly funded by the PRA holder who relinquishes the potential up-side returns that would be available from a riskier PRA portfolio.

I conclude by suggesting some extensions to the chapter's simulation model that might fine-tune the estimates of the market cost of a PRA guarantee.[5] In addition to stochastic security returns, I believe a model should recognize at least two other sources of uncertainty affecting PRA guarantees. One is the stochastic nature of wage contributions to a worker's PRA. A satisfactory simulation model should include risk-neutral processes for workers' real wages, where these wage processes might differ depending on a worker's age and industry.

Another potentially important source of uncertainty is the term structure of real interest rates. Figure 7C.3 shows that TIPS yields have changed

---

5. These extensions are detailed in Pennacchi (1999) where they are incorporated into a model for valuing a Chilean PRA guarantee.

considerably over the past few years. Randomness in real interest rates affects guarantee costs in at least two ways. First, they cause variation in the risk-neutral expected returns on PRA securities, adding more randomness to a worker's PRA balance at retirement. Second, the real interest rate that a worker faces at retirement affects the level of annuity payments that can be purchased with his or her balance. If a PRA guarantee is truly a guarantee of minimum annual retirement benefits, rather than simply a final account balance guarantee, then the guarantee's cost depends on the term structure of real interest rates at the worker's retirement date.

A risk-neutral process for real interest rates based on the Vasicek (1977) model can be combined with risk-neutral processes for security returns and real wages. This can be done while assuming a general correlation structure between these processes. Personal retirement account guarantee costs are computed using Monte Carlo simulations of these processes for different worker cohorts.

References

Croushore, Dean. 1993. Introducing: The Survey of Professional Forecasters. *Business Review,* Federal Reserve Bank of Philadelphia *Business Review* (November/December):3–13.
Feldstein, Martin. 2005. Reducing the risk of investment-based Social Security reform. NBER Working Paper no. 11084. Cambridge, MA: National Bureau of Economic Research.
Merton, Robert. 1980. On estimating the expected return on the market: An exploratory investigation. *Journal of Financial Economics* 8:323–61.
Pennacchi, George. 1999. The value of guarantees on pension fund returns. *Journal of Risk and Insurance* 66:219–37.
———. 2006. Deposit insurance, bank regulation, and financial system risks. *Journal of Monetary Economics* 53:1–30.
Vasicek, Oldrich. 1977. An equilibrium characterization of the term structure. *Journal of Financial Economics* 5:177–88.

8

Reducing Social Security PRA Risk at the Individual Level
Life-Cycle Funds and No-Loss Strategies

James M. Poterba, Joshua Rauh, Steven F. Venti, and
David A. Wise

Retirement savers in a Social Security system with a personal retirement account (PRA) component would face the challenge of deciding how to allocate their PRA portfolios across a broad range of asset classes and across many different financial products. Asset allocation decisions have important consequences for retirement wealth accumulation because they affect the expenses of investing as well as the risk of low returns. The goal of this chapter is to assess the relative risk associated with alternative asset allocation strategies in PRAs. It also offers insight on the consequences of different asset allocation rules in current private-sector defined contribution (DC) plans, such as 401(k) plans.

Quantifying the risk associated with DC pension plans, and examining how individual choices affect this risk, is an active topic of research. Samwick and Skinner (2004) compare the risks associated with defined

James M. Poterba is the Mitsui Professor of Economics at the Massachusetts Institute of Technology, and president of the National Bureau of Economic Research. Joshua Rauh is an assistant professor of finance at the University of Chicago, and a faculty research fellow of the National Bureau of Economic Research. Steven F. Venti is the DeWalt Ankeny Professor of Economic Policy and a professor of economics at Dartmouth College, and a research associate of the National Bureau of Economic Research. David A. Wise is the John F. Stambaugh Professor of Political Economy at the John F. Kennedy School of Government, Harvard University, and director of the program on the economics of aging at the National Bureau of Economic Research.

We are grateful to Tonja Bowen for outstanding research assistance, to Morningstar for providing us with mutual fund data, and to the National Institute of Aging (NIA) for research support. This research was supported by the U.S. Social Security Administration (SSA) through grant #10-P-98363-1-03 to the National Bureau of Economic Research (NBER) as part of the SSA Retirement Research Consortium. The work was also supported by NIA grant PO1-AG005842. The findings and conclusions expressed are solely those of the authors and do not represent the views of the SSA, any agency of the federal government, or of the NBER.

benefit and DC plans for workers with a set of stylized wage and employment trajectories. Many other studies have examined the risk of different investment strategies in the context of lifetime saving programs that resemble DC plans. Campbell and Viceira (2002) and Cocco, Gomes, and Maenhout (2005) explore the optimal asset allocation between stocks and bonds for life-cycle savers. Shiller (2005) tabulates the distribution of possible terminal wealth values when investors follow age-dependent asset allocation rules in a saving program that he models on a DC Social Security system. Poterba et al. (2005), hereafter PRVW (2005), examine how several different portfolio allocation strategies over the life cycle affect retirement wealth.

Previous findings about the level of retirement wealth associated with DC saving programs, and about the risk of such wealth, are very sensitive to assumptions about the expected return on corporate stock. Stocks have offered substantially higher average returns than bonds over the eighty-year sample that is often used to calibrate the return distributions. PRVW (2005) find that this has an important effect on the distribution of retirement wealth for alternative asset allocation rules. Greater exposure to stocks leads to a higher average retirement account balance. For a risk-neutral retirement saver facing the historical return distribution, and choosing a fraction between zero and 100 percent of his or her portfolio to allocate to stocks, this suggests that allocating the entire portfolio to stocks is optimal. As the risk aversion of a retirement saver increases, the optimal share of the retirement portfolio that is held in stocks declines.

Over the past three decades, PRAs, such as those in 401(k) plans and similar programs, have become the predominant form of retirement saving in the private sector. The conversion from defined benefit to DC personal account plans in the private sector has led to the introduction of financial products intended to reduce market risk. Some plan sponsors have begun to offer participants investment options that permit them to avoid asset allocation decisions. One such innovation in the financial services marketplace is the "life-cycle fund" that automatically varies the share of the saver's portfolio that is held in stocks and in bonds as a function of the saver's age or years until retirement. These funds have been one of the most rapidly growing financial products of the last decade. They offer investors the opportunity to exploit time varying investment rules, typically reducing equity exposure as retirement approaches, without the need to make active investment management choices. In this chapter, we consider the effect of such life-cycle investment strategies on the distribution of retirement wealth.

Our previous research on life-cycle asset allocation patterns, PRVW (2005), considered how life-cycle allocation affects the distribution of retirement assets and the expected utility of reaching retirement with a given asset stock. We tried to capture the potential utility of an investment strategy with a high mean retirement balance but a small probability of a very poor outcome. We recognized that wealth held outside the saver's DC plan can have an important effect on utility associated with retirement assets at retirement. We used Social Security earnings histories, rather than simple stochastic processes, to model household contribution flows to DC plans. Our results capture the wide degree of heterogeneity in household earnings experiences.

This chapter builds on our earlier methodology in several ways. First, we model the asset allocation trajectories implied by the life-cycle funds. Second, we model the returns to retirement investing using realistic expense ratios and consider the impact of expense ratios on the accumulation of retirement wealth. Third, we calculate expected utilities over a range of fixed-allocation and simple life-cycle strategies to derive the optimal strategy within a given class of strategies. We then compare the returns from typical life-cycle fund strategies with those from strategies that yield the best certainty equivalent utility. Many of the proposals for PRAs that have been discussed in policy debates in recent years would allow individuals to channel a small proportion of their Social Security taxes to a PRA. Our analysis, however, considers a setting in which a substantial fraction of salary is devoted to the PRA. We view such a system as a potential replacement for the current Social Security system. By denying participants the safety of a Social Security defined benefit "floor" under their retirement wealth, we may overestimate the riskiness of PRA investments.

We find that 100 percent stock portfolios tend to dominate when households have low risk aversion, when expected equity returns are equal to the historical average, or when households have significant amounts of non-PRA wealth. More conservative strategies yield the greatest utility for households with higher risk aversion, when expected equity returns are lower, or when households have low non-PRA wealth. The typical life-cycle investment product is valuable as a more conservative strategy, but its value is reduced by the generally high expense ratios that investors will pay. The largest expense ratios arise when the funds are invested in high-expense, actively managed equity funds, although sometimes there are surcharges for rebalancing between low-cost funds. Investors who would prefer more conservative strategies can often increase their certainty equivalent wealth through an optimally chosen fixed-proportions portfolio. If investors are incapable of rebalancing on their own, life-cycle products may add value, but whether they add value net of their expense ratios depends on the household's risk aversion and amount of non-PRA wealth.

The chapter is divided into five sections. The first section summarizes theoretical research on the optimal pattern of age-related asset allocation. It then describes the life-cycle funds that have become increasingly popular in the retirement saving market. Section 8.2 describes the algorithm that we use to simulate the distribution of retirement plan assets under different asset allocation rules during the accumulation period. This discussion draws heavily on PRVW (2005). Section 8.3 describes our strategy for calibrating the simulation model, for selecting the sample of households for analysis, and for assigning distributions of returns to each of the assets in our study. The fourth section presents the various life-cycle asset allocation rules that we consider, including some that involve age-independent asset allocation rules. It then reports our central findings about the distribution of retirement account balances under these different rules as well as the expected lifetime utility at retirement under various rules. There is a brief conclusion.

8.1   Optimal Age-Dependent Asset Allocation Rules and the Rise of Life-Cycle Funds

Financial economists have a long tradition of studying how a rational, risk-averse, long-lived consumer would choose to allocate wealth between risky and riskless assets at different ages. Samuelson (1969), in one of the first formal analyses, challenged the conventional wisdom that an investor with a long horizon should invest a larger fraction of wealth in risky assets because of the possibility to average returns over a long period. This result is related to the earlier, more general observation by Samuelson (1963) that taking repeated identical uncorrelated risks augments the risk of the final outcome, rather than reducing it. In the context of the life-cycle portfolio selection problem, when returns on the risky asset are serially uncorrelated and there is no labor income, a rational investor should hold the same fraction of wealth in risky assets at all ages. This analytical result runs counter to the suggestion of many financial advisors, who suggest that investors reduce their equity exposure as they approach retirement. Merton (1969) derives similar results in the context of a lifetime dynamic optimization framework.

Perhaps in part because this result is inconsistent with much financial practice, subsequent research has tried to uncover reasons why an investor might choose to reduce equity exposure at older ages. Bodie, Merton, and Samuelson (1992) argue that younger investors have greater flexibility in their subsequent labor supply decisions and that they should consequently be more tolerant of risk. They suggest that younger investors may rationally choose to hold a higher fraction of their portfolio in stock than older investors. Gollier (2001) and Gollier and Zeckhauser (2002) derive the conditions under which the option to rebalance a portfolio in the future affects portfolio choice. Their results suggest that under specific assumptions about the structure of utility functions, the optimal portfolio share devoted to equity will decline with age. Campbell et al. (2001) and Campbell and Viceira (2002) develop numerical solutions to dynamic models that can be used to study optimal portfolio structure over the life cycle if shocks to labor income follow specific stochastic processes and investors have power utility. Cocco, Gomes, and Maenhout (2005) solve such a model in the presence of nontradable labor income and borrowing constraints. They find that a life-cycle investment strategy that reduces the household's equity exposure as it ages may be optimal depending on the shape of the labor income profile. An important parameter is the correlation of shocks to the labor income process with investment shocks. Jagganathan and Kocherlakota (1996) demonstrate that the higher this correlation, the less the optimal asset allocation shifts away from equities as the individual ages.

The empirical evidence on age-specific patterns in household asset allocation suggests at best weak reductions in equity exposure as households age. Gomes and Michaelides (2005) survey recent research on the correspondence between theoretical models of life-cycle asset allocation and empirical evidence on actual investment patterns. Ameriks and Zeldes (2004) and Poterba and Samwick (2001) present empirical evidence on how portfolio shares for stocks, bonds, and other assets vary over the life cycle. The general conclusion is that equity shares decline very little at older ages, although Ameriks and Zeldes (2004) find some evidence that some households cash out their equity holdings when they reach retirement or annuitize their accumulated holdings in DC accounts.

To cater to the perceived desire of investors to reduce their equity exposure as they age, and to help investors overcome the problems of inertia in retirement asset allocation that are documented by Samuelson and Zeckhauser (1988), several financial institutions have created life-cycle funds. These funds are usually designed for an investor with a target retirement date. Life-cycle funds were available from Fidelity Investments as early as 1988, and there were at least 250 target-year life-cycle funds in the mutual fund marketplace in 2005. Several major mutual fund families now offer a sequence of different funds targeted to investors with different retirement dates. In some cases, the life-cycle fund is a "fund of funds" that invests in a mix of other mutual funds, while in other cases the fund manager holds a specific pool of assets and alters the asset mix as the fund ages.

Figure 8.1 shows the rapid growth in life-cycle fund assets during the last eleven years. The figure indicates that life-cycle funds held $5.5 billion in March 2000 and that their assets had grown to $47.1 billion by 2005. Many of these funds are offered in 401(k) plans. Marquez (2005) reports that Hewitt Associates estimates that 38 percent of all 401(k) plans offer life-cycle funds. At a time when Clements (2005) reports that the proliferation of investment options 401(k) plans has come under fire, life-cycle funds offer a way to combine both stock and fixed income options into a single fund and to offer investors a time varying asset allocation mix. Life-cycle funds are sometimes suggested as a natural choice for the default investment option in automatic enrollment 401(k) programs.

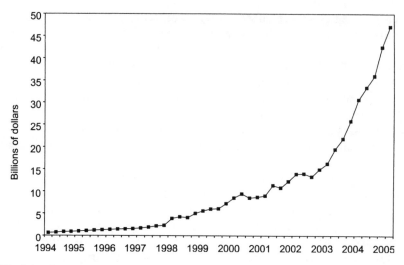

Fig. 8.1   Aggregate net assets of target-year life-cycle funds, March 1994–March 2005

Notes: This figure shows quarterly net assets of all mutual funds categorized by Morningstar as retirement or life-cycle funds that also have a target-year rebalancing feature. As of March 2005, the $47.1 billion represents assets in the following families: Barclays Global Investors LifePath, Fidelity Freedom Funds, Fidelity Advisor Freedom, Intrust Bank NestEgg, Mass-Mutual Select Destination Retire, Principal Investors Lifetime, Putnam Retirement Ready, Scudder Target, State Farm Lifepath, TIAA-CREF Institutional Lifecycle, T. Rowe Price Retirement, Vanguard Target Retirement, Vantagepoint Milestone, and Wells Fargo Outlook. Net assets for life-cycle funds were assembled from fund reports and data provided by Morningstar.

The life-cycle funds offered at different fund families follow different age-phased asset allocation rules. Table 8.1 reports summary information on the life-cycle funds offered at leading mutual fund companies, which we define as the set of mutual fund companies tracked by Morningstar. The table shows the average mix of stocks and bonds currently held by funds targeting different retirement years. Many fund prospectuses indicate the mix of various asset categories that will be held for an investor at specific ages. We have interpolated between ages, when necessary, to estimate the asset mix at a standardized set of ages.

The table also shows the net asset holdings and weighted average expense ratios of funds with different retirement years. The expenses paid by investors in these funds, which typically range between 60 and 80 basis points per year, are substantially larger than would be paid if an investor selected index mutual funds from a company offering no-load index funds with low expense ratios and then rebalanced among them over time. For example, equity index funds, government bond index funds, and money market mutual funds can be obtained from Vanguard with no load fees and expense ratios of 10 to 20 basis points. However, if investors find it difficult

Table 8.1   **Target-year life-cycle mutual fund characteristics (March 2005)**

Retirement year	Years to retirement	Net assets ($ billion)	Weighted average expense ratio (%)	No. of fund families	No. of funds	2005Q1 weighted average asset allocation (%)		
						Stocks	Bonds	Cash
2005	0	4.1	0.6	10	40	30.0	42.0	28.0
2010	5	11.2	0.8	13	45	49.4	35.4	15.3
2015	10	2.9	0.6	8	22	58.2	35.7	6.1
2020	15	14.5	0.8	13	45	69.7	24.6	5.7
2025	20	1.9	0.6	8	22	79.2	17.2	3.6
2030	25	8.3	0.8	12	39	81.7	13.8	4.5
2035	30	0.6	0.8	6	15	85.2	10.4	4.4
2040	35	3.3	0.8	11	38	88.0	8.4	3.5

Notes: Funds used in this analysis consist of all mutual funds categorized by Morningstar as retirement or life-cycle funds that also have a target-year rebalancing feature. Net assets for these funds as of March 31, 2005 were collected from fund reports and from Morningstar.com. The number of funds differs from the number of fund families for a given retirement year because funds have multiple classes of shares, and "number of funds" counts each share class as a separate fund. The weighted average expense ratio is the average expense ratio including subfund expenses weighted by fund net asset value. Asset allocations are also averaged with fund net asset value weighting. One fund family also offers funds with retirement years 2011, 2012, 2013, 2014, 2045, and 2050. The information on these funds is not used in constructing this table.

to conduct such rebalancing on their own, or for other reasons neglect planned rebalancing, they might be willing to pay the additional expenses associated with target-year life-cycle funds in which the rebalancing happens automatically.

The high expense ratios for life-cycle funds are sometimes due to expenses that the fund charges that are greater than the expenses charged by the individual funds held by the life-cycle fund. In other cases, the expenses are high because the life-cycle fund is not investing in the lowest-cost mutual fund products but rather in more expensive actively managed mutual funds.

8.2   Modeling Retirement Wealth Accumulation in Self-Directed Retirement Plans

To analyze the distribution of PRA wealth at retirement that is induced by different asset allocation strategies, we need to model the path of plan contributions over an individual's working life and to combine these contributions with information on the potential returns to holding PRA assets in different investment vehicles. We do this following the approach in PRVW (2005). Rather than using information on household earnings patterns to estimate a stochastic model for the earnings process and then using that model to simulate earnings paths for our analysis, we draw actual lifetime earnings histories from a large sample of households and carry out simulations by combining the contribution paths for various earnings histories with simulated patterns of asset returns. We focus our analysis on married couples because they are financially more homogeneous than nonmarried individuals, some of whom never married and others of whom have lost a spouse. About 70 percent of the individuals reaching retirement age are in married couples.

We assume that 9 percent of the household's earnings are contributed to a DC plan each year. We further assume that the couple begins to participate in a PRA plan when the husband is twenty-eight and that they contribute in every year in which the household has Social Security earnings until the husband is sixty-three. Households do not make contributions when they are unemployed or when both members of the couple are retired or otherwise not in the labor force. We assume that both members of the household retire when the husband is sixty-three if they have not done so already and that they do not contribute to a retirement plan after that age.

To formalize our calculations, we denote a household by subscript i, and denote their PRA contribution at age a by $C_i(a) = .09 \cdot E_i(a)$ for $E_i(a)$ the household's total earnings at age a. We assume that under this PRA system there is a fixed contribution rate of 9 percent. We express this contribution in year 2000 dollars. We do not restrict $E_i(a)$ to be covered earnings, but rather assume that contributions are made for 9 percent of all wage and salary earnings.

To find the PRA balance for the couple at age sixty-three ($a = 63$), we need to cumulate contributions over the course of the working life, with appropriate allowance for asset returns. Let $R_i(a)$ denote the net-of-expense return earned on PRA assets that were held at the beginning of the year when the husband in couple i attained age a. The value of the couple's PRA assets when the husband is sixty-three is then given by:

$$(1) \qquad W_i(63) = \sum_{t=0}^{35}\left\{\prod_{j=0}^{t}[1 + R_i(63 - j)]\right\}C_i(63 - t).$$

$R_i(a)$ depends on the year-specific returns on stocks and bonds, on the mix of stocks and bonds that the household owned when the husband was a years old, and on the expense ratio. If the couple holds an all-stock portfolio, then $R_i(a) = (1 - \theta_{stock}) \cdot R_{stock}(a)$, where θ_{stock} is the assumed annual expense ratio on an equity fund. If the couple holds all bonds, $R_i(a) = (1 - \theta_{bond}) \cdot R_{bond}(a)$. A mixture of the two is of course possible. If the couple invests in a life-cycle mutual fund, the asset return at age a will be $(1 - \theta_{bond}) \cdot R_{lifecycle}(a)$, which corresponds to the return on the mix of bonds and stocks that will be held by the life-cycle fund on behalf of an investor of age a.

We use simulation methods to estimate the distribution of $W_i(63)$, averaged over the households in our sample, for various asset allocation strategies. By comparing the distributions of retirement plan assets under each of these strategies, we can learn how these strategies affect retirement resources. The distribution of outcomes is of substantial interest, but it does not capture the household's valuation of different levels of retirement resources. It can provide information on the potential frequency of low wealth outcomes, but it does not provide a metric for comparing these outcomes with more favorable retirement wealth values.

To allow for differential valuation of wealth in different states of nature, we evaluate the wealth in the PRA account using a utility-of-terminal wealth approach. We assume that all households have identical preferences over wealth at retirement. We drop the household subscript i and assume that the utility of wealth is described by a constant relative risk aversion (CRRA) utility function

$$(2) \qquad U(W) = \frac{W^{1-\alpha}}{1-\alpha},$$

where α is the household's coefficient of relative risk aversion. The utility of household wealth at retirement is likely to depend on both PRA and non-PRA wealth, so we modify equation (2) to recognize this wealth:

$$(3) \qquad U(W_{\text{PRA}}, W_{\text{non-PRA}}) = \frac{(W_{\text{PRA}} + W_{\text{non-PRA}})^{1-\alpha}}{1-\alpha}$$

Because the effect of a change in PRA wealth on household utility is sensitive to the household's other wealth holdings, we consider other assets on the household balance sheet in our empirical analysis.

For a given household, each return history, denoted by h, generates a level of PRA wealth at age sixty-three, $W_{\text{PRA},h}$, and a corresponding utility level, U_h, where

$$(4) \qquad U_h = \frac{(W_{\text{PRA},h} + W_{\text{non-PRA}})^{1-\alpha}}{1-\alpha}.$$

We evaluate the expected utility of each portfolio strategy by the probability-weighted average of the utility outcomes associated with that strategy. These utility levels can be compared directly for a given degree of risk tolerance, and they can be translated into certainty equivalent wealth levels (Z) by asking what certain wealth level would provide utility equal to the expected utility of the retirement wealth distribution. The certainty equivalent of an all-equity portfolio, for example, denoted by the subscript SP500, is given by:

$$(5) \qquad Z_{\text{SP500}} = [EU_{\text{SP500}}(1-\alpha)]^{1/(1-\alpha)} - W_{\text{non-PRA}}.$$

When a household has non-PRA wealth, the certainty equivalent of the PRA wealth is the amount of PRA wealth that is needed, *in addition to the non-PRA wealth,* to achieve a given utility level. We treat non-PRA wealth as nonstochastic throughout our analysis.

Our approach to computing DC plan balances at retirement resembles one of the strategies developed in Samwick and Skinner (2004). Part of their empirical analysis considers the pension benefits that a sample of workers would earn under several stylized defined benefit and DC plans. It considers the benefits experience of a sample of actual workers, with actual earnings histories, under each plan. It does not, however, explore the sensitivity of retirement wealth to alternative investment strategies.

Our approach exploits the rich cross-sectional variation in household earnings trajectories. We use a large sample of Health and Retirement Survey (HRS) households to compute contribution paths for a PRA plan, and we then randomly assign return histories to these contribution paths. The result is a distribution of retirement balances for each household in the HRS sample. We combine the wealth outcomes by aggregating households into three broad educational categories to report our findings, but each entry in the following table represents an average over the outcomes for many individuals. Our strategy can be thought of as drawing an HRS household at age twenty-seven and giving it two independent draws: first a wage trajectory, which could be the actual wage trajectory for any of our sample households who have a particular education level, and then a lifetime vector of asset returns, which could be any of 200,000 draws. The return trajectory will determine the household's retirement wealth, conditional on the contribution flow.

8.3   Calibration of PRA Wealth Simulations

We select a subsample of married HRS households for analysis, construct their earnings trajectories, and measure their non-PRA wealth at retirement. We then simulate retirement wealth based on these households' Social Security earnings records. Our sample of households is larger than that in PRVW (2005). We include all HRS couples headed by men aged sixty-three to seventy-two in 2000 for which Social Security earnings histories are available. Table 8.2 shows the effects of conditioning the sample on married couples in this age range. There are 3,833 HRS households with Social Security earnings histories. The restriction to couples eliminates approximately 44 percent of that sample, and the age restriction removes an additional 19 percent, leaving a sample of 1,400 households. The age restriction removes couples with heads between the ages of fifty-nine and sixty-two. Including this group would involve forecasting earnings beyond the time period of the data.

The Social Security earnings records contain truncated information on actual earnings. No earnings above the taxable maximum income level are reported; the data are top-coded. The real value of the taxable maximum earnings level for Social Security has varied over time, and so has the dis-

Table 8.2   **Sample composition, Health and Retirement Survey (HRS) households**

	All households, head 59–72	Households 59–72, with Social Security earnings	Couples 59–72, with Social Security earnings	Couples 63–72, with Social Security earnings
Household head education less than high school				
Survey households	1,579	1,086	540	374
Population counterpart	3,769.3	2,653.4	1,324.2	938.3
Household head high school education and/or some college				
Survey households	2,793	1,954	1,076	689
Population counterpart	7,669.2	5,453.6	3,013.2	1,949.3
Household head at least college degree				
Survey households	1,132	793	526	337
Population counterpart	3,411.6	2,390.6	1,611.8	1,013.6
Total				
Survey households	5,504	3,833	2,142	1,400
Population counterpart	14,850.1	10,497.6	5,949.2	3,901.1

Source: Authors' tabulations based on the 2000 wave of the HRS and the Social Security earnings histories available for a subsample of HRS respondents. Population counterparts are calculated using the household weights provided in the HRS.

persion of earnings, so the fraction of earnings that are not captured on Social Security records varies from year to year. In some years in the early 1970s, particularly for the group with the highest education level, the top-code affects more than half of the sample. Because the payroll tax cap was not indexed for inflation during much of this period, and it changes as a result of legislative action, there are also substantial changes in this threshold during brief periods. The magnitude of the top-coding problem may, therefore, vary from year to year. We consider replacing the current Social Security system with a PRA system that allows workers to contribute a fixed fraction of their earnings without limit. To describe contributions by high-income workers, we, therefore, need to estimate earnings above the taxable maximum for workers whose data records are top-coded.

We estimate a cross-sectional tobit equation for each pre-1980 year using the reported Social Security earnings for men in our sample. In the years when a substantial fraction of earnings records are top-coded, we find that the tobit coefficients are sensitive to the set of observations we include in the estimation subsample. In particular, including men with low earnings can lead to "corrected" earnings for those at the payroll tax cap that are substantially higher than the earnings cap, regardless of other individual attributes. The tobit results are more robust when we delete individuals with very low earnings levels from our sample. We, therefore, ex-

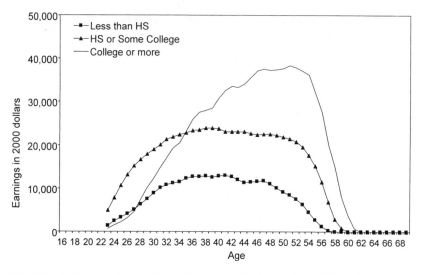

Fig. 8.2   25th percentile earnings, after top-coding correction, HRS husbands

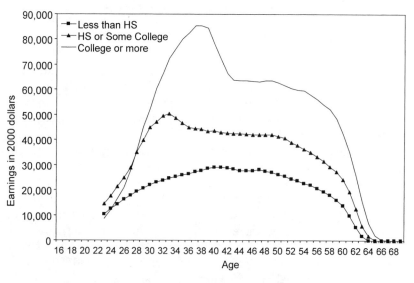

Fig. 8.3   50th percentile earnings, after top-coding correction, HRS husbands

clude anyone earning less than $2,500 (in $2000) when we estimate the to-bit equations.

Each of figures 8.2 through 8.4 shows a different part of the distribution of age-earnings profile for three different education subgroups: less than high school, high school and some college, and college and beyond, after we correct for top-coding. The median earnings path, displayed in figure

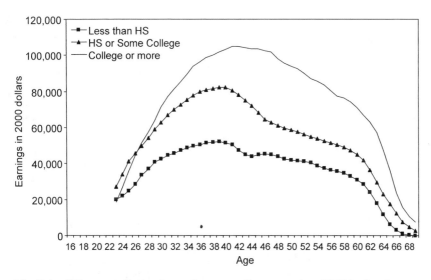

Fig. 8.4   75th percentile earnings, after top-coding correction, HRS husbands

8.3, shows an unusual "bump" in early middle age. This appears to be due to the top-coding adjustment for years in which an especially high fraction of workers were affected by the taxable earnings cap. However, this unusual pattern does not appear at the 25th or 75th percentiles, nor does it occur when we plot the means of the adjusted earnings histories. We suspect that this is because there is less variation over time in the fraction of workers affected by the tax cap at these percentiles than at the median. These figures show only the husband's earnings trajectory. We perform the same procedure for their spouses and use the imputed value of total household earnings in our simulations.

Our approach to addressing top-coding is only one of several possible approaches. Scholz, Seshadri, and Khitatrakun (2006) develop an alternative algorithm that exploits the intertemporal dependence of earnings as well as distributional assumptions to adjust top-coded earnings records. They estimate cross-sectional wage equations using Internal Revenue Service (IRS) W-2 wage reports as well as SSA earnings records, and then they back-cast the residual from the years with W-2 data to adjust the SSA earnings data for earlier years. Because HRS respondents fall in a relatively narrow age range, however, this procedure essentially uses the serial correlation structure from earnings in a later period of life, the period covered by W-2 earnings, to describe the serial correlation structure earlier in life. It is difficult to evaluate the accuracy of this assumption.

We consider our sample households as reaching retirement age when the husband is sixty-three years old. When we turn to the HRS data, however, we assume that both sixty-three- and sixty-four-year-olds in a given survey wave represent the "retiring" cohort because the HRS is carried out ever other year. We need to determine non-PRA wealth at retirement age, and the way we do this depends on the household's age. First, we consider wealth measurement for the nearly three-quarters of the sample with a household head who was either sixty-three or sixty-four in 1996, 1998, or 2000. For these households, a breakdown of nonpension wealth is available on a consistent basis in HRS waves 3, 4, and 5. We scale all household non-PRA asset values to the 2000 base year so that for each household we have an estimate of what their non-PRA wealth would have been had they turned age sixty-three in either 1999 or 2000. We implement this scaling by replacing the nominal returns on asset holdings for the two years prior to the year in which the head of household was either sixty-three or sixty-four, that is, 1994 to 1995 for the 1996 households and 1996 to 1997 for the 1998 households, with nominal returns on assets in 1998 and 1999. We calibrate our simulations using a measure of background wealth that includes only financial wealth, which is assumed to grow at a composite rate based on the national average allocation of tax-deferred financial assets between stocks, bonds, and deposits, as reported in the 2001 Survey of Consumer Finances.

Second, we consider wealth measurement for the one-quarter of the sample that reached the age sixty-four prior to 1996. We do not use the earlier waves of the HRS because the wealth questionnaire for waves 1 and 2 was different from that for later waves. Wealth values for these HRS households are imputed for each asset class based on the median measured asset growth for households between the ages of sixty-three and sixty-five, or sixty-three and sixty-seven, in the same educational category in later waves of the HRS.

Table 8.3 presents summary statistics on our estimates of household balance sheets normalized to age sixty-three to sixty-four. We report seven categories of wealth: the present discounted value (PDV) of Social Security payments, the PDV of defined benefit pensions, the PDV of other annuities, the current value of retirement accounts, the value of all other financial wealth net of debt, housing equity net of debt, and all other wealth. The top panel in table 8.3 shows medians, while the bottom panel shows means. The restriction to couples clearly raises the mean and median of the distribution. The restriction to households in the age range sixty-three to seventy-two, with full earnings histories to age sixty-three, lowers the wealth distribution somewhat by removing a group that has not yet begun to spend down their assets. The final sample of couples aged sixty-three to seventy-two has median wealth of $536,800 and mean wealth of $783,400. The median high school-educated household has 44 percent more total wealth than the median household with less than a high school education, and the median college-educated household has 61 percent more total wealth than the median high school-educated household. The differences in means are even more dramatic. In this table, to estimate defined benefit

Table 8.3   Summary statistics on household balance sheet at age 63/64, Health and Retirement Survey (HRS) households

	All HRS households				HRS couples with husband aged 63–72			
	Household head aged 59–72	Household head aged 59–72 and with SS earnings	Couples aged 59–72, with SS earnings	Couples aged 63–72, with SS earnings	All	Less than high school degree	High school and/or some college	College and/or postgraduate
Medians								
Social Security	176.1	167.2	258.0	262.5	262.5	247.4	260.9	285.5
DB pension	0.0	0.0	0.0	0.0	0.0	0.0	0.0	0.0
Other annuity	0.0	0.0	0.0	0.0	0.0	0.0	0.0	0.0
Retirement accounts	15.0	15.0	35.7	22.7	22.7	0.0	20.4	81.7
IRA	8.1	8.4	22.0	12.0	12.0	0.0	11.5	49.6
DC pension	0.0	0.0	0.0	0.0	0.0	0.0	0.0	0.0
Other financial wealth	34.6	35.2	69.6	58.0	58.0	6.4	55.7	170.5
Housing equity	76.2	72.0	90.9	92.6	92.6	60.2	90.9	125.0
Other wealth	11.5	11.0	17.7	18.1	18.1	11.0	20.0	21.9
SS + DB + Annuity	204.6	203.5	280.3	276.9	276.9	250.5	277.2	301.8
Total excluding retirement accounts	399.9	397.3	526.7	489.4	489.4	360.3	484.0	749.7
Total	439.1	435.6	587.5	536.8	536.8	370.1	531.1	856.3
Means								
Social Security	179.9	181.9	235.9	246.5	246.5	229.1	243.6	268.1
DB pension	62.4	63.1	85.2	47.7	47.7	33.9	44.4	66.6
Other annuity	4.9	5.0	5.2	5.0	5.0	0.8	7.3	4.6
Retirement accounts	107.8	113.2	154.7	136.4	136.4	36.8	83.1	330.9
IRA	73.2	72.8	95.2	77.3	77.3	29.4	67.4	140.6
DC pension	32.4	37.0	55.7	59.0	59.0	7.4	15.7	190.3

(*continued*)

Table 8.3 (continued)

	All HRS households				HRS couples with husband aged 63–72			
	Household head aged 59–72	Household head aged 59–72 and with SS earnings	Couples aged 59–72, with SS earnings	Couples aged 63–72, with SS earnings	All	Less than high school degree	High school and/or some college	College and/or postgraduate
Other financial wealth	177.4	179.3	223.1	199.7	199.7	69.6	138.7	437.3
Housing equity	113.2	103.1	125.3	115.3	115.3	78.7	106.6	165.7
Other wealth	26.2	26.5	32.8	33.0	33.0	19.2	30.1	51.3
SS + DB + Annuity	247.2	250.0	326.3	299.2	299.2	263.8	295.3	339.3
Total excluding retirement accounts	587.3	583.8	727.3	647.0	647.0	431.3	570.6	993.6
Total	694.2	695.8	881.5	783.4	783.4	468.1	653.7	1324.5
No. of households	5,504	3,833	2,142	1,400	1,400	374	689	337
Weighted size ('000s)	14,850	10,498	5,949	3,901	3,901	938	1,949	1,013

Source: Authors' tabulations based on the 2000 HRS. All entries are normalized to calendar year 2000. To estimate defined benefit (DB) and defined contribution (DC) pension wealth for HRS households, we use the pension wealth imputations from the HRS (March 2005 version). Social Security wealth is calculated as in PRVW (2005).

Notes: Other financial wealth includes stocks, equity mutual funds, bonds, fixed income mutual funds, checking and saving accounts, money market mutual funds, and certificates of deposit held outside of retirement accounts.
IRA = individual retirement account.

and DC pension wealth for HRS households, we use HRS pension wealth imputations, version 1.0, March 2005. For Social Security wealth (SSW), we follow the procedure from PRVW (2005), using cohort mortality tables and the Social Security Administration's intermediate-cost scenario discount rates to calculate the PDV of the current or projected Social Security benefits when the husband is aged sixty-three to sixty-four. We normalize the value of the wife's Social Security to be the value when the husband is aged sixty-three to sixty-four, assuming that Social Security payments start for the wife at age sixty-two if they have not started already. The present value of Social Security is determined as a joint survivor annuity.

When we calibrate our simulations with households' non-PRA wealth, we focus on the total of annuity wealth and other (i.e., nonretirement) financial wealth. We exclude housing wealth because it is not clear whether it should be viewed as a source of retirement wealth for elderly households. Venti and Wise (2004) report that elderly households rarely draw down their housing wealth, which argues against including this wealth as a source of retirement income. We also exclude defined benefit pension wealth, 401(k) wealth, and Social Security wealth as we are assuming that the PRA system we are simulating would replace those systems entirely. We view our simulations as delivering the value of DC assets that households accumulate by their retirement date. If we attributed existing 401(k) assets to these households, the amount of DC wealth that households would accumulate would be much greater than the amount that we report in our simulations.

By using the observed values of these wealth components from the HRS and treating them as nonrandom when we evaluate the expected utility of PRA retirement balances, we are implicitly assuming that changes in PRA wealth values do not affect other components of wealth. We hope to extend our analysis to allow for correlation between the returns on assets in PRA accounts and the returns on other household assets.

Table 8.4 disaggregates the household balance sheet aggregates by education level. The table underscores the substantial differences across households both within education categories and across these categories. The difference at most percentiles between the total wealth of a household that did not complete high school and one that completed college is a factor of at least two. The difference in annuities and other wealth, which we use as our primary measure of non-PRA background wealth, is substantially larger because this aggregate does not consider wealth from the current progressive Social Security system. At the 60th percentile, a household with less than high school education has $6,400 in annuity and other financial wealth, whereas a household with a college or postgraduate education has $183,000.

We assume that the three primary assets that households may hold in a PRA are corporate stock, nominal long-term government bonds, and

Table 8.4   Distribution of household balance sheet for Household and Retirement Survey (HRS) couples with husbands aged 63–72, normalized to age 63/64 in year 2000

Net worth concept	All education levels	Less than high school degree	High school and/or some college	College and/or postgraduate
20th percentile				
Total	302.0	220.9	315.1	448.1
Total excluding retirement accounts	292.2	216.8	312.2	387.8
SS + DB + Annuity	189.8	169.4	198.8	204.6
Annuities and other financial wealth	1.0	0.0	1.7	30.0
40th percentile				
Total	450.1	323.2	450.4	707.9
Total excluding retirement accounts	419.1	314.1	423.6	607.8
SS + DB + Annuity	257.0	230.7	257.3	281.2
Annuities and other financial wealth	29.7	2.0	30.0	113.0
60th percentile				
Total	637.4	441.3	622.1	1051.1
Total excluding retirement accounts	575.3	413.6	549.8	878.6
SS + DB + Annuity	295.6	265.7	296.1	338.0
Annuities and other financial wealth	62.3	6.4	58.7	183.0
80th percentile				
Total	994.5	644.1	866.4	1598.6
Total excluding retirement accounts	830.4	575.4	745.2	1229.6
SS + DB + Annuity	362.8	313.7	354.3	449.3
Annuities and other financial wealth	273.5	121.0	235.5	600.0

Source: Authors' tabulations from the 2000 HRS. Defined benefit (DB) pension wealth was calculated from the pension wealth imputations from the HRS (March 2005 version). Social Security and annuity wealth were computed as in PRVW (2005).

inflation-indexed long-term bonds (Treasury inflation-protected securities [TIPS]). Calibrating the returns on these investment alternatives is a critical step in our simulation algorithm. We assume that PRA investors hold corporate stocks through portfolios of large capitalization U.S. stocks. We do not address the possibility of poorly diversified portfolios, for example, with concentrated holdings in a single stock, as described in Munnell and Sunden (2004) and Poterba (2003). We assume that the return distribution for each asset class is given by Ibbotson Associates' (2003) empirical distribution of returns during the 1926 to 2003 period. The average annual arithmetic real return on large capitalization U.S. equities during this period was 9.2 percent, and the annual standard deviation of the real return was 20.5 percent. Long-term U.S. government bonds had a real return of 2.8 percent, on average, over this period, and a standard deviation of 10.5 percent.

We assume that TIPS offer a certain real return of 2 percent per year, approximately the current TIPS yield. Index bonds deliver a net-of-inflation certain return only if the investor holds the bonds to maturity, and selling the bonds before maturity exposes the investors to asset price risk. We nevertheless treat these bonds as riskless long-term investment vehicles. In our simulations, when we draw returns from the stock and bond return distributions for a given iteration, we draw returns for the same year from both distributions. This preserves the historical contemporary correlation structure between stock and bond returns in our simulations.

Several analysts suggest that the last several decades, or even the last century, correspond to a particularly favorable time period for equities and argue that these returns should not be extrapolated to the future. The academic literature on the equity premium puzzle, summarized, for example, in Mehra and Prescott (2002), raises the possibility that ex post returns exceeded ex ante expected returns over this period. To allow for such a possibility, we perform some simulations in which the distribution of returns from which we draw is the actual distribution except that equity returns are reduced by 300 basis points in each year. Comparing these simulations with those in our baseline indicates the sensitivity of our findings to the future pattern of equity returns.

Each iteration of our simulation algorithm involves drawing a sequence of thirty-five real stock and bond returns from the empirical return distribution. The draws are done with replacement, and we assume that there is no serial correlation in returns. We then use this return sequence to calculate the real value of each household's retirement account balance at age sixty-three under the different asset allocation strategies. For each of the 1,400 households in our sample, we simulate the PRA balance at age sixty-three 5,000 times. We then summarize these 5,000 outcomes either with a distribution of wealth values at retirement or by calculating the expected utility associated with this distribution of outcomes. We found in PRVW (2005) that roughly this number of iterations was needed to obtain robust findings, particularly at lower percentiles of the retirement wealth distribution.

8.4 Discussion of Results

We simulate eight primary asset allocation strategies for the household's PRA account. The first three involve investing in only one asset: (1) a portfolio that is fully invested in TIPS; (2) a portfolio that is fully invested in long-term government bonds, and (3) a portfolio that is fully invested in corporate stock. The next two portfolios are "heuristic portfolios" that use simple rules for life-cycle asset allocation. Portfolio (4) holds (110—age of household head) percent of the portfolio in stock, with the remaining balance in TIPS. Portfolio (5) is similar to (4) except that nominal government bonds replace TIPS for the component of the portfolio that is not held in equity. Both of these portfolios are rebalanced at the end of each period. The next two are life-cycle portfolios consisting of stocks and TIPS, and stocks and government bonds, respectively. The equity weight for each of these funds is computed based on the average of the age-specific allocations in the life-cycle funds at Fidelity, Vanguard, T. Rowe Price, Teachers Insurance and Annuity Association-College Retirement Equities Fund (TIAA-CREF); Principal, Barclays, and Wells Fargo. The life-cycle funds from these fund families are weighted equally in this calculation, and the resulting equity allocation is similar to that in table 8.1. Portfolio (6) invests the life-cycle fund average in equities and the balance in TIPS, while fund (7) holds equities and nominal government bonds in the life-cycle mix.

The final primary investment strategy we consider, strategy (8), is the "No Lose" strategy that Feldstein (2005) proposes in his analysis of individual account Social Security reforms. At each age, we calculate the share of the household's PRA contribution that would have to be invested in TIPS to guarantee at least the contributed amount in nominal terms at retirement age. The required TIPS investment is $(1 + R_{TIPS})^{-(63-a)}$, where $63 - a$ is the number of years to retirement. This strategy is fundamentally different from the other life-cycle strategies because it does not involve portfolio rebalancing at each age. Instead, the equity share of the portfolio depends on the historical pattern of TIPS yields, which in turn determine the amount available for stock investment in past years, and on the historical returns on equity assets.

In addition to these eight strategies, we also consider optimized portfolio strategies that are each derived from running multiple simulations of a given form and then selecting the optimal investment strategies from among them for a given level of risk aversion, asset class, and asset return assumption. The first of these is an optimal fixed portfolio strategy, in which we examine the outcome of investing X percent in stocks and $1 - X$ percent in TIPS at 5 percent intervals. The second is an optimal "linear" life-cycle strategy, in which we consider strategies that begin at X percent at age twenty-eight and end at $1 - X$ percent at age sixty-three. This is, of course, a restricted class of life-cycle portfolios but serves as a useful point of comparison for the commercially available products. The optimization is performed separately for each level of risk aversion, asset class, and asset return assumption. We describe this in greater detail in the following.

We assume that the returns on PRA investments equal the pretax returns on the various asset classes we consider, less the expense charge for investment management. For most of the asset classes we consider, we use two assumptions: a baseline assumption and a high-expense assumption. Our baseline assumption for equity mutual funds is a 32 basis point expense ratio, the weighted mean expense ratio on S&P 500 index funds reported in Hortaçsu and Syverson (2004). Given that government bond funds tend to have similar expense ratios to stock index funds, we assume 32 basis points as the expense ratio for government bond funds. For TIPS, we use an expense ratio of 40 basis points, on the grounds that these funds may be 20 percent more expensive than typical stock or bond index funds. Our high-expense assumption is 100 basis points for stock and bond funds. Expense ratios this high are not uncommon.

For the cost of investing in life-cycle products, we consider three possibilities. The baseline assumption we make is that the life-cycle product carries an expense ratio of 40 basis points, with investors paying a relatively small cost (8 basis points) for the automatic rebalancing. Based on the expense ratios in table 8.1, however, this baseline assumption is probably too low relative to what individuals investing in this market actually pay. We, therefore, also run simulations with the asset-weighted average expense ratio from table 8.1 of 74 basis points and for a high-expense scenario of 120 basis points.

8.4.1 The Distribution of Retirement Wealth

Table 8.5 shows the distribution of PRA balances in thousands of year 2000 dollars averaged across the 1,400 households in our sample, for each of the first eight strategies and assuming the baseline expense ratios. In the left-most panel, the simulations use the historical distribution of returns. The panel on the right reduces equity returns by 300 basis points. Households are stratified by education group within each panel. The table reports the mean wealth at retirement for each strategy, as well as 4 points in the distribution of returns. Because our interest is the comparison of wealth outcomes across different strategies, most of our following discussion focuses on a single education group, households headed by someone with a high school degree but not a college degree. The relative ranking of different strategies is similar for other education groups.

The first row of table 8.5 provides a point of reference for all of the subsequent calculations. It shows the certain wealth at retirement associated with strategy (1), holding only TIPS. For those with a high school degree and/or some college, this leads to a retirement balance of $236,700. The next panels show the results from strategy (2), holding on nominal government bonds, and strategy (3), holding only corporate stocks. Both of these strategies, as well as all of the subsequent strategies that we consider, involve risk so we report information on the distribution of outcomes.

The second panel shows that for a household with a high school degree or some college, holding only government bonds leads to a higher average

Table 8.5 **Simulated distribution of 401(k) balances at retirement ($2000), baseline expense ratios**

Investment strategy/ percentile	Empirical stock returns			Empirical returns reduced 300 basis points		
	Less than high school degree	High school and/or some college	College and/or postgraduate	Less than high school degree	High school and/or some college	College and/or postgraduate
100% TIPS	167.4	236.7	325.5	167.4	236.7	325.5
100% government bonds						
1	53.8	76.4	110.0	53.8	76.4	110.0
10	113.6	160.5	224.5	113.6	160.5	224.5
50	182.3	258.0	352.9	182.3	258.0	352.9
90	307.6	435.6	582.9	307.6	435.6	582.9
Mean	200.1	283.2	385.0	200.1	283.2	385.0
100% stocks						
1	30.9	44.3	62.4	19.0	27.2	40.1
10	186.3	265.1	355.0	101.5	143.7	200.2
50	553.5	790.4	1016.5	285.4	404.7	539.8
90	1,699.7	2,446.7	3,039.1	845.0	1,205.7	1,546.7
Mean	813.1	1,169.3	1,470.4	410.5	585.5	761.7
(110 − age)% stocks, (age + 10)% TIPS						
1	80.0	113.6	156.9	63.0	89.4	125.3
10	183.4	259.9	352.1	142.8	202.2	277.6
50	289.5	410.3	548.4	224.6	317.8	430.3
90	454.7	645.0	851.6	351.7	498.0	665.4
Mean	307.7	436.2	581.3	238.5	337.7	455.7
(110 − age)% stocks, (age + 10)% bonds						
1	62.4	87.7	122.7	49.6	69.8	99.1
10	171.1	242.6	329.9	133.5	189.1	260.7
50	308.0	436.8	581.7	238.5	337.7	455.4
90	561.2	797.7	1,041.2	431.8	612.6	809.1
Mean	344.3	488.9	646.60	266.0	377.2	505.1
Empirical life cycle, stocks and TIPS						
1	70.7	101.0	142.5	53.6	76.4	110.5
10	184.2	261.3	353.8	131.4	185.9	258.2
50	329.8	469.8	615.6	227.7	322.8	434.3
90	611.0	876.3	1,114.7	409.9	584.0	761.7
Mean	372.4	532.2	690.0	254.7	362.0	481.7
Empirical life cycle, stocks and bonds						
1	58.6	82.6	116.1	44.4	62.7	90.4
10	174.4	247.7	335.2	124.3	176.0	244.4
50	342.3	487.9	638.7	236.1	334.8	449.8
90	697.6	1,000.8	1,270.2	467.6	666.7	867.2
Mean	401.8	574.5	742.5	274.1	389.7	516.8

Table 8.5   (continued)

Investment strategy/ percentile	Empirical stock returns			Empirical returns reduced 300 basis points		
	Less than high school degree	High school and/or some college	College and/or postgraduate	Less than high school degree	High school and/or some college	College and/or postgraduate
		Feldstein (2005) "No Lose" plan				
1	123.6	174.6	245.5	120.3	169.7	239.4
10	175.5	248.9	339.0	145.1	204.9	285.0
50	314.0	448.9	581.6	209.8	297.6	400.4
90	774.2	1,120.6	1,379.3	424.0	607.4	776.1
Mean	421.9	607.8	768.0	260.0	370.9	487.8

Source: Authors' tabulations of simulation results. See text for further details.
Note: TIPS = Treasury inflation-protected securities.

retirement wealth, $283,200, than holding TIPS. The average wealth at retirement is nearly 20 percent greater than the value with TIPS, but the median wealth of $265,100 is less than 10 percent above the TIPS outcome. Moreover, there are many outcomes with retirement wealth values below the TIPS case. The 10th percentile outcome is $160,500, and the 1st percentile is $76,400.

When the PRA is invested in corporate stock, the average retirement balance is much higher than that with either TIPS or nominal government bonds: $1,169,300. This value is roughly four times greater than the outcome with nominal government bonds. Because the mean return on stocks is so much higher than that on either nominal or inflation-indexed bonds, even the low outcomes are often above the mean outcomes with bonds. The 10th percentile retirement wealth value with the all-stocks portfolio is not far below average outcome with a nominal government bond portfolio. The 1st percentile outcome, however, $44,300, is below the correspondingly low outcomes for the nominal bonds strategy.

The next two portfolios, (4) and (5), are "heuristic" life-cycle investment strategies with a mix of stocks and TIPS, or stocks and long-term nominal government bonds. In both cases, the average value of retirement wealth falls between the value with an all-stock investment and that with an all-bond portfolio. When the nominal government bond share of the portfolio is (age + 10) percent, the average value of retirement wealth using historical equity returns is $488,900 for a household with a high school education. The proportional dispersion in the retirement wealth value is smaller than that for an all equity portfolio and greater than that for the bond portfolio. The difference between the 90th percentile and the 10th percentile retirement wealth value with an all-stock strategy is 1.87 times the mean value, and the corresponding measure for the all-bond portfolio is 0.97. With the nominal bond-stock heuristic life-cycle portfolio, the 90-10 spread is 1.14 times the mean outcome. The 1st percentile outcomes with the two heuristic life-cycle portfolios are $113,600 and $87,700, both larger than 1st percentile outcomes with either the all-stock or all-bond portfolios.

The next two portfolios, (6) and (7), are the life-cycle portfolios that correspond to the average of the portfolios from various mutual fund complexes. While the age-specific equity allocation is somewhat different from the foregoing heuristic portfolios, the distribution of PRA wealth at retirement is similar. In particular, the mean value of retirement wealth is $532,200 when we combine TIPS and stocks, and $574,500 when we combine nominal long-term government bonds and stocks. The difference is due to TIPS offering a lower real yield than the historical average real return on nominal bonds during our sample period. The 1st percentile outcome when we combine TIPS with stocks is lower than that of the heuristic strategy with TIPS and stocks. Similarly, the 1st percentile outcome of the bonds-stocks mutual fund product is lower than that of the heuristic strategy with TIPS and bonds. The empirical life-cycle products are therefore higher mean but also somewhat riskier than the heuristic strategies.

The eighth and last strategy in this table is the Feldstein (2005) No Lose plan. This strategy offers a mean return that is broadly similar to the mean returns on the life-cycle strategies. The mean retirement wealth for a high school educated household is $607,800, which is between the mean wealth values with a life-cycle fund that holds TIPS and one that holds nominal government bonds. The important difference among this strategy and the life-cycle strategies and the all-stocks and all-nominal bonds strategies is found in the lower tail of the wealth outcomes. Because the No Lose strategy holds TIPS, the 1st percentile wealth value is $174,600, greater than any of the strategies other than investing 100 percent in TIPS.

The assumption that the equity return is drawn from its historical distribution is important for the absolute level of retirement wealth under most of the strategies that we consider and also for the magnitude of the differences across strategies. The fourth, fifth, and sixth columns in table 8.5 present results assuming that equity returns are reduced by 300 basis points. The all-stock strategy is the one that is most affected by this change. The average wealth at retirement for this strategy falls from $1,169,300 to $585,500. The 10th percentile wealth value drops from $265,100 to $143,700 in this case, and the 1st percentile value drops to $44,300 from $27,200. This very low outcome emphasizes the risk associated with holding stocks: a very small chance of a very poor outcome. The average retirement wealth values for the various heuristic and empirical life-cycle funds decline when we reduce the value of the mean equity return. The mean wealth value for the No Lose strategy falls relative to the life-cycle strategies because the No Lose strategy has relatively more equity exposure than any of the life-cycle plans.

The distribution of retirement balances shown in table 8.5 is conceptually similar to the distribution reported in Shiller's (2005) analysis of personal accounts Social Security reform, although there are differences in the simulation procedure that affect the results. The most important difference is that Shiller (2005) uses data on stock and bond returns from a longer time period than we consider. This means that he assumes a distribution of equity returns with a lower mean value than the mean of the distribution we consider. Our results when the average return on stocks is set at 300 basis points below the historical mean in our sample are closer to those in Shiller (2005) than our results that assume that returns are drawn from the actual return distribution for 1926–2002.

Table 8.6 shows the distributions of outcomes from table 8.5 but under the higher expense ratio scenario (100 basis points for stocks and bonds, 120 basis points for the life-cycle products). This table demonstrates the detrimental effects of high expense ratios on retirement wealth accumulation. The outcomes are 7 to 15 percent lower than under the baseline expense ratio scenario.

8.4.2 Expected Utility of Retirement Wealth

Results like those in table 8.5 and 8.6 do not provide any information on the household utility associated with a particular retirement wealth outcome. To address this issue, we evaluate the expected utility associated with various wealth outcomes from our simulation runs, using the procedure described in equation (5). We focus in this analysis on CRRA parameters of 2 and 4.

We first calculate for each education category (less than high school, high school and/or some college, college and/or postgraduate), risk aversion (2 and 4), return assumption (empirical and 300 basis points reduced), and non-PRA wealth assumption (none and annuity plus other financial wealth) an "optimal" fixed proportions strategy and "optimal" linear life-cycle strategy. This is done by searching over grids at 5 percent intervals. For example, in finding the optimal fixed proportions we start with 100 percent stocks and 0 percent TIPS, then simulate 95 percent stocks and 5 percent TIPS, and so on until we get to 5 percent stocks and 95 percent TIPS. In finding the optimal linear life-cycle portfolio, we start with a strategy that begins 100 percent in stocks and declines linearly to 0 percent in stocks with the rest of the allocation going to TIPS. We then simulate a strategy that begins 95 percent in stocks and declines linearly to 5 percent, and so on, until we get to 55 percent stocks declining to 45 percent stocks. We calculate these using the baseline expense ratios, and we assume that individuals pay the baseline expense ratios for the stock and TIPS funds (32 and 40 basis points, respectively).

Table 8.6   **Simulated distribution of 401(k) balances at retirement ($2000), higher expense ratios**

Investment strategy/ percentile	Empirical stock returns			Empirical returns reduced 300 basis points		
	Less than high school degree	High school and/or some college	College and/or postgraduate	Less than high school degree	High school and/or some college	College and/or postgraduate
100% TIPS	148.9	210.3	291.6	148.9	210.3	291.6
100% government bonds						
1	48.1	68.2	99.1	48.1	68.2	99.1
10	100.0	141.2	199.3	100.0	141.2	199.3
50	159.3	225.3	310.9	159.3	225.3	310.9
90	267.1	377.7	509.9	267.1	377.7	509.9
Mean	174.5	246.8	338.5	174.5	246.8	338.5
100% stocks						
1	27.5	39.5	56.1	17.1	24.6	36.5
10	161.5	229.5	310.1	89.2	126.2	177.4
50	474.4	676.4	876.9	247.2	350.2	471.2
90	1,446.5	2,078.4	2,599.4	724.5	1,031.8	1,333.3
Mean	694.3	996.5	1,262.2	353.5	503.4	660.3
(110 − age)% stocks, (age + 10)% TIPS						
1	70.8	100.6	140.0	56.0	79.5	112.4
10	161.2	228.3	311.8	126.0	178.3	246.9
50	253.8	359.2	484.0	197.5	279.2	381.2
90	397.7	563.3	749.4	308.4	436.2	587.5
Mean	269.6	381.7	512.7	209.6	296.5	403.3
(110 − age)% stocks, (age + 10)% bonds						
1	55.1	77.5	109.5	44.0	62.0	88.8
10	149.2	211.3	290.0	117.0	165.5	230.2
50	267.0	378.2	507.9	207.5	293.5	399.3
90	484.2	687.0	904.0	373.6	529.3	704.9
Mean	298.0	422.5	563.6	231.1	327.2	442.0
Empirical life cycle, stocks and TIPS						
1	64.8	92.5	131.5	49.5	70.5	102.6
10	166.4	235.9	321.4	119.5	169.0	236.2
50	295.6	420.6	554.7	205.4	290.8	393.9
90	544.2	779.3	997.2	366.9	522.1	685.3
Mean	333.1	475.4	620.3	229.1	325.3	435.8
Empirical life cycle, stocks and bonds						
1	53.7	75.8	107.2	41.0	57.9	84.0
10	157.5	223.5	304.4	113.0	159.9	223.5
50	306.8	436.7	575.2	212.8	301.5	407.7
90	621.2	890.0	1,136.1	418.5	595.9	779.9
Mean	359.2	513.0	667.1	246.4	350.0	467.2

Table 8.6   (continued)

	Empirical stock returns			Empirical returns reduced 300 basis points		
Investment strategy/ percentile	Less than high school degree	High school and/or some college	College and/or postgraduate	Less than high school degree	High school and/or some college	College and/or postgraduate
	Feldstein (2005) "No Lose" plan					
1	110.8	156.4	221.7	108.0	152.3	216.5
10	154.6	219.0	300.9	129.0	182.1	255.4
50	271.0	386.7	505.5	183.7	260.2	353.2
90	657.5	949.9	1,177.6	364.1	520.6	670.7
Mean	361.6	520.0	662.5	225.9	321.7	427.0

Source: Authors' tabulations of simulation results. See text for further details.
Note: TIPS = Treasury inflation-protected securities.

Table 8.7 shows the strategies that yield the highest expected utility for each set of characteristics. When there is no other wealth, risk aversion of 2, and historical empirical stock returns, the optimal fixed proportions strategy is 100 percent stocks and 0 percent TIPS for all education categories. Under the lower returns assumption, the optimal fixed proportion is 65 percent stocks and 35 percent TIPS for the lower two education categories, and 70 percent stocks and 30 percent TIPS for the college or more category. With risk aversion of 4, the optimal fixed proportion declines to 55 to 60 percent in stocks under the historical empirical distribution and 35 percent in stocks under the reduced return assumption. When there is other wealth of annuities and other financial assets, the optimal fixed proportion allocation varies from 40 percent to 100 percent depending on the education level, return assumption, and risk aversion. Lower optimal equity shares are associated with the lower return assumption, the lower levels of education, and the higher levels of risk aversion. The education patterns reflect the fact that lower-education households typically have much less non-PRA wealth than higher-education households. If alpha is 0 or 1 (not shown in the table), the optimal fixed proportion is always 100 percent stocks.

The optimal linear life-cycle strategy among the class of strategies we simulate is in many cases the one with the flattest profile. However, a profile that begins 60 to 65 percent in stocks and declines linearly to 40 to 35 percent in stocks is optimal among the class of linear life-cycle portfolios for couples with risk aversion of 4, no other wealth, and facing the historical distribution of equity returns. A more downward-sloping profile that begins 80 percent in stocks and declines linearly to 20 percent in stocks is

Table 8.7   Optimal asset allocations calculations (5% grid)

	Empirical stock returns (%)			Empirical stock returns reduced 300 basis points (%)		
	Less than high school degree	High school and/or some college	College and/or postgraduate	Less than high school degree	High school and/or some college	College and/or postgraduate
No other wealth						
alpha = 2						
Optimal fixed proportions:						
% stocks (rest TIPS)	100	100	100	65	65	70
Optimal linear life cycle:						
starting % stocks	55	55	55	55	55	55
alpha = 4						
Optimal fixed proportions:						
% stocks (rest TIPS)	55	55	60	35	35	35
Optimal linear life cycle:						
starting % stocks	65	65	60	80	80	80
Annuities and other financial wealth						
alpha = 2						
Optimal fixed proportions:						
% stocks (rest TIPS)	100	100	100	80	85	100
Optimal linear life cycle:						
starting % stocks	55	55	55	55	55	55
alpha = 4						
Optimal fixed proportions:						
% stocks (rest TIPS)	70	75	90	40	45	55
Optimal linear life cycle:						
starting % stocks	55	55	55	75	70	65

Note: TIPS = Treasury inflation-protected securities.

optimal for households with risk aversion of 4, no other wealth, and facing the reduced equity returns. In general, lower returns and higher risk aversion are correlated with a greater shift from stocks toward TIPS as the individual ages.

Table 8.8 shows the expected utility generated by the distribution of retirement resources for each of the eight primary portfolio strategies, as well

Table 8.8   Certainty equivalent wealth ($2000) for different asset allocation rules and different expected stock returns, no other wealth

Investment strategy/risk aversion	Empirical stock returns			Empirical stock returns reduced 300 basis points		
	Less than high school degree	High school and/or some college	College and/or postgraduate	Less than high school degree	High school and/or some college	College and/or postgraduate
alpha = 2						
Baseline expense ratios						
100% TIPS	167.4	236.7	325.5			
100% government bonds	171.9	242.9	334.3			
100% stocks	389.1	553.7	731.0	207.9	294.5	403.3
Heuristic: (110 − age)% stocks, rest TIPS	271.5	384.8	516.4	210.8	298.4	405.7
Heuristic: (110 − age)% stocks, rest bonds	278.0	393.9	528.7	215.8	305.5	415.3
Empirical life cycle, stocks and TIPS	322.5	458.9	605.5	224.4	317.9	430.2
Empirical life cycle, stocks and bonds	323.5	460.3	607.9	225.2	319.0	432.1
Feldstein "No Lose" plan	297.1	423.5	557.5	212.7	301.6	407.8
Optimal fixed proportions (stocks and TIPS)	389.1	553.7	731.0	224.2	317.6	430.8
Optimal linear life cycle	298.4	423.9	562.8	220.1	311.7	421.9
Average expense ratios						
Empirical life cycle, stocks and TIPS	299.1	425.3	563.6	209.0	295.8	402.1
Empirical life cycle, stocks and bonds	300.0	426.6	565.8	209.7	297.0	403.9
High expense ratios						
100% TIPS	148.9	210.3	291.6			
100% government bonds	150.5	212.7	295.1			
100% stocks	335.9	477.7	635.1	181.6	257.2	354.7
Empirical life cycle, stocks and TIPS	268.8	381.9	509.0	189.0	267.3	365.5
Empirical life cycle, stocks and bonds	269.7	383.1	511.0	189.7	268.4	367.2
Feldstein "No Lose" plan	258.4	367.7	487.8	186.9	264.6	360.7

(*continued*)

Table 8.8　　　　(continued)

	Empirical stock returns			Empirical stock returns reduced 300 basis points		
Investment strategy/risk aversion	Less than high school degree	High school and/or some college	College and/or postgraduate	Less than high school degree	High school and/or some college	College and/or postgraduate
alpha = 4						
Baseline expense ratios						
100% TIPS	167.4	236.7	325.5			
100% government bonds	150.0	211.8	294.9			
100% stocks	204.2	288.3	398.1	116.3	164.2	234.5
Heuristic: (110 − age)% stocks, rest TIPS	239.4	339.1	458.3	186.3	263.6	361.0
Heuristic: (110 − age)% stocks, rest bonds	226.2	320.2	435.5	176.6	249.8	344.1
Empirical life cycle, stocks and TIPS	263.1	372.6	501.7	186.8	263.8	363.9
Empirical life cycle, stocks and bonds	247.5	350.6	473.8	176.5	249.3	345.0
Feldstein "No Lose" plan	245.8	348.7	468.9	191.2	270.4	370.3
Optimal fixed proportions (stocks and TIPS)	256.3	363.5	490.1	0 193.8	274.3	374.6
Optimal linear life cycle	256.7	364.1	489.1	197.3	278.9	381.3
Average expense ratios						
Empirical life cycle, stocks and TIPS	244.8	346.6	468.6	174.6	246.4	341.3
Empirical life cycle, stocks and bonds	230.5	326.3	442.8	165.0	233.0	323.9
High expense ratios						
100% TIPS	148.9	210.3	291.6			
100% government bonds	131.9	186.2	261.3			
100% stocks	178.3	252.9	351.3	102.9	145.8	209.7
Empirical life cycle, stocks and TIPS	221.0	312.9	425.4	158.6	223.9	311.8
Empirical life cycle, stocks and bonds	208.2	294.8	402.7	150.0	211.8	296.3
Feldstein "No Lose" plan	215.5	305.5	413.9	168.9	238.7	329.5

Source: Authors' tabulations from simulation analysis. See text for further discussion.

Note: TIPS = Treasury inflation-protected securities.

as the two derived optimal strategies, using a certainty equivalent wealth measure to value the potential outcomes. In this table, we assume that the PRA balance is the household's only wealth. The values in the upper half of table 8.8 are based on risk aversion of 2. This panel shows that under the empirical stock return scenario, the 100 percent stocks strategy is the best among all of the strategies that we simulated for households with this level of risk aversion. The amount by which this strategy outperforms the other strategies is rather considerable in the empirical return scenario. It is roughly 20 percent greater than the empirical life-cycle strategies, assuming that investors can obtain the empirical life cycle for 40 basis points. It is roughly 30 percent greater than the empirical life-cycle strategies under the average expense ratio of 74 basis points. The certainty equivalent for 100 percent stocks is at least 40 percent greater than the heuristic strategies, and it is more than 120 percent better than the all bonds strategies. When expense ratios are raised, the 100 percent stock allocation is still optimal (as the higher expense ratio scenario also involves higher expense ratios for bonds and TIPS) but the household is 13 to 14 percent worse off.

When returns are reduced by 300 basis points, the 100 percent stock strategy is no longer optimal. The empirical life-cycle strategy under the baseline expense assumption (40 basis points) yields the best outcome. For example, for a household with a high school education, the certainty equivalent of the empirical life-cycle fund is $319,000, compared to $294,500 from investing entirely in stocks and $236,700 from investing entirely in bonds. Note that the amount by which the best strategy outperforms the next best alternative is smaller in both percentage terms and dollar terms than the amount by which the stocks strategy outperformed in the empirical stock returns scenario. In particular, the best fixed proportions strategy, which table 8.7 found to be 65 percent stocks for the lower two education categories and 70 percent stocks for the highest category, falls below the best strategy by less than $2,000. The broad magnitudes of all of the strategies that involve some equity investment are not far from the optimal strategy. Obtaining reasonably low expense ratios is critical, however, as the average and high expense ratio simulations show that the household loses substantial value relative to the baseline expense ratio certainty equivalents. Certainty equivalents under the higher expense ratios are 10 to 15 percent lower than those under the baseline expense ratios. Furthermore, the empirical life-cycle products are much less competitive when we consider the premiums that investors generally pay in terms of expense ratios.

The lower panel of table 8.8 shows a similar analysis to the upper panel but with a risk aversion of 4. Under the historical empirical distribution of equity returns and baseline expense ratios, the empirical life cycle consisting of stocks and TIPS generates the highest certainty equivalents relative to the other strategies. However, this assumes that investors will not pay a large premium in expenses for the life-cycle fund. The average expense ratio life-cycle fund (74 basis points) performs worse than the optimal linear life-cycle or optimal fixed proportions strategies because these are achieved at lower cost (32 basis points when in stocks, 40 basis points when in TIPS). Under the reduced equity return assumptions, the optimal linear life-cycle strategy beats the other strategies assuming the baseline expense ratios. When expense ratios are high, the Feldstein No Lose plan generates higher certainty equivalents than the other strategies considered.

Although not shown here, we also conducted simulations with risk aversion of 0 (linear utility) and risk aversion of 1 (log utility). In both of these cases, 100 percent equity is always the optimal strategy. Risk aversion of 0 is equivalent to considering the mean returns from tables 8.5 and 8.6. The log level of risk aversion reduces the certainty equivalent value of the all-stock portfolio strategy relative to other strategies, but this strategy continues to generate the highest expected utility for all education groups. This outcome obtains when the expected stock return is set equal to its historical average and when it is reduced by 300 basis points.

Table 8.8 considers the certainty equivalent of different investment strategies when retirement wealth from a PRA plan is the only source of wealth at retirement. By assuming that the household is solely dependent on PRA wealth, these calculations exaggerate the level of retirement income risk faced by the household. Holding constant the household's relative risk coefficient, when the household has other sources of wealth, it will behave as though it were less risk averse.

Table 8.9 presents results with the alternative assumptions about non-PRA wealth at retirement, namely that it equals annuity and other financial wealth. The households in this case are less averse to holding high fractions of their wealth in stocks. For a relative risk aversion of two, for example, the certainty equivalent value of contributing to a PRA that is invested in the empirical life-cycle fund at average expense ratios with stocks and TIPS is $425,300 when households with a high school education have no wealth at retirement other than their retirement wealth. This value can be found in table 8.8. When other financial wealth is combined with retirement account wealth in determining the utility of retirement wealth, the certainty equivalent of the same strategy rises to $442,100. These values represent the certainty equivalent of just the PRA account balance. This is the amount in addition to other wealth that would be needed to generate the expected utility associated with the uncertain retirement wealth distribution.

Allowing for nonretirement account wealth raises the attractiveness of riskier strategies relative to other investment options. Under the empirical returns scenario, the 100 percent stocks investment dominates when alpha is 2, under both the baseline expense and higher expense ratio scenarios. When returns are reduced, the optimal fixed strategy generates the highest certainty equivalent for the lower two education categories. As shown in

Table 8.9   Certainty equivalent wealth ($2000) for different asset allocation rules and different expected stock returns, other wealth equal to annuities (excluding defined benefit [DB] plans and Social Security) and non-retirement financial wealth

Investment strategy/risk aversion	Empirical stock returns			Empirical stock returns reduced 300 basis points		
	Less than high school degree	High school and/or some college	College and/or postgraduate	Less than high school degree	High school and/or some college	College and/or postgraduate
alpha = 2						
Baseline expense ratios						
100% TIPS	167.4	236.7	325.5			
100% government bonds	176.1	252.0	351.7			
100% stocks	419.0	618.9	861.7	229.4	340.5	492.5
Heuristic: (110 − age)% stocks, rest TIPS	275.9	394.3	535.4	214.8	306.9	422.2
Heuristic: (110 − age)% stocks, rest bonds	285.5	410.2	560.9	222.5	319.9	443.1
Empirical life cycle, stocks and TIPS	330.4	476.4	639.3	230.7	331.6	456.0
Empirical life cycle, stocks and bonds	334.2	483.7	653.5	233.8	337.7	467.5
Feldstein "No Lose" plan	306.2	443.8	597.0	217.3	311.6	426.8
Optimal fixed proportions (stocks and TIPS)	419.0	618.9	861.7	235.4	344.1	492.5
Optimal linear life cycle	304.0	436.1	586.9	224.8	321.9	441.6
Average expense ratios						
Empirical life cycle, stocks and TIPS	306.7	442.1	595.8	215.0	309.0	426.6
Empirical life cycle, stocks and bonds	310.3	449.1	609.3	217.9	314.7	437.6
High expense ratios						
100% TIPS	148.9	210.3	291.6			
100% government bonds	154.4	221.0	310.9			
100% stocks	363.7	538.1	755.6	201.4	299.4	436.3
Empirical life cycle, stocks and TIPS	276.0	397.6	539.1	194.6	279.6	388.3
Empirical life cycle, stocks and bonds	279.3	404.3	551.8	197.3	285.0	398.5
Feldstein "No Lose" plan	266.8	386.2	523.5	191.0	273.7	377.7

(*continued*)

Table 8.9 Certainty equivalent wealth ($2000) for different asset allocation rules and different expected stock returns, other wealth equal to annuities (excluding defined benefit [DB] plans and Social Security) and non-retirement financial wealth

Investment strategy/risk aversion	Empirical stock returns			Empirical stock returns reduced 300 basis points		
	Less than high school degree	High school and/or some college	College and/or postgraduate	Less than high school degree	High school and/or some college	College and/or postgraduate
alpha = 4						
Baseline expense ratios						
100% TIPS	167.4	236.7	325.5			
100% government bonds	157.6	227.9	325.5			
100% stocks	250.0	387.1	593.0	148.4	232.1	365.9
Heuristic: (110 − age)% stocks, rest TIPS	248.1	357.7	495.1	194.0	280.0	392.8
Heuristic: (110 − age)% stocks, rest bonds	240.3	350.2	494.6	189.0	276.0	394.9
Empirical life cycle, stocks and TIPS	277.3	404.0	561.8	198.0	288.2	409.7
Empirical life cycle, stocks and bonds	266.3	391.4	552.8	191.3	281.3	406.0
Feldstein "No Lose" plan	257.1	373.6	518.6	197.0	283.2	395.3
Optimal fixed proportions (stocks and TIPS)	275.0	408.0	569.9	199.3	287.4	405.7
Optimal linear life cycle	266.8	386.3	533.3	203.0	291.8	407.0
Average expense ratios						
Empirical life cycle, stocks and TIPS	258.5	376.6	525.7	185.3	269.7	384.7
Empirical life cycle, stocks and bonds	248.4	365.3	518.0	179.2	263.6	381.8
High expense ratios						
100% TIPS	148.9	210.3	291.6			
100% government bonds	138.8	201.0	289.1			
100% stocks	220.8	343.7	529.7	132.5	208.0	329.5
Empirical life cycle, stocks and TIPS	233.8	340.9	478.6	168.6	245.5	352.1
Empirical life cycle, stocks and bonds	225.0	331.4	472.6	163.3	240.4	350.1
Feldstein "No Lose" plan	225.9	328.3	459.0	174.2	250.3	351.9

Source: Authors' tabulations from simulation analysis. See text for further discussion.

Note: TIPS = Treasury inflation-protected securities.

table 8.7, this strategy requires 80 percent and 85 percent in stocks, respectively, for households with less than high school education and households with a high school education. For the top education category, the 100 percent equity strategy dominates. This is also the optimal fixed-proportions strategy.

When alpha is 4, the situation with baseline and average expense ratios is similar to that when the household has no other wealth, in that the empirical life-cycle portfolio is a good choice when it can be obtained at a low cost. There are some differences, however. Now the optimal fixed proportions strategy does slightly better than the empirical life-cycle portfolio for the higher two education categories under baseline expense ratios and historical equity returns. A 100 percent stocks strategy actually dominates for these education groups under the high expense ratio scenario, as their background wealth makes them effectively less risk averse, while the life-cycle funds here cost 120 basis points compared to the equity fund's 100 basis points.

The pattern of results when the household has non-PRA wealth is quite similar to the pattern when it has no other wealth. There is often an optimal fixed proportions and optimal linear life-cycle portfolio that generates certainty equivalents at least as high as those from the empirical life-cycle funds, especially when we consider the higher average expense ratios that investors actually pay in empirical life-cycle funds.

8.5   Conclusions

This chapter presents evidence on the distribution of balances in PRA retirement saving accounts under various assumptions about the asset allocation strategies that investors choose. In addition to a range of age-invariant strategies, such as an all-bond and an all-stock strategy, we consider several different "life-cycle funds" that automatically alter the investor's mix of assets as he or she ages. These funds offer investors a higher portfolio allocation to stocks at the beginning of a working career than as they approach retirement, but in many cases charge higher expense ratios. We also consider a No Lose allocation strategy for retirement saving, in which households purchase enough riskless bonds at each age to ensure that they will have no less than their nominal contribution when they reach retirement age and then invest the balance in corporate stock. This strategy combines a riskless floor for retirement income with some upside investment potential.

Our results suggest several conclusions about the effect of investment strategy on retirement wealth. The expected utility associated with different PRA asset allocation strategies, and the ranking of these strategies, is very sensitive to four assumptions: the expected return on corporate stock, the relative risk aversion of the investing household, the amount of non-

PRA wealth that the household will have available at retirement, and the expenses associated with the given investment strategies. At modest levels of risk aversion, or when the household has access to substantial non-PRA wealth at retirement, the historical pattern of stock and bond returns implies that the expected utility of an all-stock investment allocation rule is greater than that from any of the more conservative strategies.

When we reduce the expected return on stocks by 300 basis points relative to historical values, however, other strategies dominate the all-equity allocation for investors with high levels of relative risk aversion. For a risk aversion parameter of 2, the expected utility associated with investing in an optimally chosen mix of stocks and TIPS, or in an inexpensive life-cycle product, is highest. For a risk aversion parameter of 4, the expected utility associated with an optimally chosen fixed portfolio of stocks and TIPS or an optimally chosen linear life-cycle product is highest and is substantially higher than investing 100 percent in stocks. The actual life-cycle products available to investors often generate lower certainty equivalents than our derived optima, but this is partly related to the expense ratios charged by those products.

When households are calibrated to have non-PRA wealth, 100 percent stocks is optimal for a risk aversion parameter of 2, and is not far from optimal even when equity returns are reduced by 300 basis points. For a risk aversion parameter of 4, an optimally chosen fixed portfolio of stocks and TIPS, or a life-cycle product obtained at low cost, performs the best.

The analysis underscores the fact that avoiding high expense ratios is critical for households saving for retirement in a PRA. Many of the available life-cycle products have higher expense ratios than could be achieved by the household simply holding a stock index fund and some TIPS (or bonds) and either holding them in fixed proportions throughout their lifetime or rebalancing toward TIPS (or bonds) as they get older. Households who are unable to do this on their own will not do terribly in life-cycle funds, but they will lose money relative to what they could get if they executed very simple investing strategies on their own.

Our analysis of life-cycle funds suggests three issues that warrant future research. First, it is possible that life-cycle funds should be different for single individuals than for married couples. The focus in these funds so far has been on accumulating wealth for retirement, and the conceptual justification for age-phased equity exposure would be age-related variation in household risk aversion. Single individuals may have fewer opportunities to respond to an adverse economic shock than married couples, so their tolerance of equity market risk in their retirement accounts may be different from that for married couples.

Second, we have focused on only a limited set of outcome measures associated with different asset allocation strategies. While we consider various percentiles of the retirement wealth distribution, as well as the mean value of wealth at retirement, and the expected utility associated with this wealth value, other metrics may also deserve consideration. One possibility is the risk of shortfall associated with one strategy relative to another. The Feldstein (2005) No Lose strategy eliminates the shortfall risk associated with a DC investment strategy relative to investing all contributions to a DC plan in a zero-yield cash account. Shortfall risk measures could be computed for a range of other strategies.

Third, we have not introduced any of the market imperfections or elements of behavioral economics that might affect the estimated benefits of life-cycle funds. For example, we have not allowed retirement ages to vary as a function of the household's accumulated PRA balance. Allowing for additional years of work when returns are unfavorable would reduce the cost of low accumulation values. We have also assumed that when we assign households to fixed proportions strategies, they successfully rebalance their portfolio so that they maintain the designated proportions. If households fail to do so, strategies such as life-cycle investing that automate such portfolio decisions may affect expected utility in ways that we have not captured.

References

Ameriks, John, and Stephen Zeldes. 2004. Do household portfolio shares vary with age? Columbia University, Graduate School of Business. Mimeograph.

Bodie, Zvi, Robert C. Merton, and William Samuelson. 1992. Labor supply flexibility and portfolio choice in a lifecycle model. *Journal of Economic Dynamics and Control* 16:427–49.

Campbell, John Y., Joao Cocco, Francisco Gomes, and Pascal Maenhout. 2001. Investing retirement wealth: A life-cycle model. In *Risk aspects of investment-based Social Security reform,* ed. John Y. Campbell and Martin Feldstein, 439–73. Chicago: University of Chicago Press.

Campbell, John Y., and Luis M. Viceira. 2002. *Strategic asset allocation: Portfolio choices for long-term investors.* New York: Oxford University Press.

Clements, Jonathan. 2005. Plan paralysis: Why a wealth of choices in 401(k)s may not make investors rich. *Wall Street Journal,* May 4, 2005, C1.

Cocco, Joao, Francisco Gomes, and Pascal Maenhout. 2005. Consumption and portfolio choice over the life cycle. *Review of Financial Studies* 18 (2): 491–533.

Feldstein, Martin. 2005. Reducing the risk of investment-based Social Security reform. NBER Working Paper no. 11084. Cambridge, MA: National Bureau of Economic Research.

Gollier, Christian. 2001. *The economics of risk and time.* Cambridge, MA: MIT Press.

Gollier, Christian, and Richard J. Zeckhauser. 2002. Horizon length and portfolio risk. *Journal of Risk and Uncertainty* 24:195–212.

Gomes, Francisco, and Alexander Michaelides. 2005. Optimal life cycle asset allocation: Understanding the empirical evidence. *Journal of Finance* 60:869–904.

Hortaçsu, Ali, and Chad Syverson. 2004. Search costs, product differentiation, and welfare effects of entry: A case study of S&P 500 index funds. *Quarterly Journal of Economics* 119 (4): 403–56.

Ibbotson Associates. 2003. *Stocks, bonds, bills, and inflation: 2003 yearbook: Market results for 1926–2002.* Chicago: Ibbotson Associates.

Jagganathan, Ravi, and Narayana Kocherlakota. 1996. Why should older people invest less in stocks than younger people? *Federal Reserve Bank of Minneapolis Quarterly Review* 20 (3): 11–23.

Marquez, Jessica. 2005. Lifecycle funds can help companies mitigate risk and boost employee savings. *Workforce Management,* April 1, 65–67.

Mehra, Rajneesh, and Edward Prescott. 2002. The equity premium puzzle in retrospect. In *Handbook of economics of finance,* ed. G. Constantinides, M. Harris, and R. Stulz. Amsterdam: North Holland.

Merton, Robert C. 1969. Lifetime portfolio selection under uncertainty: The continuous time case. *Review of Economics and Statistics* 51:247–57.

Munnell, Alicia, and Annika Sunden. 2004. *Coming up short: The challenge of 401(k) plans.* Washington, DC: Brookings Institution.

Poterba, James M. 2003. Employer stock and 401(k) plans. *American Economic Review* 93 (May): 398–404.

Poterba, James M., Joshua Rauh, Steven F. Venti, and David A. Wise. 2005. Utility evaluation of risk in retirement savings accounts. In *Analyses in the economics of Aging.* Vol. 10, ed. David A. Wise, 13–52. Chicago: University of Chicago Press.

Poterba, James M., and Andrew Samwick. 2001. Household portfolio allocations over the lifecycle. In *Aging issues in the U.S. and Japan,* ed. S. Ogura, T. Tachibanaki, and D. A. Wise, 65–103. Chicago: University of Chicago Press.

Samuelson, Paul. 1963. Risk and uncertainty: The fallacy of the law of large numbers. *Scientia* 98:108–13.

———. 1969. Lifetime portfolio selection by dynamic stochastic programming. *Review of Economics and Statistics* 51:239–46.

Samuelson, William, and Richard J. Zeckhauser. 1988. Status quo bias in decision making. *Journal of Risk and Uncertainty* 1:7–59.

Samwick, Andrew, and Jonathan Skinner. 2004. How will 401(k) plans affect retirement income? *American Economic Review* 94:329–43.

Scholz, J. Karl, Ananth Seshadri, and Surachrai Khitatrakun. 2006. Are Americans saving optimally for retirement? *Journal of Political Economy* 114:607–43.

Shiller, Robert. 2005. The life cycle personal accounts proposal for Social Security: A review. NBER Working Paper no. 11300. Cambridge, MA: National Bureau of Economic Research.

Venti, Steven F., and David A. Wise. 2004. Aging and housing equity: Another look. In Perspectives on the economics of aging, ed. David A. Wise, 127–75. Chicago: University of Chicago Press.

Comment   Douglas W. Elmendorf

This chapter by Jim Poterba, Josh Rauh, Steve Venti, and David Wise considers an important practical issue that would be associated with the intro-

Douglas W. Elmendorf is a senior fellow at the Brookings Institution.

duction of personal retirement accounts. Deciding that people should accumulate assets and use those assets to finance their retirements is just the starting point. Among the myriad further decisions is choosing which assets to hold—and that choice might ultimately matter a great deal. This chapter extends earlier work by these authors and others to investigate the implications of alternative portfolio allocations.

I enjoyed reading about this research and learned a lot from it. Detailed simulations of the sort undertaken here are crucial in evaluating the impact of alternative proposals for Social Security reform. The authors provide a clear description of the various choices they needed to make for these complex simulations, and those choices seem sensible to me. The authors also do an admirable job of testing the robustness of their findings to alternative assumptions, especially when one recognizes the thousands of iterations of multiperiod lifetimes that underlie each figure in the tables. Thus, I do not have much to say about the specifics of the calculations. Instead, I will use my limited time to discuss the interpretation of the results, making four points in declining order of importance.

The Equity Premium

The "equity premium puzzle" plays a critical role in interpreting the results in this chapter, as it does in so many analyses regarding equity investment of retirement funds. This point is not a surprise to the authors or to other participants in this conference. However, given its overriding importance here and in other research, tracing its effects through the chapter is worthwhile.

In tables 8.5 and 8.6, the authors present the mean and various percentiles of the distribution of retirement wealth under different portfolio choices and different assumptions about investment conditions. One problem in thinking about these tables is simply the number of numbers shown. Although the robustness checks are very important, it may be difficult to see the forest for the trees. Therefore, I use a diagram to summarize the information in the tables. Figure 8C.1 is a version of the familiar mean-variance diagram, with the vertical axis showing mean retirement wealth and the horizontal axis showing the difference in retirement wealth between the 90th and 10th percentiles (because the authors do not report standard deviations).

The solid diamonds plot the outcomes of alternative investment strategies for people with a high school education facing baseline expenses and empirical stock returns. Naturally, the line slopes upward, with the all-

I am grateful to Greg Duffee and Jason Furman for helpful conversations. This comment was presented at a conference supported by the U.S. Social Security Administration (SSA) through grant #10-P-98363-1-03 to the National Bureau of Economic Research (NBER) as part of the SSA Retirement Research Consortium. The views expressed are my own and do not represent the views of the NBER or the Social Security Administration.

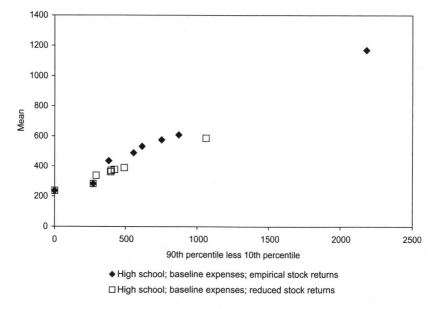

Fig. 8C.1   **Retirement wealth with alternative investment strategies**

Treasury inflation-protected securities (TIPS) strategy on the far left and the all-stock strategy on the far right.[1] The hollow squares plot the outcomes of alternative investment strategies for this same group facing baseline expenses but reduced stock returns. For any investment strategy that includes stocks, lower stock returns trim both the mean and range of retirement wealth.

I constructed similar diagrams to examine retirement wealth for people facing higher expenses and for the college-educated sample. The results were straightforward. Compared with the baseline shown with the solid diamonds, higher expenses reduce the mean and range of retirement wealth for all investment strategies. However, they have smaller effects than reduced stock returns for investment strategies that include stocks because annual returns are reduced by 60 to 80 basis points rather than 300 basis points. College-educated individuals accumulate more wealth than high school-educated individuals because they save more, but the picture is qualitatively very similar.

These calculations simply trace out the efficient frontier (after allowing for expenses). Tables 8.8 and 8.9 turn to the utility consequences. Once again, I have consolidated the large amount of information in the tables.

1. One strategy seems to be dominated in the sense of being off the efficient frontier—holding long-term bonds. That result is not surprising given the model of asset returns used in the chapter, as I discuss later.

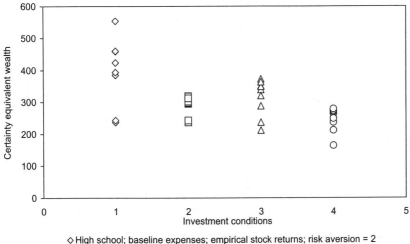

◇ High school; baseline expenses; empirical stock returns; risk aversion = 2
□ High school; baseline expenses; reduced stock returns; risk aversion = 2

Fig. 8C.2   Retirement wealth with alternative strategies and investment conditions

Figure 8C.2 shows the dispersion of certainty equivalent wealth across alternative strategies and investment conditions. The first vertical column shows the range of wealth outcomes for the baseline case, the second column shows the same for reduced stock returns, the third for higher risk aversion, and the fourth for the combination of reduced returns and higher risk aversion.

The sizes of the ranges are strikingly different for different assumptions. At the far left, the best portfolio choice produces almost 2.5 times the certainty equivalent wealth of the worst portfolio choice; in the other three columns, the best choice is only about 1.5 times as good as the worst choice. That is, under the baseline assumptions, one's portfolio choice matters a lot, but under other assumptions, it matters much less.

Why? One more type of picture is helpful. The solid diamonds in figure 8C.3 plot, for the baseline case, certainly equivalent wealth against the average share of the portfolio in stocks during a lifetime. I had to guess some of the stock shares based on information in the chapter, and I skipped the No Lose plan because I did not know how to make an educated guess. With that caveat in mind, the figure shows that portfolios invested more heavily in stocks appear to have a higher risk-adjusted return.

This result should not surprise us: it is just the equity premium puzzle. We know that if one applies a fairly low degree of risk aversion to historical equity returns, it appears that people should hold more stock than they do. Indeed, the authors find that the optimal fixed portfolio share is 100 percent in this case. However, unless one decides that the resolution of the equity premium puzzle is that people have just been wrong about their in-

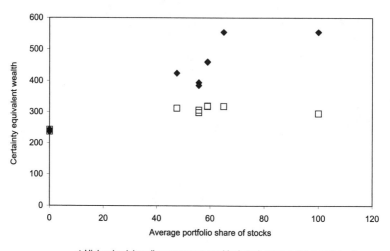

Fig. 8C.3   Stockholding and utility

vestment choices over the past century, I do not know what one can take from this finding.

The hollow squares represent the corresponding points assuming reduced equity returns. This bit of revisionist history diminishes the equity premium puzzle—and it also eliminates the upward-sloping relationship of the solid diamonds, suggesting that one's portfolio choice does not matter much. This result also should not surprise us: if we have done the certainty equivalence calculation correctly, risk should play no systematic role in the outcomes. Indeed, because risk is the main difference across these strategies, there is now very little difference of any sort. The corresponding figure assuming higher risk aversion rather than lower stock returns looks quite similar.

In sum, we know that economists cannot rationalize the observed distribution of asset returns using a standard utility function with values of risk aversion that seem plausible. Therefore, using such a utility function to compare wealth outcomes generated with the observed distribution of asset returns is problematic at best. Put differently, making utility comparisons for different investment strategies using a utility function and a distribution of historical asset returns that are not consistent with each other will produce results whose interpretation is very unclear.

Time Varying Equity Shares

One motivation for the chapter is the traditional piece of financial advice that investors should reduce their equity exposure as they get older. The simulation results are consistent with this advice, but that appears to be a matter of happenstance rather than a reflection of the fundamental economics underlying the simulations. Let me explain.

The authors note that simple economic models do not justify this traditional advice, but that more complicated models do. These complications generally offer ways to rebalance portfolios in the event of financial shocks or ways to adjust labor supply and labor income to compensate for financial shocks. However, the simulations in this chapter include neither of these features and thus appear to provide no rationale for a downward profile of stock holding over a lifetime.

Why, then, do the so-called optimal linear life-cycle asset allocations reported in table 8.7 involve such a downward tilt? One clue is the authors' statement that the optimal strategy "is in many cases the one with the flattest profile." Yet the analysis does not allow for completely flat or upward-sloping profiles, so the results reveal only the optimal *downward-sloping* linear strategy. Whether a flat or upward-sloping profile would generate higher certainty equivalent wealth is not apparent.

However, the full story is more complicated, because the authors also report some cases where the optimal stock holding profile is not the flattest available profile. These results seem to arise because all of the portfolios are constrained to *average* a 50 percent equity share over the life cycle. Because the total size of a portfolio increases with age, less wealth is subjected to the equity return with a downward tilt in the equity share than with a flat equity share at the same average level. The results in question do not reveal a preference for a downward slope per se but rather a preference for a smaller *effective* equity share on average over a lifetime. In the conditions under which investors would prefer a larger share of equities—like the baseline case—the preferred slope of equity holding is flat because that maximizes the amount of wealth receiving the equity return. In the conditions under which investors would prefer a smaller share of equities—like reduced equity returns—the preferred slope is a steep one.

In sum, the simulation results pointing to a downward tilt in stock holding reflect limitations on the portfolio allocations considered rather than underlying economic factors. Incorporating the factors that would generate a preferred downward profile would represent a very interesting—but very complex—extension to this chapter.

Time Variation in Asset Returns

The model used in the chapter does not allow for time variation in the distribution of asset returns. This restriction is quite understandable in terms of computational feasibility, but it matters for some of the results.

We know that portfolios should not be efficient simply in a static, mean-variance sense, but should hedge against future changes in investment opportunities. Of course, such dynamic hedging arises only because of time variation in expected returns or volatilities. Because this chapter assumes that the TIPS yield and the distributions of returns on other assets are fixed over time, dynamic hedging is not a consideration in the simulations or in the optimal portfolio allocations derived from those simulations.

One effect of the lack of dynamic hedging is a missing motivation for holding long-term bonds. In the real world, long-term bonds can provide an intertemporal hedge against variation in short-term interest rates because their prices rise when (expected) short-term rates fall. This role for long-term bonds does not appear in the sort of diagram I drew earlier and does not appear in the model and simulations in this chapter. Those simulations seem to imply that people should never hold long-term bonds—but that conclusion would be inappropriate, and the authors carefully do not draw it. More broadly, the optimal portfolio shares of stocks and TIPS can look quite different in models that incorporate time varying returns and dynamic hedging than in models like the one in this chapter.

Mutual Fund Expenses

The authors show a significant effect on retirement wealth of the level of expenses, as we would expect. This effect would be even larger if the simulations showed investments cumulating for longer—for example, if the analysis included the draw-down period of retirement accounts.

The chapter also raises the concern that so-called life-cycle funds may have higher expenses. However, I see little reason to believe that a life-cycle feature substantially increases the true costs of running a mutual fund, which suggests that competition is likely to whittle away at the expenses charged. Even today, the expense ratios at Vanguard for their total stock index fund, long-term Treasury bond index fund, and "target retirement" funds are 0.19 percent, 0.26 percent, and 0.21 percent, respectively. Thus, Vanguard is charging essentially nothing for the life-cycle approach. For analysis of the sort done in this chapter, I would look beyond the current, higher expenses of such funds and focus on the possible desirability of automatic portfolio reallocation over time.

Changing Progressivity as a Means of Risk Protection in Investment-Based Social Security

Andrew A. Samwick

9.1 Introduction

Around the globe, traditional pay-as-you-go Social Security systems are facing financial challenges due to demographic changes. With fertility rates at or below replacement levels in developed countries and life expectancy in retirement projected to continue increasing, the ratio of beneficiaries to workers will rise over the coming decades, increasing annual costs relative to income. The imminent retirement of the baby boom generation in many developed countries has focused attention on the need for reform.[1]

Over the past decade and more, many analysts have proposed that at least some of the financial shortfalls be eliminated through the prefunding of future benefits in order to ameliorate the increase in pay-as-you-go tax rates on future generations of workers that would otherwise be required.[2]

Andrew A. Samwick is a professor of economics and director of the Nelson A. Rockefeller Center at Dartmouth College, and a research associate of the National Bureau of Economic Research.

I thank Mike Hurd and conference participants at the National Bureau of Economic Research (NBER) Program on Aging's 2006 Conference on Retirement Research and 2007 Summer Institute for helpful comments. This research was supported by the U.S. Social Security Administration (SSA) through grant #10-P-98363-1-03 to the NBER as part of the SSA Retirement Research Consortium. The findings and conclusions expressed are solely those of the author and do not represent the views of the SSA, any agency of the federal government, or of the NBER. Any errors are my own.

1. The Social Security trustees report (Board of Trustees 2006) projects an increase in the number of beneficiaries per hundred workers from thirty in 2005 to forty-nine in 2040 to fifty-three in 2080 (table IV.B2). For an international description of the demographic challenge, see World Bank (1994).

2. The Office of the Chief Actuary at the Social Security Administration has formally analyzed over two dozen proposals. See the memoranda at http://www.ssa.gov/OACT/solvency/.

Prefunding can more readily take place in a system of decentralized personal retirement accounts (PRAs) than in the Social Security trust fund, particularly when it is desired to exploit the risk-return trade-off inherent in the equity premium and to separate the incremental saving due to higher Social Security taxes from the rest of the federal government's budget.[3]

The possibility that Social Security benefits paid from personal accounts would be subject to financial risk due to stock return volatility, in turn, has focused attention on ways to limit the risk in investment-based Social Security reform. Financial risk is of particular concern with respect to low-income beneficiaries, for whom Social Security benefits make up a disproportionate share of their retirement income. Two principal methods of limiting financial risk have been explored in the recent literature. The first is to offer a guarantee to workers that benefits will not fall below a particular threshold (e.g., 90 percent of scheduled benefits). Feldstein and Ranguelova (2001a,b) demonstrate that such guarantees can be implemented via long-term options on a stock market index in a manner similar to conventional portfolio insurance. The second method is to follow popular financial planning strategies that reduce the portfolio allocation in equities as a worker approaches retirement. Poterba et al. (2006) explore the efficacy of using such life-cycle strategies in this context.

These two mechanisms share the feature that they introduce bonds (preferably as inflation-indexed securities) into the portfolio in order to lessen the exposure to equity risk. However, in doing so, these mechanisms give up the equity premium and thus lose one very important rationale for including PRAs in the reform. In contrast, the following analysis considers an alternative approach based on modifications to the traditional benefit to protect low-earning workers while leaving all workers free to choose their own PRA portfolios. Such an approach may prove to be useful, particularly because any restrictions on the portfolio allocations in the PRAs beyond the determination of which investment choices will be offered are likely to be untenable as the accounts become larger and more popular.

The most direct way to make sure that low-earning workers do not fall into poverty in old age is to increase the progressivity of the benefit formula in the scaled-down version of the traditional system that remains after reform. Doing so would lessen the need to provide insurance against possibly low returns in the PRAs because low-income retirees would depend less on the PRAs to stay out of poverty. To be sure, there have been discussions of progressive reductions in the traditional benefits as part of a plan to close the financial gap while protecting low-earning workers. This chapter adds to the literature by quantifying the effect of such changes to the tra-

---

3. See Samwick (1999, 2004) for further discussion of the role of PRAs in prefunding future entitlement benefits.

ditional benefit formula on the need to invest PRAs in equity rather than bonds to achieve a given level of welfare.

This chapter illustrates the link between progressivity and risk using a stylized framework based on simulations of earnings trajectories and portfolio returns. The simulations are based on the projected experience of a cohort of workers corresponding roughly to those born in 1973. To calibrate the simulations, traditional retirement benefits are reduced by 40 percent, an amount comparable to what is projected to be required to restore annual balance to the system in the long term.[4] The simulations pair reductions in the traditional benefits of this magnitude with PRAs funded by contributions of 2 percent of covered earnings each year. The main comparisons are between the utility-maximizing portfolio allocations to equities across the new configurations of the traditional benefit that are more versus less progressive.

The key finding is that under baseline parameters, the most progressive traditional benefit—a flat benefit independent of earnings—allows the bottom 30 percent of the earnings distribution to achieve a higher expected utility than under proportional reductions to the current benefit formula even if they reduce their PRA investments in equity to zero. An additional 30 percent of earners can lessen their equity investments to some degree without loss of welfare relative to those available under a proportionally scaled-back current formula. Under more realistic and less extreme changes to the traditional benefit, such as that proposed by Liebman, MacGuineas, and Samwick (2005), about half of the equity risk can be eliminated for the lowest earnings decile, and some equity risk can be eliminated for the bottom six deciles. The optimal allocation to equities in the PRA is not particularly sensitive to the progressivity of the reductions in the traditional benefits—in most simulations, the share in equities increases slightly for low earners and decreases slightly for high earners with more progressive reductions in the traditional benefits.

The remainder of the chapter is organized as follows. Section 9.2 lays out the simulation framework for both the traditional benefits and the new system of PRAs. Section 9.3 discusses the combinations of PRA asset allocations and reductions in the traditional benefits that will be analyzed. Section 9.4 derives the certainty equivalent measure of expected utility that will be used in the comparisons. Section 9.5 presents the baseline results, and section 9.6 includes sensitivity tests and a comparison to life-cycle investment strategies. Section 9.7 concludes.

---

4. In 2080, the latest year of the projections in the Social Security trustees report 2006 (table IV.B1), the annual gap is 5.38 percentage points of taxable payroll, compared to a cost rate (excluding disability insurance benefits) of 16.27 percentage points of taxable payroll. Thus, the required reduction is 5.38/16.27 = 33 percent. However, this figure assumes that all benefits—including those of current retirees—can be cut by this amount. The need to protect benefits already in payment would lead to a higher cut to benefits yet to be paid.

9.2   The Simulation Framework

The model used in the analysis focuses on a cohort of workers who should expect to have their traditional benefits reduced at some point when the Social Security system is restored to solvency. Specifically, the analysis simulates the experience of the birth cohort of 1973, who will reach their normal retirement age in 2040, just as the Social Security trust fund is presently projected to be exhausted. Trust fund exhaustion will necessitate changes to the system, even if they have not been made before that time. The analysis assumes, counterfactually, that the workers have been in the new system since they entered the workforce.

The distribution of earnings at an initial age is assumed to be log-normal, allowing its parameters to be estimated from the mean and median of a sample of data. Kunkel (1996) reports the mean and quartiles of the distribution of earnings by age group for the years 1980 to 1993 based on a detailed sample of Social Security records. The population of thirty-year-olds in this analysis is approximated by the twenty-five to thirty-four-year-old cohort in Kunkel's data, and parameters of the log-normal are estimated for each year of Kunkel's sample.[5] These parameters are averaged across all the sample years, and the resulting distribution is scaled up by the growth in the average wage index in Social Security through 2003, the last year for which an estimate of that index is currently available in SSA (2006). To allow for the analysis of the distributional consequences of changes to the Social Security benefit formula, the log-normal distribution is approximated by ten workers who fall at the midpoints of the deciles of that distribution.

For each such worker, earnings evolve over the life cycle due to deterministic changes in expected earnings and stochastic shocks to earnings around expected earnings. The results of the following analyses are the distributions of simulated benefits, where simulations are conducted with 5,000 independent replicates for each of the ten workers representing the deciles of the initial distribution of earnings. The processes for the growth in expected earnings are assumed to be identical for all replicates of all workers. Expected earnings grow each year due to the growth in the national average wage, approximated here by the average real growth rate of Social Security covered wages during the 1952 to 2003 period, or 1.1 percent per year. Expected earnings also follow an age-earnings profile, reflecting changes in individual productivity and hours worked over the life cycle. Each worker is assumed to face the age-earnings profile for the least-

5. The median and mean of a lognormal distribution are given by $\exp(\mu)$ and $\exp(\mu + 0.5 \cdot \sigma^2)$, respectively, where $\exp(\ )$ denotes the exponential function and μ and σ are the mean and standard deviation of the underlying normal distribution. The median, therefore, identifies μ and the ratio identifies σ. The estimated parameters for the group discussed in the text are $\{10.2056, 0.5271\}$.

educated group of workers analyzed by Hubbard, Skinner, and Zeldes (1994).[6] Stochastic deviations from expected earnings follow an AR(1) process with a correlation coefficient of $\rho = 0.95$ and a standard deviation of 15 percent.[7] Given these parameters, annual earnings are backcasted from the initial distribution at age thirty (deterministically, at the average rate of earnings growth) to age twenty-one and then forecasted to age sixty-seven.[8]

The Social Security benefit formula depends on the growth in the national average wage in two places: to determine the maximum taxable earnings on which payroll taxes are paid and to index each year of earnings for the growth of aggregate earnings during a worker's career. Because the framework focuses on the deciles of a single age cohort, the growth in the national average wage is approximated by the growth rate of this cohort's average earnings over its career. Maximum taxable earnings subject to the payroll tax are projected forward and backward from 2003 (age thirty) using this growth rate. With these few assumptions, it is possible to get a reasonable approximation of Social Security benefits by applying the benefit formula to the simulated earnings profiles.

In each of the policy scenarios, the traditional benefit is reduced by 40 percent in the aggregate and is augmented by the benefits payable from a PRA. Personal retirement account contributions are 2 or 3 percent of earnings (depending on the scenario) up to the maximum taxable earnings level. Asset returns are based on the annual total returns in tables 2 to 5 of Ibbotson Associates (2006) for the years 1926 to 2005. Asset classes include large stocks, small stocks, long-term corporate bonds, long-term government bonds, intermediate-term government bonds, and Treasury bills. These returns are further combined in to an equity portfolio (75 percent large stocks and 25 percent small stocks), the corporate bond portfolio, and a government bond portfolio (one third in each of the long-term, intermediate-term, and bills). Each age (e.g., forty-five) in each of the 5,000 replicates is assigned a random year of returns (e.g., 1973) from this eighty-year span. Each of the ten workers, corresponding to the deciles of the initial distribution of earnings, therefore, receives the same sequence of return years. Portfolio allocations are as specified for each scenario. At retirement, PRA balances are converted to inflation-indexed annuities at a

---

6. This profile is approximated by having real earnings grow at annual rates of 2.5 percent between ages twenty-one and thirty, 1.7 percent between thirty-one and forty, 0.5 percent between forty-one and fifty, and –1.3 percent through age sixty-seven. This growth is in addition to the growth in the national average wage.

7. See Topel and Ward (1992) for other, comparable estimates of the wage process.

8. Largely because the sample is constructed around a single deterministic age-earnings profile and is assumed to be fully employed each year, it understates the cross-sectional variation in annual earnings each year. For example, the ratio of the 75th to the 25th percentiles of the earnings distribution at age fifty (or the age group forty-five to fifty-four) in the simulation is 2.59, compared to 3.30 in Kunkel's (1996) sample.

real interest rate of 3 percent, matching the long-term bond return in the trustees report.[9]

9.3   Combining Personal Accounts with a Smaller Traditional Benefit

Several approaches to reducing traditional pay-as-you-go benefits are considered, all of which reduce aggregate payouts by 40 percent (because all are designed to restore solvency to the same degree). They differ in the extent to which they protect the benefits of low earners, whose total retirement incomes are more vulnerable to the financial risk that may come from PRAs. At one extreme is a proportional reduction in the traditional benefits, in which the entire benefit formula is scaled down by 40 percent. This approach leaves the progressivity of the traditional benefit unchanged and is referred to as the *proportional reduction*. At the other extreme, the most progressive way to reduce traditional benefits is to pay each beneficiary the same amount, regardless of earnings. In this case, Social Security would play a flat benefit equal to the mean benefit in the system (scaled down by 40 percent). This method is referred to as the *uniform benefit* in the following.

Between these two extremes lie other possible approaches. One possibility is to use a weighted average of the two extremes. The following simulations consider a half-and-half benefit formula that combines the proportional reduction and uniform benefit and then divides the total by two. Another approach is to reduce benefits progressively based on features of the current benefit formula. For example, in the reform plan presented by Liebman, MacGuineas, and Samwick (2005), the replacement rates are lowered by 25 percent below the first bend point in the formula (from 90 to 67.5 percent) and 50 percent above the first and second bend points (from 32 and 15 percent to 16 and 7.5 percent).[10]

In a reformed system, PRAs are added to the traditional benefits to help maintain total retirement replacement rates. The asset allocation decision in PRAs in this framework is simply a question of equity relative to bonds. The following simulations consider time-invariant allocations to equity ranging from 0 to 100, effectively assuming annual rebalancing to meet this allocation target.[11] For purposes of comparison, three life-cycle strategies

9. The annuity factor is derived from the period life table from 2002, available at http://www.ssa.gov/OACT/STATS/table4c6.html. A dollar of PRA balance translates into $1/13.15 in annual inflation-indexed benefits. The denominator in this figure is the average of the two factors for men (12.3) and women (14.0), respectively.

10. See SSA (2006) for a description of the Social Security benefit formula. See Goss and Wade (2005) for an evaluation of the Liebman, MacGuineas, and Samwick (2005) plan. Both documents can be found at http://www.nonpartisansplan.com for reference.

11. In reality, a worker might choose to vary the allocation to equities over time as a response to realizations of both earnings and investment returns. The assumption of constant allocations throughout the life cycle greatly simplifies the analysis, in order to focus on the main trade-off of progressivity in the benefit formula against the need for low-earning workers to exploit the equity premium. The extension to a dynamic programming that solves for the optimal portfolio is a subject for future work.

are also simulated, in which the allocation to stocks averages 50 percent but declines linearly with age at rates of 1.0, 1.5, or 2.0 percentage points per year.

When it evaluates Social Security reform plans, the Office of the Chief Actuary at the Social Security Administration assigns mean returns by asset type. In recent evaluations, such as Goss and Wade (2005), mean returns have been assumed to be 6.2 percent for equity, 3.2 percent for corporate bonds, and 2.7 for government bonds, net of both inflation and a modest 30 basis point administrative cost. The baseline simulations utilize these assumptions. To capture the volatility around the mean, the historical variation in asset returns from 1926 to 2005 reported by Ibbotson Associates (2006) is utilized. Standard deviations are 22.2 percent for equity, 9.2 percent for corporate bonds, and 6.6 percent for government bonds. All simulations preserve these standard deviations but change the mean returns (by the difference between the specified mean return and the mean of the historical data), allowing for potentially lower equity premiums going forward than what SSA's Office of the Actuary has assumed.[12]

9.4   Evaluating Risk in Retirement Benefits

In the main simulations, workers are assumed to have constant relative risk aversion (CRRA) utility functions, defined over total retirement benefits, b, with risk aversion coefficient γ:

$$u(b) = \frac{b^{1-\gamma}}{1 - \gamma}$$

Expected utility for the worker representing each decile of the initial wage distribution is calculated as the average value of $u(b)$ across 5,000 independently drawn replicates. It, therefore, encompasses the uncertainty in both portfolio returns and earnings, while also allowing for comparisons across different deciles in the initial earnings distribution.[13] As a basis for comparison across configurations of the traditional benefit formula and the PRA asset allocation rules, we can calculate the certainty equivalent benefit:

---

12. Social Security reform proposals that include PRAs often stipulate that the balance can be bequeathed. Bequests are not modeled in this analysis, but this is not an important omission. Allowing for bequests would simply raise the required contribution rate to the PRA to ensure that the 2 or 3 percentage points specified in the simulations go to fund the annuities.

13. Defining the deciles with respect to initial earnings is appropriate in the current framework in which workers are assumed to adopt a single, time-invariant allocation to equities in their PRAs. An alternative approach to doing distributional analysis would use a measure of average lifetime earnings to assign workers to deciles. For example, some workers in the lowest initial earnings decile receive a number of very positive earnings draws and wind up higher in the distribution of lifetime earnings. For comparison, assigning workers to deciles based on their average indexed monthly earnings yields an allocation to deciles with a correlation of 0.83 with the deciles of the initial earnings distribution.

$$b_{CE} = \{(1 - \gamma)E[u(b)]\}^{1/(1-\gamma)} = [E(b^{1-\gamma})]^{1/(1-\gamma)}$$

The certainty equivalent is the retirement benefit that, if received with certainty, would make the individual equally well off as facing the uncertain benefit distribution. For a risk averse individual, the certainty equivalent will be less than the expected benefit level, $E(b)$. A higher certainty equivalent indicates a higher expected utility, and differences in certainty equivalents correspond to risk premiums measured in dollar terms.

By construction, the aggregate expected benefits from the traditional system are identical across all policy scenarios, conditional on the earnings realizations. This is not true within each decile, as some benefit formulas are designed to be more progressive than others and thus provide differential expected benefits to different deciles. Other differences in certainty equivalents across the policy scenarios reflect different exposure to risk, whether through the traditional benefit formula or the PRA investment portfolio, or different expected benefits through the PRA investment portfolio.

9.5   Trading off Progressivity and Risk

Figure 9.1 illustrates the impact of the benefit formula and the equity share of the PRA portfolio on expected benefits. The graph shows the relationship between expected benefits and the equity share in the PRA portfolio for the highest and lowest earnings deciles under three different benefit formulas: proportional reduction, progressive, and uniform benefit. The curves for the top decile earner go in that order, and the curves for the

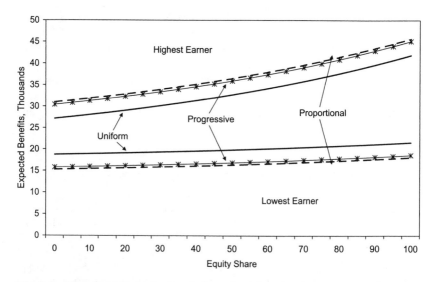

Fig. 9.1   **Expected benefits by benefit formula and equity share**

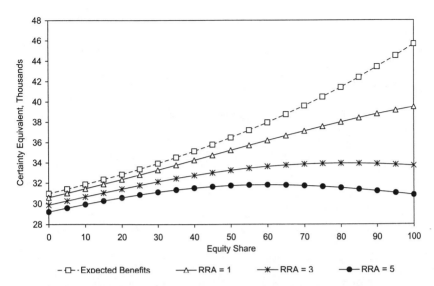

Fig. 9.2   Expected benefits and certainty equivalents, top decile, baseline case

bottom decile go in the reverse order. The proportional reduction is most generous for the top decile and least generous for the bottom decile. The uniform benefit is the opposite—most generous for the bottom decile and least generous for the top decile. The progressive benefit reduction actually tracks the proportional reduction fairly closely. The half-and-half benefit formula (not shown) would fall exactly between the proportional reduction and uniform benefit.[14] Because the risk premium on equities is positive, expected benefits increase in all cases with the portfolio share in equities. For workers in the bottom (top) decile, increases in the equity share in the PRA portfolio and increases (decreases) in the progressivity of the traditional benefit formula are two different ways to increase the expected benefit level.

Figure 9.2 shows the impact of benefit risk on the expected utility of portfolio choices in the PRA. The horizontal axis shows the portfolio share of the PRAs invested in equities, and the vertical axis shows the dollar amount of the expected benefits or expected utility (expressed as a certainty equivalent). The highest curve shows the expected benefits from a traditional benefit based on the current formula, reduced by 40 percent to

14. For the bottom decile, the reductions in the average traditional benefit relative to current law are 40, 37.6, 32.2, and 24.3 percent for the proportional, progressive, half-and-half, and uniform benefit formulas, respectively. For the top decile, the corresponding reductions are 40, 41.7, 45.6, and 51.1 percent. Table 9A.1 contains the mean benefits by earnings decile for each traditional benefit formula and for 2 percent PRAs with investments ranging from 0 to 100 percent equity, in 25 percentage point increments.

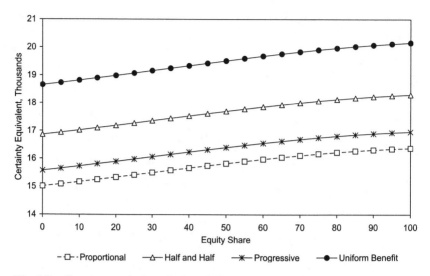

Fig. 9.3   **Certainty equivalents by benefit formulas and equity shares, baseline case, decile 1**

restore solvency, combined with a PRA funded by contributions of 2 percent of taxable payroll per year. (This is the same curve as the top curve in figure 9.1.) The graph is for the highest decile of the earnings distribution. Expected benefits increase slightly faster than linearly with the equity share of the portfolio. With a coefficient of relative risk aversion of 1, the certainty equivalent is increasing with the equity share in the portfolio, though the increase occurs at a decreasing rate. The optimal equity share is, therefore, 100. As the coefficients of relative risk aversion increase to 3 and 5 in the next two curves, the optimal equity share falls to 80 percent and 60 percent, respectively.[15]

Figures 9.3 to 9.6 and table 9.1 combine the elements of the first two figures to compare certainty equivalents by earnings decile and equity portfolio share for each of the four possible formulas for the traditional benefit. Figure 9.3 shows the results for the lowest earnings decile in the baseline case: PRAs funded by contributions of 2 percent of taxable payroll, a coefficient of relative risk aversion equal to 3, and real rates of return on asset classes—equity, corporate bonds, and government bonds—having the values assumed by Goss and Wade (2005) in the Social Security Adminis-

15. The extent of risk aversion can be illustrated by considering how much an individual would pay to avoid a specified risk. Consider a 50-50 chance of having wealth increase or decrease by 25 percent. An individual with a coefficient of relative risk aversion of 3 would pay about 9.1 percent of his or her wealth to avoid this risk. An investor with log utility (a coefficient of 1) would pay only 3.2 percent, while an investor with a coefficient of relative risk aversion of 5 would pay 13.5 percent.

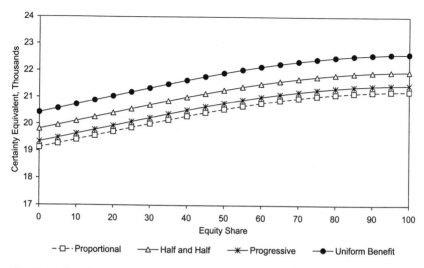

Fig. 9.4   **Certainty equivalents by benefit formulas and equity shares, baseline case, decile 4**

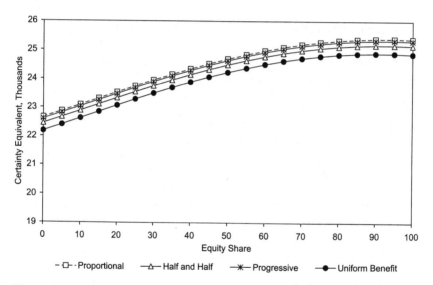

Fig. 9.5   **Certainty equivalents by benefit formulas and equity shares, baseline case, decile 7**

tration's official scoring of reform proposals: 6.2, 3.2, and 2.7 percent, respectively.

The four curves in figure 9.3 correspond to the certainty equivalents as a function of the PRA portfolio share in equity for the proportional reduction, progressive, half-and-half, and uniform benefit formulas. In all

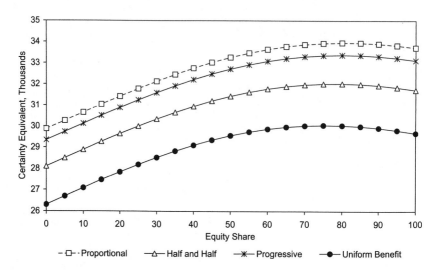

Fig. 9.6 Certainty equivalents by benefit formulas and equity shares, baseline case, decile 10

cases, the highest certainty equivalent occurs at a portfolio share of 100 percent in equities, where the curves intersect the right vertical axis. The differing degree of progressivity across the benefit formulas means that the formulas differ in the level of the certainty equivalents at this optimal portfolio share, with the most progressive benefit formula having the highest certainty equivalent. With a more progressive traditional benefit, a worker could choose to reduce the equity share—and with it, the volatility of the PRA benefit—while still surpassing the expected utility afforded by a less progressive benefit formula. For example, with the uniform benefit and the half-and-half benefit formula, a worker could allocate none of the PRA portfolio to equity and still have a higher certainty equivalent than with the proportional reduction benefit formula and a 100 percent allocation to equity. This can be seen in figure 9.3 in the greater height of the uniform benefit and half-and-half curves on the *left* vertical axis than the proportional reduction achieves on the right vertical axis. For the progressive formula, an equity share as low as 50 percent is enough to exceed the certainty equivalent generated by the proportional reduction and its optimal 100 percent equity share.

These comparisons are summarized in table 9.1. The first panel shows the maximum certainty equivalents for each benefit formula (in the columns) and each decile of the earnings distribution (in the rows), where the maximum is chosen over equity shares that are multiples of 5 between 0 and 100. The second panel shows, for each earnings decile and benefit formula, the equity share that gives that maximum certainty equivalent. Finally, the bottom panel shows, for all benefit formulas that are not the pro-

Table 9.1   **Optimal portfolio shares in equity, baseline case**

Decile	Proportional	Progressive	Half and half	Uniform
		Highest certainty equivalent		
1	16,362	16,948	18,288	20,151
2	18,373	18,817	19,819	21,185
3	19,862	20,194	20,934	21,925
4	21,236	21,466	21,968	22,621
5	22,571	22,700	22,974	23,307
6	23,914	23,950	24,011	24,044
7	25,395	25,333	25,170	24,888
8	27,212	27,035	26,606	25,946
9	29,587	29,268	28,509	27,375
10	33,956	33,381	32,029	30,058
		Optimal equity share of PRA portfolio		
1	100	100	100	100
2	100	100	100	100
3	100	100	100	100
4	100	100	100	100
5	100	100	100	100
6	95	95	95	95
7	95	95	90	90
8	90	90	90	85
9	85	85	85	85
10	80	80	80	75
		Lowest equity share with higher expected utility than proportional		
1		50	0	0
2		60	15	0
3		70	35	0
4		75	50	30
5		80	65	50
6		90	80	80

Notes: Personal retirement accounts (PRAs) are funded by 2 percent contributions. Equity returns average 6.2 percent (net of inflation and administrative costs). Utility is constant relative risk aversion, with a coefficient of 3.

portional reduction, the lowest equity share (again, in multiples of 5), that will surpass the maximum certainty equivalent available under the proportional reduction. This panel will only have rows for earnings deciles in which this is possible. For example, a uniform benefit with an equity share of zero surpasses a proportional reduction with any equity share (including the maximum, at 100 percent) for the lowest three earnings deciles.

Figure 9.4 shows the same relationships for the earnings decile that is fourth from the bottom (roughly the 35th percentile). The curves are in the same order as in figure 9.3, and the maximum certainty equivalents continue to occur at portfolio allocations of 100 percent equity. However, the vertical distances between the curves have narrowed because benefit formulas that have the same average payout but differ in progressivity will redistribute relatively less to the 4th decile than they do to the bottom decile. The maximum certainty equivalent for the proportional reduction formula can now be surpassed with equity allocations as low as 30 percent, 50 percent, and 75 percent for the uniform benefit, half-and-half, and progressive benefit formulas, respectively. The bottom panel of table 9.1 shows that there is some potential for reducing the required exposure to equity by having a more progressive benefit formula for each of the bottom six deciles, though the potential shrinks at higher deciles.

Figure 9.5 shows the same curves for the 7th decile (roughly the 65th percentile) of the earnings distribution. The ordering of the curves has now switched, with the proportional reduction offering the highest certainty equivalents for each possible equity share, followed by the progressive, half-and-half, and uniform benefit formulas. This is not surprising, as the redistribution toward the lower earning deciles must be paid for by those in higher earning deciles if the reforms have the same aggregate payouts but differ in their progressivity. The optimal equity allocations have fallen slightly, to 95 percent in equity for the proportional reduction and progressive formulas and to 90 percent in equity for the half-and-half and uniform benefit formulas. All of the curves are quite close together, indicating very little scope for trading off exposure to equity by switching benefit formulas. Figure 9.6 shows the curves for the top decile of the earnings distribution. The curves retain the same ordering from figure 9.5, but the gaps between the different formulas are now much wider. The optimal share in equity also falls to 75 percent for all four of the benefit formulas.

Figure 9.7 suggests why the progressivity of the benefit formula is such a

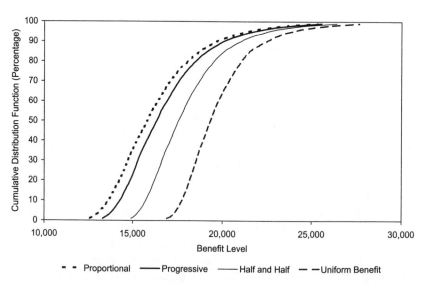

Fig. 9.7   CDFs for benefits, 2 percent PRAs, 50 percent equity shares, decile 1

powerful tool in comparison to the equity share of the PRA portfolio in affecting workers in the lower earnings deciles. The figure shows the cumulative distribution functions for the four different benefit formulas, holding constant the equity share of the PRA portfolio at 50 percent, for the bottom earnings decile. For any given benefit level, the height of the curve shows the probability of the specified benefit formula generating a benefit level that is at or below the given level. For curves that do not cross, the curve that is everywhere the lowest represents the most preferred benefit formula. As noted in the preceding, for this low-earning worker, that is the uniform benefit. Indeed, for this benefit formula, all of the variation in benefit levels is due to the variation in asset returns in different scenarios. Moving right to left on the graph, the other benefit formulas lower average benefits and add successively more earnings risk into the benefit distributions. The differences in the lowest benefit amounts across formulas (measured by the horizontal distance between the curves near the horizontal axis) are quite large. These differences also persist fairly high into the distribution of benefits, disappearing only at the highest benefit levels. Given risk averse workers, the level and likelihood of very low outcomes are of particular concern.

Figure 9.8 shows the variation in this decile's benefit distributions holding the benefit formula fixed (at proportional reduction) while varying the equity share in the portfolio from 0 to 100 percent in increments of 25 percentage points. At the very lowest benefit levels, the differences across the portfolio allocations are quite small in comparison to those shown in figure 9.7. (The scales on the axes are identical across the figures.) Low bene-

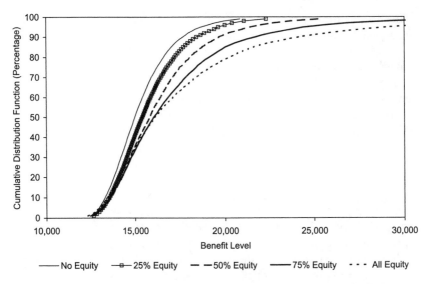

Fig. 9.8   CDFs for benefits, 2 percent PRAs, proportional reduction, decile 1

314 Andrew A. Samwick

fit outcomes are primarily due to the factor held constant across the curves—the traditional benefit formula—rather than the factor varying across the curves—the equity share in the PRA portfolio. To the extent that there are differences, both the "all equity" and "zero equity" portfolios have lower minimum benefits than more balanced portfolios. At the low end of the earnings distribution, reducing the equity share from 100 percent does not even generate a lower likelihood of very bad outcomes.

These figures establish the main results of the analysis. Given the assumed average returns on equities and bonds and their historical variation, workers with CRRA utility and a coefficient of relative risk aversion of 3 typically choose high equity shares in their PRA portfolios, regardless of the formula used to compute the traditional benefit. However, switching from a proportional reduction in the traditional benefits to any of the three more progressive benefit formulas increases the traditional benefits going to the bottom six deciles of the earnings distribution. This increase in traditional benefits gives the worker room to lower the equity share in the PRA portfolio while still achieving the same certainty equivalent available with the optimal equity share in the PRA under the proportionally reduced benefit. In the case of the maximally progressive benefit formula, in which the traditional benefit is a uniform benefit unrelated to the worker's earnings, the equity share could fall to zero for the lowest three deciles. Higher deciles or less extreme changes to the progressivity of the benefit formula result in somewhat smaller possible reductions in equity exposure.

9.6 Sensitivity Tests

In this section, the robustness of the main results is assessed by varying the degree of risk aversion, the constancy of the coefficient of relative risk aversion, the equity premium, and the size of the PRAs measured by the annual contributions as a percentage of earnings. More risk aversion, declining relative risk aversion, a lower equity premium, and larger PRAs generally reduce the optimal portfolio allocations in equities and slightly compress the differences in the allocations across configurations of the traditional benefit that achieve the same certainty equivalent. This section concludes with a discussion of life-cycle portfolio strategies.

9.6.1 Risk Aversion

The baseline choice of the coefficient of risk aversion is consistent with assumptions found in the literature on insurance and risk. Table 9.2 repeats the analysis of table 9.1 for a higher coefficient of relative risk aversion equal to 5. The first consequence of higher relative risk aversion is that all of the certainty equivalents in the top panel of table 9.2 are lower than their counterparts in table 9.1. Consistent with figure 9.2, a worker with higher risk aversion would pay a greater risk premium to avoid a given risk. The

Table 9.2   **Optimal portfolio shares in equity, higher risk aversion**

Decile	Proportional	Progressive	Half and half	Uniform
	Highest certainty equivalent			
1	15,808	16,419	17,801	19,705
2	17,582	18,059	19,124	20,547
3	18,927	19,298	20,111	21,168
4	20,173	20,447	21,032	21,762
5	21,405	21,578	21,934	22,349
6	22,622	22,706	22,858	22,982
7	23,966	23,952	23,885	23,703
8	25,648	25,515	25,179	24,630
9	27,787	27,519	26,869	25,866
10	31,823	31,297	30,054	28,223
	Optimal equity share of PRA portfolio			
1	95	95	100	100
2	85	85	90	90
3	85	85	85	85
4	80	80	80	80
5	75	75	75	75
6	75	75	75	75
7	70	70	70	70
8	70	70	70	65
9	65	65	65	60
10	60	60	60	55
	Lowest equity share with higher expected utility than proportional			
1		25	0	0
2		35	0	0
3		45	10	0
4		50	25	0
5		55	35	20
6		60	50	45

Notes: Personal retirement accounts (PRAs) are funded by 2 percent contributions. Equity returns average 6.2 percent (net of inflation and administrative costs). Utility is constant relative risk aversion, with a coefficient of 5.

next panel of table 9.2 shows that the workers seek to avoid this risk by reducing their equity shares in the PRA portfolio.[16] For example, with the proportional reduction, optimal equity shares are 95 percent in the lowest earnings decile, falling to 60 percent by the highest earnings decile.

As shown in the bottom panel of the table, changes in the progressivity of the traditional benefit allow for reductions in equity exposure in the PRA portfolio that are comparable to those for the less risk averse workers in table 9.1. For example, it is still the case that the bottom six earnings deciles have room to lower their equity exposure with more progressive tra-

16. In other words, the certainty equivalents would be even lower if the workers were constrained to hold the equity shares at the levels in the middle panel of table 9.1.

ditional benefit formulas. In addition, the allowable percentage point reductions in the equity shares are similar. For example, with a uniform benefit, the bottom four deciles can now eliminate their equity exposure entirely. With the progressive benefit formula, the equity share for the bottom earnings decile can fall from 95 to 25 percent without a loss in expected utility. Thus, the main results are robust to a higher coefficient of relative risk aversion.

9.6.2   Declining Relative Risk Aversion

The results in the middle panels of tables 9.1 and 9.2 show that the optimal allocation to equity declines at higher earnings deciles. This pattern arises due to the maintained assumption in the simulations that workers have no other sources of retirement income apart from the traditional benefit and the PRA. Because even the current Social Security formula is progressive, workers in lower earnings deciles have a greater proportion of their retirement benefits insulated from investment risk. With a homothetic expected utility function, this enables lower earning workers to take on more equity risk in their PRA portfolios.[17]

This pattern is counterfactual—in reality, investment allocations to equity rise dramatically with earnings.[18] One way to make the simulations more consistent with observed investment behavior is to modify the expected utility function to exhibit declining, rather than constant, relative risk aversion. The simplest such modification to make is to introduce a "subsistence level" of retirement benefit into the utility function, via the parameter k in:

$$u(b) = \frac{(b - k)^{1-\gamma}}{1 - \gamma}.$$

Note that $k = 0$ corresponds to CRRA utility and that with k greater than zero, utility is not defined for retirement benefit levels below k. For retirement benefit levels above k, utility is measured relative to the subsistence level. Because low-earning deciles have benefits closest to this subsistence level, they will lower their equity allocations relative to the CRRA case. The certainty equivalent for this declining relative risk aversion (DRRA) expected utility function is given by:

$$b_{CE} = k + \{(1 - \gamma)E[u(b)]\}^{1/(1-\gamma)} = k + \{E[(b - k)^{1-\gamma}]\}^{1/(1-\gamma)}.$$

17. This assumption also generates the tendency for more progressive benefit formulas to have higher optimal allocations to equity for the bottom earnings deciles and lower optimal allocations to equity for the top earnings deciles. Greater progressivity results in more non-PRA benefits at low earnings deciles and less non-PRA benefits, relative to lifetime earnings, at high earnings deciles.

18. See, for example, the tabulations in Bucks, Kennickell, and Moore (2006) or the multivariate estimates in Poterba and Samwick (2003), both based on data from the Surveys of Consumer Finances.

Table 9.3   **Optimal portfolio shares in equity, declining relative risk aversion**

Decile	Proportional	Progressive	Half and half	Uniform
		Highest certainty equivalent		
1	15,199	15,946	17,516	19,558
2	17,010	17,605	18,842	20,398
3	18,423	18,894	19,856	21,028
4	19,746	20,101	20,809	21,634
5	21,094	21,320	21,760	22,240
6	22,386	22,510	22,724	22,893
7	23,858	23,862	23,819	23,648
8	25,691	25,555	25,206	24,626
9	28,002	27,711	27,014	25,941
10	32,366	31,796	30,454	28,472
		Optimal equity share of PRA portfolio		
1	75	80	90	95
2	75	75	80	85
3	75	75	80	80
4	75	75	75	80
5	75	75	75	75
6	70	70	75	70
7	70	70	70	70
8	70	70	70	65
9	70	70	65	65
10	65	65	60	60
		Lowest equity share with higher expected utility than proportional		
1		0	0	0
2		20	0	0
3		30	0	0
4		40	15	0
5		50	30	15
6		55	45	35

Notes: Personal retirement accounts (PRAs) are funded by 2 percent contributions. Equity returns average 6.2 percent (net of inflation and administrative costs). Utility is declining relative risk aversion, with a coefficient of 3 and subsistence level of 10,000.

Tables 9.3 and 9.4 repeat the analyses in tables 9.1 and 9.2 using this DRRA expected utility function. The subsistence level is assumed to be $10,000, which is close to the minimum benefit for the lowest earning decile shown in figure 9.7. The top panels of the tables show that the certainty equivalents are lower when expected utility exhibits declining rather than constant relative risk aversion.[19] The middle panels of the tables show that optimal equity allocations are also lower with declining relative risk aversion.

19. The degree of relative risk aversion for any expected utility function is given by $-b \cdot u''(\ )/u'(\ )$. For the DRRA utility function, this expression is $\gamma^* b/(b-k)$, which is equal to the constant γ for $k = 0$. When $k > 0$, this expression declines toward γ as b increases.

Table 9.4   **Optimal portfolio shares in equity, higher and declining relative risk aversion**

Decile	Proportional	Progressive	Half and half	Uniform
		Highest certainty equivalent		
1	14,533	15,356	17,018	19,109
2	16,100	16,791	18,166	19,822
3	17,324	17,913	19,053	20,358
4	18,510	18,986	19,891	20,872
5	19,783	20,120	20,749	21,391
6	20,898	21,154	21,585	21,939
7	22,305	22,414	22,564	22,577
8	24,063	24,010	23,827	23,418
9	26,088	25,889	25,377	24,524
10	30,199	29,705	28,529	26,748
		Optimal equity share of PRA portfolio		
1	55	60	65	75
2	50	55	60	65
3	55	55	60	60
4	50	55	55	60
5	55	55	55	55
6	50	50	50	50
7	50	50	50	50
8	50	50	50	45
9	50	50	50	45
10	45	45	45	40
	Lowest equity share with higher expected utility than proportional			
1		0	0	0
2		0	0	0
3		10	0	0
4		15	0	0
5		25	0	0
6		30	10	0
7		40	30	30

Notes: Personal retirement accounts (PRAs) are funded by 2 percent contributions. Equity returns average 6.2 percent (net of inflation and administrative costs). Utility is declining relative risk aversion, with a coefficient of 5 and subsistence level of 10,000.

However, comparisons of the changes in the optimal equity allocations by earnings decile and across traditional benefit formulas relative to the CRRA case are not straightforward. For example, with $\gamma = 3$, equity shares with a proportional reduction in the traditional benefit fall from 75 to 65 percent over the earnings deciles, compared to a decline from 100 to 80 percent in the CRRA case, indicating less sensitivity to earnings decile. However, with a uniform benefit, they fall from 95 to 60 percent over the earnings deciles, compared to a decline from 100 to 75 percent in the CRRA case, indicating more sensitivity to earnings decile. Similar results hold for the higher risk aversion in table 9.4 and in the differences across columns in the respective cases.

Nonetheless, the bottom panels of the tables show that changing from a proportional reduction to a more progressive benefit formula can lessen equity exposure by as much or more than in the CRRA case. For example, with $\gamma = 3$, the bottom six deciles can again have their equity exposure reduced. With a uniform benefit, the bottom four deciles can reduce equity exposure to zero without falling behind the proportional reduction. The 6th decile can lower its equity share from 70 to 35 percent, compared to a reduction from 95 to 80 percent in the CRRA case shown in table 9.1. With the progressive formula, the bottom decile can reduce its equity exposure down to zero, and the 6th decile can reduce its equity share from 75 to 55 percent (compared to a reduction from 95 to 90 percent in the CRRA case). The results in table 9.4 at higher risk aversion levels are even more pronounced. Thus, the main results shown in the previous section are robust to and strengthened by a switch to an expected utility function that exhibits declining rather than constant relative risk aversion.

9.6.3   Lower Equity Premium

The sustainability of the premium that has existed to investments in equities historically has been the subject of considerable debate. Particularly in the case of financial market returns, past performance may be an unreliable guide to future outcomes. For example, if over the past thirty years, systematic risk in the stock market fell, then the appropriate rate of return to assume going forward would be lower. However, during this period of time that risk fell, the reduction in risk would have generated abnormally high returns to equity. These high holding period returns would have arisen precisely because future ex ante returns had fallen and would thus be a poor guide to forecasting those future returns.[20]

In light of such considerations, table 9.5 reports the results of simulations in which the expected return on equities is lowered from 6.2 percent to 4.7 percent. Personal retirement account contributions remain 2 percent of earnings per year, and the comparisons are shown for a CRRA utility function with a relative risk aversion coefficient of 3. As expected, the 150 basis point reduction in the equity premium lowers the certainty equivalents for all earnings deciles and benefit formulas, shown in the top panel. The lower equity premium also shifts the optimal portfolio allocations to lower equity. For the proportional reduction, equity shares range from 85 to 55 percent, compared to 100 to 80 percent in table 9.1. For the uniform

---

20. For a discussion of the issues associated with choosing a real return on stocks for the long term, see the papers by John Campbell, Peter Diamond, and John Shoven in Social Security Advisory Board (2001).

Table 9.5   **Optimal portfolio shares in equity, lower equity returns**

Decile	Proportional	Progressive	Half and half	Uniform
		Highest certainty equivalent		
1	15,473	16,045	17,355	19,178
2	17,265	17,694	18,662	19,984
3	18,596	18,916	19,628	20,580
4	19,820	20,040	20,522	21,147
5	21,023	21,146	21,407	21,723
6	22,220	22,255	22,312	22,340
7	23,549	23,490	23,334	23,061
8	25,162	24,994	24,588	23,963
9	27,275	26,972	26,256	25,192
10	31,185	30,639	29,366	27,510
		Optimal equity share of PRA portfolio		
1	85	90	90	95
2	80	80	80	85
3	75	75	75	75
4	75	75	75	75
5	70	70	70	70
6	65	65	65	65
7	65	65	65	60
8	60	60	60	60
9	60	60	55	55
10	55	55	50	50
		Lowest equity share with higher expected utility than proportional		
1		0	0	0
2		15	0	0
3		25	0	0
4		35	5	0
5		45	25	5
6		55	50	45

Notes: Personal retirement accounts (PRAs) are funded by 2 percent contributions. Equity returns average 4.7 percent (net of inflation and administrative costs). Utility is constant relative risk aversion, with a coefficient of 3.

benefit, equity shares range from 95 to 50 percent, compared to 100 to 75 percent in table 9.1.

With a lower equity premium, there is greater scope for changes in the progressivity of the benefit formula to substitute for higher equity allocations. The bottom panel of table 9.5 shows that with a uniform benefit, the bottom four deciles can reduce their equity shares to zero to keep pace with the optimal allocations of 75 to 85 percent in the proportional reduction case. The 6th decile can reduce its equity share to 45 percent from 65 percent. In table 9.1, with the higher equity premium, this decile could reduce its equity share only to 80 percent from 95 percent. Possible reductions in equity exposure for other benefit formulas are smaller than with the uniform benefit formula but similarly larger than their counterparts with the higher equity premium in table 9.1. Thus, the main results in the previous section are robust and even strengthened in the presence of a lower equity premium.

9.6.4   Larger Personal Retirement Accounts

Compared to the investment-based reform plans that have been proposed (see note 2), a PRA funded by only a 2 percent contribution is fairly small. The ability of progressivity in the traditional benefit to offset financial risk in the PRAs depends on the relative size of the two benefits. To investigate this dependence and extend the analysis to cover more of the range of proposed reforms, table 9.6 presents the results of simulations in

Table 9.6 **Optimal portfolio shares in equity, larger personal retirement accounts (PRAs)**

Decile	Proportional	Progressive	Half and half	Uniform
		Highest certainty equivalent		
1	17,628	18,231	19,608	21,522
2	20,000	20,460	21,500	22,921
3	21,780	22,126	22,898	23,936
4	23,440	23,681	24,213	24,908
5	25,066	25,205	25,503	25,874
6	26,725	26,771	26,854	26,921
7	28,569	28,515	28,371	28,118
8	30,872	30,698	30,279	29,639
9	33,896	33,578	32,824	31,702
10	39,522	38,941	37,579	35,590
		Optimal equity share of PRA portfolio		
1	100	100	100	100
2	95	95	100	100
3	95	95	95	95
4	90	90	90	90
5	85	85	85	85
6	85	85	85	85
7	80	80	80	80
8	80	80	80	75
9	75	75	75	75
10	70	70	70	65
	Lowest equity share with higher expected utility than proportional			
1		50	0	0
2		60	25	0
3		65	35	10
4		70	50	30
5		70	60	45
6		80	70	65

Notes: PRAs are funded by 3 percent contributions. Equity returns average 6.2 percent (net of inflation and administrative costs). Utility is constant relative risk aversion, with a coefficient of 3.

which the annual PRA contribution is increased from 2 to 3 percent of earnings. The certainty equivalents in the top panel are all naturally higher than their counterparts in table 9.1 because the additional 1 percent contributions are not accounted for by reduced consumption elsewhere in this framework. The middle panel of the table shows that optimal equity allocations are slightly lower with the larger PRAs. As the PRAs get larger relative to the traditional benefit, workers seek to mitigate their risk exposure through lower allocations to equity.

The bottom panel shows that the ability to offset equity exposure through more progressive traditional benefit formulas can be slightly lower or higher, depending on the earnings decile and benefit formula. With a uniform benefit, the bottom two deciles can reduce their equity shares to zero to keep pace with the optimal allocations of 95 to 100 percent in the proportional reduction case. In table 9.1, with the smaller PRAs, the bottom three deciles could eliminate all equity exposure. The 6th decile can reduce its equity share to 65 percent from 85 percent, compared to a reduction to 80 percent from 95 percent in table 9.1. For the progressive benefit formula, reductions in equity exposure relative to the proportional reduction formula are comparable to those in table 9.1.

9.6.5   Life-Cycle Portfolios

As noted in the preceding, prior studies have analyzed the use of life-cycle investment strategies to mitigate financial risk in PRAs. Figure 9.9 compares a portfolio with an age-invariant allocation of 50 percent to equity with three life-cycle strategies that shift from equity to bonds as re-

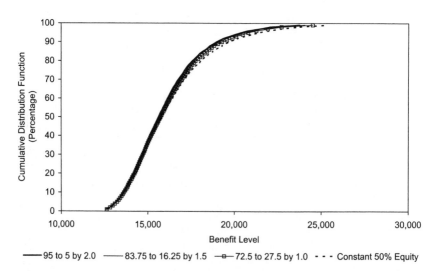

Fig. 9.9   CDFs for benefits, life-cycle allocations, baseline, proportional reduction, decile 1

tirement approaches. The first starts at a 95 percent equity share and decreases 2 percentage points per year, reaching 5 percent on the eve of retirement. The second starts at an 83.75 percent equity share and decreases 1.5 percentage points per year, reaching 16.25 percent on the eve of retirement. The third starts at a 72.5 percent equity share and decreases by 1 percentage point per year, reaching 27.5 percent on the eve of retirement. All three strategies are centered on a 50 percent equity share, based on the simple average of the allocation rules by age. The figure pertains to the lowest earnings decile and shows the cumulative distribution functions for each of the four investment options.

There are two important features of the graph. First, the curves all lie virtually on top of each other. There cannot be much of an improvement in expected utility by switching to a life-cycle strategy if such a strategy results in a distribution of benefits that is so similar to the age-invariant portfolio allocation. Second, the life-cycle strategies lie above the age-invariant portfolio for all but the very lowest percentiles of the distributions, the more so the greater the decline in the equity allocation with age. The reason is that the life-cycle strategies do not have the same expected benefits as the age-invariant portfolio because the life-cycle strategies focus the high-equity allocations on the early years, when many years of contributions are yet to be made.

Thus, life-cycle strategies may be desirable, but this is so in the current context primarily because they serve to reduce the overall level of equity exposure. This may be a desirable goal—for example, if the equity premium is low enough or volatility of returns is high enough—but it can be achieved more straightforwardly with a simple reduction in the age-invariant portfolio share in equities given the parameters used in the preceding simulations.

9.7 Conclusions

Policymakers seeking to design investment-based Social Security reform proposals have wrestled with the issue of how much financial risk is appropriate for individuals to bear. Suggested methods of alleviating risk have focused on strategies that amount to requiring more bonds relative to equity in the PRAs, whether through the purchase of guarantees or life-cycle investment strategies. It is worth emphasizing that most of the simulations in this chapter suggest fairly high optimal allocations to equities, particularly by those in the lowest deciles of the earnings distribution. Direct restrictions on equity holding in PRAs are likely to prove unpopular, particularly among those whose opportunities are most broadened by the chance to invest their mandatory contributions in equities. This chapter suggests another possibility for alleviating the consequences of financial risk, namely, increasing the progressivity of the traditional benefit. Doing so insulates workers in the lower part of the benefit distribution against possibly adverse shocks to financial returns without constraining them to not invest in equities.

The main simulations in the chapter compare proportional reductions in traditional benefits with more progressive reductions. The key finding is that under baseline parameters, the most progressive traditional benefit—a flat benefit independent of earnings—allows the allocation to equities to be reduced to zero for the lowest three earnings deciles relative to the optimal allocation when the traditional benefits are reduced proportionately based on the current formula. The next three deciles are able to achieve some reduction in equity exposure as well. Under less extreme changes to the traditional benefit, such as that proposed by Liebman, MacGuineas, and Samwick (2005), the allocation to equities can be decreased by half for the lowest earnings decile and by smaller fractions for an additional five deciles. Sensitivity tests show that optimal allocations to equities typically decrease with higher risk aversion, declining risk aversion, a lower equity premium, or larger accounts, but the general pattern of results persists and in some cases allows for greater equity reduction through higher progressivity in the traditional benefit formula.

The results in this chapter suggest two avenues for further research. First, the present analysis used a very stylized model of the initial earnings distribution and its evolution over time to simulate the distribution of future benefits. Actual data and more sophisticated time series estimates could be incorporated. Second, the present analysis focused on time-invariant portfolio allocations in the PRAs, which were further assumed to be the worker's only source of investment wealth. While the latter might be a reasonable approximation for the lowest earning households, higher earning households are likely to have existing holdings of equities that make the portfolio allocation decision in the PRA less consequential. Extending the current framework to allow for optimal, age-dependent portfolio allocations and for saving in accounts other than the PRAs would provide better estimates of the extent to which greater progressivity can protect low earners from investment risk and of the size of the welfare costs paid by higher earners for providing this protection.

Appendix

Table 9A.1 **Mean benefits by earnings decile**

Decile	Traditional benefits				
	Current law	Proportional	Progressive	Half and half	Uniform
1	22,033	13,220	13,739	14,949	16,678
2	23,851	14,311	14,666	15,494	16,678
3	25,127	15,076	15,317	15,877	16,678
4	26,212	15,727	15,870	16,203	16,678
5	27,227	16,336	16,388	16,507	16,678
6	28,181	16,908	16,874	16,793	16,678
7	29,177	17,506	17,382	17,092	16,678
8	30,304	18,182	17,956	17,430	16,678
9	31,726	19,036	18,682	17,857	16,678
10	34,130	20,478	19,907	18,578	16,678
All	27,797	16,678	16,678	16,678	16,678

	Real annuities from 2% PRAs, real equity returns average 6.2%				
	No equity	25% equity	50% equity	75% equity	All equity
1	2,069	2,532	3,125	3,884	4,858
2	2,840	3,481	4,307	5,377	6,769
3	3,451	4,226	5,225	6,516	8,184
4	4,015	4,915	6,075	7,575	9,524
5	4,590	5,621	6,948	8,659	10,871
6	5,234	6,402	7,896	9,813	12,278
7	5,974	7,321	9,056	11,298	14,198
8	6,901	8,448	10,435	12,996	16,302
9	8,185	10,021	12,379	15,426	19,382
10	10,498	12,907	16,008	20,009	25,171
All	5,376	6,587	8,145	10,155	12,754

	Real annuities from 2% PRAs, real equity returns average 4.7%				
	No equity	25% equity	50% equity	75% equity	All equity
1	2,069	2,303	2,570	2,875	3,220
2	2,840	3,166	3,544	3,981	4,489
3	3,451	3,844	4,298	4,822	5,424
4	4,015	4,471	4,996	5,604	6,306
5	4,590	5,113	5,715	6,409	7,206
6	5,234	5,822	6,493	7,259	8,132
7	5,974	6,658	7,446	8,355	9,401
8	6,901	7,681	8,576	9,605	10,786
9	8,185	9,106	10,164	11,383	12,793
10	10,498	11,715	13,113	14,713	16,541
All	5,376	5,988	6,692	7,500	8,430

Note: PRA = personal retirement account.

References

Board of Trustees, Federal Old-Age and Survivors Insurance and Federal Disability Insurance Trust Funds. 2006. *Annual report.* Washington, DC: GPO. http://www.ssa.gov/OACT/TR/TR06/tr06.pdf.

Bucks, Brian K., Arthur B. Kennickell, and Kevin B. Moore. 2006. Recent changes in U.S. family finances: Evidence from the 2001 and 2004 Survey of Consumer Finances. *Federal Reserve Bulletin* 92 (February): A1–A38. http://www.federal reserve.gov/pubs/oss/oss2/2004/bull0206.pdf.

Feldstein, Martin S., and Elena Ranguelova. 2001a. Accumulated pension collars: A market approach to reducing the risk of investment-based Social Security reform. In *Tax policy and the economy 2000,* ed. James M. Poterba. Cambridge, MA: MIT Press.

———. 2001b. Individual risk in an investment-based Social Security system. *American Economic Review* 91 (4): 1116–25.

Goss, Stephen C., and Alice H. Wade. 2005. Estimated financial effects of "A nonpartisan approach to reforming Social Security—A proposal developed by Jeffrey Liebman, Maya MacGuineas, and Andrew Samwick." Social Security Administration. Manuscript, November 17. http://www.ssa.gov/OACT/solvency/Liebman_20051117.pdf.

Hubbard, R. Glenn, Jonathan S. Skinner, and Stephen P. Zeldes. 1994. The importance of precautionary motives in explaining individual and aggregate saving. *Carnegie Rochester Conference Series on Public Policy* 40:59–125.

Ibbotson Associates. 2006. *Stocks, bonds, bills, and inflation yearbook 2006.* Chicago: Ibbotson Associates.

Kunkel, Jeffrey L. 1996. Frequency distribution of wage earners by wage level. Actuarial Note no. 135. Washington, DC: Social Security Administration, Office of the Actuary, July. http://www.ssa.gov/OACT/NOTES/pdf_notes/note135.pdf.

Liebman, Jeffrey, Maya MacGuineas, and Andrew Samwick. 2005. Nonpartisan Social Security reform plan. Harvard University. Manuscript, December. http://www.ksg.harvard.edu/jeffreyliebman/lms_nonpartisan_plan_description.pdf.

Poterba, James M., Joshua Rauh, Steven F. Venti, and David A. Wise. 2006. Lifecycle asset allocation strategies and the distribution of 401(k) retirement wealth. National Bureau of Economic Research Working Paper no. 11974. Cambridge, MA: National Bureau of Economic Research, January. http://www.nber.org/papers/w11974.

Poterba, James M., and Andrew A. Samwick. 2003. Taxation and household portfolio composition: U.S. evidence from the 1980s and 1990s. *Journal of Public Economics* 87 (January): 5–38.

Samwick, Andrew A. 1999. Social Security reform in the United States. *National Tax Journal* 52 (December): 819–42.

———. 2004. Social Security reform: The United States in 2002. In *Pensions: Challenges and reform,* ed. Einar Overbye and Peter A. Kemp, 53–69. Aldershot, UK: Ashgate.

Social Security Administration, Office of Policy (SSA). 2006. *Annual statistical supplement to the Social Security bulletin, 2005.* Washington, DC: Social Security Administration, February. http://www.socialsecurity.gov/policy/docs/statcomps/supplement/2005/.

Social Security Advisory Board. 2001. Estimating the real rate of return on stocks over the long term. Social Security Advisory Board, August. http://www.ssab.gov/Publications/Financing/estimated%20rate%20of%20return.pdf.

Topel, Robert H., and Michael P. Ward. 1992. Job mobility and the careers of young men. *Quarterly Journal of Economics* 107 (2): 439–79.
World Bank. 1994. *Averting the old age crisis: Policies to protect the old and promote growth.* New York: Oxford University Press.

Comment   Michael Hurd

An important aspect of the debate about personal retirement accounts concerns their investment in equities. On the one side, a main reason for having personal retirement accounts is that indeed they can be invested in equities that historically have a greater rate of return than bonds and a much greater rate of return than the internal rate of return on Social Security contributions. On the other side is the risk that comes with the higher mean rate of return: there are significant chances that a worker could end up worse off than under a Social Security system that has no personal retirement accounts. Of particular concern is the risk to low-wage workers who are unlikely to have other resources to buffer against bad outcomes. Consequently, there have been a number of proposals to provide insurance against these unfavorable outcomes. This chapter points out that the debate need not be restricted to personal retirement accounts within the structure of the existing Social Security system. Some of the risk from low rates of return in private retirement accounts could be partially offset by increased progressivity in the Social Security program. This is an interesting alternative to insurance against bad outcomes on rates of return and in some ways would be preferable: insurance has the undesirable effect of reducing the mean rate of return on equities because of the cost of insurance. Or said differently, insurance reduces the amount invested in equities partly offsetting the main reason for having personal retirement account in the first place.

The simulations show that there is considerable scope for investing in equities in personal retirement accounts while protecting the bottom part of the income distribution via an increase in the progressivity of the Social Security system. For example, in figure 9.1, the "half-and-half" progressivity structure with no investment in equity will provide greater expected utility for a typical worker in the bottom income decile than the existing structure fully invested in equities. At the same time, those in the top income decile could invest about 80 percent in equities and achieve greater expected utility than under the present structure but with no equities (figure 9.6). Said differently, compared with the present situation, the bottom decile could have greater expected utility and no investment risk, and the top decile

Michael Hurd is a senior economist and director of the RAND Center for the Study of Aging, and a research associate of the National Bureau of Economic Research.

could have greater expected utility with investment risk. If we think those in the bottom part of the income distribution do not want any investment risk as evidenced by their having few (if any) equities in their portfolios, while those in the upper income deciles can handle investment risk as evidenced by their risk taking in other parts of their portfolios, we might favor this altered situation. It should be pointed out, however, that scenario is similar to having insurance against bad outcomes in that the total amount invested in equities is less than optimal.

The key to this proposal is to increase progressivity. However, greater progressivity means that Social Security contributions will become more of a tax and less of an investment. At the extreme of a flat benefit, it is completely a tax, which has possible labor supply effects and corresponding deadweight losses. Possibly more important are political economy effects. Social Security enjoys widespread political support for several reasons, but probably a leading reason is that it is viewed as an earned right and that greater participation leads to greater benefits. I believe that policymakers should be very cautious to disturb that political equilibrium.

The metric used in the chapter to compare the various options is expected utility. I have some reservations about this approach. Total public pension benefits are the sum of Social Security benefits and the income flow resulting from annuitizing the personal retirement account. Expected utility is calculated by assuming that consumption equals total benefits. For most people, however, consumption is not equal to this flow because they have other economic resources. For example, a well-to-do person will finance consumption out of public pension benefits, employer-sponsored pension benefits including 401k plans, interest and dividends, and from savings (spend-down of capital). The 2 percent of Social Security earnings with the current contribution cap is a very small part of the economic resources of such a person. Thus, the variation in the value of a personal retirement account due to the stochastic rate of return on equities will not cause much variation in consumption as a fraction of total consumption. Said differently, for a well-to-do person, the utility function is practically linear over the relevant amount of variation induced by stochastic rates of return. This would not be true of someone who has little other financial resources. At the extreme would be someone with no other resources. Old-Age and Survivors Insurance (OASI) taxes are 10.6 percent of taxable earnings so that the 2 percent personal retirement account contribution would amount to about 16 percent of total economic resources at retirement under the assumption that both Social Security contributions and the personal retirement account have the same rate of return.[1] Thus, stochastic variation in

1. Of course, if the personal retirement account delivers a much greater rate of return, as would be the case if it were invested in equities at historical market rates of return, it would accumulate to a much greater fraction of economic resources at retirement.

rates of return in the personal retirement account would translate directly into variation in consumption and in utility.

Samwick does not directly address this issue, but does consider an alternative utility function that admits to variation in risk aversion with economic status. He observes that low-wealth households have a large fraction of their portfolios in riskless Social Security, which should lead them to hold a large fraction of their assets in equities. However, just the opposite is observed in the data: low-wealth households are unlikely to hold equities. A possible resolution is that the underlying utility function of low-wealth households exhibits greater risk aversion. Thus, he proposes an alternative to the constant relative risk aversion (CRRA) utility:

$$u(b) = \frac{(b - k)^{1-\gamma}}{1 - \gamma},$$

where b is consumption and k is necessary expenditures. Under this utility function, relative risk aversion declines with b, which means that low-spending households are less likely to hold risky portfolios. While this utility function probably leads to a better description of behavior with respect to portfolio choice, it does not really address the issue of alternative sources of finance for consumption. Furthermore, as implemented, households at the low end of the consumption distribution become very risk averse. For example, in figure 9.7, the 20th percentile of consumption is about $1,400, and with $k = \$10,000$, a household at the 20th percentile would have a relative risk aversion parameter of about 10.5. This is an extreme value of risk aversion.

Because of the inability to account for other resources that can be used for consumption, there is an imprecise correspondence between variation in total benefit outcomes and variation in utility. Therefore, I prefer analysis of the distributions of actual benefit outcomes as in figures 9.7 and 9.8. For example, in figure 9.7 with proportional reduction (which has the current Social Security benefit structure but at a reduced level), the median benefit would be about $1,600. There is a 10 percent chance that benefits would be less than approximately $1,350 and a 10 percent chance they would be more than approximately $1,950. In my view, this is substantial benefit risk: the range of the middle 80 percent of the distribution is $600, which is about 0.38 of the median.

A good deal of the variation in benefits appears to arise from earnings risk. This can be seen from figure 9.7 for the "uniform benefit" scenario. Under this scenario, the Social Security benefit is independent of earnings. All the variation in benefit comes from the personal retirement account part of the benefit. Some is due to investment risk and some due to earnings risk because the contribution to the personal retirement account is proportional to earnings. Even so, the curve is beginning to look like a step function, which would be the case with no risk. Indeed, the ratio of the range of the middle 80 percent to the median is about 0.23. The importance of pure earnings risk is further shown in figure 9.8 for the "no equity" simulation. The same measure of risk is about 0.37.

Apparently earnings risk is an important determinant of the results. It affects the amount in personal retirement accounts even in the absence of rate-of-return risk because a fixed percentage of earnings is put into the account. It affects the benefit from Social Security, but its importance depends on the progressivity of the benefit schedule. It would be useful to present some information about the contribution of earnings risk to total risk. But rather than presenting certainty equivalents as in most of the tables, it would be better to present the ranges of the benefit outcomes.

In summary, the chapter provides an additional way of thinking about protection against unfavorable outcomes were some part of personal retirement accounts invested in equities. However, the political economy of the present public support of the Social Security system should be carefully considered before implementing increased progressivity.

IV

Demographics, Asset Flows, and Macroeconomic Markets

10

The Decline of Defined Benefit Retirement Plans and Asset Flows

James M. Poterba, Steven F. Venti, and David A. Wise

Many analysts have suggested that population aging will adversely affect the assets of baby boomers when they retire. They argue that when a large population cohort is working and accumulating resources for retirement, their demand for wealth is high, and this raises the price of financial assets and other stores of wealth. Conversely, when a large cohort retires, the argument suggests that cohort members are likely to sell their assets to finance consumption and thereby to drive down asset prices. This argument suggests that the rapidly increasing population of older people in the United States and around the world might lead to lower returns in financial markets in the decades ahead.

This chapter examines the effect of population aging on the demand for financial assets in retirement saving plans, particularly defined benefit (DB) plans, in the United States. It is part of a larger project that aims to evaluate the potential empirical importance of demographic trends on financial market returns in the United States. Our analysis focuses on re-

James M. Poterba is the Mitsui Professor of Economics at the Massachusetts Institute of Technology, and president of the National Bureau of Economic Research. Steven F. Venti is the DeWalt Ankeny Professor of Economic Policy and a professor of economics at Dartmouth College, and a research associate of the National Bureau of Economic Research. David A. Wise is the John F. Stambaugh Professor of Political Economy at the John F. Kennedy School of Government, Harvard University, and director of the program on the economics of aging at the National Bureau of Economic Research.

This research was supported by the U.S. Social Security Administration (SSA) through grant #10-P-98363-1-03 to the National Bureau of Economic Research (NBER) and by the National Institute of Aging (NIA) under grant PO1-AG005842 to the National Bureau of Economic Research. The findings and conclusions expressed are solely those of the authors and do not represent the views of any agency of the federal government or the NBER. We thank Jonathan Skinner, Annamaria Lusardi, and participants in the Woodstock Conference on Retirement Research for their comments.

tirement saving programs because the future effect of demographic trends on financial asset demand is likely to be most pronounced in asset holdings in retirement saving plans. The inflows and outflows from these plans, particularly DB plans, are sensitive to demographic trends. Thus, a key stepping stone in understanding the effect of population age structure on asset returns is forecasting the effect of demographic trends on the net cash flows to retirement saving plans and the stock of assets in these plans.

Over the past two and a half decades, there has been a fundamental change in saving for retirement in the United States. There has been a rapid shift from saving through employer-managed DB pensions to defined contribution (DC) retirement saving plans that are largely controlled by employees. Just two or three decades ago, employer-provided DB plans were the primary means of saving for retirement in the United States. But since that time, 401(k) and other personal retirement accounts have become the principal form of retirement saving in the private sector. Defined benefit plans have remained an important form of retirement saving for federal employees and for state and local employees, although even for these employees, personal retirement accounts are becoming increasingly important. More than 80 percent of private retirement plan contributions in 2000 and 2001 were to 401(k) and other personal accounts. Contributions to personal retirement plans accounted for only 12 percent of total contributions to federal pension plans in 2000, but had increased to 17 percent by 2004. Thus, to understand the effect of demographic trends on the demand for retirement assets in the coming decades, it is important to evaluate the likely flows into and out of both 401(k) and DB plans.

In Poterba, Venti, and Wise (2008), we described the rise of 401(k) plans and the implications of this rise for the flow of assets into and out of 401(k) plans over the next four decades. In this chapter we describe the decline in DB plans and assess its implications for the flow of assets into and out of DB plans over the next four decades. We then bring together projections of net pension flows to both DB and DC plans. Schieber and Shoven (1997) consider the implications of population aging for private pension fund saving and project saving as a percent of payrolls. Their projection method differs from ours, and it does not consider the rising importance of self-directed DC plans.

There is a substantial and growing literature on the link between population age structure and returns in financial markets. The U.S. Government Accountability Office (2006) provides a recent review of related research. Several studies have used an overlapping-generations framework to explore the theoretical effects of a transitory increase in the population growth rate, a "baby boom," on the equilibrium rate of return. These studies, while based on stylized models, offer valuable insight on the direction of asset market effects. Other research has taken a more empirical approach and explored the reduced from relationship between summary measures of demographic structure and the returns to investors holding bonds and stocks. The existing findings, illustrated, for example, in Brooks (2002), Geanakoplos, Magill, and Quinzii (2004), and Poterba (2005), span a range of different potential outcomes. Most of the existing work adopts a closed-economy approach, either studying how a baby boom in a single economy will affect returns in that economy or examining the correlation between a nation's population structure and financial market returns in that nation. Recent analyses, however, such as Boersch-Supan, Ludwig, and Winter (2005) and Krueger and Ludwig (2006), move beyond this setting and examine how demographic trends affect international capital flows as well as domestic asset markets.

Very few studies have used household-level data on asset accumulation to project future asset demand. This chapter on DB plans and our companion paper on 401(k) plans begin with a disaggregated analysis of current asset flows in and out of the pension system and use these flows as a base to project pension assets in future years. These projections are a critical input to assessing the effect of demographically induced asset flows on market rates of return.

This chapter is divided into ten sections. In the first, we present a cohort description of the decline in the participation rate of *employed* persons in DB plans over the past two decades. Then we describe a series of analyses that provide the basis for projections of future assets in DB plans. We begin section 10.2 with a cohort description of the dollar amount of pension benefits received by persons over age fifty-five, and we develop projections of DB benefits in the future. In section 10.3, we present a parallel cohort description of the probability of receipt of DB benefits by persons over the age of fifty-five. In section 10.4, we return to the estimation of DB participation during the working years. While in the first section we considered DB participation profiles for *employed* persons, here we consider analogous profiles for *all persons* in the population. The estimates obtained in this section are used to supplement the estimates obtained in section 10.3 to project benefits after retirement for all persons in the population. In section 10.5, we combine the information described in the previous three sections to develop projections of the total value of DB benefits in future years. Section 10.6 presents projections of DB pension wealth for cohorts retiring between 1982 and 2040 and, for each cohort, compares DB wealth to projected 401(k) assets from Poterba, Venti, and Wise (2008). In section 10.7, we consider projections of the total value of assets in DB trust funds. Section 10.8 brings together projections for both DB and 401(k) plans to explore the flow in and out of the pension system as a whole. It is the change in the assets in DB trust funds combined with the change in the assets in personal retirement accounts that may affect the rate of return on the investments of future generations of retirees. In section 10.9, we discuss what our projections imply for the relative change in asset demand in the future. Section 10.10 summarizes our findings.

10.1   Participation of Employees in DB Plans

Defined benefit participation data were obtained form the several waves of the Survey of Income and Program Participation (SIPP) for the years 1984, 1987, 1991, 1993, 1995, 1998, and 2003. Our analysis here and in subsequent sections is based on organization of the data by cohort. We sometimes define cohorts by the age of the cohort in 1984 and sometimes by the year in which the cohort attains age sixty-five. When referring to the cohort age in 1984, the age is proceeded by "C." When referring to the year the cohort attains age sixty-five, the year is proceeded by "A." Thus, C65 and A1984 identify the same cohort.

To project DB participation in the future, or to predict DB participation in earlier years, we must make projections beyond the range of the observed SIPP data. The cohorts for which data are observed, and the ages for which data are observed, are shown in table 10.1. The table also shows the cohorts, and ages, for which projections are made. Data for all years spanned by the SIPP surveys are available for cohorts C25 through C45. Data for some of the survey years are available for cohorts C9 to C24 and for cohorts C46 to C64. The cohorts for which some SIPP data are available are noted in bold in the table.

Figure 10.1 shows the data for selected cohorts. It is clear that the DB participation rate of employed persons declined consistently with successively younger cohorts. For example, at age forty-five, the participation

Table 10.1   Cohorts, observed data, and projected data for defined benefit participation given employment

Cohort defined by age in 1984	Age in 1984	Age in 2003	Cohort defined by year age 65 is attained
C-1	−1	18	A2050
C0	0	19	A2049
C1	1	20	A2048
C8	8	27	A2041
C9	9	28	A2040
C25	25	43	A2024
C45	45	63	A2004
C64	64	83	A1985
C65	65	84	A1984
C100	100	119	A1949

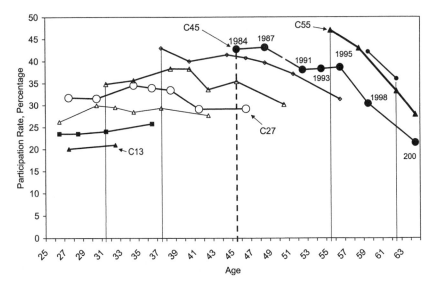

Fig. 10.1   DB participation rate of employed persons, selected cohorts

rate of those who attained age forty-five in 1984, the C45 cohort, was about 43 percent. But the participation rate of the C27 cohort, which attained age forty-five in 2002, was about 29 percent. Comparisons at other ages show similar differences.

Not only is there a cohort effect, with younger cohorts having a successively lower participation rate at all ages, but there is also a *within-cohort* decline in the participation rate with age. The within-cohort decline with age for older cohorts is likely explained in part by retirement. Defined benefit plans typically provide incentives to retire early, and DB participants, on average, retire earlier than persons without these plans; some participants may retire as early as age fifty-five. But even for younger cohorts, there is typically a within-cohort decline in DB participation rates with age.

For comparison, similar cohort data for 401(k) plans and other personal retirement plans are shown in figure 10.2. At age forty-five, the 401(k) participation rate of the cohort that attained age forty-five in 1984 was only 8 percent. But the participation rate of the cohort that attained age forty-five in 2002 was about 47 percent.

Figure 10.3 shows DB participation rates for every other cohort. Again, it is clear that with few exceptions, the data show consistently lower participation rates with successively younger cohorts.

Because we rely on the SIPP data, we have compared the SIPP participation rates by age with rates by age from the Bureau of Labor Statistics (BLS). The comparisons are shown in table 10.2. The SIPP data pertain to

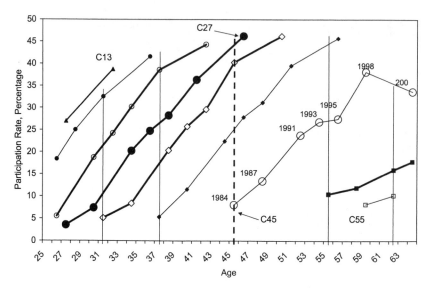

Fig. 10.2   401(k) participation rate of employed persons, selected cohorts

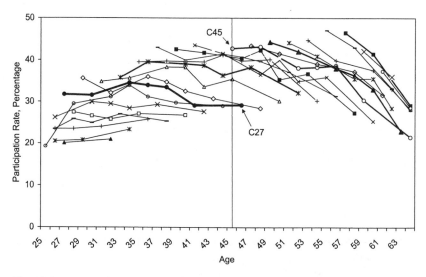

Fig. 10.3   DB participation rate for employees, every other cohort

all employees age twenty-five to sixty-four, including persons employed in private-sector firms, self-employed persons, and persons in federal, state, or local government employment. The BLS data pertain to employees of all ages, but exclude the self-employed and federal employees. Thus, the comparison is imperfect. For the four years that a direct comparison can

Table 10.2   **Defined benefit participation rate by age, based on Survey of Income and Program Participation (SIPP) and Bureau of Labor Statistics (BLS), for employed persons aged 25–64**

Year	BLS private firms	BLS private and state and local	SIPP
1984			39.4
1985			
1986			
1987			36.8
1988			
1989			
1990	35	43	
1991	34	41	34.9
1992	32	40	
1993	28	37	34.2
1994	28	36	
1995		35	31.6
1996	27	35	
1997		35	
1998		30	29.9
1999	21		
2000	19		
2001			
2002			
2003	20		26.1

Source: Wiatrowski (2005).

be made, the data show that the SIPP estimates are below the BLS estimates as might be expected given the differences in the coverage of the two series. All three series show the same downward trend over time.

The cohort data shown in figures 10.1 and 10.2 allow comparisons between the participation rates of some cohorts at a given age—say forty-five—but these data alone do not allow comparisons that include very young or very old cohorts who were not represented in the SIPP data. For example, we cannot compare the participation rates at age forty-five of cohorts C55 and C13—marked in figure 10.1. To do this, we need to project forward the future participation rates of younger cohorts at older ages and project backward the participation rates of older cohorts at younger ages.

We have made these projections by fitting the cohort data and then using the estimated parameters to predict outside range of the observed data, while relying on estimated cohort effects. The detailed estimates are not shown in the chapter but are available on request. The data represented in figures 10.1 to 10.3 are based on employed persons. As explained in the following, we need to develop estimates based on the percent of all persons who are covered by a DB plan. These projections are explained in section 10.4.

10.2   DB Pension Benefits of Recipients and Projections

We now begin a series of analyses that provide the basis for projections of future assets in DB plans. We begin in this section with a cohort description of the dollar amount of the DB benefits of *persons* who received DB benefits at ages over fifty-five and then describe how we project benefit amounts in the future. In section 10.3, we present a parallel description of the percent of older persons that receives DB benefits.

Data on DB benefits received by retirees, like the participation data for employed persons shown in the preceding, are obtained from SIPP waves for the years 1984, 1987, 1991, 1993, 1995, 1998, and 2003. And, as with the participation data, we first present a cohort description of the observed data. We then fit the observed data and use the fitted model to project benefits outside the range of the observed data. Table 10.3 describes the observed data and the cohorts for which data must be projected. We obtain data on benefits received for persons aged fifty-five to eighty-five. Some SIPP data are available for cohorts C36 to C67. Benefits received for younger cohorts—C47 to C35—and for older cohorts—C68 to C102—must be projected. The numerical amounts table 10.3 show monthly pension benefits observed in the SIPP. An "X" indicates that a pension benefit amount is not observed in the SIPP and that the amount must be estimated. Partial data are available for cohorts C36 to C48. Cohort C36 was age fifty-five in 2003, and thus SIPP data are available for only one year (2003) for this cohort. For successively older cohorts through C48, data are available for more years. Beginning with cohort C55—that was age fifty-five in 1984—data are available for all seven years that the SIPP data are available. Complete data are available for all cohorts through C66, that was age eighty-five in 2003, the last year of SIPP data. For cohorts C67 through C85, successively fewer years of data are observed in the SIPP. Cohort C85 was age eighty-five in 1984, and thus SIPP data for this cohort are only available in that year.

By fitting the observed data on the receipt of benefits, we can interpolate values for years between the years for which data are available. In addition, the model used to fit the data can be used to project benefits for cohorts outside of the range of the observed data. The cohorts and ages for which such projections must be made are indicated by "X" in table 10.3. We project benefits received back to A1947 because members of this cohort attain age 100 in 1982 and may thus be receiving benefits in the initial year (1982) of our DB asset projections. We project benefits received forward as far out as 2096 to allow calculation of employer DB pension liabilities, described in the following.

Figure 10.4 shows the actual data for the monthly level of benefits for selected cohorts. The data are for all persons age fifty-five to eighty-five and include persons who are receiving benefits from federal or state and local re-

Table 10.3 More detailed description of cohort data and projections for the amount of defined benefit pension benefit received

Cohort

Age	A2096 … / C-47	A2014 / C35	A2013 / C36	A2012 / C37	A2008 / C41	A2007 / C42	A2001 … / C48	A1994 … / C55	A1983 / C66	A1982 / C67	A1973 / C76	A1972 / C77	A1965 … / C84	A1964 / C85	A1965 / C86	A1947 … / C101	A1947 / C102
55	X	X	1613	X	1325	X	813	661	X	X	X	X	X	X	X		
56	X	X	X	1624	x	1313	x	x	X	X	X	X	X	X	X		X
57	X	X	X	X	x	x	1065	778	X	X	X	X	X	X	X		X
58	X	X	X	X	x	x	1375	752	X	X	X	X	X	X	X		X
59	X	X	X	X	1592	1555	x	x	X	X	X	X	X	X	X		X
60	X	X	X	X	x	x	x	x	X	X	X	X	X	X	X		X
61	X	X	X	X	X	X	1139	856	X	X	X	X	X	X	X		X
62	X	X	X	X	X	X	x	x	X	X	X	X	X	X	X	X	X
63	X	X	X	X	X	X	x	x	X	X	X	X	X	X	X	X	X
64	X	X	X	X	X	X	x	879	X	X	X	X	X	X	X	X	X
65	X	X	X	X	X	X	x	x	X	X	X	X	X	X	X	X	X
66	X	X	X	X	X	X	x	938	499	X	X	X	X	X	X	X	X
67	X	X	X	X	X	X	1152	x	x	478	X	X	X	X	X	X	X
68	X	X	X	X	X	X	X	x	558	x	X	X	X	X	X	X	X
69	X	X	X	X	X	X	X	839	562	518	X	X	X	X	X	X	X
70	X	X	X	X	X	X	X	x	x	546	X	X	X	X	X	X	X
71	X	X	X	X	X	X	X	x	x	x	X	X	X	X	X	X	X
72	X	X	X	X	X	X	X	x	x	x	X	X	X	X	X	X	X
73	X	X	X	X	X	X	X	x	588	559	X	X	X	X	X	X	X
74	X	X	X	X	X	X	X	953	x	x	X	X	X	X	X	X	X
75	X	X	X	X	X	X	X	X	689	x	X	X	X	X	X	X	X
76	X	X	X	X	X	X	X	X	x	633	375	X	X	X	X	X	X
77	X	X	X	X	X	X	X	X	756	x	x	378	X	X	X	X	X
78	X	X	X	X	X	X	X	X	x	718	470	450	X	X	X	X	X
79	X	X	X	X	X	X	X	X	757	x	415	467	X	X	X	X	X
80									x	x	x	X	X	X	X	X	X
81									x	X	X	X	X	X	X	X	X
82									724	X	X	X	X	X	X	X	X
83									X	X	457	X	X	X	X	X	X
84									X	X	x	X	x	X	X	X	X
85	X	X	X	X	X	X			X	X	X	X	303	X	X	X	X
86	X	X	X	X	X	X	X	X	756	X	452	X	X	307	X	X	X
87	X	X	X	X	X	X	X	X	X	X	X	X	X	X	X	X	X
⋮																	
99	X	X	X	X	X	X	X	X	X	X	X	X	X	X	X	X	X
100	X	X	X	X	X	X	X	X	X	X	X	X	X	X	X	X	X

Partial data for cohorts C36 to C48

Complete (all SIPP survey years) for cohorts C55 to C66

Partial data for cohorts C67 to C85

x, x interpolated between observed data

X projected data

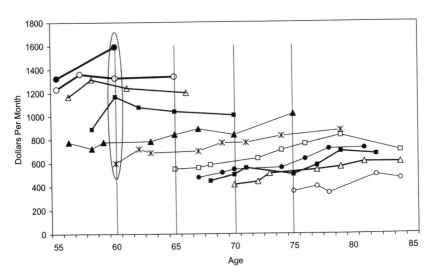

Fig. 10.4   DB benefit receipt for selected cohorts

tirement programs, as well as from private-sector pensions plans.[1] Two features of the data stand out. One is that benefits of younger cohorts are much greater than benefits of older cohorts. For example, the benefit at age sixty for the cohort that attained that age in 1984 was about $600 per month; the benefit for the cohort that attained age sixty in 2003 was about $1,600 per month (circled in the figure). The other feature of the data is that within-cohort benefits increase with age. In part this results from the indexing of benefits from some DB plans, especially federal and state and local plans. In addition, private employer plans, which are typically not indexed, sometimes grant cost-of-living increases on an ad hoc basis after retirement.

We fit the cohort data on benefits with the following specification:

$$B_{ac} = \alpha_{a \le 60} A_1 + \alpha_{60 < a \le 65} A_2 + \alpha_{65 < a \le 70} A_3 + \alpha_{70 < a \le 75} A_4 + \alpha_{>75} A_5 + \sum_{c=1971}^{2013} c_c C_c$$

Here, B is the dollar amount of monthly pension benefits, and cohorts are defined by the year the cohort attains age sixty-five—the C_c indicator variable—and the variables A_1 through A_5 specify age as piecewise linear with break points at sixty, sixty-five, seventy, and seventy-five.

---

1. The level of DB benefits received is derived from SIPP data on receipt of income from the following sources: pension from company or union; federal civil service or other federal civilian employee pension; U.S. military retirement pay; National Guard or reserve forces retirement; state government pension; local government pension; U.S. government railroad retirement; veterans compensation or pension. We have assumed that all monthly income received from these sources is DB income although it is possible that withdrawals of DC assets may be included.

The parameter estimates are presented in table 10A.1. We use the estimated parameters from this specification to project benefits forward for the younger cohorts and to project benefits backward for the older cohorts. There are at least two years of observed SIPP data for cohorts as old as A1970 (observed at age seventy-nine in 1984 and age eighty-two in 1987). There are not enough SIPP observations to reliably estimate cohort effects for cohorts younger than A2012. We obtain benefit estimates for cohorts attaining age sixty-five prior to 1970 by shifting the A1970 benefit profile by according to the Social Security Administration's average wage index. That is, we assume that the pension benefit growth paralleled wage growth between 1949 and 1970. We only use benefits received in calendar years 1982 and later. For cohort A1970, for example, we use estimates beginning at age seventy-seven, in 1982. We use the wage index to estimate cohort effects for cohorts that retired before 1970, but we only project for older ages (after 1982) for each cohort.

The more important projections are for cohorts younger than the A2012 cohort. Which specific extrapolation to use, however, is open to question. The following figures show some of the relevant data. Figure 10.5 shows the estimated cohort effects for cohorts A1982 to A2012. An exponential fit over all of the cohort effects—with an R^2 value of 0.99—suggests that, on average, benefits increase by 4.5 percent with each successively younger cohort. But the figure also shows that the rate of change in the cohort effects may have declined over time. The estimated rate of change was only

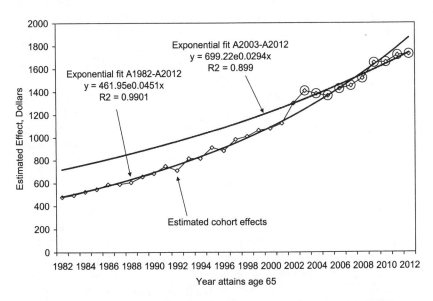

Fig. 10.5   Estimated cohort effect from benefit regression by year cohort attains age 65

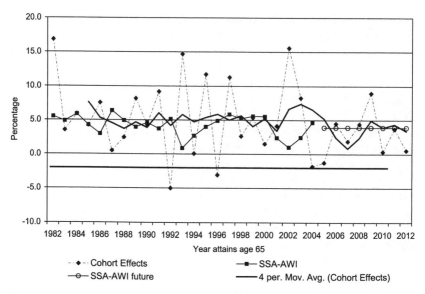

Fig. 10.6   Percent change in estimated benefit cohort effect versus the Social Security average wage index (AWI), by year cohort attains age 65

2.94 percent for the A2003 to A2012 cohorts. (The cohort effects for these years are circled in figure 10.5.)

Figure 10.6 shows a different view of the data, beginning with the change in the estimated cohort effects from one cohort to the next younger cohort. It is clear that the percent changes vary substantially from one cohort to the next. The figure also shows the four-year moving average of these changes. It is clear from the moving average that the average change from one cohort to the next younger cohort was close to 5 percent over most of the period but declined to close to 1 percent around 2006. The figure also shows the Social Security average wage index over the years 1982 to 2003. These data suggest a noticeable correspondence between the four-year moving average of the change in the estimated cohort effects and the wage index. After 2003, the SSA assumes a wage increase of 3.9 percent annually. On average, the change in the cohort effects was only about 2.9 percent over these years.

Based on these data, we have assumed that for younger cohorts benefits will increase at 3.9 percent for each successively younger cohort, the same as the SSA intermediate assumption for the average wage index. Figure 10.7 shows benefit profiles for selected cohorts, including projected profiles for cohorts A2013 to A2050 (dashed lines in the figure) and the fitted cohort profiles for cohorts A1974 to A2012 (solid lines). Profiles for cohorts older than A1974 are not shown (these cohorts are relatively unimportant because our projection of DB assets begins in 1982). All profiles are in year

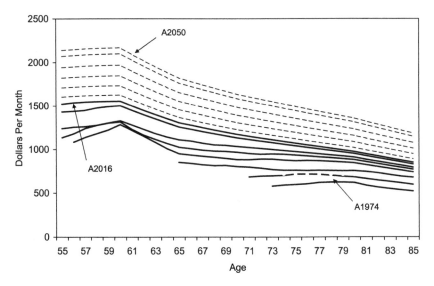

Fig. 10.7   Fitted and projected benefit profiles, selected cohorts (in year 2000 dollars)

Notes: Last fitted profile graphed is A2012. First projected profile graphed is A2016.

2000 dollars. The benefit model parameter estimates show that cohort age profiles in *current* dollars are slightly upward sloping, perhaps due to the indexing of government pensions and ad hoc cost-of-living increases for other pension benefits. The age profiles in 2000 dollars in the figure slope downward, however.

10.3   Receipt of DB Pension Benefits

In the previous section, we discussed the dollar amount of the DB benefits of persons who received DB benefits at each age. To obtain an estimate of the total dollar amount of DB benefits, we need also to determine the proportion of persons who receive benefits at each age. We now consider the probability of benefit receipt.

We begin with cohort data on the percentage of persons receiving DB benefits at each age. Figure 10.8 shows data for selected cohorts (essentially every other cohort). Two features of the data are evident. First, the cohort effects are rather small, with the exception of the older cohorts. In other words, the profile of benefit receipt by age is about the same for all the cohorts represented in the SIPP data (with the exception of the oldest cohorts). For example, among cohorts observed at age seventy, the probability of receipt of benefits ranges from about 45 percent for the youngest cohort to 49 percent for the oldest cohort. Second, the age at which the maximum percent of persons receive benefits is about seventy.

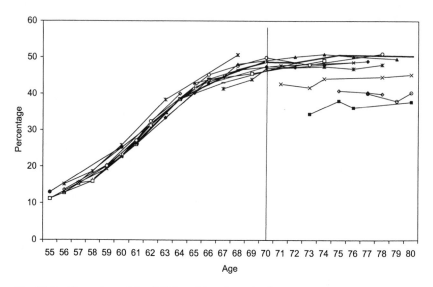

Fig. 10.8   Percent receiving DB benefits, selected cohorts

To project benefit receipt for future (younger) cohorts that are not observed in the SIPP data, we assume the age-benefit-receipt profile shown in figure 10.8 continues to apply. However, we allow this profile to shift (downward) for younger cohorts. We first estimate age and cohort effects for cohorts observed in the SIPP. Then we predict benefits for younger cohorts, assuming that—except for the cohort effects—the age-benefit-receipt profile in the same for younger cohorts as it has been for older cohorts observed in the SIPP.

We fit the benefit receipt data using a probit model and a piecewise linear specification for age like the one presented in the preceding. The sample consists of the same persons age fifty-five to eighty-five used in the previous section to estimate the level of benefits. The specification is

$$R_{ac} = \alpha_{a \leq 60} A_1 + \alpha_{60 < a \leq 65} A_2 + \alpha_{65 < a \leq 70} A_3 + \alpha_{70 < a \leq 75} A_4$$

$$+ \alpha_{75 < a} A_5 + \sum_{c=1969}^{c=2012} c_c C_c,$$

where R is the receipt of benefits, and cohorts are defined by the age the cohort attains age sixty-five. The estimated cohort effects are shown in table 10A.2. Figure 10.9 shows that the estimated cohort effects are essentially unchanged for cohorts that attained age sixty-five between 1982 and 2003. The cohort effects were smaller but increasing for cohorts that attained age sixty-five between 1969 and 1981. The larger cohort effects for cohorts that attained age sixty-five in 2004 and later years are based on very few SIPP observations and pertain only to persons who were receiving benefits at

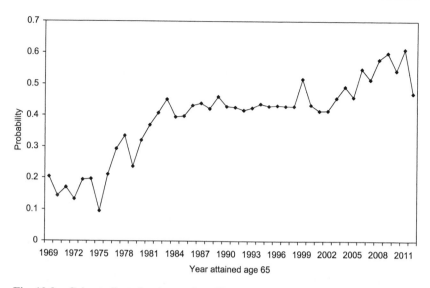

Fig. 10.9   **Cohort effects for the receipt of benefits by year attained age 65**

young ages. For example, data for the A2004 cohort are only observed through age sixty-four and for the A2012 cohort only for age fifty-six.

Because we cannot reliably estimate cohort effects for cohorts younger that A2003, we assume that the benefit receipt rates of successively younger cohorts follow the same pattern as the DB participation rates of these same cohorts when they were in the labor force. The assumption is that if fewer persons in a particular cohort participated when young, then fewer persons will receive benefits after retirement. We do this by first calculating the maximum DB participation rate over ages twenty-five to sixty-four for each cohort. We use this maximum rate to predict benefit receipt when the cohort is retired. We use cohort-to-cohort changes in the maximum DB participation rate, and the 2003 fitted age-benefit receipt profile, to project benefit receipt for cohorts A2004 through A2060. Before presenting these projections, we describe the population-based DB participation rates that are required to make the calculations.

10.4   Population-Based DB Participation Rates

The previous two sections have developed projections for the level of benefits (conditional on receipt) and for the probability of receiving DB benefits after retirement. As noted in the preceding, the probability of receiving benefits cannot reliably be estimated for cohorts retiring after 2003 using the SIPP data. These cohorts are not observed after age fifty-five in the data. However, these same cohorts are observed at younger ages when they are in the labor force. We infer the probability of benefit receipt after

Table 10.4   Defined benefit (DB) participation and ratio of employment to population, all persons aged 25–64

Year	DB participation given employment	Employment to population ratio	(DB participation) × (Employment to population ratio)
1984	39.4	0.752	29.6
1987	36.8	0.767	28.2
1991	34.9	0.778	27.2
1993	34.2	0.771	26.4
1995	31.6	0.777	24.6
1998	29.9	0.778	23.3
2003	29.7	0.763	22.7

Source: Authors calculations from Survey of Income and Program Participation Surveys.

retirement from the DB participation rates of these cohorts when they were in the labor force. This section develops estimates of DB participation that are closely related to those presented in section 10.1 for *employed* persons. Here we consider the participation rate of *all persons in the population* because we will use our estimates to infer benefit receipt for all retirees (not just those who were employed).

The employment-based participation rates and the population-based rates can differ substantially. To see this, note that the percent of population that participates in a DB plan at age a is given by

$$\left(\frac{DB}{P}\right)_a = \left(\frac{E}{P}\right)_a \Pr[DB_a \mid E_a],$$

where E is employment, and P is population, and a denotes age. Table 10.4 shows the probability that a person has a DB plan given that the person is employed and the employment to population ratio for each year of SIPP data available between 1984 and 2003. These data show that the last term, $\Pr[DB_a \mid E_a]$, has declined between 1984 and 2003, but the fraction of the population employed $(E/P)_a$ increased between 1984 and 1998 but fell in 2003.[2] The percentage of employed persons participating in a DB plan declined from 39.4 percent to 29.7 percent over this period.

The overall effect of these trends is that cohort effects are smaller when *all* persons are used as the base than when *employed* persons are used as the base. This can be seen by comparing figure 10.1 with figure 10.10, which are shown together in the following. For example, at age forty-five, the difference in the participation rates of cohorts 27 and 45 is about 13 per-

2. The employment to population ratio for persons sixteen and over reported by the BLS shows an increase from 59.5 percent in 1984 to 64.1 percent in 1998 and then a drop to 62.3 percent in 2003. The SIPP data we use are for ages twenty-five to sixty-four.

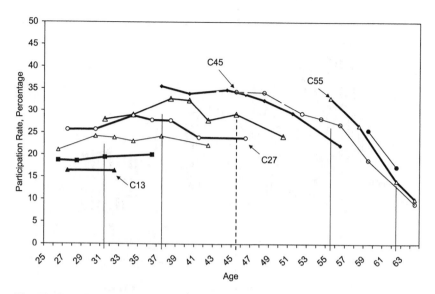

Fig. 10.10   DB participation rate for all persons, selected cohorts

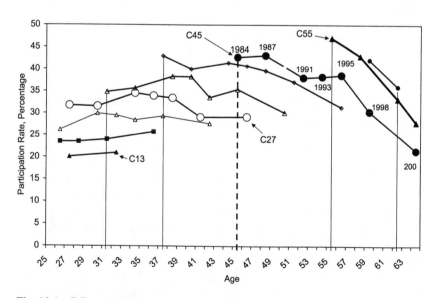

Fig. 10.1   DB participation rate of employed persons, selected cohorts

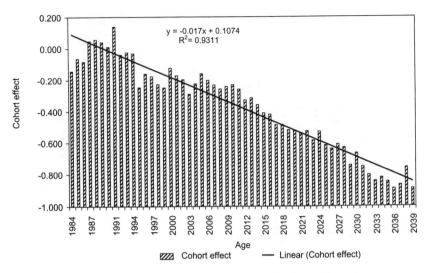

Fig. 10.11   DB participation for all persons, estimated cohort effects, by year attained age 65

centage points based on those employed but only about 10 percentage points based on all persons.

As with the participation based on employed persons, we fit the population-based participation data using a probit model with this specification:

$$DB(\text{Pop})_{ac} = \alpha_{a \leq 30}A_1 + \alpha_{30 < a \leq 35}A_2 + \alpha_{35 < a \leq 40}A_3 + \alpha_{40 < a \leq 45}A_4 + \alpha_{45 < a \leq 50}A_5$$

$$+ \alpha_{50 < a \leq 55}A_6 + \alpha_{55 < a \leq 60}A_7 + \alpha_{60 < a}A_8 + \sum_{c=9}^{c=65} c_c C_c$$

The estimated cohort effects from this specification (defined here by age in 1984) are shown in figure 10.11, while the complete estimation results are shown in table 10A.3.

Selected fitted cohort profiles together with the corresponding cohort data are shown in figure 10.12. We judge that the fitted profiles represent the data quite well. We then use the model estimates to predict population-based participation rates at all ages (twenty-five to sixty-four) for each of the cohorts for which we are able to estimate cohort effects. These predictions are shown (as solid lines) in figure 10.13 for selected cohorts. We predict at all ages for each cohort because we want to determine the age at which the participation rate is at a maximum for each of the cohorts. The use of this calculation is explained in the following. Predicting at older ages for the younger cohorts suggests that by the time these cohorts reach retirement age, their participation in DB plans will be very low. For example, based on these predictions, the DB participation rate of persons in the C11

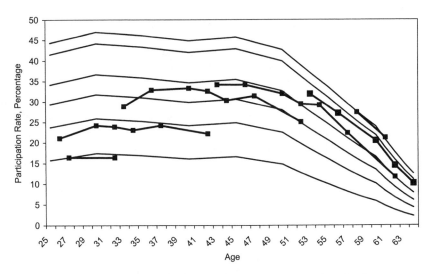

Fig. 10.12   Actual versus fitted DB participation profiles for selected cohorts (all persons)

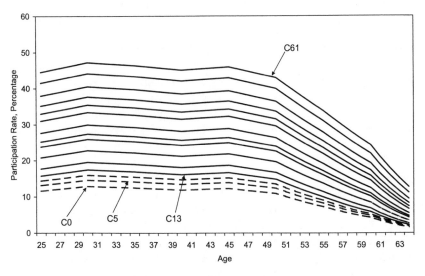

Fig. 10.13   DB participation for all persons, projections to younger cohorts (dotted), (2.1% decline for cohorts that retire 2040–2050)

cohort will be only 8.8 percent when that cohort attains age fifty-five (cohort C11 attains age sixty-five in 2038).

The youngest cohort in the SIPP data is A2040. For later use, we will need cohorts as young as A2050. Figure 10.11 shows that the decline in the estimated cohort effects, with successively younger cohorts, is close to linear—at –0.017 per cohort. Thus, we extrapolate the estimated cohort effects linearly to project the effects for younger cohorts. This extrapolation yields profiles for the younger cohorts shown as dashed lines in figure 10.13.

All of the projections we make are subject to substantial uncertainty. These projection in particular raise the prospect that the past trend may not be a good predictor of the future trend. For example, several large companies have recently announced that traditional DB pension plans would be phased out. Other companies could follow this lead more rapidly than our projections suggest. This would lead to a faster-than-projected decline in DB assets.

10.5   Projected Benefits Paid

To develop projections of the total value of benefits paid by DB plans, we combine estimates of the level of benefits in section 10.2 with estimates of the probability of benefit receipt in section 10.3. To help to forecast benefit receipt for younger cohorts (retiring after 2003), we use estimates of DB participation of these younger cohorts during their working ages. In particular, we use the population-based estimates of DB participation by cohort discussed in section 10.4 to predict pension receipt after retirement. The necessary data is set out in table 10.5. We first use the estimates of probability of benefit receipt for cohorts A1982 to A2003 to predict the percent of each of these cohorts that receives benefits at age seventy (recall from figure 10.8 that age seventy is the age at which the maximum percent of persons receive benefits). As discussed in section 10.3, for these cohorts there are a sufficient number of SIPP observations to obtain reasonably reliable estimates of benefit receipt. These probabilities are shown in column (3) of table 10.5. The probabilities are also graphed in figure 10.14 for the years 1982 through 2003.

We next need to project benefits at age seventy for younger cohorts (A2004 to A2040). To make these projections, we use the population-based DB participation rates, discussed in section 10.4. From these data, we have calculated the maximum participation rates, over ages twenty-five to sixty-four, for each cohort. These estimates are shown in column (5) of table 10.5. We use the maximum participation rate during working years to predict the probability of benefit receipt at age seventy for cohorts A2004 and younger. We assume that the year-to-year percent change in the probability of receipt of benefits at age seventy is the same as the year-to-year percent change in the maximum DB participation rate. Thus, for example, the last cohort for which the receipt probability is observed is A2003 (47.3 percent). We project the 2004 receipt probability by assuming it declines by the same percentage amount as the maximum participation probability (from 38.6 percent for A2003 to 37.7 percent in 2004). The prediction for 2004,

Table 10.5　　　**Projections of the probability of benefit receipt at age 70, by cohort**

Year cohort attains age 65 (1)	Age of cohort in 1984 (2)	Probability receive benefits at age 70 (from benefit receipt data) (3)	Projected probability receive benefits at age 70 (4)	DB participation maximum (from DB participation data) (5)
1982	67	45.5		
1983	66	47.0		
1984	65	48.8		
1985	64	46.5		39.7
1986	63	46.6		42.9
1987	62	48.0		42.1
1988	61	48.3		47.2
1989	60	47.6		45.4
1990	59	49.1		47.6
1991	58	47.9		47.0
1992	57	47.7		45.8
1993	56	47.4		50.9
1994	55	47.7		43.8
1995	54	48.2		44.4
1996	53	47.9		44.2
1997	52	48.0		35.8
1998	51	47.9		39.1
1999	50	47.9		38.4
2000	49	51.4		36.6
2001	48	48.0		35.7
2002	47	47.3		40.5
2003	46	47.3		38.6
2004	45		46.1	37.7
2005	44		41.9	34.2
2006	43		44.9	36.6
2007	42		47.9	39.1
2008	41		45.9	37.5
2009	40		44.5	36.4
2010	39		43.4	35.4
2011	38		44.1	36.0
2012	37		44.6	36.4
2013	36		43.3	35.4
2014	35		40.3	32.9
2015	34		40.9	33.4
2016	33		38.9	31.8
2017	32		36.7	29.9
2018	31		36.3	29.6
2019	30		33.5	27.3
2020	29		33.5	27.4
2021	28		32.1	26.2
2022	27		31.9	26.0
2023	26		31.2	25.5
2024	25		31.9	26.0
2025	24		29.5	24.1

(*continued*)

Table 10.5 (continued)

Year cohort attains age 65 (1)	Age of cohort in 1984 (2)	Probability receive benefits at age 70 (from benefit receipt data) (3)	Projected probability receive benefits at age 70 (4)	DB participation maximum (from DB participation data) (5)
2026	23		31.7	25.9
2027	22		28.4	23.1
2028	21		27.5	22.5
2029	20		28.6	23.4
2030	19		27.9	22.7
2031	18		23.9	19.5
2032	17		26.5	21.7
2033	16		23.6	19.3
2034	15		21.9	17.9
2035	14		20.7	16.9
2036	13		21.4	17.4
2037	12		20.6	16.8
2038	11		19.3	15.7
2039	10		20.0	16.3
2040	9		19.5	15.9

Note: DB = defined benefit.

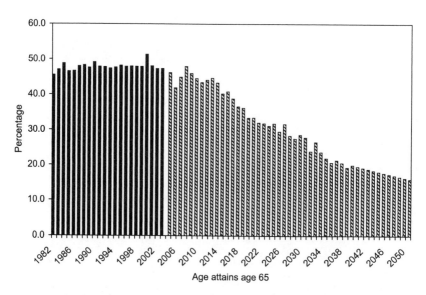

Fig. 10.14 **Percent receiving benefits at age 70, by cohort (solid is fitted SIPP estimate, and striped is projected)**

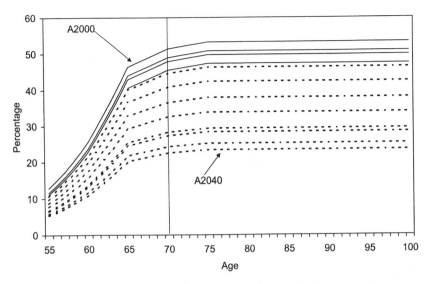

Fig. 10.15   Projected percent receiving benefits for selected cohorts attaining age 65 in years 1982 through 2040 (solid is fitted SIPP estimate, and dotted is projected)

46.2 percent (shown in column [4]) is 47.3% × (37.7%/38.6%). The same calculations are continued to project the probability of receiving benefits at age seventy for cohorts A2004 through A2040. For cohorts younger than A2040 (not shown in the table) a 2 percent decline is assumed. This is an extrapolation of the decline for the cohorts A2031 to A2040.

From the percent that receives benefits at age seventy, we predict the percent that receives benefits at each age, as described in section 10.3. These estimates are shown for selected cohorts in figure 10.15.

10.6   Present Value of DB Benefits at Sixty-Five

We have projected the average level of the DB benefits of recipients, by age and cohort, B_{ac}, for cohorts attaining age sixty-five in the years 1982 through 2050. We have also projected the probability of benefit receipt for each age and cohort. First, we obtain for each cohort the average present value (PV) of benefits at age sixty-five for persons who *receive* DB benefits, given by:

$$(1) \qquad \text{PV(recipients)}_{c,65} = \sum_{a=65}^{100} \left(\prod_{t=65}^{a} S_{t,c} \right) \left(\frac{B_{a,c}}{(1 + r)^{(a-65)}} \right),$$

where $S_{t,c}$ is the cohort-specific probability of survival to age t conditional on being alive at $t - 1$, and r is the discount rate. Second, we calculate the present value of DB benefits at age 65 for *all* cohort members, both those with and those without a DB plan. The expected average benefit received

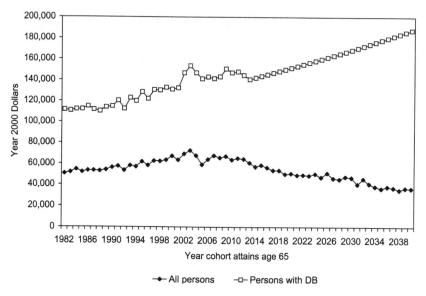

Fig. 10.16   Present value DB benefits at age 65: All persons and persons with a DB

by all persons of age a in cohort c is $\overline{B}_{ac}$ = Pr[benefit receipt] · [benefits$_{ac}$ | benefit receipt] = $B_{ac} \cdot P_{ac}$. Thus the present value of benefits averaged over *all* persons is given by:

$$(2) \qquad \text{PV(all persons)}_{c,65} = \sum_{a=65}^{100}\left(\prod_{t=65}^{a} S_{t,c}\right)\left(\frac{B_{a,c} \cdot P_{ac}}{(1+r)^{(a-65)}}\right).$$

Figure 10.16 graphs both of these present value calculations. The present value amounts have been converted to constant year 2000 dollars. A real discount rate of 3 percent and average SSA age-specific survival probabilities are assumed. For these calculations, pension benefits received prior to age sixty-five have been ignored. The top profile shows that the average present value of DB benefits for persons that receive DB benefits will be greater for cohorts retiring in the future than for cohorts retiring today. This is because we assume that nominal benefits increase by 3.9 percent annually, and the inflation rate is 2.8 percent. However, the lower profile shows that the PV of DB wealth, averaged across all persons, will decline in the future as fewer persons participate. Indeed, these projections show DB wealth peaking in 2003 at about $73,000 and falling to about $50,000 by 2020.[3]

---

3. These estimates indicate that in 2000 the average of DB benefits over all persons was $67,386. Based on HRS data, Johnson, Burman and Kobes (2004), estimate that the mean present value of employer-sponsored pension income for persons sixty-five to sixty-nine in 2000 was $50,203. Our estimate should be larger than theirs because we include persons of all ages. In particular, average benefits increase with age because death rates selectively leave in the sample persons with higher benefits and because of ad hoc cost-of-living increases and indexed benefits in many government plans.

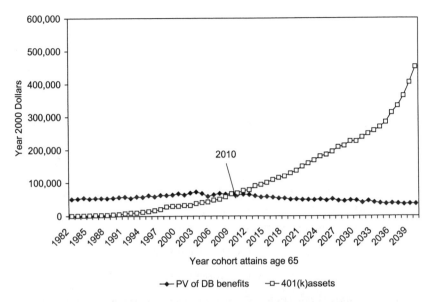

Fig. 10.17   Present value DB benefits at age 65 and 401(k) assets at age 65, all persons—Historical rates of return

For comparison, we show the average present value of 401(k) assets at age sixty-five, reported in Poterba, Venti and Wise (2008).[4] The comparison between the average present value of DB benefits at age sixty-five and average 401(k) assets at age sixty-five is graphed in figures 10.17 and 10.18 for *all* persons. The comparisons in figures 10.19 and 10.20 pertain to persons *with* plans. Figures 10.17 and 10.19 show 401(k) assets at retirement assuming that the return on equities in the future will be equal to the historical average. Figures 10.18 and 10.20 show 401(k) assets assuming that the return on equities in the future will be 300 basis points less than historical average return.

Assuming historical rates of return, figure 10.17 shows that average 401(k) assets of *all persons* reach the average PV of DB benefits of all persons in 2010 when both are about $67,000. Thereafter, assets in 401(k) accounts continue to grow, reaching about $137,000 in 2020, $226,000 in 2030, and $452,000 in 2040. Assuming historical rates of return less 300 basis points, average 401(k) assets reach the average PV of DB benefits of all persons in 2011 when both are about $66,000. Thereafter, assets in 401(k)

4. These projections use actual annual pretax returns through 2005. Beginning in 2006, we assume that the average annual nominal return on equities is 12 percent and that the average nominal return on corporate bonds is 6 percent. Ibbotson Associates (2006) reports that the historical arithmetic mean of pretax returns on long-term corporate bonds has been 6.2 percent per year, while large-capitalization stocks have returned an average of 12.3 percent over the period 1926 to 2005. These returns are the pretax total return available on a portfolio with no management fees. We have not as yet accounted for asset management fees.

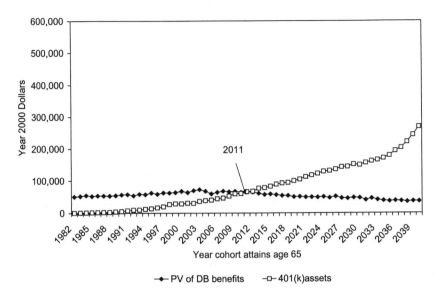

Fig. 10.18   Present value DB benefits at age 65 and 401(k) assets at age 65, all persons—Historical rates of return minus 300 basis points

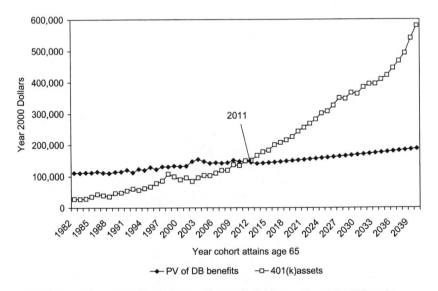

Fig. 10.19   Present value of DB benefits at age 65 for persons with a DB and 401(k) assets at age 65 for persons with a 401(k)—Historical rates of return

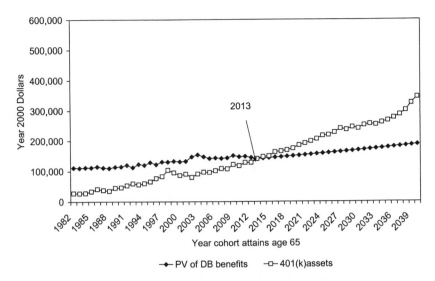

Fig. 10.20   Present value of DB benefits at age 65 for persons with a DB and 401(k) assets at age 65 for persons with a 401(k)—Historical rates of return minus 300 basis points

accounts continue to grow, reaching about $104,000 in 2020, $149,000 in 2030, and $269,000 in 2040. The lower rate of return on equities substantially reduces the accumulation of assets in 401(k) plans. Even with the lower rate of return on equities, however, by 2040 the accumulation of assets in 401(k) plans would be 3.7 times as large as the historical maximum level of assets (fully funded) in DB plans, which was realized in 2003.

Figure 10.19 shows the present value of DB benefits for persons who have a DB plan and the 401(k) assets for persons who have a 401(k) plan, assuming the average historical equity return. For these persons, balances in 401(k) accounts reach the PV of DB benefits in 2011, when both are about $148,000. Thereafter, the 401(k) assets continue to grow, reaching about $243,000 in 2020, $363,000 in 2030, and $580,000 in 2040. For persons *with DB* plans, the average present value of benefits also continues to grow, reaching $187,000 by 2040. By 2040, the accumulation of 401(k) assets is about 3 times the PV of DB assets. Figure 10.20 shows 401(k) assets assuming that the rate of return on equities is 300 basis points lower than the historical average. Here the assets of persons with 401(k) accounts reach the level of the PV of DB benefits for persons who receive benefits in 2014, when both are about $145,000. Thereafter, the 401(k) assets continue to grow, reaching about $185,000 in 2020, $241,000 in 2030, and $345,000 in 2040. For persons *with DB* plans, the average present value of benefits also continues to grow, reaching $187,000 by 2040. Thus, for persons with plans, by 2040 the accumulation in 401(k) plans is about 1.8 times the PV of DB assets at sixty-five.

Our 401(k) asset projections do not account for legislated increases in the contribution limits between 2003 and 2007. The limit increases are large for all income groups, with the largest increases for persons with incomes between $15,000 and $20,000. Only a small proportion of persons are currently contributing at the maximum. However, as incomes increase, a larger and larger fraction of employees are likely to be contributing at the new limits. For this reason, it is likely that future contributions to 401(k) plans will be greater than our assumptions (projections) suggest. In addition, we have not accounted for the effects of the Pension Protection Act of 2006, which gives employers latitude to set more "saving friendly" defaults in 401(k) plans. Beshears et al. (2008) survey some of the recent evidence on how changing defaults for enrollment, contribution rates, and asset allocations can significantly increase retirement saving.

10.7   Assets in DB Trust Funds and Total DB Benefits Paid

Finally, we want to estimate the level of total assets in DB trust funds. These estimates are likely to be particularly important for assessing future changes in the demand for financial assets. We made similar calculations with respect to 401(k) and other personal retirement account assets in Poterba, Venti, and Wise (2008). We believe the DB component, together with the 401(k) component, represent a substantial fraction of the demography-induced change in asset demand.

There are at least two general ways to predict future assets in DB plans. One way is to predict total benefits paid in future years and then to suppose that assets in a year are sufficient to pay the present value of these future obligations. We take this approach here. We believe, however, that this approach should yield fully funded current assets that are greater than actual assets. A second way is to predict future assets based on an extrapolation of current assets compared to fully funded liabilities. A possible extrapolation procedure, for example, is to assume that assets will continue to be a given percent below the fully funded level. We have not pursued this approach here.

To obtain the present value of future obligations, we must first calculate total DB benefits paid each year. As described in the preceding, we have projected the average level of DB benefits of recipients by age and cohort (or, alternatively, by age and calendar year). We have also projected the conditional probability of receiving benefits for each age and year. We now combine these projections with demographic projections obtained from the Social Security Administration to obtain total DB benefits paid in each year. More precisely, we calculate the total dollar value of DB benefits paid to all persons in year t as:

(3)
$$DB_t = \sum_{a=55}^{100} N_{a,t} P_{a,t} B_{a,t},$$

where $N_{a,t}$ is the number of persons age a in year t, $P_{a,t}$ is the probability that benefits are received by a person age a in year t, and $B_{a,t}$ is the average benefit received (conditional on benefit receipt) by a person of age a in year t.

Figure 10.21 shows these totals for the years 1982 to 2004, together with a constructed series that sums together private-sector DB benefits, benefits paid to federal employees, and benefits paid to state and local employees. The private-sector data are from the Form 5500 data and exclude benefits paid directly by insurance carriers. Federal DB benefits include payments made by the Civil Service Retirement System, the Federal Employees Retirement System, and the Military Service Retirement System. Defined benefit and DC benefits are not reported separately for state and local plans. The data used here include DC as well as DB benefits. Thus, our projected DB benefits should be somewhat smaller than sum of these reported government and private-sector benefits.

The projected totals are close to the constructed totals in the early years but are smaller than the constructed totals in the later years. The discrepancy is due in part at least to the growing importance of 401(k)-like accounts in the state and local government plans. Thus, we believe that the comparison lends credence to our estimates, based on SIPP data, for these years. Our forward projections depend on the assumptions we have made to project benefit levels and benefit receipt for future cohorts not represented in the SIPP data.

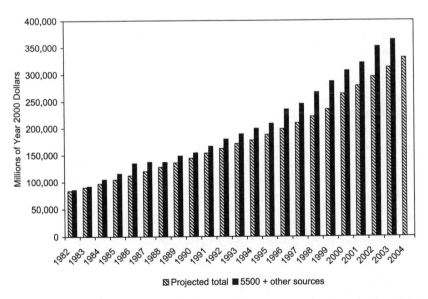

Fig. 10.21   DB benefits paid: Projected versus 5500 plus other sources, 1982 to 2004

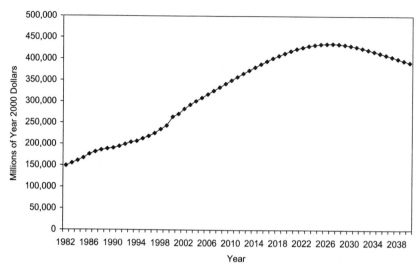

Fig. 10.22   Projected DB benefits paid: By year

Our projected estimates of total DB benefits in future years are shown in figure 10.22 in year *2000 dollars.* Total benefits paid from DB plans continue to increase until 2027. The profile turns down eventually because the probability that benefits are received (at age seventy) reaches a maximum with the cohort that attains age sixty-five in 2007, although this cohort continues to receive benefits after 2007. From a peak of $435,000 in 2027, the real value of total benefits paid declines modestly to $392,000 by 2040. As noted in figures 10.17 to 10.20, the real level of benefits increases through the end of the projection period, so the decline in total benefits in figure 10.22 is driven by the decline in the probability of benefit receipt.

For comparison, projected benefits paid from DB plans are graphed against amounts withdrawn from 401(k) plans in figure 10.23.[5] Benefits from DB plans exceed withdrawals of 401(k) assets until 2028, assuming historical rates of equity returns. After 2028, the value of DB benefits falls each year, and 401(k) withdrawals increase rapidly thereafter. If the future average rate of return on equities is assumed to be the average historical rate less 300 basis points, the benefits from DB plans exceed withdrawals of 401(k) assets until 2034.

We use our projections of benefits to be paid from DB plans to help to project future assets in DB trust funds. Suppose that in each year assets held by DB plan sponsors were equal to the present value of future obliga-

---

5. The 401(k) withdrawals shown in this figure are projected amounts disbursed when account owners are alive and do not include balances that remain in accounts when account owners die.

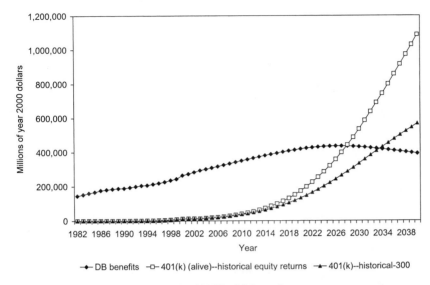

Fig. 10.23   DB benefits paid versus 401(k) withdrawals

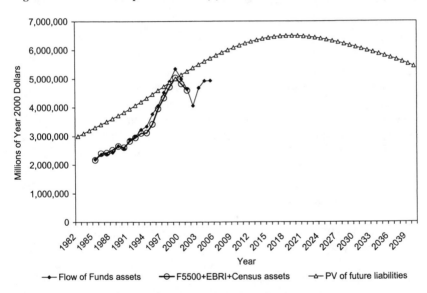

Fig. 10.24   Present value of DB liabilities versus DB assets

tions. If future liabilities are discounted at 3 percent and firms have a twenty-year planning horizon, the present value of liabilities each year is shown in figure 10.24. The figure also shows two series representing re-ported total assets in DB plans. The first is from the flow of funds accounts that include private-sector DB plans and the value of assets in DB and DC

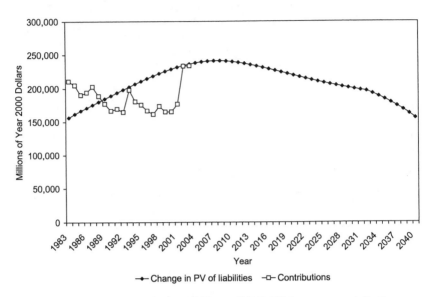

Fig. 10.25   Change in present value of future DB liabilities versus contributions

plans for government sponsors. The second series is composed of private-sector DB assets from Form 5500 reports, federal DB assets from various federal agency annual reports, and the sum of DB and DC assets for state and local governments from the Census Bureau's series on state and local government retirement systems. Actual assets, for the years they are available, are substantially below our calculation of the present value of liabilities in all years, with the possible exception of 1999. But the gap between actual assets and fully funded assets declined between 1985 and 1999. During this period, contributions to DB plans sometimes exceeded and sometimes fell short of the change in the present value of liabilities, as shown in figure 10.25. The gap closed in the late 1990s largely because of the stock market boom.

It is perhaps not surprising that actual assets are less than our estimates of the assets employers would have to hold to fully fund projected liabilities. Private-sector plan sponsors have substantial latitude in the assumption of interest rates, investment returns, when benefits will be paid, and other features that determine funding levels.[6] The former director of the Pension Benefit Guaranty Corporation (PBGC), Bradley Belt (2005), estimated that private DB plans were underfunded by $450 billion in 2004. There are even fewer restrictions on the funding of federal, state, and local plans, and many are thought to be substantially underfunded.

6. Bergstresser, Desai, and Rauh (2006) discuss these issues in the context of earnings manipulation.

Our fully funded method yields assets that are well above actual assets in DB plans, at least in recent years. We know of no way to confidently predict future funding levels, however. Thus, we have projected future assets levels according to the fully funded method described in the preceding.

10.8   DB and 401(k) Assets Combined

What will be the change in asset levels for all pension plans—DB and 401(k) plans combined—in future years? The evolution of total assets depends on three components: contributions, withdrawals, and the internal buildup. In our prior work, we projected assets held in 401(k) plans. These 401(k) assets, DB plan liabilities (fully funded DB assets), and the sum of both series are shown in figure 10.26 and 10.27, assuming historical equity returns and historical returns minus 300 basis points, respectively. If equities in 401(k) plans earn the historical return, then 401(k) asset balances overtake DB balances in 2009. If equities earn 300 basis points less than the historical average, then 401(k) assets first exceed DB assets in 2010.

We also consider total contributions to DB and 401(k) plans and total withdrawals from DB and 401(k) plans. Figure 10.28 shows contributions to 401(k) plans, the annual change in DB liabilities (a rough measure of contributions to a fully funded DB plan), and the sum of these contributions. The sum is relatively flat between 2000 and 2040. In contrast, the sum of benefits paid grows rapidly through 2040, especially if historical equity rates of return are assumed. Withdrawals from 401(k) plans, DB benefits

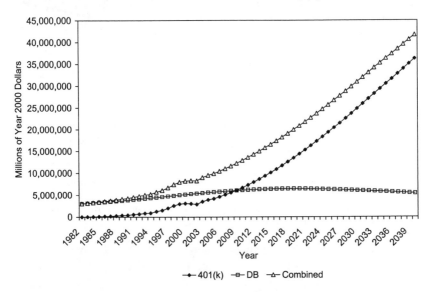

Fig. 10.26   Projected assets: 401(k), DB, and combined—Historical equity rates of return

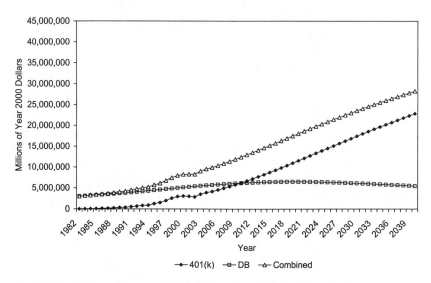

Fig. 10.27   Projected assets: 401(k), DB, and combined—Historical equity return minus 300 basis points

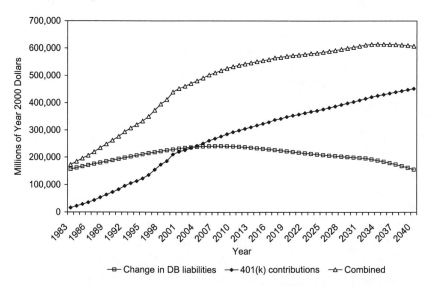

Fig. 10.28   Projected contributions: 401(k), DB (change in liabilities), and combined—Historical equity returns

paid, and the sum of the two are shown in figure 10.29 using historical equity returns and figure 10.30 using the historical return less 300 basis points.

Figure 10.31 shows the total projected contributions to and withdrawals from DB and 401(k) plans combined. Withdrawals assuming historical eq-

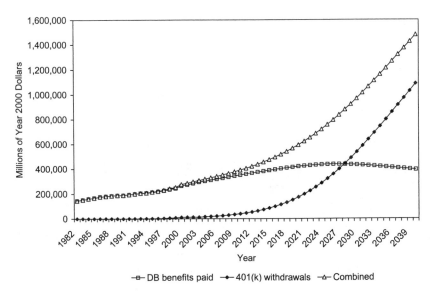

Fig. 10.29 Projected withdrawals: 401(k), DB (benefits paid), and combined—Historical equity returns

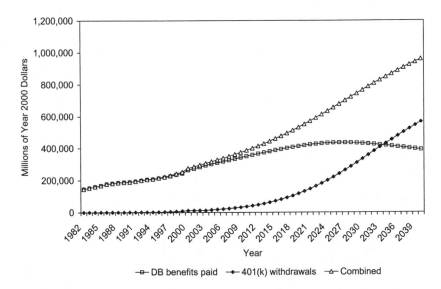

Fig. 10.30 Projected withdrawals: 401(k), DB (benefits paid), and combined—Historical equity returns minus 300 basis points

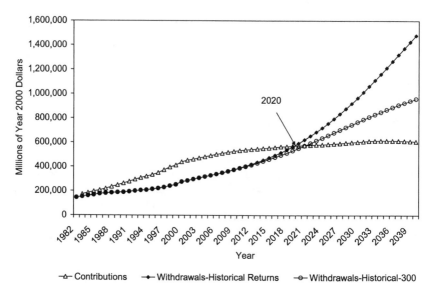

Fig. 10.31   Projected contributions and withdrawals: DB and 401(k) plans combined

uity rates of return and withdrawals assuming the historical return minus 300 basis points are shown in the figure. Withdrawals exceed contributions after 2020 and 2021 for these two withdrawal series, respectively. Figure 10.32 shows the combined withdrawals minus contributions. Again, withdrawals exceed contributions after 2020 if historical equity rates of return are assumed and after 2022 if historical rates minus 300 basis points are assumed. The excess of withdrawals over contributions reaches about $872 billion by 2040 (in year 2000 dollars) when historical rates of return are assumed but only about $353 billion if historical rates minus 300 basis points are assumed. Because of internal buildup, however, under either equity return scenario total assets in pension plans continue to grow through 2040. This is shown in figures 10.26 and 10.27.[7]

10.9   Demographically Sensitive Assets and Rates of Return

Whether demographically induced changes in DB and DC assets will have an appreciable effect on the rates of return on equities and other fi-

7. Schieber and Shoven (1997) consider the implications of population aging for private pension fund saving and project saving as a percent of payrolls. Their projection method is very different from ours, and it does not focus on the rising importance of self-directed DC plans in the way that ours does. Nevertheless, their results are qualitatively similar to ours. They project that total private pension withdrawals will exceed contributions beginning in 2024, reversing the pattern of earlier years.

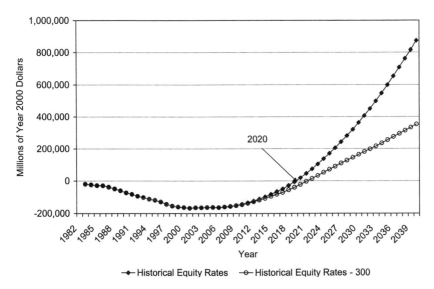

Fig. 10.32   Projected withdrawals minus contributions: DB and 401(k) plans combined

nancial assets depends on the magnitude of these changes relative to the other components of asset demand. Other changes in asset demand may reinforce or counterbalance them. Because asset markets are global, domestic demand for financial assets is not the only force determining the returns on stocks and bonds in the United States. Several recent studies have explored how demographic change in the currently developed world will affect global asset demand. Our estimates of the future demand for pension assets in the United States, if replicated in other countries, could be an important input to such studies. Whether international capital flows will reinforce or moderate the demographic pressures on asset returns that may arise from changes in the population age structure in the United States depends critically on the future rate of development of currently young economies and on the age structure of other developed nations.

When evaluating how demographic change affects the demand for financial assets in general, and specifically corporate equities, one must remember that a large fraction of financial assets are owned by a small fraction of the population. This group of high net worth investors is likely to be less sensitive to age-related changes in asset demand than other investors who have life-cycle motives for saving. Kennickell (2006) reports that in the 2004 Survey of Consumer Finances, the wealthiest 5 percent of households owned 65.6 percent of equities, including mutual funds, and 79.1 percent of equities, excluding mutual funds. Pension assets represent a smaller share of the assets of this group than of other less-affluent sectors of the population.

Retirement plan assets are one of the most, if not the most, demographically sensitive components of the household financial balance sheet. There are clear demographic effects on assets in DB plans, which are typically paid out as benefit annuities at the time of retirement. The link between demographic structure and 401(k) plan assets is less mechanical because older households have discretion over the rate at which they draw down assets in retirement. There is uncertainty both about the date at which withdrawals will begin and the rate of such withdrawals once they start. At present, many 401(k) participants do not begin to make withdrawals until they are required to do so at age 70.5. In the future, the average age of first withdrawal is likely to increase even for those who do not wait until 70.5 to begin withdrawals because the average age of retirement is likely to rise. This is likely to result both from the increase in the normal Social Security retirement age from sixty-five to sixty-seven by 2027, and from the conversion from DB plans, with strong incentives to leave the labor force early, to personal retirement accounts without these incentives. Longer working lives will probably delay withdrawals from personal retirement accounts and increase the accumulation of retirement assets.

For households that are constrained by the mandatory withdrawal requirements from personal retirement accounts, withdrawals of DC plan assets are likely to overstate the decline in asset demand at older ages. There is no requirement that households consume their minimum distributions, and households that would prefer not to make any withdrawals from their 401(k) plans or individual retirement accounts (IRAs) may simply reinvest the mandatory payouts in other investment options. It is possible that such households will bequeath a substantial portion of their tax-deferred assets to their heirs, who may continue to accumulate assets in a tax-deferred setting for many years. Recent legislation has facilitated such transfers of personal retirement account assets. While this consideration suggests that 401(k) assets may remain substantial even for households at very advanced ages, it is also possible that the financial burden of health care in retirement will be greater for future retirees than for past cohorts and that this will necessitate greater expenditures during retirement. If the cost of health care continues to increase, future retirees are likely to spend more on health care than current retirees. This could affect not only the accumulation of retirement assets, but could accelerate withdrawals from retirement accounts as well.

The many uncertainties that arise in trying to link one source of asset demand to equilibrium rates of return make us reluctant to attempt to quantify the impact of demographically induced changes in retirement asset accumulation on prospective stock or bond returns. There is also a fundamental circularity in this question. Our projections of future DC assets are based on assumptions about the rate of return that plan assets will earn in the next few decades. This underscores the importance of consid-

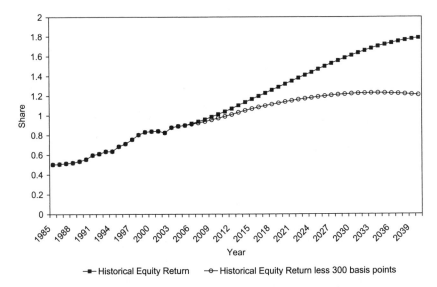

Fig. 10.33   **Total pension assets as share of GDP—Historical return and historical return minus 300 basis points**

ering the sensitivity of future retirement asset projections to rate of return assumptions. This concern notwithstanding, we have developed one metric to provide some indication of the quantitative importance of the demographically induced changes in retirement asset demand.

Figure 10.33 shows our projected demand for all pension plan assets, including both bonds and equities, as a percentage of the Social Security Administration intermediate gross domestic product (GDP) projection. The figure shows that pension assets grow from 50 percent of GDP in 1985 to 100 percent in 2010 to 179 percent in 2040. If the return on equity is 300 basis points lower than the historical return, then total pension assets grow to about 120 percent of GDP by 2040. Both of these projections suggest a very substantial increase retirement saving over the coming decades.

Figure 10.34 shows the projected demand for corporate equity in both DB and DC plans as a percentage of the Social Security Administration intermediate GDP projection: one based on the historical equity rate of return and the other based on the historical return less 300 basis points.[8] Historically, pension equities grew from about 30 percent of GDP in 1985 to about 55 percent in 2005. Our projections suggest continued growth between now and 2040, to 142 percent of GDP when the projection is based on the historical equity return and 84 percent of GDP when the assumed rate of return is the historical value minus 300 basis points. The shape of

8. The equity share is based on projected accumulated equity assets, which depends on the assumed rate of return on equities. We assume no rebalancing in 401(k) plans.

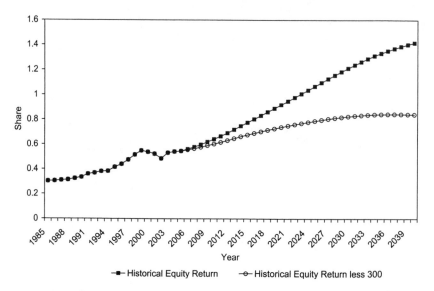

Fig. 10.34   Pension equity as share of GDP—Historical return and historical return minus 300 basis points

the projected growth path is also affected by the different rate of return assumptions. For example, the one-year growth rate of pension assets between 2039 and 2040 is 1.0 percent in the former case and –0.2 percent when we assume the lower equity return. The figure shows that even when we make the lower rate of return assumption, the stock of pension assets continues to increase for the next three decades, even relative to the aggregate economy. The projections do not suggest a sharp decline in pension assets, either in absolute dollars or relative to GDP, when the baby boom cohort reaches retirement age. If low returns depress the growth of 401(k) assets, however, there may be some years in which total retirement assets as a share of GDP are stable or decline slightly.

10.10   Summary

A key component to any effort to analyze how demographic trends may affect future returns on financial assets is a careful analysis of how these trends will affect assets in DB and DC pension plans. This chapter on DB pension plan assets and our earlier companion paper on 401(k) assets explore this issue. The dramatic decline in DB participation in the past three decades stands in contrast to the rapid expansion of 401(k)-like plans. We develop projections of the DB benefits of cohorts retiring between now and 2040 and use them to project the total assets held in DB plans through

2040. The projections are based on extrapolation of cohort data from many waves of the SIPP along with demographic projections from the Social Security Administration.

We project the present value of DB benefits at age sixty-five for cohorts who reach age sixty-five in each year from 1982 to 2040, and we compare these projections to projections of 401(k) assets. Our projections suggest that the average (over *all persons*) of the present value of real DB benefits at age sixty-five attained an historical maximum in 2003, when the value was $72,637. Our projections also suggest that the average value of 401(k) assets at age sixty-five surpasses the average present value of DB benefits at age sixty-five in about 2010. Thereafter, the value of 401(k) assets grows rapidly, attaining levels much greater than the maximum present value of DB benefits. If equity returns between 2006 and 2040 are comparable to those observed historically, by 2040 average projected 401(k) assets will be over six times larger than the historical maximum level of DB benefits at age sixty-five, attained in 2003. Even if equity returns average 300 basis points below their historical value, we project that average 401(k) assets in 2040 would be 3.7 times as large as the value of DB benefits in 2003.

The projected growth of real 401(k) assets more than offsets the projected decline in real DB plan assets during the next three decades. Focusing on DB assets alone suggests that an aging population, in conjunction with a shift away from DB plans, will lead to a decline in the real value of pension assets averaged across all retirees in future cohorts. When we combine projected 401(k) assets with projected DB assets, however, we find that real pension assets not only increase, but increase substantially, in future decades.

Our findings underscore the need for further analysis of the factors that determine the diffusion of 401(k) plans across corporations, especially small companies with low-wage workers, as well as the contribution behavior and withdrawal behavior of 401(k) participants. The growing role of 401(k)-type plans in the retirement landscape suggests that understanding asset accumulation and draw-down in these plans is a critical component of any analysis of the effect of demographic change on financial markets.

Appendix

Table 10A.1   **Regression estimates for the level of pension benefits**

Cohort		Parameter estimates		
Age in 1984	Year age 65	Coefficient	Standard error	t-statistic
86	1963	41.84	59.67	0.70
85	1964	−22.90	75.76	−0.30
83	1966	−42.08	50.39	−0.84
82	1967	27.12	55.60	0.49
81	1968	110.47	62.20	1.78
80	1969	55.35	68.64	0.81
79	1970	132.11	59.10	2.24
78	1971	206.22	55.86	3.69
77	1972	156.01	53.63	2.91
76	1973	151.60	50.57	3.00
75	1974	171.49	51.14	3.35
74	1975	246.42	48.08	5.12
73	1976	232.83	51.14	4.55
72	1977	264.87	48.86	5.42
71	1978	312.69	51.26	6.10
70	1979	328.91	50.51	6.51
69	1980	352.85	49.27	7.16
68	1981	410.67	49.83	8.24
67	1982	479.79	48.30	9.93
66	1983	496.66	49.11	10.11
65	1984	526.01	49.72	10.58
64	1985	548.35	50.30	10.90
63	1986	589.81	49.88	11.83
62	1987	592.74	49.54	11.97
61	1988	607.28	50.00	12.15
60	1989	657.08	50.77	12.94
59	1990	685.37	51.76	13.24
58	1991	748.48	53.73	13.93
57	1992	710.96	51.80	13.73
56	1993	815.37	53.83	15.15
55	1994	815.87	53.67	15.20
54	1995	911.54	55.21	16.51
53	1996	883.43	55.71	15.86
52	1997	983.28	58.73	16.74
51	1998	1,009.20	60.24	16.75
50	1999	1,063.51	60.98	17.44
49	2000	1,079.51	61.99	17.41
48	2001	1,124.29	63.02	17.84
47	2002	1,299.43	71.18	18.25
46	2003	1,407.14	71.53	19.67
45	2004	1,381.55	77.27	17.88
44	2005	1,364.24	75.67	18.03
43	2006	1,425.66	84.44	16.88

Table 10A.1   (continued)

| Cohort | | Parameter estimates | | |
Age in 1984	Year age 65	Coefficient	Standard error	t-statistic
42	2007	1,452.48	83.95	17.30
41	2008	1,516.71	84.13	18.03
40	2009	1,652.97	114.61	14.42
39	2010	1,658.59	116.33	14.26
38	2011	1,720.02	123.20	13.96
37	2012	1,729.32	127.80	13.53
Intercept Age		−131.08	54.89	−2.39
55–60		52.53	7.38	7.11
60–65		−13.07	5.73	−2.28
65–70		10.55	4.29	2.46
70–75		17.93	4.20	4.27
75–80		16.91	4.85	3.49
> 80		0.92	5.84	0.16
No. of observations	32,388			
$F(56, 32331)$	69.53			
R^2	0.1112			
Root MSE	802.96			

Note: MSE = mean square error.

Table 10A.2   **Probit estimates for receipt of pension benefits**

| Cohort | | Parameter estimates | | |
Age in 1984	Year age 65	Coefficient	Standard error	t-statistic
80	1969	0.20	0.14	1.43
79	1970	0.14	0.13	1.11
78	1971	0.17	0.12	1.40
77	1972	0.13	0.12	1.09
76	1973	0.19	0.12	1.60
75	1974	0.20	0.12	1.65
74	1975	0.10	0.12	0.83
73	1976	0.21	0.12	1.84
72	1977	0.29	0.11	2.66
71	1978	0.34	0.11	3.04
70	1979	0.24	0.11	2.17
69	1980	0.32	0.11	2.93
68	1981	0.37	0.11	3.38
67	1982	0.41	0.11	3.77
66	1983	0.45	0.11	4.17
65	1984	0.40	0.11	3.64

(*continued*)

Table 10A.2 (continued)

Cohort		Parameter estimates		
Age in 1984	Year age 65	Coefficient	Standard error	*t*-statistic
64	1985	0.40	0.11	3.68
63	1986	0.43	0.11	3.98
62	1987	0.44	0.11	4.09
61	1988	0.42	0.11	3.92
60	1989	0.46	0.11	4.28
59	1990	0.43	0.11	3.98
58	1991	0.43	0.11	3.95
57	1992	0.42	0.11	3.85
56	1993	0.42	0.11	3.91
55	1994	0.44	0.11	4.01
54	1995	0.43	0.11	3.94
53	1996	0.43	0.11	3.95
52	1997	0.43	0.11	3.91
51	1998	0.43	0.11	3.91
50	1999	0.52	0.11	4.71
49	2000	0.43	0.11	3.94
48	2001	0.41	0.11	3.74
47	2002	0.41	0.11	3.73
46	2003	0.46	0.11	4.07
45	2004	0.49	0.11	4.36
44	2005	0.46	0.11	4.00
43	2006	0.55	0.11	4.80
42	2007	0.51	0.11	4.51
41	2008	0.58	0.12	4.78
40	2009	0.60	0.12	4.95
39	2010	0.54	0.12	4.41
38	2011	0.61	0.12	4.94
37	2012	0.47	0.12	3.82
Intercept Age		−6.94	0.38	−18.31
55–60		0.10	0.01	15.45
60–65		0.11	0.00	23.08
65–70		0.03	0.00	5.25
70–75		0.01	0.01	1.78
75–80		0.00	0.01	0.01
No. of observations	78,686			
Pseudo R^2	0.0593			
Wald χ^2 (49)	4,943.32			

Table 10A.3   **Probit estimates for participation using population base**

Cohort		Parameter estimates		
Age in 1984	Year age 65	Coefficient	Standard error	t-statistic
65	1984	−0.143	0.122	−1.17
64	1985	−0.064	0.107	−0.59
63	1986	−0.083	0.105	−0.79
62	1987	0.046	0.092	0.51
60	1989	0.056	0.091	0.62
59	1990	0.040	0.091	0.44
58	1991	0.010	0.094	0.11
57	1992	0.139	0.094	1.48
56	1993	−0.040	0.098	−0.40
55	1994	−0.025	0.095	−0.26
54	1995	−0.031	0.096	−0.32
53	1996	−0.247	0.096	−2.56
52	1997	−0.160	0.096	−1.67
51	1998	−0.177	0.090	−1.98
50	1999	−0.227	0.087	−2.62
49	2000	−0.249	0.084	−2.95
48	2001	−0.124	0.081	−1.52
47	2002	−0.173	0.080	−2.17
46	2003	−0.198	0.078	−2.52
45	2004	−0.290	0.079	−3.65
44	2005	−0.225	0.078	−2.88
43	2006	−0.160	0.077	−2.07
42	2007	−0.202	0.077	−2.63
41	2008	−0.232	0.078	−2.99
40	2009	−0.257	0.078	−3.31
39	2010	−0.241	0.078	−3.09
38	2011	−0.230	0.077	−2.97
37	2012	−0.259	0.078	−3.31
36	2013	−0.327	0.078	−4.18
35	2014	−0.313	0.078	−4.02
34	2015	−0.358	0.077	−4.62
33	2016	−0.410	0.077	−5.29
32	2017	−0.419	0.077	−5.44
31	2018	−0.486	0.077	−6.31
30	2019	−0.485	0.077	−6.31
29	2020	−0.519	0.077	−6.76
28	2021	−0.525	0.077	−6.84
27	2022	−0.543	0.077	−7.05
26	2023	−0.526	0.077	−6.82
25	2024	−0.586	0.078	−7.47
24	2025	−0.530	0.078	−6.76
23	2026	−0.618	0.079	−7.81
22	2027	−0.640	0.080	−8.03
21	2028	−0.610	0.079	−7.68
20	2029	−0.631	0.080	−7.91

(continued)

Table 10A.3   (continued)

Cohort		Parameter estimates		
Age in 1984	Year age 65	Coefficient	Standard error	t-statistic
19	2030	−0.743	0.081	−9.16
18	2031	−0.667	0.081	−8.24
17	2032	−0.750	0.082	−9.20
16	2033	−0.803	0.082	−9.79
15	2034	−0.842	0.082	−10.27
14	2035	−0.821	0.082	−10.02
13	2036	−0.846	0.083	−10.19
12	2037	−0.889	0.085	−10.51
11	2038	−0.866	0.092	−9.38
10	2039	−0.756	0.092	−8.23
9	2040	−0.888	0.096	−9.28
Intercept Age		−0.519	0.229	−2.27
<30		0.013	0.008	1.75
30–35		−0.004	0.006	−0.67
35–40		−0.006	0.006	−1.15
40–45		0.004	0.006	0.76
45–50		−0.015	0.006	−2.59
50–55		−0.048	0.007	−7.29
55–60		−0.056	0.008	−6.64
>60		−0.111	0.015	−7.26
No. of observations	216,969			
Pseudo R^2	0.021			
Wald χ^2 (64)	1,930.12			

References

Belt, Bradley D. 2005. Testimony before the Committee on Education and the Workforce, United States House of Representatives, March 2.

Bergstresser Daniel, Mihir A. Desai, and Joshua Rauh. 2006. Earnings manipulation and managerial investment decisions: Evidence from sponsored pension plans. *Quarterly Journal of Economics* 121 (1): 157–95.

Beshears, John, James Choi, David Laibson, and Brigitte Madrian. 2008. The importance of default options for retirement saving outcomes: Evidence from the United States. In *Lessons from pension reform in the Americas,* ed. Stephen J. Kay and Tapen Sinha, 59–87. Oxford, UK: Oxford University Press.

Boersch-Supan, Axel, Alexander Ludwig, and Joachim Winter. 2005. Aging, pension reform, and capital flows: A multi-country simulation model. NBER Working Paper no. 11850. Cambridge, MA: National Bureau of Economic Research.

Brooks, Robin. 2002. Asset market effects of the baby boom and Social Security reform. *American Economic Review* 92 (May): 402–06.

Geanakoplos, John, M. Michael Magill, and Martine Quinzii. 2004. Demography and the long-run predictability of the stock market. *Brookings Papers on Economic Activity,* Issue no. 1:241–325.

Ibbotson Associates. 2006. *Stocks, bonds, bills, and inflation, 2006 yearbook.* Chicago: Ibbotson Associates.

Johnson, Richard, Leonard Burman, and Deborah Kobes. 2004. *Annuitized wealth at older ages: Evidence from the Health and Retirement Study.* Final Report to the Employee Benefits Security Administration, U.S. Department of Labor. Washington, DC: Urban Institute.

Kennickell, Arthur B. 2006. Currents and undercurrents: Changes in the distribution of wealth, 1989–2004. Federal Reserve Board of Governors, Working Paper.

Krueger, Dirk, and Alexander Ludwig. 2006. On the consequences of demographic change for rates of return to capital and the distribution of wealth and welfare. Goethe University, Frankfurt. Mimeograph.

Poterba, James M. 2005. The impact of population aging on financial markets in developed countries. In Global demographic Change: Economic Impact and challenges, ed. Gordon H. Sellor, 163–216. Kansas City, MO: Federal Reserve Bank of Kansas City.

Poterba, James M., Steven F. Venti, and David A. Wise. 2008. New estimates of the future path of 401(k) assets. *Tax Policy and the Economy* 22:43–80.

Schieber, Sylvester, and John Shoven. 1997. The consequences of population aging for private pension fund saving and asset markets. In *The economic effects of aging in the United States and Japan,* ed. M. Hurd and N. Yashiro. 111–30. Chicago: University of Chicago Press.

U.S. Government Accountability Office. 2006. Retirement of baby boomers is unlikely to precipitate dramatic decline in market returns, but broader risks threaten retirement security. Report no. GAO-06-718. Washington, DC: GPO, July.

Wiatrowski, William. 2005. Documenting benefits coverage for all workers. USDOL/BLS, December. http://www.bls.gov/opub/cwc/cm20040518ar01p1.htm.

Comment   Jonathan Skinner

Everyone knows that the United States is embarking on a fundamental demographic shift as the baby boomers age, but there's less agreement on how it will affect the financial security of future retirees. James M. Poterba, Steven F. Venti, and David A. Wise (2007b) have provided some critical answers to this larger question by charting the course of defined benefit plans and their future inflows and outflows. The chapter is remarkable not because the results are shocking—indeed, they appear quite reasonable—but because of the incredible attention to detail in building up from the micro-level patterns of data to aggregate predictions. By harnessing millions of individual-level observations from a variety of sources and years, they not only provide a solid foundation for the aggregate estimates, but they also

Jonathan Skinner is the John Sloan Dickey Third Century Chair of Economics and the John French Professor of Economics at Dartmouth College, and a research associate of the National Bureau of Economic Research.

allow for checks on the data predictions to ensure that they're not being misled by any single source of data. This chapter is, therefore, of interest both as a methodological exercise and as providing reliable estimates of future flows and stocks of defined benefit assets.

Still, the authors must ultimately confront several unknowable measures regarding future growth in wages and in rates of return and, hence, future growth. The most difficult to predict, of course, is the rate of return on assets. As they note, the historical nominal return on equity has been 12.3 percent and on bonds 6.2 percent, and they make the assumption that similar returns will continue during their analysis. Predicting future rates of return (and the gap between stock and bond returns) is, of course, a difficult business, and there is little agreement on even the premium of expected stock returns over bond returns, (e.g., Geanokoplos, Mitchell, and Zeldes 1999), without even trying to guess what will be the level of each. Still, it seems prudent to focus on rates of return somewhat less stellar than those experienced in the past, and so I will focus on the authors' calculations assuming rates of return 300 basis points below the historical record.

I consider three questions. First, what is the partial-equilibrium shift in all assets (including defined contribution and Social Security trust funds) caused by these demographic change? Second, how much would we expect this shift to affect the gross rate of return on assets? And third, by how much would this change in the rate of return affect the future income of retirees?

What Is the Partial-Equilibrium Shift in Demand for Assets?

There are three basic sources of assets most relevant to this exercise. The first is private retirement accounts, which include both defined benefit plans and defined contribution (or 401[k]) plans. In a companion piece, Poterba, Venti, and Wise (2007a) have performed a similar exercise for defined contribution plans such as 401(k)s, and in this chapter, the authors combine both defined contribution and defined benefit flows.

Figure 10.5 in this volume shows the Poterba, Venti, and Wise best estimate of the net flows from these two sources combined. As noted in the preceding, I will focus on the lower rates of return, and under this assumption, they predict a net outflow from combined defined benefit and defined contribution plans. They find that defined benefit assets will exhibit little change over time, with the loss in participants offset by the higher per-worker benefits of those remaining. However, defined contribution plans are projected to both grow rapidly, and then to decline as baby boomers draw down their assets, leading to significant net outflows. By 2020, the systems are in equipoise, with contributions balanced by withdrawals, but by 2040, the floodgate has burst, resulting in a net outflow of just less than 400 billion dollars annually.

The second is the Social Security trust fund. Currently under intermediate projections, it is predicted to grow to about $3.5 trillion in 2020 before

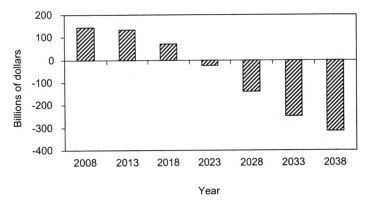

**Fig. 10C.1   Inflows and outflows of the OASDI trust fund
(intermediate projections)**
Source: Social Security Administration trustees report, 2006. Annualized changes calculated
from predicted levels of assets and assigned to midpoint year.

beginning its march toward bankruptcy by 2040. The implicit *annual* flows
out of the trust fund (as Treasury bonds are sold off) is shown in figure
10C.1, where once again the trust shows little net flows around 2020, but
after 2035 there is a dramatic decline the stock of treasury bonds held by
the Social Security Administration being sold off to make up for the budgetary shortfalls. Of course, by 2040, that outflow stops when there are no
longer assets to sell, and taxes must either be raised or benefits cut. And if
the Social Security Administration takes action before the last dollar is
drained from the trust fund, there would be further moderation of the outflows.

The third category is private wealth. The primary reason for why demographic changes would affect wealth and saving behavior is simply because
of a change in the age structure, more retirees and fewer younger people.
However, it is difficult to pin down this specific number. First, the defined
benefit and defined contribution flows noted in the preceding already reflect much of the traditional life-cycle saving that is done through tax-
preferred retirement plans. Second, the pure life-cycle effects are likely at-
tenuated by the substantial fraction of wealth held by the extremely
wealthy, and thus unlikely to be subject to life-cycle deaccumulation
(United States Government Accounting Office [USGAO] 2006). Third, as
noted in Dynan, Skinner, and Zeldes (2004), elderly households show at
best modest levels of dissaving (or even positive saving). Finally, as shown
in figure 10C.2, predicted changes in wealth holdings owing to shifts in the
demographic structure are modest because the fraction of the population
at peak saving ages—those forty-five to sixty-four—declines only slightly,
from 20.2 to 20 percent, between 2000 and 2040 (Goyal 2004). There is a
sizeable increase in the elderly population sixty-five and over, but the in-

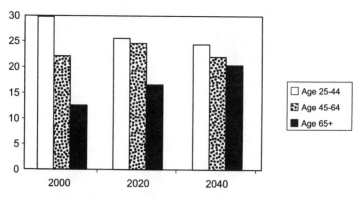

Fig. 10C.2   Projections of the age distribution in the U.S., 2000–2040
Source: Goyal (2004).

crease is largely offset by a decline in the proportion of younger age groups, but these younger groups tend to have modest saving rates as well.

In sum, by 2020 we should not expect to observe any large change in the demand for assets, but by 2040 we might expect an outflow of as much as $750 billion—more if private nonretirement saving scales back substantially, less if Social Security reforms are implemented before the trust fund goes bust. While large in dollar terms, this shift is still relatively modest in comparison to projected U.S. gross domestic product (GDP) of 23.8 trillion (2005$) in 2040 (Social Security Trustees 2006). Shifts in implied saving rates of 3 percent (e.g., 750 billion divided by 23.8 billion) are not out of the ordinary, particularly with respect to recent declines in aggregate saving rates, and the magnitude would be even smaller in the presence of potential capital inflows from developing countries such as China or India.

How Will This Shift in Demand Affect the Rate of Return on Assets?

In the simplest model, a fall in national saving rates should lead to a decline in the capital-labor ratio and, hence, a *rise* in the interest rate. An offsetting effect, of course, is the change in the age distribution and, hence, in the net number of workers. Krueger and Ludwig (2007) have addressed these two effects in the context of a general equilibrium simulation model for the United States and other countries and conclude that on net, the decline in labor dominates the decline in capital, thus leading to between a 12 and 89 basis point decline in the interest rate. Their estimated effects are quite sensitive to whether taxes are raised to maintain Social Security solvency (the former estimate) or whether benefits are cut (the latter). As it turns out, the open-economy and closed-economy estimates are quite similar, largely because other countries are experiencing the same shift in the age distribution.

Missing from these estimates, however, is the possibility of a more short-term demand effect going in the opposite direction—that a (flow) decline in the demand for assets will lead to a drop in stock market and bond returns (e.g., Poterba 2004). A recent comprehensive review of the literature suggested at best modest effects, with results again bounded largely by a decline of .5 percent (USGAO 2006). Again, these effects are consistent with the modest magnitude of the expected shift in demand.

How Will Changes in the Rate of Return Affect Retiree Welfare?

The Krueger and Ludwig (forthcoming) estimate of an 89 basis point decline is the largest estimate I've seen of how the aging baby boomers will affect asset returns, so it is useful to put this difference in perspective. Certainly small differences in the rate of return can exert a large impact on wealth accumulation; the difference between $1,000 invested at 4 percent and $1,000 invested at 4.89 percent over twenty years is $2,191 versus $2,598, which is real money. On the other hand, many retirees depend primarily on annuity flows, for example, from Social Security benefits, and so interest rates will have relatively less impact on overall retiree income. (Lower interest rates may further improve the U.S. government's ability to pay Social Security benefits given that it tends to issue debt.) More to the point, it's not unusual to find differences in administrative fees for mutual funds of 100 basis points or more. So one could put the 89 basis points in another context—it's smaller in magnitude than the difference in return between the administrative fees from keeping one's money in a retail brokerage account, paying a 2 percent administrative fee, versus a Charles Schwab, Vanguard, or Fidelity low-fee account. It seems likely that baby boomers will face more insidious risks in the future.

References

Dynan, Karen, Jonathan Skinner, and Stephen Zeldes. 2004. Do the rich save more? *Journal of Political Economy* 112 (April): 397–444.
Geanakoplos, John, Olivia Mitchell, and Stephen P. Zeldes. 1999. Social Security money's worth. In *Prospects for Social Security reform,* ed. Olivia S. Mitchell, Robert J. Meyers, and Howard Young, 79–151. Philadelphia: University of Pennsylvania Press.
Goyal, Amit. 2004. Demographics, stock market flows, and stock returns. *Journal of Financial Quantitative Analysis* 39 (1): 115–43.
Krueger, Dirk, and Alexander Ludwig. 2007. On the consequences of demographic change for rates of return to capital and the distribution of wealth and welfare. *Journal of Monetary Economics* 54(1): 49–87.
Poterba, James. 2004. The impact of population aging on financial markets. NBER Working Paper no. 10851, October.
Poterba, James M., Steven F. Venti, and David A. Wise. 2007a. New estimates of the future path of 401(k) assets. NBER Working Paper no. 13083, May.

————. 2007b. The decline of defined benefit retirement plans and asset flows. NBER Working Paper no. 12834, January.

Social Security Trustees. 2006. *The 2006 annual report of the board of trustees of the Federal Old-Age and Survivors Insurance and Federal Disability Insurance Trust Funds.* Washington, DC: GPO.

U.S. Government Accounting Office USGAO. 2006. Baby boom generation: Retirement of baby boomers is unlikely to precipitate dramatic decline in market returns, but broader risks threaten retirement security. Report no. GAO-06-718. Washington, DC: GPO.

11

Demographic Change, Relative Factor Prices, International Capital Flows, and Their Differential Effects on the Welfare of Generations

Alexander Ludwig, Dirk Krüger, and
Axel Börsch-Supan

11.1 Introduction

In all major industrialized countries the population is aging, over time reducing the fraction of the population in working age. This process is driven by falling mortality rates followed by a decline in birth rates. This reduces population growth rates; in some countries, population will even decline. While demographic change occurs in all countries in the world, extent and timing differ substantially. Europe and some Asian countries have almost passed the closing stages of the demographic transition process,

Alexander Ludwig is head of macroeconomics research unit at the Mannheim Research Institute for the Economics of Aging, University of Mannheim. Dirk Krüger is a research professor at the Mannheim Research Institute for the Economics of Aging, University of Mannheim, an associate professor of economics at the University of Pennsylvania, and a faculty research fellow of the National Bureau of Economic Research. Axel Börsch-Supan is director of the Mannheim Research Institute for the Economics of Aging, University of Mannheim, and a research associate of the National Bureau of Economic Research.

This chapter is in part based on D. Krüger and A. Ludwig's "On the Consequences of Demographic Change for Rates of Return to Capital, and the Distribution of Wealth and Welfare," *Journal of Monetary Economics,* 51 (1), 49–87, 2007. We thank conference participants and researchers at several places for their helpful comments, in particular Martin Floden, Ayse İmrohoroğlu, Jim Poterba, Sandra Svaljek, and an anonymous referee. This research was supported by the U.S. Social Security Administration (SSA) through grant #10-P-98363-1-03 to the National Bureau of Economic Research (NBER) as part of the SSA Retirement Research Consortium and by the sponsors of the Mannheim Research Institute for the Economics of Aging (MEA), the Land of Baden-Württemberg, the German Association of Insurers (GDV) and the German Science Foundation (DFG). The findings and conclusions expressed are solely those of the author(s) and do not represent the views of the SSA, any agency of the federal government, the NBER, or any other sponsor. This chapter was prepared for the 2006 NBER Conference on Social Security research from the Retirement Research Center in Woodstock, Vermont.

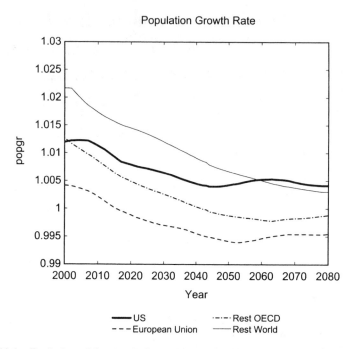

Fig. 11.1   Evolution of the population growth rate in 4 regions

while Latin America and Africa are only at the beginning (Bloom and Williamson 1998; United Nations 2002).

Figure 11.1, based on United Nations (UN) population projections (United Nations 2002), illustrates the differential impact of demographic change on population growth rates for the period 2000 to 2080. They are defined as the growth rate of the adult population, aggregated into four mutually exclusive regions of the world: the United States, the European Union (EU), the rest of the Organization for Economic Cooperation and Development (OECD [ROECD]) and the rest of the world (ROW).

Population growth rates are predicted to decline in all regions, but to remain positive in the United States and in the ROW region throughout the twenty-first century. In contrast, they will become negative in the EU by about 2016 and in the ROECD by about 2042, such that their populations start shrinking, while the populations of the other two world regions continue to grow.

These striking differences in demographic change will change the global balance and induce differential factor price changes and international flows of labor, capital, and products. All this will affect the welfare of the people living in these regions. This is the topic of this chapter. As we will see, welfare is affected differentially not only across regions but also across generations.

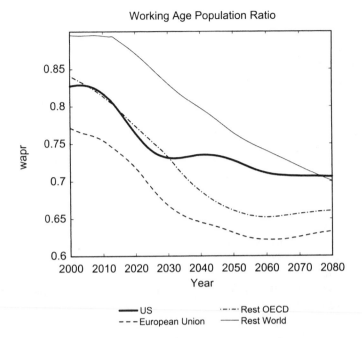

Working Age Population Ratio

Legend:
—— US
– – – European Union
·—·—· Rest OECD
—— Rest World

Fig. 11.2   Evolution of working age to population ratios in 4 regions

Figure 11.2 shows the impact of demographic change on working-age population ratios—the ratio of the working-age population (of age twenty to sixty-four) to the total adult population (of age twenty to ninety-five). This indicator, which will turn out to be crucial in our analysis, illustrates that the EU is the oldest, whereas the ROW is the youngest region in terms of the relative size of the working-age population. The United States and the rest of the OECD region initially have the same level of working-age population ratios, but the dynamics of demographic change differ substantially in the United States relative to the other regions. While working-age population ratios decrease across all regions, the speed of this decrease significantly slows down for the United States in about 2030.

The chapter continues a line of research by Börsch-Supan (1996); Börsch-Supan, Ludwig, and Winter (2002, 2006); and, especially, Krüger and Ludwig (2007) that aim to quantify the effects of demographic change on macroeconomic developments and welfare. What are the effects of these long-run developments on relative factor prices and welfare? What are the additional effects of ongoing pension reforms that convert the pay-as-you-go (PAYGO) pension systems into multipillar systems with potentially large capital stocks?

The basic effects are intuitive: first, the changes in the population structure will alter aggregate labor supply and aggregate savings. This will change factor prices for labor and capital. Because labor will become scarcer, relative to capital, real wages will increase and real rates of return to capital will decrease. Second, if countries reform their PAYGO pension systems, the additional supply of capital increases the downward pressure on the rates of return. This will have differential effects on the welfare of generations. The young may gain through higher wages, while the old may lose due to lower capital returns.

While these basic mechanisms are intuitive, their quantification is difficult, especially in an international context. Quantification, however, is important in order to understand the implications for Social Security reform. If capital returns decline very little, welfare implications will also be small. If returns decline catastrophically, like suggested by some proponents of the so-called asset meltdown hypothesis, pension reforms, that substitute parts of the PAYGO Social Security system by prefunded accounts, may create large welfare losses for future pensioners.

This chapter feeds the demographic projections by the United Nations into a computable overlapping generations model of the type pioneered by Auerbach and Kotlikoff (1987). We extend the model to a multicountry version as in Börsch-Supan, Ludwig, and Winter (2006) and enrich the model by uninsurable idiosyncratic uncertainty, as in İmrohoroğlu, İmrohoroğlu, and Joines (1995, 1999); Conesa and Krüger (1999); and Krüger and Ludwig (2007).

Both extensions are indispensable for the welfare questions we want to address. First, employing a multicountry view is essential as capital markets are global and populations age differentially; for instance, the countries that supply capital to the United States age faster than the United States. In our model, capital can freely flow between different regions in the OECD (the United States, the EU and the rest of the OECD). These capital flows may mitigate the decline in rates of return and the increase in real wages from the perspective of fast-aging economies such as the European countries.

Second, uninsurable idiosyncratic uncertainty will endogenously give rise to some individuals deriving most of their income from returns to capital, while the income of others is mainly composed of labor income. Abstracting from this heterogeneity does not allow a meaningful analysis of the distributional consequences of aging-induced changes in factor prices. This model feature also adds a precautionary savings motive to the standard life-cycle savings motive of households, which makes life-cycle savings profiles generated by the model more realistic.

We find that the rate of return to capital decreases by roughly 80 to 90 basis points if capital is allowed to freely flow across regions. Our simulations indicate that capital flows from rapidly aging regions to the rest of the world will initially be substantial but that trends are reversed when households decumulate savings. However, due to the high correlation of long-run demographic developments among OECD countries in terms of trends in the working-age population ratio, compare figure 11.2, these capital flows do not affect much the long-run decrease of the rate of return. The latter does not change much whether we assume the United States (or Europe) to be closed or open economies.

In order to evaluate the welfare consequences of the demographic transition, we ask the following question: suppose a household economically born in 2005 would live through the economic transition with changing factor prices induced by the demographic change (but keeping its own survival probabilities constant at their 2005 values); how would its welfare have changed, relative to a situation without a demographic transition? We find that for young households with little assets, the increase in wages dominates the decline in rates of return. Abstracting from Social Security and its reform, newborns in 2005 gain in the order of 0.6 to 0.9 percent in terms of lifetime consumption. Older, asset-rich individuals, on the other hand, tend to lose because of the decline in interest rates. If the demographic transition, in addition, makes a reform of the Social Security system necessary, then falling benefits or increasing taxes reduce the welfare gains for newborn individuals. An increase in the retirement age to seventy, on the other hand, mitigates some of these negative consequences.

Our chapter borrows model elements from, and contributes to, three strands of the literature. Starting with Auerbach and Kotlikoff (1987), a vast number of papers has used large-scale overlapping generations (OLG) models to analyze the transition path of an economy induced by a policy reform. Examples include Social Security reform (see, e.g., Conesa and Krüger 1999) and fundamental tax reform (see, e.g., Altig et al. 2001; Conesa and Krüger 2006).

A second strand of the literature (often using the general methodology of the first strand) has focused on the economic consequences of population aging in closed economies, often paying special attention to the adjustments required in the Social Security system due to demographic shifts. Important examples include Huang, İmrohoroğlu, and Sargent (1997), De Nardi, İmrohoroğlu, and Sargent (1999) and, with respect to asset prices, Abel (2003).

The contributions discussed so far assume that the economy under investigation is closed to international capital flows. However, as the population ages at different pace in various regions of the world, one would expect capital to flow across these regions. The third strand of the literature our chapter touches upon, therefore, is the large body of work in international macroeconomics studying the direction, size, cause, and consequences of international capital flows and current account dynamics, reviewed comprehensively in Obstfeld and Rogoff (1995).

Our chapter is most closely related to work that combines these three strands of the literature, by using the methodology of large-scale OLG models to study the consequences of demographic change in open economies. The work by Attanasio, Kitao, and Violante (2006, 2007) construct a two-region (the North and the South) OLG model to study the allocative and welfare consequences of different Social Security reforms in an open economy. Compared to their model, we include endogenous labor supply and idiosyncratic income shocks.

Similar to our own work, Fehr, Jokisch, and Kotlikoff (2005) investigate the impact of population aging on the viability of the Social Security system and its reform. Building on earlier work by Brooks (2003), who employs a simple four-period OLG model, Henriksen (2002), Feroli (2003), and Domeij and Floden (2006) use large-scale simulation models similar to Börsch-Supan, Ludwig, and Winter (2006) to explain historical capital flow data with changes in demographics, rather than, as we do, to study the welfare and distributional implications of *future* changes in demographics. Relative to this literature, we see the contribution of our chapter in evaluating the welfare consequences of the demographic transition per se and not just the alternative Social Security reform scenarios, as well as in the analysis of the distributional consequences of changing factor prices due to population aging.

The chapter is organized as follows. Section 11.2 presents a simple two-period OLG model to illustrate the relationship between demographic change, per capita consumption, and welfare. Section 11.3 contains the description of our large-scale quantitative simulation model, and section 11.4 presents our main results. Finally, section 11.5 concludes.

11.2   A Simple Model

Key for understanding the results in section 11.4 is to notice that per capita consumption and individual welfare are entirely different concepts in OLG economies. Per capita consumption and output are cross-sectional measures referring to all households currently alive, whereas welfare is a cohort-based measure. Relevant for utility over the life cycle are wages, interest rates, and how consumption and leisure are weighted at different ages. Due to discounting, utility from future consumption is lower than from current consumption, giving more weight to consumption and leisure at young ages.

As societies are aging, labor becomes relatively scarce and capital relatively abundant, which leads to increases of wages and decreases in rates of return. This implies that the consumption profile is tilted over the life cycle such that the young consume relatively more than the old. In per capita consumption, allocations are weighted with cohort sizes. Hence, as a consequence of demographic change, the size of those who consume more—the young—decreases, whereas the size of those who consume less—the old—increases. If this compositional effect is stronger than the direct effect of a decrease in size of the overall population, per capita consumption decreases.

However, if the higher consumption at young ages has a higher utility weight than the lower consumption at older ages, individual welfare increases. This leads to a result that is counterintuitive at first sight: per capita consumption and welfare may move into different directions. Demographic change leads to a reduction of per capita consumption, yet, at the same time, it also leads to an increase of the newborns' lifetime welfare, at least in the absence of Social Security.

We now illustrate these insights using a simplified version of the Diamond (1965) model. Krüger and Ludwig (2007) develop an open-economy version of the model with Social Security in order to illustrate the various interactions between demographic change, Social Security and international capital flows. Here, we do not address all these issues and focus on a closed economy without Social Security. We also abstract from technological progress.[1]

11.2.1   Households

There are N_t young households who live for two periods and have preferences over consumption c_t^y, c_{t+1}^o representable by the utility function

$$\log(c_t^y) + \beta \log(c_{t+1}^o).$$

In the first period of their lives, households work for a wage w_t, and in the second period, they retire. Because we ignore Social Security, the budget constraints read as

$$c_t^y + s_t = w_t$$

$$c_{t+1}^o = (1 + r_{t+1})s_t,$$

where r_{t+1} is the real interest rate between period t and $t + 1$.

11.2.2   Firms

The production function is given by

$$Y_t = K_t^\alpha N_t^{1-\alpha},$$

where Y_t is output, and K_t is the aggregate capital stock.

The production technology is operated by a representative firm that behaves competitively in product and factor markets. Assuming that capital depreciates fully after its use in production, profit maximization of firms implies that

---

1. These results on per capita consumption and welfare also hold in an open-economy model where relative prices are driven by the impact of the countries' relative sizes; see Krüger and Ludwig (2007) for more details.

$$1 + r_t = \alpha k_t^{\alpha-1}$$

$$w_t = (1 - \alpha)k_t^{\alpha},$$

where

$$k_t = \frac{K_t}{N_t}$$

is the capital intensity.

11.2.3   Aggregation

Market clearing requires that

$$K_{t+1} = N_t s_t,$$

from which we also have that

$$k_{t+1} = \frac{s_t}{\gamma_{t+1}^N},$$

where γ_t^N is the gross growth rate of the young cohort between periods $t - 1$ and t. It also measures the working age to population ratio (the higher is γ_t^N, the higher is that ratio), which allows us to map the predictions of this model to the data plotted in figure 11.2.[2]

Equilibrium in this model can be characterized analytically. To do so, we first solve the household problem and then aggregate across households.

Optimal savings of the young are given as

$$s_t = \frac{\beta}{1 + \beta} w_t.$$

Substituting out for wages from the preceding gives

$$s_t = \frac{\beta(1 - \alpha)}{1 + \beta} k_t^{\alpha}.$$

From the capital market clearing condition, we now get that

---

2. The population at time t is given by $P_t = N_t + N_{t-1}$ and the working age to population ratio is given by

$$\frac{N_t}{N_t + N_{t-1}},$$

which we can rewrite as

$$\frac{1}{1 + 1/\gamma_t^N}.$$

Thus, γ_t^N is a measure both of the population growth rate as well as the working age to population ratio.

$$k_{t+1} = \frac{(1 - \alpha)\beta}{(1 + \beta)\gamma^N_{t+1}} k^\alpha_t.$$

In the steady state, we have that $\gamma^N_t = \gamma^N$ and $k_{t+1} = k_t = k^*$, where k^* is the steady-state capital stock given by

$$k^* = \left(\frac{\phi}{\gamma^N}\right)^{1/(1-\alpha)}$$

where $\phi = (1 - \alpha)\beta/(1 + \beta)$.

11.2.4   Analysis

Steady-state consumption when young and old can now be written as

$$c^y = \frac{1 - \alpha}{1 + \beta} k^\alpha$$

$$c^o = \beta\alpha k^{\alpha-1} c^y.$$

From the utility function, we can then derive that

$$u = \ln(c^y) + \beta \ln(c^o)$$

$$= \psi - \frac{[\alpha(1 + \beta) - \beta(1 - \alpha)]}{1 - \alpha} \ln \gamma^N,$$

where ψ is some constant term that is independent of the exogenous variable γ^N.

It now immediately follows that utility decreases in γ^N (or increases in $\ln k$) if and only if

$$\alpha(1 + \beta) - \beta(1 - \alpha) > 0$$

$$\Leftrightarrow \alpha > \frac{(1 - \alpha)\beta}{1 + \beta}.$$

Notice that this is just the same condition as requiring the economy to be dynamically efficient because the golden rule capital stock maximizing per capita consumption is given by

$$k^{**} = \left(\frac{\alpha}{\gamma^N}\right)^{1/(1-\alpha)},$$

that is, if $\alpha > (1 - \alpha)\beta/(1 + \beta)$ then $k^{**} > k^*$.

We, therefore, have the result that in a dynamically efficient economy, utility is increased as the population growth rate is reduced.[3] But from this

---

3. These results are reminiscent of the serendipity theorem of Samuelson (1975); see also Michel and Pestieau (1993) as well as Jaeger and Kuhle (2007).

we cannot conclude that decreases of the population growth rate lead to increases in per capita consumption because a decrease of γ^N leads to an increase of k^{**} and k^*.

To clarify this, we now derive analytic expressions for per capita output and consumption. Let P be total population. Notice that we can write steady-state per capita output as

$$\frac{Y}{P} = \frac{k^\alpha N}{P} = \frac{k^\alpha \gamma^N}{1 + \gamma^N}.$$

Using the equilibrium for the steady-state capital intensity, we can rewrite this expression as

$$\frac{Y}{P} = \phi^{\alpha/(1-\alpha)}\gamma^{N-[\alpha/(1-\alpha)]}\frac{\gamma^N}{1 + \gamma^N}.$$

We, therefore, have that

$$\frac{\partial(Y/P)}{\partial\gamma^N} = \phi^{\alpha/(1-\alpha)}\gamma^{N-[\alpha/(1-\alpha)]}\frac{1}{1 + \gamma^N}\left(\frac{1}{1 + \gamma^N} - \frac{\alpha}{1 - \alpha}\right).$$

That is, per capita output increases in γ^N if and only if

$$\alpha < \frac{1}{2 + \gamma^N},$$

which becomes less strong as γ^N is smaller (that is, in economies with a shrinking population).

As for per capita consumption, we have that

$$\frac{C}{P} = \frac{c^y N^y + c^o N^o}{N^y + N^o}$$

$$= \frac{c^y N^o(\gamma^N + \beta\alpha k^{\alpha-1})}{N^0(\gamma^N + 1)}$$

$$= (1 + \alpha\beta\phi^{-1})\frac{1 - \alpha}{1 + \beta}\phi^{\alpha/(1-\alpha)}\gamma^{N-[\alpha/(1-\alpha)]}\frac{\gamma^N}{1 + \gamma^N},$$

which, apart from the constant, has the same form as the equation for per capita output. Therefore, the same condition as before applies (which is due to the fact that the saving rate is constant in this simple model).

We can summarize these findings as follows: starting from an initial steady state, then if γ^N falls we have—in the new steady-state that the economy converges to—that (1) welfare of newborns is unambiguously higher if the economy is dynamically efficient, that is, if $\alpha > (1 - \alpha)\beta/(1 + \beta)$ and (2) per capita output and consumption are lower than in the initial steady state if $\alpha < 1/(2 + \gamma^N)$.

11.3   The Quantitative Model

The quantitative model we use to evaluate the consequences of demographic changes for international capital flows, returns to capital and wages, as well as the welfare consequences emanating from these changes is the same as in Krüger and Ludwig (2007). We focus on the industrialized world decomposed into three regions: the United States, the European Union (EU), and the rest of the OECD (ROECD).

We can think of our simulation model as an engine for the following thought experiment: we allow country-specific survival, fertility, and migration rates to change over time, inducing a demographic transition. Induced by the transition of the population structure is a transition path of the economies of the model, both in terms of aggregate variables as well as cross-sectional distributions of wealth and welfare. Summary measures of these changes will provide us with answers as to how the changes in the demographic structure of the economy, by changing returns to capital and wages, impact the distribution of welfare. Eventually, given by the assumption of a stable demography in the very far future, the economies will reach a steady state that permits the computation of the transition paths.

Specifically, we start computations in year 1950 assuming an artificial initial steady state. We then use data for a calibration period, 1950 to 2004, to determine several structural model parameters. We then compute the model equilibrium from 1950 to 2050, the transition path of interest, and further onward until the new steady state is assumed in 2300, far into the future.[4]

11.3.1   Demographics

The demographic evolution in our model is taken as exogenous.[5] It is the main driving force of our model in addition to the design of the Social Security system; see section 11.3.4. Households start their economic life at age twenty, retire at age sixty-five, and live at most until age ninety-five. Because we do not model childhood of a household explicitly, we denote its twentieth year of life by $j = 0$, its retirement age by $jr = 45$, and the terminal age of life by $J = 75$. Households face an idiosyncratic, time- and country-dependent (conditional) probability to survive from age j to age $j + 1$, which we denote by $s_{t,j,i}$.

For each country i, we have data or forecasts for populations of model age $j \in \{0, \ldots, 75\}$ in years $1950, \ldots, 2300$. From now on, we denote year 1950 as our base year $t = 0$, and year 2300 as the final period T, and the de-

---

4. The steady-state year of 2300 is chosen far into the future in order to avoid any contamination of the transition path between 2005 and 2050.

5. While the UN demographic forecasts include a projection of future fertility rates, mortality rates, and migration flows, these projections are not modified by our model output.

mographic data for periods $t \in \{0, \ldots, T\}$ by $N_{t,j,i}$. For simplicity, we assume that all migration takes place at or before age $j = 0$ in the model (age twenty in the data), so that we can treat migrants and individuals born inside the country of interest symmetrically.

11.3.2 Technology

In each country, the single consumption good is being produced according to a standard neoclassical production function

$$Y_{t,i} = Z_i K_{t,i}^{\alpha} (A_t L_{t,i})^{1-\alpha},$$

where $Y_{t,i}$ is output in country i at date t, $K_{t,i}$ and $L_{t,i}$ are capital and labor inputs, and A_t is total labor productivity, growing at a constant country independent rate g. The scaling parameters Z_i control relative total factor productivities across countries, whereas the parameter α measures the capital share and is assumed to be constant over time and across countries. In each country, capital used in production depreciates at a common rate δ. Because production takes place with a constant returns to scale production function and because we assume perfect competition, the number of firms is indeterminate in equilibrium and, without loss of generality, we assume that a single representative firm operates within each country.

11.3.3 Endowments and Preferences

Households value consumption and leisure over the life cycle according to a standard time-separable utility function

$$E\left[\sum_{j=0}^{J} \beta^j u(c_j, 1 - l_j)\right],$$

where β is the raw time discount factor, and expectations are taken over idiosyncratic mortality shocks and stochastic labor productivity. In particular, the expectations operator E encompasses the survival probabilities $s_{t,j,i}$.

We assume that the per-period utility function is a standard nested constant relative risk aversion (CRRA)-Cobb-Douglas function given by

$$u(c_j, 1 - l_j) = \frac{1}{1 - \sigma}[c_j^{\omega}(1 - l_j)^{1-\omega}],$$

where σ is the coefficient of relative risk aversion—the inverse of the intertemporal substitution elasticity—and ω is the consumption share parameter.

Households are heterogeneous with respect to age, a deterministic earnings potential, and stochastic labor productivity. These sources of heterogeneity affect a household's labor productivity, which is given by

$$\theta_k \varepsilon_j \eta.$$

First, households' labor productivity differs according to their age: ε_j denotes average age-specific productivity of cohort j. Second, each household belongs to a particular group $k \in \{1, \ldots, K\}$ that shares the same average productivity θ_k. Differences in groups stand in for differences in education or ability, characteristics that are fixed at entry into the labor market and affect a group's relative wage. We introduce these differences in order to generate part of the cross-sectional income and, thus, wealth dispersion that does not come from our last source of heterogeneity, idiosyncratic productivity shocks. Last, a household's labor productivity is affected by an idiosyncratic shock, $\eta \in \{1, \ldots, E\}$, that follows a time-invariant Markov chain with transition probabilities

$$\theta_k \varepsilon_j \eta.$$

We denote by Π the unique invariant distribution associated with π.

11.3.4   Government Policies

Key government policy in, and the second exogenous driving force of, our model is pension policy. The main ingredients are country-specific PAYGO public pension systems whose taxes and benefits will adjust to the demographic changes in each country. On the revenue side, households pay a flat payroll tax rate, $\tau_{t,i}$, on their labor earnings. Retired households receive benefits, $b_{t,k,i}$, that are assumed to depend on the household type, θ_k, but are independent of the history of idiosyncratic productivity shocks. Social Security benefits are, therefore, given by

$$b_{t,k,i} = \rho_{t,i}\theta_k(1 - \tau_{t,i})w_{t,i},$$

where $\rho_{t,i}$ is the pension system's net replacement rate.

We assume that the budget of the pension system is balanced at all times such that taxes and benefits are related by

$$\tau_{t,i}w_{t,i}L_{t,i} = \sum_k b_{t,k,i} \sum_{j \geq jr} N_{t,j,k,i},$$

where $N_{t,j,k,i}$ denotes the population in country i at time t of age j and type k.

In order to shed light on the interaction between the implications of demographic change and the type of Social Security system, we apply four different scenarios for the future evolution of the Social Security system:

- Scenario 1 models a defined contribution PAYGO system in which taxes are held constant, and replacement rates adjust according to the demographic change.
- Scenario 2 models a defined benefit PAYGO system in which replacement rates are held constant, and taxes adjust according to the demographic change.

- A third scenario models an increase in the retirement age and, in addition, adjusts benefits, if needed, to assure budget balance.
- Finally, as a benchmark, our fourth scenario has no PAYGO system altogether such that all old-age provision is done via private savings modeled by the life-cycle saving and consumption decisions of the households.

In addition to its role as governor of the Social Security system, the government also distributes accidental bequests left by those households who die before age *J*. It collects their assets and redistributes them in a lump-sum fashion among the remaining citizens of the country.

11.3.5   Market Structure

In each period, there are spot markets for the consumption good, for labor, and for capital services. While the labor market is a national market where labor demand and labor supply are equalized country by country, the markets for the consumption good and capital services are international where goods and capital flow freely, and without any transaction costs, between countries. The supply of capital for production stems from households in all countries who purchase these assets in order to save for retirement and to smooth idiosyncratic productivity shocks. As sensitivity analysis, we explore how countries would be affected by their demographic changes if they were closed economies where capital stocks and accumulated assets coincide by definition.

11.3.6   Equilibrium

A competitive equilibrium in this economy is defined by sequences of individual decision functions, sequences of production plans for firms, sequences of policies by the government, prices, transfers, and cross-sectional measures such that (1) households and firms behave optimally, (2) the government budget constraint holds, and (3) aggregation conditions hold and (4) markets clear. A stationary equilibrium is a competitive equilibrium in which all individual functions are constant over time and all aggregate variables grow at a constant rate. A formal definition of equilibrium is given in Krüger and Ludwig (2007).

11.3.7   Calibration

Calibration of the model is based on the minimum-distance method developed in Ludwig (2005). Tables 11.1 and 11.2 summarize the information on the values of technology and preference parameters, respectively. Notice that some of these parameters are restricted to be identical across regions, while others are allowed to differ. In particular, total factor productivities, Z_i, are scaled such as to match labor productivities and consumption share parameters, ω_i, are determined such as to match hours worked in the three regions of our model.

Table 11.1   Technology parameters

Parameter	United States	European Union	ROECD
Capital share α		0.33	
Growth rate of technology g		0.018	
Depreciation rate δ		0.04	
Total factor productivity Z_i	1.0	0.88	0.65

Note: ROECD = rest of the Organization for Economic Cooperation and Development.

Table 11.2   Preference parameters

Parameter	United States	European Union	ROECD
Coefficient of RRA σ		1.0	
Time discount factor β		0.9378	
Consumption share parameter ω_i	0.463	0.446	0.442

Note: ROECD = rest of the Organization for Economic Cooperation and Development; RRA = relative risk aversion.

Data for calibrating the Social Security system are taken from various sources. For the United States, we calculate Social Security contribution rates from National Income and Product Accounts (NIPA) data taken from the Bureau of Economic Analysis (BEA) table 3.6. For the other world regions, we proxy the time path of Social Security contribution rates by using time path information on total labor costs taken from the Bureau of Labor Statistics (BLS) and scale these data by the social security contribution rates reported by the OECD. Using these contribution rates and the demographic data, we back out replacement rates by the PAYGO budget constraint.

11.3.8   Solution Method

For given structural model parameters, we solve for the equilibrium of the model in separate outer and inner loop iterations. Throughout, we take as length of the period one year. Outer loop iterations search for equilibrium interest rates, contribution rates, and accidental bequests using a modification of the familiar Gauss-Seidel algorithm (see Ludwig 2007). Recursive methods are used to solve the household model in inner loop iterations, which are described in detail in Krüger and Ludwig (2007).

11.4   Results

In order to isolate the direct effects of demographic changes on returns to capital, international capital flows, and the distribution of wealth and welfare, we first abstract from Social Security in our analyses of sections 11.4.1 through 11.4.3. In section 11.4.4, we quantify the additional effects that are implied by the adjustments of Social Security parameters to demographic change.

One element that distinguishes our model from the earlier work in Börsch-Supan, Ludwig, and Winter (2006) is idiosyncratic risk. This enables us to characterize the distributional consequences of demographic change in a more realistic setting. In section 11.4.5, we address its implications for the general equilibrium rates of return and wages as well as for welfare. Throughout, we assume that capital flows freely between regions in the OECD.

11.4.1 Dynamics of Aggregate Statistics

In figure 11.3, we display the evolution of the real return to capital from 2000 to 2080. In the same figure, we plot, as a summary measure of the age structure of the population, the fraction of the world adult population with age above sixty-five (by assumption these individuals are retired in our model); this statistic is one minus the working age to population ratio. We observe that the rate of worldwide return to capital is predicted to fall by almost 1 percentage point in the next sixty years and then to settle down at that lower level.

Pretax wages are related to the interest rate by

$$w_{t,i} = (1 - \alpha)Z_i A_t \left(\frac{\alpha Z_i}{r_t + \delta} \right)^{\alpha/(1-\alpha)}$$

and, thus, detrended (by productivity growth) real wages follow exactly the inverse path of interest rates, documented in figure 11.3. These detrended wages are predicted to increase by roughly 4 percent between 2000 and 2050 in all regions in our model.

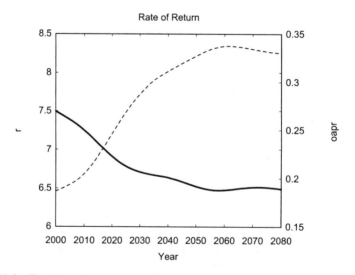

Rate of Return

Fig. 11.3   Evolution of world interest rates

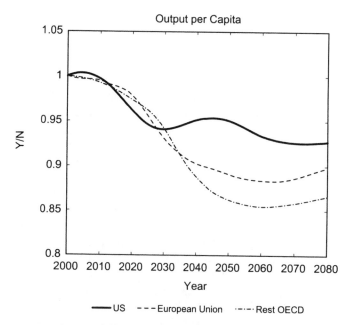

Fig. 11.4   Evolution of GDP per capita in 3 regions

In figure 11.4, we plot the evolution of detrended output per capita in the three regions, normalized to 1 in the year 2000. Notice that per capita here refers to the adult population aged twenty to ninety-five. We observe substantial declines of 7 to 13 percent in the three regions. The decline is least pronounced in the United States because there the decrease of the fraction of households in working age is more modest after 2030, as we saw in figure 11.2. During the transition period from 2005 to 2050, the negative effects of decreasing working age to population ratios, therefore, dominate the positive effects on output per worker (see the discussion in section 11.2).

11.4.2   Quantifying International Capital Flows

In order to analyze the direction and size of international capital flows, we will document the evolution of the net foreign asset position and the current account of the countries/regions under consideration. The current account is given by the change in the net foreign asset position and, thus, by the difference of country i's saving and investment.[6]

---

6. Note that in a closed economy, $F_{t,i} = C_{t,i} = 0$, and that in a balanced growth path of an open economy, $CA_{t,i} = g(A_{t,i} = K_{t,i})$ Furthermore, net asset positions and current accounts evidently have to sum to zero across regions:

$$\sum_i F_{t,i} = \sum_i CA_{t,i} = 0 \text{ for all } t.$$

$$CA_{t,i} = F_{t+1,i} - F_{t,i}$$
$$= S_{t,i} - I_{t,i}.$$

When reporting these statistics, we always divide them by output $Y_{t,i}$. We start with investigating national saving and investment rates and then discuss the implied current account and net foreign asset positions.

The most direct effect of an aging population is that labor, as a factor of production, becomes scarce. As a result, for unchanged aggregate saving, the return to capital has to fall and gross wages have to rise. This is what we observe in figure 11.3. However, the decline in interest rates may reduce the incentives of households to save, depending on the relative size of the income and substitution effect. In addition, with the aging of society, the age composition of the population shifts toward older households who are dissavers in our life-cycle model. Consequently, savings rates in all regions in our model decline over time. For the next twenty years, the fall in savings rates is most pronounced for the United States because there, during this time period, the large cohort of baby boomers moves into retirement. The same is true for other regions of the world, albeit to a lesser degree on average.[7] After the large cohort of baby boomers have left the economy (i.e., died), the U.S. saving rate is predicted to rebound (in about twenty-five to thirty-five years) and then to stabilize, whereas in the EU and the rest of the OECD, savings rates continue to fall until about 2040 and then stabilize.

The other side of the medal (that is, of the current account) is the investment behavior in the different regions. Given that savings rates decline globally due to population aging, investment rates have to do so as well, on average, because the world current account has to balance to zero. As the population ages and the labor force declines, it is optimal to reduce the capital stock with which these fewer workers work. Thus investment rates fall. This fall is by far the least pronounced for the United States. Furthermore, in the United States, the investment rate stops falling by about 2020, roughly a decade earlier than its saving rate. This is due to the fact that the fall in the working age to population ratio is completed around that date in the United States. On the other hand, in the EU and the rest of the OECD, this ratio continues to fall until 2035. Because capital- (effective) labor ratios have to be equalized, capital allocated to these regions has to fall (relative to the United States) and so do investment rates in these regions.

Figure 11.5 shows the current account to output ratios resulting from these dynamics of saving and investment rates. It depicts a clear deterioration of the U.S. current account of about 2 percent of gross domestic product (GDP) that is expected to occur in the next thirty years as capital flows

7. Notice that the evolution of demographic variables and the simulated time paths of savings may differ substantially across the countries within each country block; see, for example, Börsch-Supan, Ludwig, and Winter (2006).

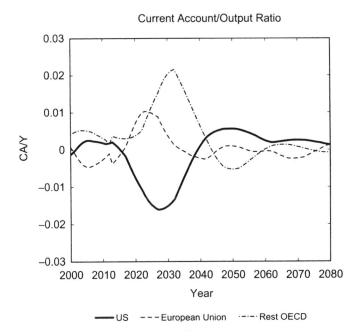

Current Account/Output Ratio

—— US   – – – European Union   ·–··– Rest OECD

Fig. 11.5   Evolution of the current account in 3 regions

from the EU and, with a slight time delay, from the rest of the OECD, into the United States. By 2040, this process is completed, and the current account of all countries returns to roughly zero from that point on. The predicted deterioration in the U.S. current account is due to an investment rate that falls less than in other countries (because the population in the United States ages slower and, thus, the labor force falls less) as well as a (temporary) sharp decline in the U.S. savings rate in the next twenty years due to the gradual retirement of the baby boomers.

11.4.3   Distributional and Welfare Consequences of Demographic Change

In the previous sections, we have documented substantial changes in factor prices induced by the aging of the population, amounting to a decline of about 1 percentage point in real returns to capital and an increase in gross wages of about 4 percent in the next decades. In this section, we want to quantify the distributional and welfare effects emanating from these changes.

Evolution of Inequality

In figure 11.6, we display the evolution of income inequality over time in the three regions. Income is composed of labor income (which later will in-

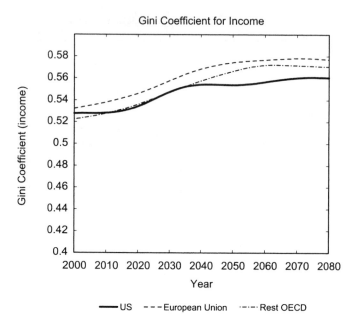

Fig. 11.6   Evolution of income inequality in 3 regions

clude pension income) and capital income as well as transfers from accidental bequests.

We observe a significant increase in income inequality between 2000 and 2080, of about 5 points in the Gini coefficient for the EU and the ROECD and 3.5 points in the United States. The reason for this increase is mainly a compositional effect. Retired households have significantly lower income, on average, than households in working age. The demographic transition toward more retired households, therefore, is bound to increase inequality, especially in those regions where the increase in the fraction of retired households among the population is very pronounced. This explains the more modest increase in income inequality in the United States. Note that consumption inequality follows income inequality trends fairly closely in the three regions (and, thus, is not shown here), but increases in consumption inequality are less pronounced. Also notice that the ordering of countries in the figure will be reversed once we add pension systems—then, income will be least equally distributed in the United States.

The fact that it is *not* a rise in capital income inequality that drives the increase in total income inequality becomes clear when plotting wealth inequality over time (see figure 11.7). There is no discernible increase in the same period; evidently, the same is true for capital income inequality because capital income is proportional to wealth.

In contrast to income, wealth follows a hump-shaped pattern over the

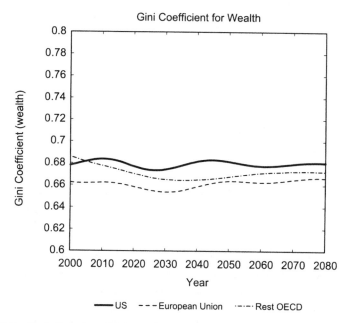

Fig. 11.7 Evolution of wealth inequality in 3 regions

life cycle (on average), with the elderly and the young being wealth-poor. Thus, in contrast to income inequality, the aging of the population does not lead to an increase in wealth inequality because the demographic change increases the fraction of the elderly but reduces the fraction of the young. Consequently, income and wealth inequality do not follow the same trend over time, nor is the ranking in inequality across regions the same for income and wealth.

We, therefore, conclude that the opposite general equilibrium effects on wages and interest rates have little impact on the income and wealth distribution across generations.

Welfare Consequences of the Demographic Transition

A household's welfare is affected by two consequences of demographic change. First, her lifetime utility changes because her own survival probabilities increase; this is in part what triggers the aging of the population. Second, due to the demographic transition, she faces different factor prices and government transfers and taxes (from the Social Security system and from accidental bequests) than without changes in the demographic structure. Specifically, households face a path of declining interest rates and increasing wages, relative to the situation without a demographic transition.

We want to isolate the welfare consequences of the second effect. For this we compare lifetime utility of individuals born and already alive in 2005

Table 11.3   Welfare consequences, United States—pure demographic effects (%)

Productivity η_1	Productivity η_2
0.9	0.6

under two different scenarios. For both scenarios, we fix a household's individual survival probabilities at their 2005 values; of course, they fully retain their age-dependence. Then we solve each household's problem under two different assumptions about factor prices (and later taxes/transfers, once we have introduced Social Security). Let $\overline{W}(t, i, j, k, \eta, a)$ denote the lifetime utility of an individual at time $t \geq 2005$ in country I with individual characteristics (j, k, η, a) that faces the sequence of equilibrium prices as documented in the previous section, but constant 2005 survival probabilities, and let $\overline{W}_{2005}(t, i, j, k, \eta, a)$ denote the lifetime utility of the same individual that faces prices and taxes/transfers that are held constant at their 2005 value. Finally, denote by $g(t, i, j, k, \eta, a)$ the percentage increase in consumption that needs to be given to an individual (t, i, j, k, η, a) at each date and contingency in his or her remaining lifetime (keeping labor supply allocations fixed) at fixed prices to make him or her as well off as under the situation with changing prices.[8] Positive numbers of $g(t, i, j, k, \eta, a)$ thus indicate that households obtain welfare gains from the general equilibrium effects of the demographic changes; negative numbers mean welfare losses. Of particular interest are the numbers $g(t = 56, i, j = 0, k, \eta, a = 0)$, that is, the welfare consequences for newborn individuals in 2005 ($t = 56$)—remember that newborns start their life with zero assets.

Table 11.3 documents these numbers for θ-type 1 for the United States, differentiated by their productivity shock η. The results for θ-type 2 are nearly identical.[9]

We make several observations. First, newborn individuals experience welfare gains from changing factor prices and transfers induced by the demographic transition (compare the discussion in section 11.2). Apart from changing preferences through higher longevity (an effect we control for in our welfare calculations), the demographic transition substantially in-

---

8. For the Cobb-Douglas utility specification for $\sigma \neq 1$, the number $g(t, i, j, k, \eta, a)$ can easily be computed as

$$g(t, i, j, k, \eta, a) = \left(\frac{\overline{W}(t, i, j, k, \eta, a)}{\overline{W}_{2005}(t, i, j, k, \eta, a)} \right)^{1/[\omega_i(1-\sigma)]}.$$

A similar expression holds for $\sigma = 1$.

9. The welfare consequences are very similar for other countries. In fact, in the benchmark model, the only difference across countries and types stems from accidental bequests, which are redistributed in a lump-sum fashion and whose dynamics varies slightly across countries. Because these transfers are small in magnitude, however, so are the cross-country and cross-type differences in welfare.

creases the real wage over time, reduces the interest rate and first increases, and then (after 2040) somewhat reduces transfers from accidental bequests. The effect from changes in transfers is small, at least for newborns. The dominating effect for newborn individuals is the substantial increase in wages, partially because these individuals have not yet accumulated assets and, thus, do not suffer from a loss of capital income on already accumulated financial wealth, in contrast to older households. Of course, a lower interest rate makes it harder for these households to accumulate assets for retirement. Because borrowing is ruled out the decline in interest rates alone, therefore, has unambiguously negative consequences for welfare.

Second, individuals born with low productivity will experience somewhat higher welfare gains than individuals that start their working life with high productivity. Low-productivity individuals expect higher productivity in the future and, thus, benefit more strongly from the increasing wage profile induced by the demographic transition than the currently highly productive, whose productivity is going to fall in expectation.

Given that the welfare impact of changing factor prices constitutes a trade-off between increasing wages and falling returns to capital, one would expect that those members of society for whom labor income constitutes a smaller part of (future) resources than capital income benefit less from the demographic transition. An advantage of our model with uninsurable idiosyncratic income shocks and, thus, endogenous intracohort wealth heterogeneity is that it allows us to document how the welfare consequences are distributed across the population, both across and within cohorts. Figure 11.8 plots the welfare gains for individuals of age sixty in 2005.

These households have most of their working life behind them and, thus, are fairly unaffected by the wage changes and simply experience lower returns on their accumulated savings. We see that individuals in this cohort suffer welfare losses that increase substantially by the amount of financial assets they have already accumulated. To give a sense of how many individuals there are at different points in the asset distribution, the support of this distribution for the sixty-year-old ranges roughly to $a = 12$ (about 19 times GDP per capita), with median asset levels around 4 (10) times GDP per capita for the low η-low (high) type individuals and about 4.1 (10.8) times GDP per capita for the high η-low (high) type individuals. Overall, a fraction of 38 percent of individuals economically alive in 2005 gain from the changing factor prices. These tend to be young individuals with little assets and currently low labor productivity.

11.4.4   The Role of Social Security

So far, we have abstracted from government policies. An idealized PAYGO public pension system can respond to an increase in the share of

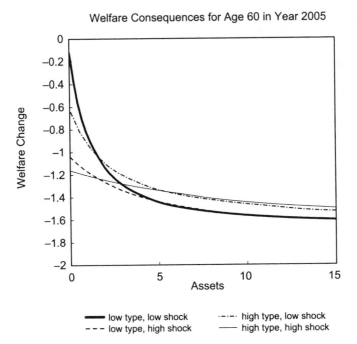

Fig. 11.8   Welfare change

pensioners in the population by (a combination of) at least three ways: cutting benefits, increasing Social Security contribution rates, or increasing the retirement age. While a likely response will include all elements, we now present results for the model with a PAYGO Social Security system that responds to population aging by either holding tax rates fixed (and, thus, cutting benefits), by holding replacement rates fixed (and thus raising taxes), or by increasing the retirement age.[10]

Because of the strong influence of a public pension system on private savings behavior, we expect that these different reform scenarios may have substantially different implications for the evolution of factor prices and the size and direction of international capital flows as well as the distribution of welfare. This conjecture turns out to be correct. Note that for all exercises we recalibrate production and preference parameters such that each economy (with the different Social Security systems) attains the same calibration targets for the 1950 to 2004 period.

In table 11.4, we show how the evolution of macroeconomic aggregates and prices differs across the various scenarios for Social Security. Com-

---

10. In our experiment, we increase the mandatory retirement age by five years in 2005 and keep contribution rates fixed. When needed, benefits are adjusted to retain budget balance of the Social Security system.

Table 11.4   Evolution of aggregates in the United States, 2005–2050 (%)

Variable	No Social Security	τ fixed	ρ fixed	Adj. of jr
r	−0.86	−0.82	−0.26	−0.79
w	4.1	3.8	1.2	3.6
τ	0	0	5.9	0
ρ	0	−7.1	0	−3.1
Y/N	−5.2	−5.2	−9.5	−3.8
C/N	−4.7	−4.7	−7.4	−2.6

paring the no-Social Security scenario to a world with Social Security in which payroll tax rates are held constant (and, thus, benefits decline), we observe that changes in factor prices are roughly the same between the two scenarios.[11] One big difference, however, is the change in Social Security benefits required to cope with the demographic transition, which implies a decline in replacement rates by about 5 percentage points in the scenario with Social Security. Column (4) demonstrates that keeping pension benefits constant and adjusting taxes, on the other hand, has dramatic consequences for the evolution of interest rates and wages, relative to the benchmark scenario of fixing tax rates for Social Security. With fixed benefits, the incentives to save for retirement are drastically reduced, relative to the benchmark. In addition, the substantial increase in tax rates of 6 percentage points and the corresponding reduction in after tax wages make it harder to save. Therefore, despite the decline in the fraction of households in working age (and diminished incentives to work because of higher payroll taxes), now the capital-labor ratio remains roughly unchanged because of the large reduction of household savings. Consequently, the increase in wages and decline in returns is much less pronounced in this scenario. Finally, the last column of table 11.4 shows that an increase in the retirement age by five years, while leaving the change in factor prices roughly the same as in the benchmark, implies a much smaller decline in benefits as with a retirement age of sixty-five (see column [3]).[12] Because of the expansion in labor supply, output per capita falls significantly less in this scenario than in all others.

Given these substantial differences in changes of allocations, it is not surprising that the welfare consequences differ across these two scenarios as well. Table 11.5 summarizes the welfare losses from the demographic tran-

11. Remember that we recalibrate our model so that in all scenarios, the pre-2005 equilibrium features the same capital-output ratio.

12. A further increase in the retirement age has no substantial effect on labor supply because households are not very productive beyond age seventy because we do not account for the effects of improved health on productivity. Consequently, the effects reported in table 11.4 may be biased, and the accompanying welfare consequences of increases in retirement ages for newborns reported in table 11.5 are at the lower bound.

Table 11.5   Welfare consequences, newborns in the United States (%)

Type	No Social Security		τ fixed		ρ fixed		Adj. of *jr*	
	η_1	η_2	η_1	η_2	η_1	η_2	η_1	η_2
K_1	0.9	0.6	0.8	0.2	−1.6	−1.8	1.4	0.6
K_2	0.9	0.6	0.4	0.0	−1.8	−1.9	0.8	0.3

sition for newborns in the United States in 2005.[13] We find that, because of the decline in benefits or the increase in taxes, the welfare implications from the demographic change are less favorable in a world with Social Security than without. The policy option of keeping benefits constant and letting tax rates increase implies especially large welfare losses from population aging for newborns, and even more so for future generations (not shown here). If, in contrast, the retirement age is increased to age seventy, low-type households who enter the labor market unproductive are especially benefiting. These households expect productivity to be higher in the future, face increasing wages, and can exploit these longer now as they can work until age seventy. It is, therefore, this group for which the increase in wages presents a good opportunity to intertemporally substitute labor supply; consequently, the benefit of being able to work longer and, thus, the overall welfare gains from changing factor prices are largest for this group. For older individuals, the welfare losses from the demographic transition are significantly smaller with an expansion of the retirement age, relative to simply holding contribution rates fixed and letting benefits decline (results not shown). Older households are given the option to endogenously respond to lower benefit levels by expanding their labor supply for five more years.

Thus, we conclude that the option of increasing the retirement age leads to less welfare losses (and even welfare gains for some groups) from population aging than adjusting taxes or benefits alone.

11.4.5 The Role of Idiosyncratic Risk

We now investigate the role of idiosyncratic risk and ask whether our quantitative predictions change when we ignore idiosyncratic risk as has been done in earlier analyses (e.g., Börsch-Supan, Ludwig, and Winter 2006). In order to illustrate the interactions between relative price changes and the insurance role of the pension system, we here take as a benchmark

13. Note that the numbers of table 11.6 do permit a meaningful welfare comparison of different Social Security reform scenarios to deal with the demographic change. In order to achieve this comparability in our welfare computations (and in these only), we always use the same parameters for all scenarios, those calibrated for the no Social Security benchmark. The table does not, however, permit an assessment as to whether households are better off in a world with or without Social Security.

Table 11.6   **U.S. aggregates, 2005–2008—the role of risk (%)**

Variable	τ fixed	τ fixed − no risk
r	−0.82	−0.75
w	3.8	3.5
τ	0	0
ρ	−7.0	−6.3
Y/N	−5.2	−3.9
C/N	−4.7	−3.0

Table 11.7   **Welfare consequences—the role of risk (%)**

Type	τ fixed		τ fixed − no risk
	η_1	η_2	
K_1	0.8	0.2	0.7
K_2	0.4	0.0	0.5

scenario a Social Security system with fixed contribution rates. We then re-calibrate the model such as to meet the same calibration targets on the aggregate level. Because a precautionary savings motive is not at work in an economy without risk, we have to increase the discount factor by 2 percentage points to make households sufficiently impatient such as to meet the calibration target of the capital output ratio. Our results for macroeconomic aggregates are summarized in table 11.6. Relative price changes are stronger in the scenario with risk because hours worked decrease more strongly and, therefore, Social Security benefits are more strongly reduced. As a consequence of the interplay of both effects, the capital output ratio increases by more and, therefore, the relative price effects are slightly stronger than in the scenario without risk.

Finally, table 11.7 compares the welfare consequences of demographic change across the two scenarios. In these welfare comparisons, we isolate the role of idiosyncratic risk by holding preference parameters constant (as before in table 11.5) and by evaluating the welfare consequences for the equilibrium prices that resulted from our pure τ-fixed scenario. With the exception of low-type, low-shock households, all households are better off in a world without risk. By the mean reverting pattern of our wage processes, uncertainty about future wage income represents a chance for low-type, low-shock households.

11.5   Conclusions

In all major industrialized countries, the population is aging, bringing with it a potentially large impact on the returns to the production factors capital and labor. This chapter reports that the rate of return to capital can be expected to decrease by about 80 to 90 basis points until 2050, with a corresponding increase of wages if PAYGO Social Security systems are reformed such that contribution rates are held constant. Under such a reform, the welfare consequences from population aging through increasing wages and declining rates of return are positive in the order of up to 1 percent in lifetime consumption for newborns in 2005. This number masks important distributional shifts: households that have already accumulated assets lose from the decline in rates of return. As an interesting policy effect, our chapter also shows that increasing the mandatory retirement age by five years is shown to substantially mitigate these losses and to significantly increase welfare gains of newborns.

The welfare gains for newborns are actually larger than what we compute because in addition, these newborns are expected to live longer than the current generation. Similarly, the welfare losses for older asset holders are smaller because they also have a longer life expectancy. Quantifying the utility gains from living longer is beyond the scope of this chapter.

Future research will be devoted to several valuable additions. One important channel of adjustment to a shrinking labor force that we have abstracted from is endogenous human capital accumulation. Higher returns to human capital in the form of higher wages may make it optimal for young (and possibly older) households to obtain a better education, increasing the supply of effective labor. This effect may counteract some of the increase in the capital-labor ratio and, hence, mitigate the impact of population aging on factor prices. Another addition will be to differentiate among asset types. For example, out-of-life-cycle investment motives one may expect a stronger decrease of the rate of return on risk free assets and, thus, an increase of the equity premium. Finally, our analysis has focused on open capital markets within OECD countries, and we thereby did not address the potentially important roles of the upcoming demographic changes in China and India for international capital flows and welfare from a U.S. perspective. The literature has not reached a conclusion on the relative importance of these countries.[14] All these issues are left for future research.

References

Abel, A. 2003. The effects of a baby boom on stock prices and capital accumulation in the presence of Social Security. *Econometrica* 71:551–78.

14. While the computations for a worldwide capital market scenario in Börsch-Supan, Ludwig, and Winter (2006) suggest that the effects of including these countries on equilibrium rates of return and wages will be relatively small, Fehr, Jokisch, and Kotlikoff (2007) arrive at a different conclusion.

Altig, D., A. Auerbach, L. Kotlikoff, K. Smetters, and J. Walliser. 2001. Simulating fundamental tax reform in the U.S. *American Economic Review* 91:574–95.
Attanasio, O., S. Kitao, and G. Violante. 2006. Quantifying the effects of the demographic transition in developing economies. *Advances in Macroeconomics* 2, Article 2. Available at http://www.bepress.com/bejm/advances/vol6/iss1/art1.
———. 2007. Global demographic trends and Social Security reform. *Journal of Monetary Economics* 54 (1): 144–98.
Auerbach, A., and L. Kotlikoff. 1987. *Dynamic fiscal policy*. Cambridge, UK: Cambridge University Press.
Bloom, D., and J. Williamson. 1998. Demographic transitions and economic miracles in emerging Asia. *World Bank Economic Review* 12 (3): 419–55.
Börsch-Supan, A. 1996. The impact of population aging on savings, investment and growth in the OECD area. In *Future global capital shortages: Real threat or pure fiction?*, ed. OECD, 103–41. Paris: OECD.
Börsch-Supan, A., A. Ludwig, and J. Winter. 2002. Aging and international capital flows. In *Aging, financial markets and monetary policy,* ed. A. Auerbach and H. Hermann, 55–83. Heidelberg, Germany: Springer.
———. 2006. Aging, pension reform, and capital flows: A multi-country simulation model. *Economica* 73:625–58.
Brooks, R. 2003. Population aging and global capital flows in a parallel universe. *IMF Staff Papers* 50:200–221.
Conesa, J., and D. Krüger. 1999. Social Security reform with heterogeneous agents. *Review of Economic Dynamics* 2:757–95.
———. 2006. On the optimal progressivity of the income tax code. *Journal of Monetary Economics* 53 (7): 1425–50.
De Nardi, M., S. İmrohoroğlu, and T. Sargent. 1999. Projected U.S. demographics and Social Security. *Review of Economic Dynamics* 2:575–615.
Diamond, P. A. 1965. National debt in a neoclassical growth model. *American Economic Review* 55:1126–50.
Domeij, D., and M. Floden. 2006. Population aging and international capital flows. *International Economic Review* 47 (3): 1013–32.
Fehr, H., S. Jokisch, and L. Kotlikoff. 2005. The developed world's demographic transition—The role of capital flows, immigration and policy. In *Social Security reform—Financial and political issues in international perspective,* ed. R. Brooks and A. Razin, 11–43. Cambridge, UK: Cambridge University Press.
———. 2007. Will China eat our lunch or take us to dinner? Simulating the transition paths of the United States, the European Union, Japan, and China. In *Fiscal policy and management: NBER-East Asia Seminar on Economics.* Vol. 16, ed. T. Ito and A. K. Rose, 133–98. Chicago: University of Chicago Press.
Feroli, M. 2003. Capital flows among the G-7 nations: A demographic perspective. Finance and Economics Discussion Series no. 2003-54. Washington, DC: Board of Governors of the Federal Reserve System.
Henriksen, E. 2002. A demographic explanation of U.S. and Japanese current account behavior. Carnegie Mellon University. Mimeograph.
Huang, H., S. İmrohoroğlu, and T. Sargent. 1997. Two computations to fund Social Security. *Macroeconomic Dynamics* 1:7–44.
İmrohoroğlu, A., S. İmrohoroğlu, D. Joines. 1995. A life-cycle analysis of Social Security. *Economic Theory* 6:83–114.
———. 1999. Social Security in an overlapping generations economy with land. *Review of Economic Dynamics* 2:638–65.
Jaeger, K., and W. Kuhle.. 2007. The optimum growth rate for population reconsidered. *Journal of Population Economics,* forthcoming.
Krüger, D., and A. Ludwig. 2007. On the consequences of demographic change for

rates of returns to capital, and the distribution of wealth and welfare. *Journal of Monetary Economics* 54 (1): 49–87.
Ludwig, A. 2005. Moment estimation in Auerbach-Kotlikoff models: How well do they match the data? MEA, University of Mannheim. Mimeograph.
———. 2007. The Gauss-Seidel-Quasi-Newton method: A hybrid algorithm for solving dynamic economic models. *Journal of Economic Dynamics and Control* 31:1610–32.
Michel, P., and P. Pestieau. 1993. Population growth and optimality: When does serendipity hold? *Journal of Population Economics* 6 (4): 353–62.
Obstfeld, M., and K. Rogoff. 1995. The intertemporal approach to the current account. In *Handbook of international economics.* Vol. 3, ed. G. Grossman and K. Rogoff, 1731–99. Amsterdam: Elsevier.
Samuelson, P. A. 1975. The optimum growth rate of population. *International Economic Review* 16 (3): 531–37.
United Nations. 2002. *World population prospects: The 2002 revision.* New York: United Nations Population Division, United Nations.

Comment   James M. Poterba

This chapter makes an important contribution to the rapidly-growing literature on the financial market consequences of demographic change. It is both technically sophisticated and substantively important. The technical innovations include the construction of a multicountry overlapping generation (OLG) model that is solved under the assumption of perfect foresight and the careful modeling of uncertainty in the labor income process facing individuals. Allowing such uncertainty induces both precautionary as well as life-cycle motives for individual saving, thereby moving beyond many previous studies that have counterfactually assumed that there are no intergenerational wealth transfers.

The substantively important conclusions in this chapter concern the impact of demographic change on wages, the return to capital, and the pattern of international capital flows. There is broad theoretical consensus on the direction of change in each of these variables that follows from a decline in the birth rate and a corresponding increase in average population age. Yet whether the resulting effects are likely to be large or small is critically important for a range of issues, including the structure of long-term fiscal policy and the appropriate level of saving by households that are preparing for retirement. Simulation models are the best way to develop reliable answers to questions about the magnitude of the effects of population aging, but one always worries that these models may neglect important factors

James M. Poterba is the Mitsui Professor of Economics at the Massachusetts Institute of Technology, and president of the National Bureau of Economic Research.

that are quantitatively significant. The model developed in this chapter addresses a number of concerns that have been raised with earlier simulation studies, and in the process, provides greater confidence about the likely quantitative importance of the financial market consequences and other effects of population aging.

The authors divide the developed world into three "nations": the United States, the European Union (EU), and the rest of the Organization for Economic Cooperation and Development (OECD). They draw population projections by age from United Nations benchmark forecasts, and they find the transition paths of the three economies over the next forty-five years given the projected age structure. They solve the model to evaluate the "autarky" case for the United States, and they compare this outcome with the result when there are capital flows between the three hypothetical "countries." They also introduce a stylized Social Security system into each country. Because current tax and benefit structures are not sustainable in many nations, including the United States, the authors consider several ways of restoring balance to the Social Security system, and they evaluate the economic effects of each alternative. One of the key contributions of the analysis is the quantification of the differential effects of restoring Social Security balance by changing the replacement rate for retirees, and restoring balance by increasing tax rates, on wages, rates of return to capital, and cohort-specific welfare.

The baseline findings suggest that the demographic transition that is already underway is likely to reduce the rate of return to capital. While the magnitude of this decline depends on the degree of capital market openness, a decline of 50 basis points appears possible in the next two decades, and 90 basis points in the next half century. There are also important changes in the economywide average real wage, stemming from variation in the capital-labor ratio over time. Comparison of closed-economy results for an economy like the United States, and open-economy results for a hypothetical global economy that combines the United States, the EU, and the rest of the OECD, shows substantial fluctuations in the U.S. capital account as a result of demographic change. In the near term, global demographic pressures encourage the United States to import capital because the rest of the OECD is, on average, older than the United States and, therefore, has a greater domestic capital to labor ratio. One virtue of the simulation model in this chapter is the careful quantification of the importance of capital market openness.

The model begins with hypothetical households that make labor supply and saving decisions and that face wage shocks. Such disaggregate modeling makes it possible to evaluate how population aging will affect hypothetical households of different ages in 2007, as well as households that have, as a result of their past earnings shocks, accumulated different levels of financial assets. The simulation findings offer detailed evidence on the cohort-specific welfare effects associated with population aging. They quantify the extent to which individuals born into large cohorts, like the baby boomers, suffer from reduced lifetime utility as a result of lower life-time wages, the consequence of supplying labor when it is plentiful, as well as lower rates of return on their investments. The central findings suggest that while those in large cohorts are less well off than those in smaller co-horts, the adverse effect translates to a reduction in lifetime consumption of less than 1 percent, and, in some cases, less than one-half of 1 percent. Within the cohort that is currently alive and working, the cost of prospec-tive population aging is greatest for those who have substantial wealth holdings. Substantial wealth-holders lose the most from the demography-induced decline in rates of return.

This chapter is among the first to offer insights on the disaggregate pat-terns within cohorts of the welfare changes associated with population ag-ing. This is an important contribution, and it should spur substantial further work. There is great heterogeneity in wealth holdings, wage rates, and other attributes that affect lifetime utility within cohorts. The differences in the effects of population aging within cohorts may be as large as the differences across cohorts, and this chapter begins the analysis of such differences.

One of the chapter's most important innovations is the introduction of stylized Social Security programs in each nation and the analysis of how changes in Social Security policy might attenuate or reinforce the conse-quences of population aging. The authors identify a key interaction be-tween the generosity of the publicly provided pay-as-you-go Social Secu-rity system and the aggregate effects of population aging on financial market returns. If the Social Security system is reformed in a way that re-duces the generosity of the unfunded public program at the same time the demographic shift is increasing the capital-labor ratio in the economy, this will exacerbate the downward pressure on returns associated with popula-tion aging. The key assumption underlying this result is the crowd-out of private capital accumulation by the Social Security program. Any Social Security reform that induces more private saving will reinforce the increase in saving associated with population aging. Within cohorts, the house-holds with substantial wealth will be most affected by the changes in wealth accumulation associated with Social Security reform because they have the largest interest in prospective returns.

One of the important conclusions of the Social Security analysis is that demographic changes have a larger effect on welfare in the presence of un-funded retirement income programs than in the absence of such programs. When the population ages in a nation with a pay-as-you-go Social Security system, preserving fiscal stability requires either benefit reductions or higher taxes. Regardless of which alternative policymakers choose, there will be welfare reductions for some of the households alive at the time of the demographic transition. This chapter traces through the economic effects of each of these alternatives. Within the set of benefit reductions, it distinguishes between a policy of raising the retirement age and one of preserving the retirement age but adopting a lower income replacement rate. The analysis provides valuable evidence on how the alternative policies will affect both the distribution of welfare across cohorts as well as the pattern of lifetime utility levels within cohorts.

By embedding a hypothetical "U.S. economy" in a hypothetical "global" economy, the chapter provides important insights about the economic effects of global aging. The presence of international capital markets makes the rate of return in a given economy a function not only of its own demographic mix, but also of that in other nations. One interesting conclusion for those concerned about population aging in the United States is that international capital flows accentuate, rather than reduce, the downward prospective pressure on rates of return because the rest of the OECD, on average, ages faster and more dramatically than the United States. The chapter nevertheless shows that the welfare consequences of working with a closed-economy rather than an open-economy model are small. This is precisely the type of quantitative evidence that makes this simulation exercise so valuable.

While there is much to applaud about the open-economy modeling in this chapter, this aspect of the analysis also raises questions that require further attention. One potentially important shortcoming of the current model is the omission of developing countries, particularly the BRICs (Brazil, Russia, India, and China). These countries are likely to experience rapid economic growth over the next few decades, and they may emerge as important suppliers of global financial capital by 2050. Even though they account for a relatively small fraction of global capital supply today, their rapid growth and their prospective aging make them important components of any long-term analysis. Thus, while the near-term findings, those for the next ten to twenty years, may not be particularly sensitive to the omission of these countries, the longer-term results could be affected by this modeling assumption.

Considering the role of the BRICs in the current model underscores the uncertainties of any long-horizon projection such as the one developed here. Once one recognizes that the effect of population aging in the developed world on asset returns in 2050 is likely to depend on the intervening growth rate of the BRICs, one realizes that some parameters that are very difficult to predict—such as that growth rate—may be consequential for the modeling exercise. Even in developed countries, there are important uncertainties that should be recognized. The average age at retirement in the United States fell by five years between 1950 and 2000, yet in the current model, preferences and public policies are relatively stable, so such a dramatic change would not occur. Yet substantial changes could occur within the forecast horizon, and they could result in substantial divergences from the baseline analysis.

One of the most intriguing possibilities is a link between aggregate population age structure and the rate of productivity growth. Because demographic changes like those considered in this chapter take place over decades, any change in the rate of productivity growth over the simulation period can have large cumulative effects. This draws attention to potential shifts in the rate of productivity growth, which is treated as exogenous in this model. If older workers are more reliable, absent less often, and more committed to their jobs, this may lead to higher productivity growth when the average age in the workforce is higher and, consequently, alter the standard of living for households alive in 2050. Because there is little empirical evidence on the nature of such linkages, it would be premature for the authors to attempt to capture such effects in their modeling. However, recognizing the possibility of such effects suggests that all long-horizon simulation results should be viewed with some caution. This warning does does not diminish the importance of using simulation tools to evaluate how various policy interventions or other shocks might affect the evolution of the economy.

Another potential extension of the model, like including the BRICs, which again flows naturally from the open-economy setting, is the analysis of immigration policy. The current model takes age structure as given, so it implicitly adopts the immigration and emigration rates assumed by the United Nations. One way OECD countries may expand the number of young workers and blunt the potential effects of population aging is by opening their borders to immigrants to a greater extent than they have in the recent past. There may be important differences across nations in the capacity to make such adjustments, and a model like the one developed here could be used to address the resulting impact on economic circumstances. The treatment of immigration may be particularly important for the analysis of Social Security programs and their impact on different cohorts. Institutional details matter in this context because the net effect of greater immigration on the financial status of Social Security depends on whether the immigrants are legal or illegal and on whether benefits are paid to individuals who return to their home country in retirement.

Another concern with this model, which could be addressed in future work, involves the costs of raising children and the divergence between the treatment of young and old dependents. While elderly dependents are explicitly recognized in the model because they receive Social Security benefits and draw down their wealth holdings, there are no children. Economic agents are born at age twenty, fully educated and ready to enter the labor force. In practice, countries with high birth rates usually incur substantial costs in raising children. These costs include direct outlays for schooling, health care, and other essentials, as well as reductions in labor force activity of parents. The model does not recognize that a decline in birth rates that underlies the demographic transition of the next half century is likely to result in reduced outlays for child-raising. Adding this effect would potentially raise the level of per-adult output during part of the period when the population is aging. There are also potential effects on government budgets because governments are most directly involved in providing services to the young and the old. An analysis that focuses only on Social Security, but neglects school spending, overstates the fiscal effects of population aging.

These suggestions for enhancing the model to tackle additional issues, or to add realism on some dimensions, do not detract from the substantial and valuable contributions of the current analysis. The authors have made great strides in developing a realistic and insightful multicountry model that can be used to study a wide range of different issues relating to population aging. I expect that this powerful new tool, which has already generated important findings in the current chapter, will in the future yield further discoveries on a variety of other issues.

Mortality Projections

12

Is the U.S. Population Behaving Healthier?

David M. Cutler, Edward L. Glaeser, and
Allison B. Rosen

Understanding changes in population health is a key input into public and private decision making. People who live longer have more years of life to enjoy, but also need to prepare for more older years, through increased saving and possibly delayed retirement. Rational decision makers will take into account forecasts of longevity and quality of life in making their work and savings decisions. Public policy must account for this as well. Every additional year of life after age sixty-five is associated with about $15,000 of Social Security and medical care spending, and years spent disabled result in substantially greater medical spending than years spent without disability (Trends in Health and Aging 2007).

Health outcomes are a product of several inputs. Peoples' behaviors and genetic predisposition put them at risk for disease. The medical system then alleviates or treats these risks. Distinguishing the role of behavioral risk factors from medical care is important for several reasons. One reason is the impact on medical spending. Improved behaviors generally lower medical spending, at least in the short term, while treating adverse risk profiles increases costs. Thus, knowing whether health behaviors are

David M. Cutler is dean for the social sciences and the Otto Eckstein Professor of Applied Economics at Harvard University, and a research associate of the National Bureau of Economic Research. Edward L. Glaeser is the Fred and Eleanor Glimp Professor of Economics at Harvard University, and a research associate of the National Bureau of Economic Research. Allison B. Rosen is an assistant professor in the department of internal medicine at the University of Michigan Health System.

We are grateful to Ioana Petrescu for research assistance and James P. Smith for comments. This research was supported by the U.S. Social Security Administration (SSA) through grant #10-P-98363-3 to the National Bureau of Economic Research (NBER) as part of the SSA Retirement Research Consortium. The findings and conclusions expressed are solely those of the authors and do not represent the views of the SSA, any agency of the federal government, or of the NBER.

improving is important in forecasting medical costs. In addition, behavioral trends are essential in predicting future disease burden. A population that behaves in a healthier way will have higher quality of life compared to one with a more adverse behavioral profile, even given length of life. Finally, changes in behaviors are a good guide to the "demand" for better health, which can be used to develop models of health demand and supply. In this chapter, we consider what has happened to the population's health behaviors over time and consider various scenarios for trends in the future.

Past trends in behavioral risk factors have not been in a common direction. Some measures of population risk have improved markedly, while others have deteriorated. Smoking rates have fallen by more than a third since 1960 (Anonymous 1999), and alcohol consumption has declined by 20 percent since 1980 (Lakins, Williams, and Yi 2006), both leading to better health. Demographically, the population is better educated, and better-educated people live longer than less-educated people (Elo and Preston 1996). On the other hand, obesity rates have doubled in the past two decades (Flegal et al. 2002), and diabetes has increased as a result (Gregg et al. 2005). Further, the population has a higher share of minority groups, for whom life expectancy is lower. The net impact of these risk factor trends on population health expectations is uncertain (Preston 2005).

Our analysis has two parts. We start by aggregating these different health trends into a single measure of population risk. We focus on the most common risk factors: smoking, drinking, obesity, hypertension, high cholesterol, and diabetes. We weight the different risk factors by their impact on predicted ten-year mortality, as determined through multiple regression analysis. We show that overall health trends in the past three decades have improved markedly. For the entire population aged twenty-five and older, the age-adjusted probability of dying in ten years, conditional on the same level of medical care, fell from 9.8 percent in the early 1970s to 8.4 percent around 2000, a 14 percent reduction. The largest contributors to this trend were reductions in smoking and improved blood pressure control.

The second part of our analysis considers the impact of a continuation of future trends. Our conclusions here are not as rosy. We show that if current obesity trends continue, the population mortality risk could increase, even with continued reductions in smoking. We estimate that about a third of the past gains would be reversed within twenty years. The increase in obesity is the proximate cause of this. But even given the increase in obesity, the health impact would be substantially blunted if more people took medication to control blood pressure, cholesterol, and diabetes.

Our chapter has five sections. The first section discusses important risk factors; the second section shows trends in risk factors. The third section evaluates mortality risk from the early 1970s through the early 2000s. The fourth section then considers alternative scenarios for future risk trends. The last section concludes.

12.1 Health Behaviors

We are interested in measuring the population's health profile over time. Health is a product of many features: the individual risk factor profile; the disease environment; and the impact of medical care. We focus on individual behaviors because that is (perhaps) the easiest to forecast and tells us the most about the demand for health.

To understand our analysis, consider a simple model. Individuals live for up to two periods; health is defined as the probability that a person survives to period 2. If alive, people get consumption c. For simplicity, we assume no borrowing or lending, and no discounting. The lifetime utility function is then:

$$(1) \qquad V = U(c) + \pi(b) \cdot U(c),$$

where $\pi(b)$ is the probability of survival to period 2, depending on behavior b. Define the behavior as improving health, so $\pi' > 0$. Action b has a cost, p per unit. The cost may be monetary (the cost of a gym membership) or psychological (the implicit cost of dieting). In equilibrium, people will consume item b until the marginal benefit is equal to the marginal cost. This is given by:

$$(2) \qquad \pi' \cdot U(c) = p.$$

Equilibrium b will change over time for two reasons. The first is that the population becomes richer. This shows up as increasing c. As long as people are not sated in goods consumption, increases in income will raise the utility of living longer and, hence, lead to a greater investment in b. The second change is in the cost of better health. This cost may increase or decrease over time. To the extent that b involves hiring people (e.g., a personal trainer), and all wages increase in the economy, the cost of b will increase. Some aspects of technical change will also increase b. For example, technology that makes food more readily available will increase the psychological cost of denying ourselves food. Cutler, Glaeser, and Shapiro (2003) suggest that this is why obesity has increased over time. In other cases, b might fall over time, as we develop new medications or ways of improving health.

The net impact of economic changes on health behaviors is thus indeterminate, depending on the demand for better health relative to the cost of health improvements.

Empirically, we delineate the risk factors we consider into four groups: demographics, genetics, behaviors, and biological factors. The relations between these are shown in figure 12.1. Demographic factors included age,

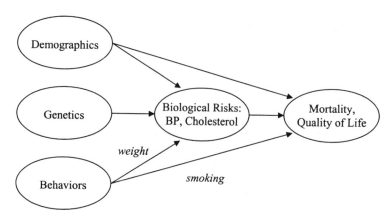

Fig. 12.1   Conception of risk factors affecting health

sex, race, and education. Age, sex, and race are standard risk measures. Education is strongly related to health, although the reason for this is unclear (Cutler and Lleras-Muney 2008). Because some evidence suggests that the education effect is causal (Lleras-Muney 2005; Oreopoulos 2007; Arendt 2005; Spasojevic 2003), we consider this as a demographic risk factor. Of course, to the extent that education reflects other underlying characteristics of people such as position in the social hierarchy (Wilkinson 1996; Link and Phelan 1995) or discount rates (Fuchs 1982), we will be overstating the impact of educational changes on health.

A variety of genetic factors predispose people to disease. The data that we have do not render genetic profiles. Because it is unlikely that the population's genetic profile would change markedly in a few decades—particularly controlling for gender and race—we do not consider the possible impact of genetic changes.

There are a number of behavioral risk factors that are important for health. Mokdad et al. (2004) rank the impact of risk factors on mortality; our results largely confirm these rankings. The most important behavioral risk factor is smoking. Mokdad et al. estimate that smoking accounts for about 435,000 deaths annually. Obesity is second in importance, though the impact is controversial (Flegal et al. 2005; Willett et al. 2005). The impact of obesity on mortality ranges from about 100,000 deaths per year to about 400,000 deaths per year.

Other behaviors are of much less quantitative importance than smoking and obesity. Excessive alcohol use is the third important risk factor, accounting for 85,000 deaths. Remaining risk factors include exposure to microbial agents (75,000 deaths) or toxic agents (55,000 deaths), motor vehicle accidents (43,000 deaths), guns (29,000 deaths), sexual behaviors (20,000 deaths), and illicit drug use (17,000 deaths). Many of these latter risk factors disproportionately affect the young. For purposes of Social Security and Medicare, our focus is primarily on the elderly. Thus, we limit our analysis of behavioral risks to smoking, obesity, and alcohol use.

Finally, we consider two biological risk factors: blood pressure and cholesterol. Both blood pressure and cholesterol are products of other behaviors, most importantly obesity. We consider this link extensively in our forecasting analysis.

Not all important risk factors are included in our analysis of risk. For example, the composition of diet matters as well as overall caloric intake. Among biological risks, the most important omissions are hemoglobin A1c (i.e., diabetes status) and some of the more novel risk factors (such as C-reactive protein or albuminuria). None of these risk factors were measured in the early National Health and Nutrition Examination Survey (NHANES).

12.2   Data

Risk factor analysis requires data on physical measures of the population, not just self-reports. Not everyone with high blood pressure knows they are hypertensive, for example, and the share of people with this knowledge will change over time. In the United States, the leading survey with both physical examination and laboratory measurements is the NHANES. More detail on the survey design and operation is reported elsewhere (Miller 1973; NCHS 2006).

We use two NHANES surveys, the first from 1971 to 1975 (NHANES I), and the second from 1999 to 2002 (NHANES IV). Our analysis began with the NHANES I because that is the first population health survey that asked about smoking status, a key variable in health risk.

In each case, our initial sample is the population aged twenty-five to seventy-four. The upper age restriction matches the sampling frame of NHANES I. To focus on the elderly and nonelderly population in specific, we also consider the population aged fifty-five and older.

Table 12.1 shows the characteristics of the sample in the two time periods. The first set of columns are for the entire population, and the second set of columns are restricted to the population aged fifty-five and older. After eliminating people with missing risk factor information, our full age sample includes 6,764 respondents to NHANES I and 6,255 respondents to NHANES IV. The subset of older respondents is about one-third the size.

Age was categorized into ten-year age groups beginning at age twenty-five. Race was defined as white, black, or other. Education was divided into three groups: less than a high school degree; a high school degree; and at least some college. Table 12.1 shows that these risk factors moved in the expected direction over time. In particular, the share of people with at least some college education doubled over those three decades.

Table 12.1   **Characteristics of the sample (%)**

	Entire population		Population 55+	
Risk factor	NHANES I 1971–1975 (n = 6,764)	NHANES 1999–2002 (n = 6,225)	NHANES I 1971–1975 (n = 2,453)	NHANES 1999–2002 (n = 2,188)
Female	52.5	51.1	54.1	51.9
Race				
White	89.0	85.8	90.8	88.6
Black	10.0	9.9	8.5	8.0
Other race	1.0	4.3	0.7	3.5
Married	79.0	64.9	72.5	70.1
Education				
<High school	34.4	19.8	55.3	31.7
High school	37.2	24.9	26.0	27.1
At least some college	28.4	55.3	18.6	48.8
Smoking				
Current smoker	40.3	24.8	28.5	16.3
Former smoker	21.2	26.0	27.9	40.6
Never smoker	38.5	49.2	43.6	43.1
Drinking				
Heavy drinker	6.7	4.4	5.8	4.5
Light drinker	72.3	65.3	60.3	55.1
Nondrinker	20.9	30.3	33.9	40.5
Body mass index (BMI)				
Underweight, BMI < 18.5	2.8	1.7	2.9	0.9
Optimal weight, $18.5 \le BMI < 25$	47.7	30.4	40.1	25.0
Overweight, $25 \le BMI < 30$	34.6	34.7	37.5	36.4
Obese, $30 \le BMI$	14.8	33.2	19.5	37.7
Blood pressure				
Normal blood pressure	22.4	43.4	8.9	22.5
Prehypertension	38.2	38.9	28.1	43.6
Stage 1 hypertension	23.6	13.1	32.4	22.3
Stage 2 hypertension	15.7	4.6	30.6	11.7
Cholesterol				
Normal cholesterol	35.4	47.4	19.6	35.6
Borderline high	34.9	34.4	34.7	41.8
High	29.7	18.3	45.7	22.6

Note: NHANES is the National Health and Nutrition Examination Survey.

Following standard practice in the literature, smoking status was divided into three groups: current smokers, former smokers, and never smokers. Smoking status was determined by responses to two questions, "Have you ever smoked at least 100 cigarettes in your entire life?" and "Do you smoke cigarettes now?" The share of current smokers fell by a third over the time period, from 40 percent in the early 1970s to 25 percent around 2000. Two-thirds of this was people who never started smoking, and one-third was people quitting.

Drinking status was divided into heavy drinkers, light drinkers, and nondrinkers. In NHANES I, drinking status was assessed with three questions. Nondrinkers were those who answered "no" to the question, "During the past year have you had at least one drink of beer, wine, or liquor?" Among those who answered "yes," subsequent questions included "How often do you drink?" and "When you drink, how much do you usually drink over 24 hours?" Heavy drinkers were those who drink three or more drinks over twenty-four hours and reported drinking "everyday" or "just about everyday." The next possible response was "about 2 or 3 times a week." In NHANES IV, nondrinkers were defined as those who responded "zero" to the question, "In the past 12 months, how often did you drink any type of alcoholic beverage?" A subsequent question asked people, "In the past 12 months, on those days that you drank alcoholic beverages, on the average how many drinks did you have?" Heavy drinkers were those who reported drinking three or more drinks at least four times per week (i.e., four or more times per week, sixteen or more times per month, or 208 or more times per year). Both heavy and light alcohol use declined over time. Heavy drinking fell from 7 to 4 percent of the population; light drinking fell from 72 to 65 percent.

Body mass index (BMI) was based on direct measurement of height and weight. In accordance with conventional guidelines (National Institutes of Health 1998), we classified respondents as underweight (BMI < 18.5), normal weight (18.5 ≤ BMI < 25), overweight (25 ≤ BMI < 30), and obese (30 ≤ BMI). The largest change in weight has been the shift from healthy weight to overweight. Overweight and obesity were 49 percent of the population in the early 1970s; today, they are 68 percent. At the other end of the scale, fewer people are underweight now than in the past (2 percent versus 3 percent).

Blood pressure and total cholesterol were measured according to standard protocols used in the medical examination component of each survey (Burt et al. 1995; Hajjar and Kotchen 2003; Carroll et al. 2005). Blood pressure was divided into four groups following the recommendations of the seventh report of the Joint National Committee on Prevention, Detection, Evaluation, and Treatment of High Blood Pressure (JNC VII): normal blood pressure (systolic blood pressure [SBP] ≤ 120 mmHG and diastolic blood pressure [DBP] ≤ 80 mmHG); prehypertension (120 ≤ SBP < 140 or 80 ≤ DBP < 90); stage 1 hypertension (140 ≤ SBP < 160 or 90 ≤ DBP < 100); and stage 2 hypertension (160 ≤ SBP or 100 ≤ DBP). Cholesterol levels were divided into three groups based on the recommendations of the Third Report of the National Cholesterol Education Program Expert Panel on Detection, Evaluation, and Treatment of High Blood Cholesterol in Adults (NCEP 2001): normal cholesterol (total cholesterol < 200); borderline high cholesterol (200 ≤ total cholesterol < 240); and high cholesterol (240 ≤ total cholesterol).

Even with the increase in obesity, substantial gains have been made in blood pressure and cholesterol control. The share of people with stage 2 hypertension fell from 16 percent of the population in the early 1970s to 5 percent around 2000. The share with stage 1 hypertension fell nearly in half as well. Rates of high cholesterol declined by over one-third, almost certainly a result of improved medications.

12.3   The Health Profile, 1971–1975 versus 1999–2002

To gauge the impact of these differing health trends, we need to weight the various risk factors. The optimal weights to use will depend on the question being asked. One could use longevity weights, quality of life weights, or medical spending weights. In practice, the NHANES does not have data on medical spending, and quality of life data are not great. Thus, we use mortality weights.

To estimate the impact of these risk factors on mortality, we use the epidemiological follow-up conducted as part of the 1971 to 1975 NHANES. Epidemiological follow-ups were conducted at periodic intervals after the initial survey, going into the 1990s. We estimated a logit model for death from any cause within the ten years subsequent to the initial survey. We choose ten years to get the long-term impact of these risk factors, but to avoid a situation where most everyone will have died. Previous evidence shows that prediction equations from NHANES are broadly similar to those from other data sources such as the Framingham Heart Study, with the possible exception of increased importance of smoking and diabetes in NHANES data (Liao et al. 1999; Leaverton et al. 1987).

Table 12.2 shows the odds ratios for death in the subsequent ten years. The coefficients are all in the expected direction, and most are statistically significant. Among demographic factors, blacks are more likely to die than whites (OR $= 1.4$; $p = .010$), and marriage is protective of future longevity (OR $= 0.68$; $p = .001$). People with less than a high school degree have 27 percent higher mortality than people with a high school degree ($p = .036$).

Behavioral risk factors are also important. Being a current smoker increases the odds of death in the next ten years by 113 percent ($p < .001$). Heavy drinking is associated with higher mortality, and light drinking is associated with lower mortality; the net impact is thus unclear, though as we show in the following, these changes are relatively small.

Without controlling for hypertension or high cholesterol, obesity increases the odds of death by 44 percent ($p = .018$); however, this drops to 28 percent and is no longer statistically significant ($p = .112$) once blood pressure and cholesterol are controlled for. This finding parallels other research from the Framingham Heart Study, which does not include obesity in the risk equations (Anderson et al. 1991; Wilson et al. 1998), and data showing that the impact of obesity on mortality is declining in more recent

Table 12.2   **Effect of risk factors on 10-year mortality**

Variable	Odds ratio	Standard error
Race (relative to white)		
Black	1.402**	.195
Other race	.245	.221
Married	.682**	.077
Education (relative to high school graduate)		
<High school	1.269**	.144
At least some college	1.062	.191
Smoking status (relative to never smoker)		
Current smoker	2.126**	.250
Former smoker	1.233	.165
Drinking status (relative to nondrinker)		
Heavy drinker	1.021	.175
Light drinker	.771**	.094
Body mass index (BMI; relative to optimal)		
Underweight, BMI < 18.5	2.408**	.582
Overweight, 25 ≤ BMI < 30	.762**	.089
Obese, BMI ≥ 30	1.278	.197
Blood pressure (relative to normal)		
Prehypertension	.904	.166
Stage 1 hypertension	1.131	.201
Stage 2 hypertension	1.535**	.289
Cholesterol (relative to normal)		
Borderline high	1.029	.130
High	1.150	.148
N	6,525	

Source: Data from National Health and Nutrition Examination Survey I.
Note: The regression includes 10-year age dummy variables interacted with gender.
**Significant at the 5 percent level.

surveys (Flegal et al. 2005). Indeed, it is likely that some of the obesity effect we find would be reduced still further if we were able to control for diabetic status. Being underweight is associated with significantly higher mortality, likely because of the loss of lean body mass (and, therefore, weight) associated with chronic or severe illnesses (Willett et al. 2005).

Both hypertension and high cholesterol are associated with substantially increased risk. People with stage 2 hypertension have a 54 percent increase in risk ($p = .023$) above those with normal blood pressure. High cholesterol is associated with a 15 percent higher mortality risk, though this is not statistically significant ($p = .277$).

We use these coefficients to estimate the mortality risk for every person in the 1971 to 1975 and 1999 to 2002 NHANES surveys. These risks will vary with all of the risk factors. To standardize the risk assessment, we present age- and sex-adjusted risks, using the age and sex distribution of the population in 1999–2002 as weights.

Table 12.3   Impact of risk factors on predicted 10-year mortality

	Total population	Population 55+
Predicted mortality		
1971–1975	9.8%	25.7%
1999–2002	8.4	21.7
Change	−1.4	−3.9
Effect of:		
Smoking	−0.9	−1.2
Blood pressure	−0.6	−2.1
Education	−0.2	−0.9
Cholesterol	−0.2	−0.6
Drinking	0.1	0.2
Body mass index	0.3	0.6

Notes: Estimates are adjusted to the age and sex distribution of the population in 1999–2002. Effects of changes in race and marital status are not reported.

Table 12.3 reports the risk profile in the two time periods, for the population as a whole and for the near elderly and elderly populations. For the entire population, the ten-year mortality risk declined from 9.8 percent in 1971 to 1975 to 8.4 percent in 1999 to 2002 ($p < .001$), an absolute reduction of 1.4 percentage points, and a relative risk reduction of 14 percent. Among the population aged fifty-five and older, the absolute risk fell from 25.7 percent to 21.7 percent ($p < .001$), a relative reduction of 16 percent.

The lower rows of the table show which risk factor changes were most important in this health improvement. We calculate these by taking derivatives of the prediction equation evaluated at the mean risk level (in a logit model, $dp/dx = p[1 - p]\beta$). We evaluate this equation at the average probability in the population.

For the population as a whole, the largest risk factor change was the reduction in smoking, which contributed to a 0.9 percent absolute decrease in mortality risk. Better risk factor control was second in importance. Improved blood pressure control led to a reduction of 0.6 percent in risk, and better cholesterol control accounted for 0.2 percent. The increase in obesity offset some, but not all, of these risk reductions.

In the population aged fifty-five and older, the patterns were the same, although the magnitudes were larger. The most important factor for the older population was better control of medical risk: lower blood pressures contributed a 2.1 percent absolute reduction in mortality risk, and lower cholesterol contributed 0.6 percent. Second in importance was decreased smoking, accounting for a 1.2 percent reduction in risk. Improved education among the older group led to a nearly 1 percent reduction in risk. The impact of obesity was to raise risk by 0.6 percentage points.

The factors responsible for better control of hypertension and high cholesterol likely include increased use of medications and, to a lesser extent,

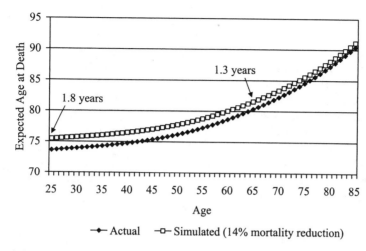

Fig. 12.2   **Effect of mortality reduction on expected age at death**

behavioral change. Use of antihypertensive medications rose markedly after the early 1970s (Burt et al. 1995), and use of HMG-CoA Reductase Inhibitors (i.e., statins) to control cholesterol increased markedly in the 1990s (Ma et al. 2005; Ford et al. 2003). Other possible factors include reduced fat and salt intake (Cutler and Kadiyala 2003).

The relatively small impact of obesity on mortality risk is in part a reflection of the fact that we control for blood pressure and cholesterol in our mortality equation. As noted in the preceding, the estimate of obesity on mortality nearly doubles without controlling for these risk factors.

Life expectancy is easier to understand than mortality rates. We simulate the impact of risk factor changes by considering how a 14 percent reduction in risk at every age would affect mortality rates at each age. Figure 12.2 shows the impact. The lower line in the figure is the expected age at death for a person alive at each age, using the 1970 Social Security life table for the United States. The upper line is the expected age at death for people at those same ages, but with a 14 percent lower mortality rate. The expected increase in longevity is 1.8 years at age twenty-five, 1.6 years at age forty-five, 1.4 years at age sixty-five, and 0.7 years at age eighty-five.

12.4   Forecasts of Future Risk

Forecasting in any field is difficult, but behaviors are particularly difficult to forecast. Still, forecasting is important in this case for two reasons. First, we want to understand how the disparate trends we have observed will play out in the future. Will the increase in obesity become significant enough to overwhelm reductions in smoking and improved risk factor control? If so, it suggests that longevity forecasts should not be as optimistic as they currently are. Second, forecasting can help evaluate the impact of different interventions. How much would increased use of medications for hypertension and high cholesterol mitigate the impact of rising obesity?

We develop a forecasting model based on the pathways laid out in figure 12.1. We forecast the impact of educational changes and behaviors for the early 2020s, twenty years after the most recent NHANES. As the horizon extends further out, the forecast becomes more speculative.

Our forecasting methodology is explicitly extrapolative. We want to understand what will happen if current trends continue. This is not a "best guess" about the future health profile, which would be based on explicit consideration of the demand for and supply of health behavioral changes. We describe each component of the forecast.

12.4.1   Education

We have reasonable data to guide our education simulation because education rarely increases after age twenty-five. Still, differential mortality by education makes the forecast difficult. For people that will be aged twenty-five to fifty-four in two decades, assume that completed education for those ages will match those observed for those same ages in 1999 to 2002. For age and sex groups aged fifty-five and older, we assume that education will be at the highest level for the pre-fifty-five cohorts. These assumptions yield a twenty-year forecast of 17 percent of people with a high school degree or less (compared to 20 percent in 1999 to 2002) and 59 percent of people with at least some college education (compared to 55 percent currently).

12.4.2   Smoking

We also have good data to guide our smoking simulation. Because people rarely start smoking after age twenty-five, the share of elderly people in the future that smoke is bounded by the share of people who smoke currently. Specifically, for people who will be age forty-five and older in two decades, we assume that the share who will be ever smokers is the same as the share for that age and sex group in 1999 to 2002. To forecast the division between current and former smokers, we use data on the trend in current smoking rates. As shown in table 12.2, current smoking rates fell by 2.7 percent per year (demographically adjusted) between 1971 to 1975 and 1999 to 2002. We assume this rate continues within each age and sex group. We then subtract the forecast of current smokers from the forecast of ever smokers to estimate the share of former smokers.

For the population twenty-five to forty-four, we do not have past experience to guide our forecasts because we do not view them as adults in 1999 to 2002. For these groups, we assume that the current smoking rate is equal to the smoking rate in 1999 to 2002 among that age group, adjusted down by 2.7 percent per year (the historical trend). We assume the same ratio of former to current smokers in those age groups as we observe in 1999 to 2002. Thus, the share of ever smokers is trending down as well.

The net impact of our forecast is that current smoking rates would decline from 25 percent of the population in 1999 to 2002 to 15 percent two decades later. The share of former smokers would be relatively constant, falling from 26 percent to 23 percent. Among the population aged fifty-five and older, current smoking rates would fall from 16 to 10 percent, and the share of former smokers would remain constant.

It is worth reiterating that our forecast is designed to extrapolate past trends, not to provide a best guess about the future. Still, some data suggest this is reasonable. Future generations of Americans will have grown up with stronger warnings about the harms from cigarettes than current generations and may, thus, smoke less. In addition, recent price increases as a result of tobacco taxes and the Master Settlement Agreement should lead additional people to stop smoking (Chaloupka and Warner 2000).

12.4.3   Drinking

We assume that heavy and light drinking will each change at the same annual rate in the next two decades as they did in the period from 1971 to 1975 to 1999 to 2002 (a decline of 1.5 percent per year for heavy drinking and 0.3 percent per year for light drinking). This leads to a forecast of 3.3 percent of the population being heavy drinkers in two decades (compared to 4.4 percent currently) and 61.2 percent being light drinkers (compared to 65.2 percent currently).

12.4.4   Obesity, Hypertension, and High Cholesterol

Forecasting obesity is difficult because obesity can change rapidly at any age (Cutler, Glaeser, and Shapiro 2003). Further, obesity is a key input into hypertension and high cholesterol, so we cannot forecast those without understanding obesity trends. Our forecast of these factors is done in several steps.

We start by extrapolating past changes in weight. Between 1971 to 1975 and 1999 to 2002, average BMI increased by 11 percent in total (from 25.6 to 28.3), or 0.4 percent annually. We assume that this annual change in BMI will continue for the next twenty years. We account for this by increasing each person's BMI in the 1999 to 2002 data uniformly by 7.4 percent for twenty years. We then calculate for each person their obesity status: underweight, normal weight, overweight, or obese. This forecast suggests that 0.6 percent of the population will be underweight (compared to 1.7 percent currently), 20.1 percent of the population will be normal weight (compared to 30.4 percent currently), 33.9 percent of the population will be overweight (compared to 34.7 percent currently), and 45.4 percent will be obese (compared to 33.2 percent currently).

It is important to note a key assumption of this weight forecast. We assume that weight increases by the same percent annually, not the same number of pounds. An increase of the same number of pounds would translate into a reduced growth rate of obesity over time. However, time series data from the Behavioral Risk Factor Surveillance Survey do not show a reduction in the rate of obesity increase in the past two decades. If anything, the rate is increasing over time.

The second step is to use these forecasts to simulate the population's blood pressure and cholesterol in two decades if there were no treatment. To do this, we use data from the 1959 to 1962 National Health Examination Survey (NHES). The NHES data were gathered from a period when blood pressure and cholesterol treatments were very scarce. They thus provide a good structural model for these risks. Following Cutler et al. (2007), we relate systolic blood pressure, diastolic blood pressure, and total cholesterol to age and age squared, interacted with gender, race dummy variables, and BMI and its square. These regressions are shown in table 12.4.

Table 12.4   Prediction equations for blood pressure and cholesterol

	Blood pressure		Total cholesterol
	Systolic	Diastolic	
Age	−.355**	.963**	4.57**
	(.148)	(.089)	(.35)
Age^2	.010**	−.009**	−.010**
	(.002)	(.001)	(.004)
Female	−8.55**	.918	35.95**
	(4.27)	(2.578)	(10.14)
Female · Age	−.116	−.162	−2.31**
	(.201)	(.121)	(0.48)
Female · Age^2	.006**	.002*	.034**
	(.002)	(.001)	(.005)
Black	6.31**	4.63**	−7.88**
	(0.77)	(0.46)	(1.83)
Other race	−7.72**	−1.40	−19.54**
	(1.78)	(1.08)	(4.20)
BMI	1.57**	1.42**	8.05**
	(0.34)	(0.20)	(0.80)
BMI^2	−.006	−.010**	−.124**
	(.006)	(.004)	(.014)
Constant	90.50**	26.23**	−14.81
	(5.46)	(3.30)	(13.01)
N	6,257	6,257	6,098
R^2	.373	.240	.244

Source: Data are from the 1959–1962 National Health Examination Survey.
Note: BMI = body mass index.
**Significant at the 5 percent level.

The general fit of the models is good, with R^2s ranging from 24 percent to 37 percent. The coefficients are all in the expected direction; most important, BMI is related to blood pressure and cholesterol.

We use these equations and the forecast of BMI from the 1999 to 2002 population to simulate systolic blood pressure, diastolic blood pressure, and total cholesterol. In performing the simulation, we first find the expected value of blood pressure and cholesterol for each person. We then add in a random normal error term, drawn from the same variance as in the 1959 to 1962 data. The latter step allows us to capture heterogeneity in actual values of blood pressure and total cholesterol.

The next step in the simulation is to consider the impact of treatment. In our benchmark simulation, we assume that treatment will be taken by the same share of people and have the same efficacy as medication use does in 1999 to 2002. The share of people taking medication is known from the 1999 to 2002 NHANES, which asks explicitly about use of antihypertensive and cholesterol-lowering medication. In those data, 60 percent of people with hypertension report taking antihypertensive medication, and 35 percent of people with high cholesterol report taking cholesterol-lowering medication.

For those taking medication, we draw values of blood pressure and cholesterol from the distribution of medication users, using the mean and standard deviation of each. This simulation suggests that people taking antihypertensive medication have a reduction of 7.9 (9.2) mmHg in systolic (diastolic) blood pressure (to mean levels of 143 [89] in systolic [diastolic] blood pressure) and that people taking cholesterol-lowering medication have a reduction of 30.5 mg/dL in total cholesterol (to a mean level of 244 mg/dL).

These simulations rest on the assumption that the structural equations for blood pressure and cholesterol are similar over time. Consideration of this assumption suggests that it is reasonable. One issue is whether there are other risk factors that would have changed over time. For hypertension, the other likely risk factor is salt intake, but this has not changed greatly (Cutler and Kadiyala 2003). For cholesterol levels, the share of fat and cholesterol in the diet is also important, but this, too, did not change greatly (Cutler and Kadiyala 2003). Thus, Cutler et al. (2007) conclude that the early data are a good guide to nontreatment blood pressure for the later population, and the same seems likely for cholesterol.

Table 12.5 shows the predicted changes in ten-year mortality risk for each of these simulations. We consider the different changes independently, although the effects will generally be additive. Continued reductions in smoking will reduce mortality risk, by roughly the same amount as changes over the past thirty years. The mortality risk for the entire population aged twenty-five and older would decline by 0.7 percent, or 8 percent of the baseline rate. The impact on the older population would be an ab-

Table 12.5   Impact of possible future risk factors on predicted 10-year mortality

	Total population	Population 55+
Predicted mortality, 1999–2002	8.4	21.7
Effect of:		
Continued reduction in smoking	−0.7	−1.0
Continued increase in education	0.0	−0.5
Continued reduction in drinking	0.1	0.2
Continued increase in obesity	1.1	1.3
Continued increase in obesity and		
more effective medications	0.0	0.1

Notes: Estimates are adjusted to the age and sex distribution of the population in 1999–2002. Effects of changes in race and marital status are not reported.

solute mortality reduction of 1.0 percent, or 5 percent of the baseline rate. Education changes would have a modest impact on mortality, larger for the older population than for the population as a whole.

The most surprising finding in table 12.5 is the impact of future changes in obesity on mortality risk. Even with existing degrees of medication use, the impact of increases in obesity, hypertension, and high cholesterol would lead to a 1.1 percent increase in mortality risk for the total population, or 13 percent of the baseline rate. In the population fifty-five and older, the increase in risk is 1.3 percent, or 5 percent of the baseline risk.

The reason for this large impact is the nonlinear relationship between BMI and weight increase, and between BMI and health risk. At higher levels of BMI, a given percent increase in weight is a greater number of pounds. And because weights are so high to begin with, further increases in weight push many more people into the obese category, where health impacts are particularly severe. Thus, the impact of BMI changes on health is becoming increasingly large.

Lack of good hypertension and cholesterol control is a major reason why increases in BMI have such large impacts on mortality risk. The last row of the table shows an alternative simulation where BMI increases the same amount, but all people with hypertension or high cholesterol are assumed to be on medication and medication is assumed to bring people to the 75th percentile of effectiveness. This is an additional reduction of 14 (7) mmHg in systolic (diastolic) blood pressure and 18 mg/dL in cholesterol. In this simulation, the impact of weight changes on mortality risk is virtually nil and is significantly smaller than the impact of continued smoking reductions. The key in this simulation is the effectiveness of medications more than getting more people to take them. Because even the typical person taking medication has high risk factor levels, increasing the share of people taking medication to 100 percent lowers the risk to only 0.1 percent for the population aged fifty-five and over (relative to 1.3 percent at the current level). If medications can be made more effective or used more regularly, however, the benefits would be much greater.

12.5 Conclusions

The impact of trends in health behaviors on longevity has not been uniform across the different behaviors over the past three decades. Fewer people smoke than used to, but more people are obese. The net impact is important, but not clear a priori. Examining these factors as a whole, we show significant improvements in the health risk profile of the U.S. population between the early 1970s and the early 2000s. Reduced smoking, better control of medical risk factors such as hypertension and cholesterol, and better education among the older population have been more important for mortality than the substantial increase in obesity.

Our results suggest substantial caution about the future, however. Where smoking reductions can be expected to have continued impacts on improved health, future changes in obesity might more than overwhelm this trend. Two-thirds of the U.S. population is overweight or obese. As a result, continued increases in weight from current levels have a bigger impact on health than did increases in weight from lower levels of BMI (Olshansky et al. 2005). A large part of the impact of BMI is moderated through its effect on hypertension and high cholesterol. Given that not everyone with these conditions takes medications, or is controlled by the medication they do take, the resulting impact of rising weight on health can be significant. The optimistic side of this picture, however, is the potential for better control. If the effectiveness of risk factor control can be increased, much of the impact of obesity on mortality risk can be blunted.

Effectiveness, as we are using the term, captures several factors. One is the effect of the medication when taken as directed. Studies show that the reduction in blood pressure from medication is about the level we predict, and that people taking antihypertensive medication in the NHANES have average blood pressures about the level of people treated in clinical trials (e.g., Cushman et al. 2002). Our predictions of cholesterol reduction, in contrast, are only half those in clinical trials (LaRosa et al. 1999). Other evidence shows that physicians do not always prescribe evidence-based therapies, and not everyone prescribed these medications takes them as directed (Lenfant 2003; Osterberg 2005). Some people take their medication sporadically, others take only part of the dosage, and still others take drug "holidays."

Understanding how to improve utilization of and adherence to recommended medications are key issues. Research has focused on two possible avenues. The first is through performance-based payment. Physicians are paid for office visits, but not for ensuring follow-up with their recommendations. The idea behind pay-for-performance systems is to reward physicians (or insurance companies) for successful efforts to increase utilization and possibly adherence. Such efforts might involve having nurse outreach, automatic medication refills, or more convenient office hours to monitor side effects. The second strategy involves use of information technology. Patients can receive electronic reminders about medication goals, information such as blood pressure can be transmitted and monitored electronically, and automated decision tools can help with dosing and medication switches. Whether these or other strategies offer the greatest promise of improved adherence is uncertain; our results suggest that evaluating these strategies in practice is a high research priority.

References

Anderson, Keaven M., Peter W. F. Wilson, Patricia M. Odell, and William B. Kannel. 1991. An updated coronary risk profile. A statement for health professionals. *Circulation* 83:356–62.
Anonymous. 1999. Achievements in public health: Tobacco use—United States, 1900–1999. *Morbidity and Mortality Weekly Report* 48:986–93.
Arendt, Jacob N. 2005. Does education cause better health? A panel data analysis using school reform for identification. *Economics of Education Review* 24:149–60.
Burt, Vicki L., Jeffrey A. Cutler, Millicent Higgins, Michael J. Horan, Darwin Labarthe, Paul Whelton, Clarice Brown, and Edward J. Roccella. 1995. Trends in the prevalence, awareness, treatment, and control of hypertension in the adult U.S. population. Data from the health examination surveys, 1960 to 1991. *Hypertension* 26:60–69.
Carroll, Margaret D., David A. Lacher, Paul D. Sorlie, James I. Cleeman, David J. Gordon, Michael Wolz, Scott M. Grundy, and Clifford L. Johnson. 2005. Trends in serum lipids and lipoproteins of adults, 1960–2002. *Journal of the American Medical Association* 294:1773–81.
Chaloupka Frank J., and Kenneth E. Warner. 2000. The economics of smoking. In *Handbook of health economics.* Vol. 1B, ed. A. J. Culyer and J. P. Newhouse, 1539–1627. Amsterdam: Elsevier.
Cushman, William C., Charles E. Ford, Jeffrey A. Cutler, et al. 2002. Success and predictors of blood pressure control in diverse North American settings: The Antihypertensive and Lipid-Lowering Treatment to Prevent Heart Attack Trial (ALLHAT). *Journal of Clinical Hypertension* 4:393–404.
Cutler, David M., Edward L. Glaeser, and Jesse M. Shapiro. 2003. Why have Americans become more obese? *Journal of Economic Perspectives* 17 (3): 93–118.
Cutler, David M., and Srikanth Kadiyala. 2003. The return to biomedical research: Treatment and behavioral effects. In *Measuring the gains from medical research,* ed. Robert Topel and Kevin Murphy, 110–62. Chicago: University of Chicago Press.
Cutler, David M., and Adriana Lleras-Muney. 2008. Education and health: Evaluating theories and evidence. In *Making Americans healthier: Social and economic policy as health policy,* ed. J. House, R. Schoeni, G. Kaplan, and H. Pollack, 29–60. New York: Russell Sage Foundation.

Cutler, David M., Genia Long, Ernst R. Berndt, et al. 2007. The value of antihypertensive drugs: A perspective on medical innovation. *Health Affairs* 26 (1): 97–100.

Elo, Irma T., and Samuel H. Preston. 1996. Educational differentials in mortality: United States, 1979–85. *Social Science and Medicine* 42:47–57.

Flegal, Katherine M., Margaret D. Carroll, Cynthia L. Ogden, and Clifford L. Johnson. 2002. Prevalence and trends in obesity among U.S. adults, 1999–2000. *Journal of the American Medical Association* 288:1723–27.

Flegal, Katherine M., Barry I. Graubard, David F. Williamson, and Mitchell H. Gail. 2005. Excess deaths associated with underweight, overweight, and obesity. *Journal of the American Medical Association* 293:1861–67.

Ford, Earl S., Ali H. Mokdad, Wayne H. Giles, and George A. Mensah. 2003. Serum total cholesterol concentrations and awareness, treatment, and control of hypercholesterolemia among U.S. adults: findings from the National Health and Nutrition Examination Survey, 1999 to 2000. *Circulation* 107:2185–89.

Fuchs, Victor. 1982. Time preference and health: An exploratory study. In *Economic aspects of health,* ed. Victor Fuchs, 93–120. Chicago: University of Chicago Press.

Gregg Edward W., Yiling J. Cheng, Betsy L. Cadwell, Giuseppina Imperatore, Desmond E. Williams, Katherine M. Flegal, Narayan K. M. Venkat, and David F. Williamson. 2005. Secular trends in cardiovascular disease risk factors according to body mass index in U.S. adults. *Journal of the American Medical Association* 293:1868–74.

Hajjar, Ihab, and Theodore A. Kotchen. 2003. Trends in prevalence, awareness, treatment, and control of hypertension in the United States, 1988–2000. *Journal of the American Medical Association* 290:199–206.

Lakins Nekisha, Gerald D. Williams, and Hsiao-ye Yi. 2006. *Apparent per capita alcohol consumption: National, state, and regional trends, 1977–2004.* Surveillance Report no. 78. Washington, DC: National Institute on Alcohol Abuse and Alcoholism.

LaRosa, John C., Jiang He, and Suma Vupputuri. 1999. Effect of statins on risk of coronary disease: A meta-analysis of randomized controlled trials. *Journal of the American Medical Association* 282:2340–46.

Leaverton, Paul E., Paul D. Sorlie, Joel C. Kleinman, Andrew L. Dannenberg, Lillian Ingster-Moore, William B. Kannel, and Joan C. Cornoni-Huntley. 1987. Representativeness of the Framingham risk model for coronary heart disease mortality: A comparison with a national cohort study. *Journal of Chronic Diseases* 40:775–84.

Lenfant, Claude. 2003. Clinical research to clinical practice—Lost in translation? *New England Journal of Medicine* 349:868–74.

Liao Youlian, Daniel L. McGee, Richard S. Cooper, and Mary Beth E. Sutkowski. 1999. How generalizable are coronary risk prediction models? Comparison of Framingham and two national cohorts. *American Heart Journal* 137:837–45.

Link, Bruce G., and Jo Phelan. 1995. Social conditions as fundamental causes of disease. *Journal of Health and Social Behavior* 36:80–94.

Lleras-Muney, Adriana. 2005. The relationship between education and adult mortality in the United States. *Review of Economic Studies* 72:189–221.

Ma, Jun, Niraj L. Sehgal, John Z. Ayanian, and Randall S. Stafford. 2005. National trends in statin use by coronary heart disease risk category. *PLoS Medicine* 2:e123.

Miller, Henry W. 1973. *Plan and operation of the Health and Nutrition Examination Survey.* United States—1971–1973. *Vital Health Statistics* 1:1–46.

Mokdad, Ali H., James S. Marks, Donna F. Stroup, and Julie L. Gerberding. 2004. Actual causes of death in the United States, 2000. *Journal of the American Medical Association* 291:1238–45.

National Center for Health Statistics (NCHS). 2006. NHANES 1999–2000 data files: Data, docs, codebooks, SAS code. http://www.cdc.gov/nchs/nhanes.htm.

National Cholesterol Education Program (NCEP). 2001. Executive summary of the third report of the National Cholesterol Education Program Expert Panel on Detection, Evaluation, and Treatment of High Blood Cholesterol in Adults (Adult Treatment Panel III). *Journal of the American Medical Association* 285:2486–97.

National Institutes of Health. 1998. Clinical guidelines on the identification, evaluation, and treatment of overweight and obesity in adults—The evidence report. National Institutes of Health. *Obesity Research* 6(Suppl. 2): S51–S209.

Olshansky, S. Jay, Douglas J. Passaro, Ronald C. Hershow, Jennifer Layden, Bruce A. Carnes, Jacob Brody, Leonard Hayflick, Robert N. Butler, David B. Allison, and David S. Ludwig. 2005. A potential decline in life expectancy in the United States in the 21st century. *New England Journal of Medicine* 352:1138–45.

Oreopoulos, Philip. 2007. Do dropouts drop out too soon? Wealth, health, and happiness from compulsory schooling. *Journal of Public Economics* 91 (11–12): 2213–29.

Osterberg, Lars, and Terrence Blaschke. 2005. Adherence to medication. *New England Journal of Medicine* 353:487–97.

Preston, Samuel H. 2005. Deadweight?—The influence of obesity on longevity. *New England Journal of Medicine* 352:1135–37.

Spasojevic, Jasmina. 2003. Effects of education on adult health in Sweden: Results from a natural experiment. New York: City University of New York Graduate Center.

Trends in Health and Aging. 2007. http://www.cdc.gov/nchs/agingact.htm.

Wilkinson, Richard. 1996. *Unhealthy societies: The afflictions of inequality.* London: Routledge.

Willett, Walter C., Frank B. Hu, Graham A. Colditz, and JoAnn E. Manson. 2005. Underweight, overweight, obesity, and excess deaths. *Journal of the American Medical Association* 294:551.

Wilson, Peter W. F., Ralph B. D'Agostino, Daniel Levy, Albert M. Belanger, Halit Silbershatz, and William B. Kannel. 1998. Prediction of coronary heart disease using risk factor categories. *Circulation* 97:1837–47.

Comment   James P. Smith

In their excellent chapter, David M. Cutler, Edward L. Glaeser, and Allison B. Rosen make several salient points. First, trends in most behavioral risk factors are strongly positive. These would include education, smoking, heavy drinking, hypertensive control, and total cholesterol. In contrast, only a few behavioral risk factors are strongly negative, most notable among them are obesity and drinking abstention. When combined into a

James P. Smith is a senior economist at Rand Corporation.

ten-year mortality analysis from National Health and Nutrition Examination Survey (NHANES) I, the good stuff beats out the bad stuff, and mortality rates are predicted to decline significantly based on observed post 1970s trends in these risk factors. More speculatively, they project that these trends will continue unabated in the future, further depressing mortality. The very large caveat they emphasize involves obesity where a continuation of past trends may eventually overwhelm all that is positive.

I think this thought provoking chapter contains a simple but powerful message that disease specific alarmists often miss. Not all is gloomy in American health trends; in fact, just the opposite is the dominant reality. The rhetoric surrounding the very real problem of rapidly rising rates of obesity would make you think the Americans can do nothing right when it comes to taking care of their health and that our health future is a gloomy one indeed. They demonstrate that, when one combines all health behaviors together, on average, Americans did pretty well in taking care of themselves with the rapid decline in smoking getting much of the credit. Their model predicts a substantial decline in mortality, which, in fact, is precisely what happened over the last thirty years.

There are several extensions that would make the chapter or subsequent ones that follow even more valuable. Some of these involve examining within group and within period trends. To illustrate my point, the top panel of table 12C.1 lists current smoking behavior for men ages twenty-five to seventy for the same three education groups used in the Cutler, Glaeser, and Rosen chapter—less than high school, high school graduate, and more than a high school graduate (Smith 2007). These are derived from three NHANES—NHANES II (1976 to 1980), NHANES III (1988 to 1994), and NHANES IV (1999 to 2002). The first three rows in this table are the fraction of men who currently smoke; the last three rows represent different measures of the changes between the waves over time.

As documented in the Cutler, Glaeser, and Rosen chapter, smoking behavior has declined rapidly over this period—almost 15 percentage points among all men between the late 1970s and the turn of this century. However, these trends were far from uniform across either education groups or over time. There was a drop in current smoking of only 6 percentage points among the least-educated compared to a fall of 16 percentage points among the most-educated men. Similarly, the decline in male smoking was much larger between NHANES II and NHANES III (11.1 percentage points) than it was between NHANES III and NHANES IV (5.5 percentage points).

The middle panel of table 12C.1 arrays data in a similar manner, but now the focus is on the fraction of men who are obese. In this case, there are not strong differences across education groups in the time series increase in rates of male obesity. For example, there is a 12.1 percentage point increase in obesity in the lowest education group compared to an 11.1 percentage

Table 12C.1	Health behaviors by education and calendar year—men ages 25–70				
	Education				
	Low	Middle	High	All	NHANES Waves
A. Smoking					
1976–1980	49.1	44.8	35.1	42.8	II
1988–1994	44.9	42.8	21.8	33.7	III
1999–2002	43.2	36.6	18.1	28.2	IV
delta	−5.9	−8.2	−16.2	−14.6	IV-II
delta	−4.2	−2.0	−13.3	−11.1	III-II
delta	−1.7	−6.2	−2.9	−5.5	IV-III
B. Obesity					
1976–1980	12.6	12.2	7.4	10.6	II
1988–1994	24.7	22.2	18.6	21.1	III
1999–2002	28.3	31.1	26.9	28.2	IV
delta	15.7	18.9	19.5	17.6	IV-II
delta	12.1	10.0	11.2	10.5	III-II
delta	3.6	8.9	8.3	7.1	IV-III
C. Education					
1976–1980	33.2	31.3	35.4		II
1988–1994	23.1	31.1	45.7		III
1999–2002	20.9	24.9	55.1		IV
delta	−12.3	−6.4	19.7		IV-II
delta	−10.1	−0.2	10.3		III-II
delta	−2.2	−6.2	9.4		IV-III

point increase in the highest education group. However, there does appear to be attenuation in the increase in male obesity over time although not as dramatic as what took place in smoking.

The bottom panel of table 12C.1 displays patterns in male education over these three NHANES waves. The decline in the fraction of men without a high school diploma was also concentrated in the 1980s and has subsequently slowed down. As larger fractions of individuals complete high school and then college, schooling advances are inevitably going to slow down. There may still be important advances in the acquisition of skills relevant for promoting good health behaviors, but years of schooling will cease to be a useful index to pick them up.

Combined, these panels of table 12C.1 demonstrate a couple of simple but important facts. First, within-time period trends are quite different across the three education groups that are used in the chapter, and it might be insightful to model them separately. For several reasons, an equally good argument would apply to estimating the mortality model separately for men and women. Second, a use of all the NHANES data available over this period indicates that there has taken place an apparent slowdown in the trends of most of the behavioral risk factors both good (smoking, education) and bad (obesity).

This possible slowdown in the average improvement in health behaviors might suggest that there may be a slowdown in the improvements in mortality as well. For a different reason outside of simple trends in health behaviors per se, that is unlikely to be the case. For example, in 1978, less than half of those with hypertension were taking some medications to deal with the disease—by 1994, this was over 80 percent (Goldman and Smith 2005). Hypertension is actually a disease that is at least partially taken into account in their mortality models. But hypertension is simply one example of many types of diseases where improved drugs, greater adherence, or more effective medical interventions have all made the consequences of disease—and not simply mortality—much less now than in the past.

The mortality predictions that they make use model coefficients based on 1970s medical technology, but things are most surely getting much better. A good useful first step would evaluate how well their model does in predicting mortality over this period. This would simply involve comparing actual mortality reductions over this period with their predictions. Because they are not taking medical advances into account in their projections, I suspect that they should severely underpredict 1970 to 2000 time-period mortality gains. The same reasoning would lead us to believe that they will also severely underpredict future mortality reductions as well. The extent of the underprediction would not be a bad measure of the medical and other improvements that were taking place at the same time.

At the end of the chapter, they abandon their optimism and start morphing into obesity alarmists. And here I have to start parting company with them. I think that there are many reasons why obesity is not going to be quite the problem that they envision may happen. Over this time period, undiagnosed diabetes fell from half of diabetics being undiagnosed to about one in five (Smith 2007). Diagnosed diabetes is surely better treated than undiagnosed diabetes.

Even though the obesity pill may not be on the near-term horizon, many new effective treatments are available for the principal diseases that are the consequences of obesity—diabetes, heart disease, and arthritis. It surely would be a lot better for them and much cheaper for all of us if more Americans were more concerned about and put more effort into reducing their weight in the first place. But it is equally true that the consequences of having the diseases that are associated with obesity are not as dire as they were twenty, ten, or even five years ago. For each of these obesity-related diseases, far more effective medical treatments are available now than before, a situation that I fully anticipate will continue in the future.

Moreover, it also seems to me highly unlikely that past obesity trends will continue at the rates of the past thirty years. That would result in the majority of Americans being obese, an implausible scenario that assumes that Americans would not react to the antiobesity campaigns and information about the poor health consequences associated with obesity. As mentioned in the preceding, we have already seen signs that there has been a slowdown in the rate at which obesity has been rising. In sum, projecting mortality consequences of obesity based largely on the medical technology of the early 1970s may seriously overstate the mortality consequences of the disease.

These quibbles on my part should not divert attention from my basic reaction. This is a excellent contribution to the literature that should be read by economists and those who work in health outside of economics. I gained some very valuable insights from this chapter, and they will as well.

References

Goldman, Dana, and James P. Smith. 2005. Socioeconomic differences in the adoption of new medical technologies. *American Economic Review* 95 (2): 234–37.
Smith, James P. 2007. Nature and causes of male diabetes trends, undiagnosed diabetes, and the SES health gradient. *Proceedings of the National Academy of Sciences* 104 (33): 13,225–31.

Contributors

Alan J. Auerbach
Department of Economics
508-1 Evans Hall, #3880
University of California, Berkeley
Berkeley, CA 94720-3880

John Beshears
Department of Economics
Littauer Center
Harvard University
Cambridge, MA 02138

Andrew Biggs
American Enterprise Institute
1150 Seventeenth Street, NW
Washington, DC 20036

Axel Börsch-Supan
Mannheim Research Institute for the
  Economics of Aging
Building L13, 17
University of Mannheim
D-68131 Mannheim, Germany

Jeffrey R. Brown
Department of Finance
340 Wohlers Hall, MC-706
University of Illinois at Urbana-
  Champaign
1206 South Sixth Street
Champaign, IL 61820-9080

Clark Burdick
Office of Research, Evaluation, and
  Statistics
Social Security Administration
400 Virginia Avenue, Suite 300
Washington, DC 20254-0001

James J. Choi
Yale School of Management
135 Prospect Street
P.O. Box 208200
New Haven, CT 06520-8200

David M. Cutler
Department of Economics
Harvard University
1875 Cambridge Street
Cambridge, MA 02138

Douglas W. Elmendorf
The Brookings Institution
1775 Massachusetts Avenue, NW
Washington, DC 20036

Martin Feldstein
Department of Economics
Harvard University
Cambridge, MA 02138

Jason Furman
The Brookings Institution
1775 Massachusetts Avenue, NW
Washington, DC 20036

John Geanakoplos
Department of Economics
Yale University
PO Box 208281
New Haven, CT 06520-8281

Edward L. Glaeser
Department of Economics
315A Littauer Center
Harvard University
Cambridge, MA 02138

Gopi Shah Goda
Robert Wood Johnson Scholars
Harvard University
1730 Cambridge Street, S410
Cambridge, MA 02138

Michael Hurd
RAND Corporation
1776 Main Street
Santa Monica, CA 90407

Dirk Krüger
Department of Economics
University of Pennsylvania
3718 Locust Walk
Philadelphia, PA 19104

David Laibson
Department of Economics
Littauer M-12
Harvard University
Cambridge, MA 02138

Ronald Lee
Departments of Demography and
  Economics
University of California, Berkeley
2232 Piedmont Avenue
Berkeley, CA 94720

Jeffrey Liebman
John F. Kennedy School of
  Government
Harvard University
79 John F. Kennedy Street
Cambridge, MA 02138

Alexander Ludwig
Mannheim Research Institute for the
  Economics of Aging
L13, 17, Room 307
University of Mannheim
68131 Mannheim, Germany

Erzo F.P. Luttmer
John F. Kennedy School of
  Government, Mailbox 25
Harvard University
79 John F. Kennedy Street
Cambridge, MA 02138

Brigitte C. Madrian
John F. Kennedy School of
  Government
Harvard University
79 John F. Kennedy Street
Cambridge, MA 02138

George G. Pennacchi
Department of Finance
University of Illinois
1206 South Sixth Street
Champaign, IL 61820

James M. Poterba
National Bureau of Economic
  Research
1050 Massachusetts Avenue
Cambridge, MA 02142-1347

Joshua Rauh
Graduate School of Business
University of Chicago
5807 South Woodlawn Avenue
Chicago, IL 60637

Allison B. Rosen
Departments of Internal Medicine and
  Health Policy and Management
300 North Ingalls, Suite 7E10
University of Michigan
Ann Arbor, MI 48109

Andrew A. Samwick
Department of Economics
6106 Rockefeller Hall
Dartmouth College
Hanover, NH 03755-3514

John B. Shoven
Department of Economics
Room 132
Stanford University
579 Serra Mall at Galvez Street
Stanford, CA 94305-6015

Jonathan Skinner
Department of Economics
6106 Rockefeller Hall
Dartmouth College
Hanover, NH 03755

Sita Nataraj Slavov
Department of Economics
Occidental College
1600 Campus Road
Los Angeles, CA 90041

Kent Smetters
Insurance and Risk Management
    Department
3000 Steinberg Hall—Dietrich Hall
The Wharton School, University of
    Pennsylvania
3620 Locust Walk
Philadelphia, PA 19104-6302

James P. Smith
RAND Corporation
1776 Main Street
P.O. Box 2138
Santa Monica, CA 90401-3208

Steven F. Venti
Department of Economics
6106 Rockefeller Center
Dartmouth College
Hanover, NH 03755

Scott J. Weisbenner
Department of Finance
340 Wohlers Hall, MC-706
University of Illinois at Urbana-
    Champaign
1206 South Sixth Street
Champaign, IL 61820

David W. Wilcox
Federal Reserve Board
20th and C Streets, NW
Washington, DC 20551

David A. Wise
John F. Kennedy School of
    Government
Harvard University
79 John F. Kennedy Street
Cambridge, MA 02138

Stephen P. Zeldes
Graduate School of Business
Columbia University
3022 Broadway
New York, NY 10027-6902

Author Index

Subject Index